Civil Litigation

Author

Stuart Sime, Barrister, BVC Course Director, The City Law School

Editor

Stuart Sime, Barrister, BVC Course Director, The City Law School

Series Editor

Julie Browne, Barrister, Senior Lecturer, The City Law School

Civil Litigation

The City Law School, City University, London

OXFORD
UNIVERSITY PRESS

OXFORD

UNIVERSITY PRESS

Great Clarendon Street, Oxford OX2 6DP

Oxford University Press is a department of the University of Oxford.
It furthers the University's objective of excellence in research, scholarship,
and education by publishing worldwide in

Oxford New York

Auckland Cape Town Dar es Salaam Hong Kong Karachi
Kuala Lumpur Madrid Melbourne Mexico City Nairobi
New Delhi Shanghai Taipei Toronto

With offices in

Argentina Austria Brazil Chile CzechRepublic France Greece
Guatemala Hungary Italy Japan Poland Portugal Singapore
South Korea Switzerland Thailand Turkey Ukraine Vietnam

Oxford is a registered trademark of Oxford University Press
in the UK and in certain other countries

Published in the United States
by Oxford University Press Inc., New York

British Library Cataloguing in Publication Data
Data available

Library of Congress Cataloging in Publication Data
Data available

Typeset by Laserwords Private Limited, Chennai, India
Printed in Great Britain on acid-free paper by
Ashford Colour Press Ltd, Gosport, Hampshire

ISBN 978–0–19–956848–2

10 9 8 7 6 5 4 3 2 1

FOREWORD

I am delighted to write this Foreword to the manuals which are written by practitioners and staff of the Inns of Court School of Law (ICSL [now The City Law School]).

The manuals are designed primarily to support training on the Bar Vocational Course (BVC). They now cover a wide range, embracing both the compulsory and the optional subjects of the BVC. They provide an outstanding resource for all those concerned to teach and acquire legal skills wherever the BVC is taught.

The manuals for the compulsory subjects are updated and revised annually. The manuals for the optional subjects are revised every two years. To complement the Series, the publishers will maintain a website for the manuals which will be used to keep them up-to-date throughout the academic year.

The manuals, continually updated, exemplify the practical and professional approach that is central to the BVC. I congratulate the staff of The City Law School who have produced them to an excellent standard, and Oxford University Press for its commitment in securing their publication. As my predecessor the Hon. Mr Justice Gross so aptly said in a previous Foreword, the manuals are an important ingredient in the constant drive to raise standards in the public interest.

Lord Justice Etherton
Chairman of the Advisory Board of the Institute of Law
City University, London

PREFACE

Virtually everybody who picks up this manual for the first time will have had previous, perhaps considerable, experience of the study of the law. However, since there is no standardisation of legal education, it is quite possible that many students will, so far, have approached the law from a purely academic premise. Others may have followed courses which have a more practical orientation. Both have their advantages and drawbacks.

The vocational course is, however, designed to prepare the aspiring barrister to meet the disciplines of everyday professional life at the Bar, and this manual has been prepared with that purpose in mind.

This manual deals with many of the major aspects of civil litigation with which an aspiring practitioner needs to be familiar. It must be stressed that this manual is intended to be a practical introduction to civil procedure, but as you progress on the course you will also have to become familiar with practitioners' books, such as *Blackstone's Civil Practice*, for more detailed guidance on the practice in the High Court and County Courts.

It is hoped that this manual will provide a means of understanding the concepts of civil litigation, rather than being a mere statement of its constituent 'nuts and bolts'. It has been designed with the hope, as has been said, of promoting an understanding of fundamental principles involved, so that the various rules and practice directions which govern civil litigation can the more easily be understood and applied.

This new edition has been revised to ensure that its contents are as up-to-date as possible. It is hoped that this work will continue to provide an invaluable source of reference well after the (hopefully successful) conclusion of the Bar Vocational Course.

OUTLINE CONTENTS

DETAILED CONTENTS

TABLE OF CASES

TABLE OF STATUTES

TABLE OF SECONDARY LEGISLATION

1

Introduction

This manual describes the way in which disputes are resolved through litigation in the civil courts of England and Wales. This chapter will first outline the steps that are normally taken in a case, from the moment a client consults a solicitor to the enforcement of any judgment obtained. It will then deal with a number of matters of general principle. The law is stated as at 6 April 2009.

Commentary on how to draft court documents for use in litigation can be found in the *Drafting* manual, and will not be discussed here. Regarding applications for orders in court, this manual will describe the procedure and the principles that are applied, sometimes in some depth. However, guidance on how to present such applications is contained in the *Advocacy* manual.

1.1 Outline of the usual steps in a case

1.1.1 Overview of stages in a common law claim

Figure 1.1 illustrates the main stages in a common law claim, whether commenced in the High Court or a County Court.

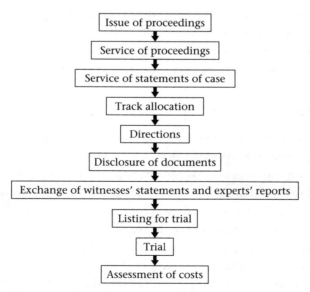

Figure 1.1 Main stages in common law claims

This manual will cover all of these stages. At this point it is helpful to provide an outline of the steps in a possible case. The steps which follow are based on a personal injury claim in the County Court.

1.1.2   Initial role of the solicitor

Let us take the example of a client who goes to see a solicitor about an accident suffered at work.

During the interview, the solicitor will need to obtain a full statement from the client. This will comprise a description of the accident, the extent of the injuries suffered, and all other relevant information, including the client's background, date of birth and National Insurance number (so the Benefits Agency can provide a certificate of State benefits paid to the client), witnesses who may be able to give evidence, etc. The solicitor may need to be shown identification evidence (if the claim exceeds 15,000 euros) to comply with the Money Laundering Regulations 2003, SI 2003/3075.

Among other matters, the client will clearly want advice as to whether any claim for compensation is likely to succeed, and if so, how much is likely to be awarded. Often, this cannot be answered immediately. Before giving such advice, medical reports will usually have to be obtained, and counsel's opinion may eventually be sought. Medical reports will often be obtained as a joint exercise in conjunction with the defendant's insurers.

Another matter which may have to be investigated is whether the proposed defendant is worth suing. After all, if the person responsible is of limited means, insolvent, untraceable or unknown, then, unless there is liability insurance, further steps may simply be a waste of time and money.

1.1.3   Cost of litigation

The client will also, not unnaturally, be concerned about how much the claim will cost, and how much, if anything, he or she will be liable to pay. In certain non-personal injuries cases State funding may be applied for under the Community Legal Service. You will find public funding discussed in **Chapter 35**. In personal injuries claims assistance under the Community Legal Service is not available, so the litigation will have to be funded by the client or through a conditional fee agreement, unless there is a trade union or insurance company prepared to foot the bill. Of course, if the client is ultimately successful, much (although usually not all) of his or her costs will be repaid by the other side. Normally the solicitor will give some indication of the likely cost, and will ask for a sum to be paid on account.

1.1.4   Pre-action protocol

It is common to have a period of negotiations before proceedings are issued. If these are successful, a great deal of time and expense should be saved. A formal system for early exchange of information and evidence has been laid down for personal injuries claims in the Pre-action Protocol for Personal Injury Claims. The idea behind the protocol is to promote contact and negotiation between the advisers for the two sides before proceedings start, with the aim of encouraging negotiated settlements and avoiding unnecessary litigation. Parties complying with the protocol have to provide each other with most of the relevant documentation and evidence relevant to assessing the merits of the claim and its value. It is hoped that compliance with the protocol will enable the parties to settle claims on a fair and informed basis. The protocol will be considered in more detail in **Chapter 2**.

1.1.5 Limitation period

The primary limitation period in personal injuries cases is three years, and usually proceedings must be issued within that time. However, the Limitation Act 1980 (LA 1980), ss 14 and 33, which are discussed at **23.3.3.4** and **23.5.2**, may sometimes assist a claimant who would otherwise be out of time.

1.1.6 Issue of the claim form

The nature of the claim must be stated on a prescribed claim form, together with its value. Further, full particulars of claim can be incorporated into the claim form, although these can be served separately.

The claim form is issued by being sealed with the court's seal: see **Chapter 3**.

1.1.7 Service of the claim form

The claimant has four months in which to take the step required for service of the claim form. If any difficulty is experienced in doing so, it may be possible to have its validity extended (see **Chapter 25**). Service is usually effected by the court by posting the claim form by ordinary first class post to the defendant. In all cases it must be accompanied by a 'Response Pack' containing forms to be used by the defendant in responding to the claim. There is no need to serve the particulars of claim with the claim form, but the claimant has the option of doing so if so desired.

1.1.8 Service of particulars of claim

The particulars of claim is the document in which the claimant sets out the nature of the claim against the defendant. Briefly, it sets out the facts that the claimant alleges and which, if proved, would establish one or more causes of action against the defendant or defendants. At the end of the document it is usual to set out a 'prayer' listing the remedies, such as damages and interest, that are sought against the defendants. The contents of the particulars of claim must be verified by a 'statement of truth' signed by the claimant or the claimant's solicitor.

If the client's condition may deteriorate in the future, a claim for provisional damages may be made in the particulars of claim: see **13.7**.

As mentioned above, the particulars of claim may be incorporated into the claim form, or be separate but served with it, or be separate from the claim form and served later. Unless time for service is extended by agreement (which is quite common) or by order of the court, the particulars of claim must be served within 14 days after service of the claim form on the defendant.

Normally, particulars of claim stand on their own. Personal injuries cases, like the case we are considering, are an exception, and in such cases the claimant must serve two documents with the particulars of claim, namely:

- a medical report dealing with all the injuries alleged in the particulars of claim; and

- a schedule of the past and future expenses and losses claimed (including out of pocket expenses and any loss of earnings and pension rights).

1.1.9 Subsequent stages

Assuming the parties are unable to agree on terms of settlement, the stages of the proceedings after service of the particulars of claim are usually as follows:

(a) Acknowledgment of service within 14 days by the defendant by returning the form to the court. A defendant may ignore this step, and simply file a defence (step (b)) within the 14-day period after service of the particulars of claim.

(b) Service of the defence by the defendant. This must be done within 14 days of service of the particulars of claim, or 28 days if an acknowledgment of service was filed.

(c) Service of the reply, if any, by the claimant within 14 days thereafter.

(d) Shortly after the defence is filed the court will send allocation questionnaires to the parties. These are five-page documents asking questions about what needs to be done to prepare the case for trial (see **Figure 7.1**).

(e) After the parties return their allocation questionnaires a District Judge at the court will decide which case management track to allocate the case to. Cases worth less than £5,000 will usually be allocated to the small claims track, those worth between £5,000 and £25,000 are usually allocated to the fast track, and those worth more than £25,000 usually go on the multi-track.

(f) At the same time as allocating a case to a track the court will usually give directions regarding the steps that need to be taken to prepare the case for trial, and which lay down a timetable within which those steps must be taken.

(g) The parties exchange lists of documents (see **Chapter 20**) in accordance with the court's directions.

(h) The parties inspect each other's documents seven days later, usually by sending copies through the post.

(i) If the claimant needs money prior to trial, for example to convert a house to provide wheelchair access or to purchase a suitable car, an application notice may be issued applying for an order requiring the defendant to make an interim payment on account of any damages that might ultimately be recovered at trial: see **Chapter 13**.

(j) The parties will prepare their cases for trial. They will take statements from witnesses, which will need to be exchanged (**Chapter 30**); they prepare the expert evidence in accordance with the court's directions; they may seek further information from the other side on questions of fact (**Chapter 22**); they may serve notices to admit facts and to prove documents (**Chapter 32**); and, if they may be relying on hearsay evidence, serve notices under the Civil Evidence Act 1995 (CEA 1995): see **Chapter 31**.

(k) The defendant may seek to protect its position on costs by making an offer to settle under Part 36: see **Chapter 27**.

(l) One of the things the District Judge will have done when giving directions at the allocation stage is to decide when the parties should return pre-trial checklists. This will generally be when the directions made on allocation should have been fully complied with. Pre-trial checklists ask detailed questions about compliance with directions and the nature of the evidence to be adduced at trial.

(m) Usually, once pre-trial checklists have been returned the court will confirm the trial date or a 'window' during which the trial will take place.

(n) Particularly in multi-track cases, but to some extent also in fast track cases, the court may hold case management hearings from time to time between filing of the defence and trial. These can take several forms, including allocation hearings, case management conferences and pre-trial reviews.

(o) Prior to trial, counsel will need to be briefed, witnesses served with witness summonses if necessary (for which see **33.12.6**), and bundles of documents prepared for the court.

(p) The trial itself is almost invariably held in open court, which means the public and press may be present. It is conducted by a circuit or district judge depending on its value. Counsel are wigged and gowned, and witnesses give oral evidence on oath or affirmation.

(q) After hearing the evidence the judge gives a reasoned judgment and considers the question of costs: see **Chapter 36**.

(r) The court will usually send the parties a sealed copy of the judgment, which is simply a record of the result of the trial, not the judge's reasons.

(s) The loser may consider an appeal: see **Chapter 39**.

(t) The winner is usually entitled to an order for costs against the loser. In fast track cases costs are usually assessed by the judge there and then. In multi-track cases costs are usually subject to detailed assessment. This is a process that can take many months, culminating in a hearing before a costs officer. It is open to the losing party to seek to agree the amount of costs payable with the successful party.

(u) If the loser fails to pay the damages and/or costs, the winner may have to go on to enforce the judgment: see **Chapter 38**.

1.2 The courts

1.2.1 Jurisdiction of the County Court

1.2.1.1 Creature of statute

The County Court owes its existence to statute, and the jurisdiction exercised by its judges and officers must be derived from the County Courts Act 1984 (CCA 1984) and the Civil Procedure Rules 1998 (CPR), failing which it will be acting *ultra vires*. The CPR are discussed further at **1.2.2.1** below.

Traditionally, it was thought that, being a creature of statute, the County Court had no inherent jurisdiction. Since *Langley v North West Water Authority* [1991] 1 WLR 697 it has been accepted that County Courts do in fact have an inherent jurisdiction.

1.2.1.2 Remedies available in the County Court

The CCA 1984, s 38(1), provides:

Subject to what follows, in any proceedings in a County Court the court may make any order which could be made by the High Court.

County Courts have no power to order the remedies available on judicial review (mandatory orders, prohibiting orders and quashing orders).

Further, the County Court Remedies Regulations 1991, SI 1991/1222, provide that County Courts shall not have power to grant search orders and that they have the power to grant freezing injunctions (see **Chapters 15** and **16**) only in limited circumstances. Exceptions, where freezing injunctions can be granted in the County Court, include injunctions over the subject matter of County Court proceedings and injunctions in aid of the execution of County Court judgments. (It should be noted, however, that search orders and freezing injunctions can be granted generally in the specialist Patents County Court and the Central London County Court Mercantile List.) Where the County Court has no power to make such an order, the application must be made in the High Court (see *Schmidt v Wong* [2006] 1 WLR 561 for the procedure).

1.2.2   Jurisdiction of the High Court

1.2.2.1   General

High Court procedure is governed primarily by the Supreme Court Act 1981 (which is to be known as the Senior Courts Act 1981 from October 1999) (SCA 1981) and the CPR. Very often the Act is expressed in wide terms, leaving the Civil Procedure Rule Committee to control the statutory powers by rules of court and the appellate courts to establish principles for the exercise of the statutory powers. If the Rule Committee exceeds its powers, its rules may be challenged as *ultra vires*. A successful challenge against one provision was made in *General Mediterranean Holdings SA v Patel* [2000] 1 WLR 272. The Committee's power to make rules is derived from the Civil Procedure Act 1997, ss 1 and 2, which is to be exercised with a view to securing that the civil justice system is accessible, fair and efficient.

Secondly, matters of practice are regulated by *Practice Directions* which supplement the main CPR.

1.2.2.2   Inherent jurisdiction

The inherent powers of the High Court derive from the fact that it is the successor to the old common law courts. By resorting to its inherent jurisdiction the court can ensure justice is done between the parties where otherwise there might appear to be a gap in the court's powers through a situation not being covered expressly in either the SCA 1981 or the CPR. The ambit of the court's inherent powers moves with the times, so in *Harrison v Tew* [1990] 2 AC 523, HL, it was held that the court's inherent jurisdiction in an area may be ousted by later statutory provisions dealing with the same subject matter. This means there is no residual inherent discretion where there are express provisions of the CPR dealing with the matter (*Tombstone Ltd v Raja* [2008] EWCA Civ 1444).

1.2.2.3   District Registries of the High Court

There are 133 District Registries, each one serving the districts of a number of County Courts. District Registries are established by SCA 1981, ss 99-103. All proceedings involving disputes in London must be commenced in the Royal Courts of Justice (RCJ); elsewhere the claimant can choose between the RCJ and the local District Registry.

1.2.2.4   Masters and District Judges

Most of this manual is concerned with various interim applications which can be made in civil proceedings. These are applications to the court, other than by way of trial or appeal, for various orders or directions. Interim procedure is dealt with in **Chapter 10**. Most interim applications are made to a Master or District Judge in the first instance. Masters exercise this jurisdiction in the High Court sitting in London (both QBD and

ChD). District Judges perform the same function in High Court cases proceeding in District Registries. Rather confusingly, the corresponding official in a County Court is also called a District Judge, and one person may be the District Judge for both a High Court District Registry and its local County Court.

County Court District Judges have jurisdiction to try small claims and fast track claims, and also certain possession proceedings and hearings to assess damages. Unless they have trial jurisdiction over the claim, and with some other exceptions, Masters and District Judges cannot grant interim injunctions. They can never try claims under the Human Rights Act 1998, s 7(1)(a), in respect of a judicial act, nor claims for declarations of incompatibility under s 4 (PD 2B).

1.3   Choosing the appropriate court

1.3.1   Which courts have jurisdiction?

Civil jurisdiction is exercised mainly by the High Court and County Courts. Magistrates' courts have limited jurisdiction over matrimonial and some other matters, and are not considered in more than outline in this manual.

1.3.2   Choice between High Court and County Court

For many types of proceedings the High Court and County Courts have concurrent jurisdiction. The decision as to where to commence proceedings in such cases will be dictated by factors such as the importance of the case, whether the case is likely to raise difficult questions of law or fact, and the convenience of the court building to the parties and lawyers involved in the case.

There are a number of rules restricting the choice between the High Court and County Courts. The most important are:

(a) Personal injuries claims *must* be brought in a County Court if the value of the claim does not exceed £50,000. This is discussed further at **1.3.6**.

(b) Consumer credit cases (based on hire purchase and related forms of agreement) *must* be brought in a County Court if the upper credit limit (broadly, the amount borrowed) does not exceed £25,000.

(c) Other money claims *may* be brought in the High Court provided the value of the claim exceeds £25,000. The result is that below £25,000 the claim must be brought in the County Court, and above that figure there is a choice.

(d) As an exception to paragraph (c) above, High Court proceedings can always be justified if they are suitable for inclusion in one of the specialist lists, such as Commercial, Patents and Companies Court matters.

(e) Equity proceedings, contentious probate proceedings, and proceedings under the Law of Property Act 1925 (LPA 1925) can be brought in the County Court *only* if the amount of the fund or the value of the land does not exceed £30,000. If the amount exceeds £30,000 the proceedings must be brought in the High Court.

(f) Claims for the possession of land must generally be commenced in the County Court for the district in which the land is situated (CPR, r 55.3).

(g) Judicial review and defamation proceedings can *only* be commenced in the High Court.

(h) Claims under the Human Rights Act 1998, s 7(1)(a), in respect of a judicial act *must* be brought in the High Court (CPR, r 7.11).

1.3.3 County Court

There are about 220 County Courts, with the country being divided into districts each being served by one or more County Courts (CCA 1984, s 1).

1.3.4 High Court

The High Court, together with the Crown Court and the Court of Appeal, forms part of the Senior Courts of England and Wales (Constitutional Reform Act 2005, s 59(1)). It is divided into three Divisions:

(a) The Chancery Division (ChD).

(b) The Queen's Bench Division (QBD).

(c) The Family Division.

Business is allocated between the Divisions in accordance with the SCA 1981, s 61, and Sch 1. Broadly:

(a) The ChD deals with land, mortgages, trusts, administration of estates, probate, bankruptcy, intellectual property and company matters.

(b) The QBD deals with judicial review, admiralty and commercial matters.

(c) The Family Division is assigned all matrimonial and related matters.

Family law and procedure are dealt with in the ***Family Law in Practice*** manual, so this manual will concentrate on procedure in the QBD and ChD. Where the subject matter is not specifically provided for, the litigant has the choice of which Division to use. In practice, most claims in tort and contract are commenced in the QBD.

1.3.5 Specialist courts

In addition, there are a number of specialised courts, most of which are part of either the QBD or ChD, although some are also part of the County Courts. Apart from the brief descriptions below, they will not be considered more than in passing elsewhere in this manual. The main specialist courts are:

(a) The Commercial Court, which is part of the QBD. Its procedures are governed by the CPR as extensively modified by CPR, Part 58, and the Admiralty and Commercial Courts Guide (the 'Commercial Court Guide'). Its administrative office at the Royal Courts of Justice is called the Admiralty and Commercial Registry.

(b) The Admiralty Court, which is part of the QBD. It shares its administrative office with the Commercial Court; and its practice follows that set out in CPR, Part 61, and the Commercial Court Guide.

(c) Mercantile Courts have been established as part of the High Court sitting in a number of District Registries and in a number of County Courts, so that commercial claims commenced in these courts can be dealt with by specialist judges with procedural rules tailored for litigation of this nature. They are governed by CPR, Part 59, and the relevant Mercantile Court Guide.

(d) Commercial arbitration matters are dealt with by the Commercial Court and Mercantile Courts. Procedural rules can be found in CPR, Part 62.

(e) The Technology and Construction Court (TCC). This is primarily part of the QBD, but some TCC claims may be started in the Central London County Court and High Court District Registries. It has its own building in Fetter Lane, near the Royal Courts of Justice. The TCC deals primarily with complex building disputes and with complex engineering and technology cases. It has its own rules set out in CPR, Part 60.

(f) The Companies Court is part of the ChD, and deals mainly with applications under the Companies Acts, and with company insolvency matters. It has its own special Practice Direction, PD 49, and, in relation to insolvency matters, PD Insolvency Proceedings.

(g) Whereas the Companies Court deals with the winding up of insolvent companies, insolvent individuals are dealt with through bankruptcy. Bankruptcy matters (like corporate insolvency) mostly fall outside the scope of the CPR, being governed instead by the Insolvency Rules 1986, SI 1986/1925. It is anticipated that a new set of Insolvency Rules will replace the Insolvency Rules 1986 (now intended to be implemented on 6 April 2011; this has been put off many times already). Bankruptcy petitions must generally be brought in the County Court having bankruptcy jurisdiction (not all County Courts do) serving the district where the debtor lives, leaving the ChD of the High Court to deal with debtors living (broadly) in Greater London and abroad (insofar as the courts of England and Wales are able to exercise jurisdiction over such people). Bankruptcy matters are governed by PD Insolvency Proceedings.

(h) The Patents Court deals with patent matters in the ChD and the Patents County Courts. It has its own rules set out in CPR, Part 63, and its own court guide.

1.3.6 Personal injuries cases

Claims for damages in respect of personal injuries where the claimant does not reasonably expect to recover more than £50,000 must be commenced in a County Court: High Court and County Courts Jurisdiction Order 1991, SI 1991/724, art 5. The term 'personal injuries' includes disease, impairment of physical or mental condition, and death. The value of the claim is determined as at the date the claim is commenced, and:

- claims for interest and costs are disregarded;
- contributory negligence is disregarded;
- if provisional damages (see **13.7**) are claimed, any possible future application for further damages is disregarded; and is calculated ignoring sums required to be paid to the Secretary of State by virtue of the Social Security (Recovery of Benefits) Act 1997 (see **Remedies** manual).

Quantification of damages for personal injuries is dealt with in the **Remedies** manual. The great majority of claims are for less than £50,000. Note that the £50,000 provided by the Order is the sum of the claim for:

- special damages for actual financial losses incurred before trial or settlement;

- general damages for pain, suffering and loss of amenity relating to the injury itself; and
- future losses, such as future loss of earnings and the cost of future medical care.

The third item is (in very general terms) calculated by multiplying the claimant's annual loss by a number of years' purchase, calculated by reference to the claimant's age, retirement age etc, with modifiers based on educational background and disability. Losses where the first two items exceed £50,000 are comparatively rare, but where the injury results in the claimant being unable to work or only capable of low-paid work, the total award is likely to justify commencing proceedings in the High Court.

1.3.7   Cost implications of commencing in the High Court

The normal rule is that the loser pays the successful party's costs. Unless there are sufficient reasons (such as complexity) for bringing a claim in the High Court, a claimant who brings proceedings in the High Court which should have been commenced in the County Court is likely to be penalised in costs, even if successful. The usual penalty is that the successful claimant's award for costs is reduced by up to 25%. See SCA 1981, s 51(8), (9).

1.3.8   Deliberate flouting

Where proceedings are commenced in the wrong court and the court is satisfied the claimant knew or ought to have known of any relevant provision allocating jurisdiction, the court may order the proceedings to be struck out: CCA 1984, ss 40(1)(b) and 42(1)(b). It was held in *Restick v Crickmore* [1994] 1 WLR 420, CA, that where the claimant knew or ought to have known that the claim should have been started in one court, but started it in the other, the court has a discretion whether to strike the claim out or to transfer it to the correct court. Normally the court will simply order a transfer and penalise the claimant in costs under SCA 1981, s 51 (see **1.3.7**). Striking out is a draconian punishment, and should only be used where it was plain that the claim was being started in the wrong court, and the claimant chose to do so in an attempt to harass the defendant, or deliberately run up unnecessary costs, or ignored a clear warning from the defendant as to the correct court, or had persistently started actions in the wrong court.

1.4   General principles

1.4.1   The overriding objective

The CPR, r 1.1, provides:

> (1) *These Rules are a new procedural code with the overriding objective of enabling the court to deal with cases justly.*
> (2) *Dealing with a case justly includes, so far as is practicable—*
> (a) *ensuring that the parties are on an equal footing;*
> (b) *saving expense;*
> (c) *dealing with the case in ways which are proportionate—*
>   (i)   *to the amount of money involved,*
>   (ii)   *to the importance of the case;*
>   (iii) *to the complexity of the issues; and*
>   (iv)   *to the financial position of each party;*

(d) ensuring that it is dealt with expeditiously and fairly; and

(e) allotting to it an appropriate share of the court's resources, while taking into account the need to allot resources to other cases.

The CPR came into force on 26 April 1999. They are, as stated in r 1.1(1), a new procedural code, replacing the Rules of the Supreme Court and the County Court Rules, which were the rules previously governing proceedings in the High Court and County Courts respectively. Being a new code means that the courts construe the CPR without being constrained by decisions made under the earlier rules, even if (as is often the case) the wording used by the CPR is very similar to that used by the old rules. One of the reasons for introducing the CPR was to make a break from the old law. This should mean that old cases should not be cited as an aid to the interpretation of the CPR (see *Biguzzi v Rank Leisure plc* [1999] 1 WLR 1926). There are a number of authorities which have nevertheless adopted principles from the pre-1999 case law. Sometimes this has been to gain inspiration on how the CPR should be applied (*Phillips v Symes (No 3)* [2008] 1 WLR 180, HL). On other occasions it has been to ensure that the application of the CPR remains consistent with underlying substantive law (*Adelson v Associated Newspapers Ltd* [2008] 1 WLR 585).

By CPR, r 1.2, the court has to give effect to the overriding objective when making decisions, and the parties are by r 1.3 expected to help the court to further the overriding objective. By r 1.4 the court must further the overriding objective by actively managing cases, which by r 1.4(2) includes:

(a) encouraging the parties to cooperate with each other in the conduct of the proceedings;

(b) identifying the issues at an early stage;

(c) deciding promptly which issues need full investigation and trial and accordingly disposing summarily of the others;

(d) deciding the order in which issues are to be resolved;

(e) encouraging the parties to use an alternative dispute resolution procedure if the court considers that appropriate and facilitating the use of such procedure;

(f) helping the parties to settle the whole or part of the case;

(g) fixing timetables or otherwise controlling the progress of the case;

(h) considering whether the likely benefits of taking a particular step justify the cost of taking it;

(i) dealing with as many aspects of the case as it can on the same occasion;

(j) dealing with the case without the parties needing to attend at court;

(k) making use of technology; and

(l) giving directions to ensure that the trial of a case proceeds quickly and efficiently.

1.4.1.1 Dealing with cases justly

The main concept in CPR, r 1.1, means that the primary concern of the court is doing justice. Shutting a litigant out through a technical breach of the rules will not often be consistent with this, because the primary purpose of the civil courts is to decide cases on their merits, not to reject them through procedural default. In *Jones v Telford and Wrekin District Council* The Times, 29 July 1999, the Master of the Rolls commented that the court must not lose sight of the fact that its primary concern is doing justice. An example is *Chilton v Surrey County Council* [1999] CPLR 525, where the Court of Appeal indicated that dealing with a claim justly involves dealing with the real claim, and allowed the claimant to rely on a revised statement of past and future loss and expense quantifying the claim at about £400,000 rather than the original statement, which indicated a claim value of about £5,000. There are conflicting cases on whether a party who starts a claim using the wrong form, or relying on the wrong statutory provision, should be granted permission to amend in order to deal with the claim justly. In

Thurrock Borough Council v Secretary of State for the Environment, Transport and the Regions The Times, 20 December 2000, permission to amend was granted, whereas in *Re Osea Road Camp Sites Ltd* [2005] 1 WLR 760 on similar facts permission was refused and the claim was struck out.

1.4.1.2 Equal footing

In *Maltez v Lewis* The Times, 4 May 1999, the concept of dealing with the parties on an equal footing was held not to extend to the court being able to prevent a party from instructing the lawyers of its choice, even if one side could not afford lawyers as expensive as those being used by the other. In *McPhilemy v Times Newspapers Ltd* [1999] 3 All ER 775, the Master of the Rolls said that if a party wanted the court to restrain the activities of another party with the object of achieving greater equality, the party making the application had to demonstrate they were themselves conducting the proceedings with a desire to limit expense so far as practical. However, the powers of the court to restrain excess did not extend to preventing a party from putting forward allegations which were central to their case. That said, it was open to the court to attempt to control how those allegations were litigated with a view to limiting costs.

1.4.1.3 Dealing with cases expeditiously, fairly and saving expense

In *Cadogan Properties Ltd v Mount Eden Land Ltd* [1999] CPLR 476, the court at first instance had made an order for service by an alternative method in circumstances where there were no grounds for doing so. That order was set aside on appeal, with the result that proceedings had not been served and the period of validity had expired. The Court of Appeal relied on CPR, r 1.1(2)(d) (the need to deal with cases fairly and expeditiously), and also on the need for proportionality (r 1.1(2)(c)), to justify making an order extending the validity of the originating process. The defendant was aware of the proceedings, and suffered no significant prejudice by the course adopted by the court. In *Re Hoicrest Ltd* [2000] 1 WLR 414 it was held that, on the facts, the case was not an appropriate one for using the Part 8 procedure (see **3.18**). Instead of striking out the proceedings (see **28.2**), the Court of Appeal allowed the claim to continue as an ordinary Chancery action, as that was more cost-effective than forcing the claimant to start again by issuing fresh proceedings.

1.4.1.4 Proportionality

Dealing with claims in ways which are proportionate to their value, importance and complexity may mean that on occasions the court will stop the parties from using the CPR to the full in order to keep the procedures followed under control. This may be reflected in dropping unnecessary steps (eg *Rosenberg v Nazarov* [2008] EWHC 812 (Ch)), or preventing a party from having a hearing to decide whether an agreed extension of time should be designated as 'final' (*TIP Communications LLC v Motorola Ltd* [2009] EWHC 212 (Pat), where the point was regarded as tactical posturing). Refusing an order because the claim form and witness statement were not signed was regarded as disproportionate in *Colliers International Property Consultants v Colliers Jordan Lee Jafaar Bhd* [2008] 2 Lloyd's Rep 368. Proportionality is very important on the issue of costs (see **Chapter 36**).

1.4.1.5 Allotting an appropriate share of the court's resources

In *Stephenson (SBJ) Ltd v Mandy* The Times, 21 July 1999, the defendant appealed against an interim order restraining him from breaching a restrictive covenant in his contract of employment. The appeal came before the Court of Appeal on 30 June, and the trial had been fixed for 20 July. Given the short period before the trial and the fact the claimant had given the usual undertaking in damages (see **14.5.2**), the court decided that considering the merits of the appeal would not be in accordance with the overriding objective. Expense would not be saved by hearing the appeal, and given the short time to trial hearing the appeal would not be a good use of the court's resources.

1.4.1.6 Cooperating

In *Chilton v Surrey County Council* [1999] CPLR 525, the Court of Appeal decided against the defendant partly because it seemed that the defendant was attempting to take tactical advantage of a mistake by the claimant's solicitors in overlooking to serve the revised statement of past and future loss and expense rather than cooperating with the claimant's solicitors to put matters right. To similar effect is *Hertsmere Primary Care Trust v Administrators of Balasubramanium's Estate* [2005] 3 All ER 274, where the defendant told the claimant that a Part 36 offer was defective, but refused to explain why. At trial it became clear there was an obvious, but technical, defect in the offer. The defendant's conduct was held to be a refusal to cooperate, and the court treated the offer as if it had been in the proper form.

1.4.2 Computation of time

The CPR, r 2.8 and r 2.9, lay down a number of rules for computing periods of time for doing any act which is fixed by the Rules or by court orders or judgments.

1.4.2.1 'Month'

'Month' means calendar month (not lunar month). Thus, if an act is required to be done within a month after 31 October, the period begins on 1 November and the last day for doing the act is 30 November.

1.4.2.2 'Clear days'

A period of time expressed as a number of days is computed as 'clear days'. This means that if an act is required to be done (say) three clear days before or after a specified date, at least that number of days must intervene between the two dates.

1.4.2.3 Short periods

When computing periods of time of five days or less, Saturdays, Sundays and bank holidays are excluded. For example, an application must be served three clear days before the return date (when the application will be heard by the Master). If the return date is Tuesday 14 October, the three 'clear days' would be Thursday 9 October, Friday 10 October and Monday 13 October, and the last day for service would be Wednesday 8 October.

1.4.2.4 Court office closed

When time expires on a day on which the court office is closed, and for that reason the act cannot be done on that day, the act will be in time if done on the next day that the court office is open.

1.4.2.5 Time applications

The CPR, r 3.1(1)(a), provides that the court may extend or shorten any time period laid down by the rules or any court order. An extension may be granted after the initial period has expired. The power to extend time may be exercised even where a rule says a step 'must' be taken within a stated period (*USF Ltd v Aqua Technology Hanson NV/SA* (2001) LTL 31/1/2001). Time applications which are issued before the time limit has expired tend to be granted unless there is any prejudice to the other side (*Robert v Momentum Services Ltd* [2003] 1 WLR 1577). An application made very close to the trial may be refused where its effect would be unfair on the other party (*Calenti v North Middlesex NHS Trust* (2001) LTL 2/3/2001). The procedure is considered further in **Chapter 10**. The costs of the application will usually be borne by the party applying for the order.

In practice, many time limits are extended by consent between the parties' solicitors. Such agreements should be in writing (usually by letter), and do not require an order being made by the court. However, the parties cannot agree to extend time if the agreement will impinge on certain 'key' dates. These include the dates set by the court for any case management conference, pre-trial review, for filing pre-trial checklists, or for the trial. Further, the parties cannot agree to extend time in relation to any step carrying a sanction in default: see CPR, r 3.9(3).

1.4.3 Errors of procedure

The CPR, r 3.10, provides:

Where there has been an error of procedure such as a failure to comply with a rule or practice direction—

> (a) *the error does not invalidate any step taken in the proceedings unless the court so orders; and*
>
> (b) *the court may make an order to remedy the error.*

The rule is worded very widely, and consequently most procedural failures will be treated as irregularities. Even a mistake as to whether a judge had authority to try a particular category of case was held to be an error of procedure in *Fawdry & Co v Murfitt* [2003] QB 104. The rule confirms the removal of an old (pre-1964) distinction between failures rendering the proceedings or step in the proceedings a nullity (and hence incapable of cure), and failures which are mere irregularities.

However, some procedural failings are not failures 'to comply with the requirements of these rules'. For example, in *Dubai Bank Ltd v Galadari (No 4)* The Times, 23 February 1990, it was assumed that the plaintiff (now called a claimant) had ceased to exist as a corporate body when the writ (the predecessor of the claim form) was issued through failing to comply with Dubai company law. Morritt J held that the requirement for a plaintiff was a basic principle of law, and if the plaintiff did not exist when the writ was issued the proceedings were a nullity and were not saved by the predecessor to r 3.10. Another example is provided by *Bank of America National Trust and Savings Association v Chrismas* [1994] 1 All ER 401, where it was held that the rule is subordinate to the Limitation Act 1980, s 35(3), which prevents certain amendments after the expiry of the limitation period. Purported service of an amended claim in breach of s 35(3) therefore could not be cured under this rule (see **24.7.3.5**).

On an application to remedy an error, it must be kept in mind that some errors are worse than others. Using an out-of-date form or returning an acknowledgment of service form to the wrong court office are clearly less serious than serving a claim form which is no longer valid for service or serving a claim form abroad without first seeking permission where that is required. Serving a claim form in Switzerland with the German language translation, but not the English language version, was regarded as probably suitable for remedy under r 3.10 in *Phillips v Symes (No 3)* [2008] 1 WLR 180, HL.

1.4.4   Discretion

An applicant for most forms of interim order will have to establish a number of basic conditions, which will be prescribed by either the SCA 1981, CCA 1984 or rules of court. Once these conditions have been satisfied, the court will then exercise its discretion whether to grant the order applied for.

At one extreme are applications where the court is given a broad, general discretion. An example is *Corfu Navigation Co v Mobil Shipping Co Ltd* [1991] 2 Lloyd's Rep 52, CA, dealing with an application for security for costs (see **Chapter 26**). Once the basic conditions in such a case have been established, counsel's arguments should be addressed to the basic principle underlying the application, and it is inappropriate to subject the judicial reasoning in previous cases to detailed and semantic analysis.

At the other extreme are applications where, once the basic conditions are satisfied, the order follows almost as of course with little scope for any residual judicial discretion. An example is an application for summary judgment where the court finds there is no real prospect of defending the claim (see **Chapter 12**, especially **12.7.1**). In such a case the court has little if any discretion, and should make the order. Of course, establishing these conditions may be far from easy, and, in the context of summary judgment, if the conditions are not satisfied the court has a very wide discretion regarding the other forms of order it may make (see **12.7.2** to **12.7.5**).

1.4.5   Interpreting the CPR

The CPR have been deliberately drafted in a plain English style in order to make them intelligible to lay people using the courts. When construing the rules the courts primarily seek to find the natural meaning of the words used. Although CPR, r 1.2(b), says that the court must seek to give effect to the overriding objective when it interprets any rule, the Court of Appeal has said this does not apply when the words of a rule are clear. In *Vinos v Marks & Spencer plc* [2001] 3 All ER 784 (approved in *Godwin v Swindon Borough Council* [2002] 1 WLR 997) May LJ said that interpretation to achieve the overriding objective does not enable the court to say that provisions which are quite plain mean what they do not mean, nor that the plain meaning of the rules should be ignored. Whether this approach will endure is open to question. In *Goode v Martin* [2002] 1 WLR 1828, it was held that what would have been the plain meaning of a provision of the CPR applying traditional rules of construction could be avoided in a case where that meaning would have infringed a party's rights under the European Convention on Human Rights. The Human Rights Act 1998, s 3(1), provides that 'so far as it is possible to do so, primary legislation and subordinate legislation must be read and given effect in a way which is compatible with the Convention rights'. To do this, the court was prepared to read additional words into a rule.

Pre-action conduct of litigation

2.1 Introduction

This chapter deals primarily with the requirements of the Pre-action Protocol for Personal Injury Claims (the personal injury protocol), which is the pre-action protocol governing fast track personal injuries cases. This protocol is similar to PD Pre-action conduct, paras 6.1 to 9.7, which lay down similar requirements as to disclosure of documents and the factual basis of each side's case where no specific protocol applies. The chapter also mentions some other topics relevant in the pre-issue period, such as sending notices and pre-action applications.

2.2 Pre-action protocols

2.2.1 Published protocols

There are published protocols for personal injury claims, medical negligence claims (also known as clinical disputes), disease and illness claims, housing disrepair claims, rent arrears claims, mortgage possession claims, building disputes, defamation claims, professional negligence claims, and judicial review. Compliance with pre-action protocols is intended to ensure an open and cooperative approach to case preparation. Compliance is also intended to promote the prospects of achieving settlements as early as possible and on an informed basis. Compliance with any relevant protocol is regarded as the normal reasonable approach for solicitors to take, with failure to adhere to a relevant protocol being punished by a harsher response to applications for extensions of time later on, and possible costs penalties and other sanctions.

2.2.2 Alternative dispute resolution (ADR)

Litigation should be seen as a last resort. The steps required to be taken by pre-action protocols are intended to ensure that other means of resolving disputes are attempted before proceedings are issued (PD Pre-action conduct, para 8.1). Lawyers on both sides are under a heavy obligation to consider alternatives to litigation, such as mediation, and to resort to proceedings only where this is really unavoidable (*Cowl v Plymouth City Council* (2001) The Times, 8 January 2002).

Each of the published protocols (other than the construction disputes protocol) requires the parties to consider whether some form of ADR would be more suitable than litigation. Both sides may be required to provide the court with evidence that ADR was considered. Proceedings should not be issued while settlement is being actively explored. Each of the protocols expressly recognises that the parties cannot be forced to mediate or enter into any form of ADR, but a failure to comply with the requirement to consider ADR may be taken into account on costs.

2.2.3 Pre-action admissions of liability

One of the purposes of the pre-action protocols is to enable defendants to assess the strength of the claim they are facing, and to decide whether to admit liability at an early stage. Usually, defendants keep to such pre-action admissions, but there have been a number of instances where the admission is abandoned if proceedings are issued. At common law there was no restriction on a defendant withdrawing a pre-action admission (*Sowerby v Charlton* [2006] 1 WLR 568). Provided the conditions set out below are satisfied, in the period before proceedings are issued, such an admission may be withdrawn only with the consent of the claimant (CPR, r 14.1A(3)(a)). After proceedings are issued, such an admission may only be withdrawn if all parties consent or if the court gives permission (r 14.1A(3)(b)).

The conditions are that the pre-action admission:

(a) was made on or after 6 April 2007;

(b) was made by a notice in writing (r 14.1A(1));

(c) was made in a claim governed by either the Pre-action Protocol for Personal Injury Claims; the Pre-action Protocol for the Resolution of Clinical Disputes; or the Pre-action Protocol for Disease and Illness Claims (PD 14, para 1.1(2)); and

(d) was made either after the defendant received a letter before claim written in accordance with the relevant pre-action protocol (r 14.1A(2)(a)) or if the admission is stated to be made under Part 14 (r 14.1A(2)(b)).

2.3 Cases not covered by pre-action protocols

In cases not covered by an approved protocol, the court will expect the parties, in accordance with the overriding objective, to act reasonably in exchanging information and documents relevant to the claim and generally in trying to avoid the necessity for the start of proceedings. The parties should follow a reasonable procedure, suitable to the particular circumstances. Normally this will involve the claimant writing a detailed letter before claim which should list the essential documents relied upon. A failure to write before issuing proceedings may be penalised in costs (*Phoenix Finance Ltd v Fédération Internationale de l'Automobile* The Times, 27 June 2002). The time a defendant should be given for giving a full response will depend on the nature of the case. In simple debt cases 14 days may be enough, whereas 30 days may be needed if the claim is likely to be met by an insurer, or 90 days if the matter is complex (PD Pre-action conduct, para 7.2). The defendant's full response should say whether liability is accepted in full or in part or denied (Annex A, para 4.1). If liability is denied, the response must give detailed reasons and list the essential documents relied upon (Annex A, para 4.2). Both parties are entitled to ask for copies of documents in the possession of the other side, which must not be used by the recipient for purposes other than resolving the dispute (para 9.2). Both parties should state whether they are prepared to enter into mediation or some other method of dispute resolution. If expert evidence is required, the parties should consider how best to minimise expense (para 9.4).

2.4 Personal injury protocol

The personal injury protocol is designed primarily for personal injuries claims worth up to £15,000 (this may be raised to £25,000) or, in other words, cases likely to be allocated to the fast track if proceedings are commenced. The spirit of the protocol should be followed in larger cases. The parties can depart from the detail in the protocol, but the court will want an explanation of the reasons for departing from it if proceedings are subsequently issued. **Figure 2.1** sets out the steps that should be taken under the protocol.

Time	Comments
Soon after being retained	Solicitor should consider whether an informal notification of the possible claim should be made to the defendant. This will not start the protocol timetable.
Letter before claim	This should be sent at least six months before the expiry of limitation to give time for compliance before limitation expires. Two copies of the letter should be sent to the defendant, or one to the defendant and one to the insurer. The letter should be written in a style consistent with the overriding objective, not in a vituperative tone calculated to annoy the other side (*King v Telegraph Group Ltd* [2005] 1 WLR 2282). Also, (i) The letter should contain a clear summary of the facts, the nature of the injuries and details of the financial losses claimed. An example of such a letter is illustrated as **Figure 2.2**. (ii) If possible the letter before claim should indicate which documents should be disclosed by the defendant at this stage. Detailed lists of the types of documents that should be disclosed for different types of personal injuries cases are set out in annexes to the protocol. By way of example, the list for road traffic accident cases is set out as **Figure 2.3**. There are even more detailed lists for accidents at work, especially in cases where specific statutory provisions apply. No charge should be made for providing copy documents under the Protocol.
21 days	Defendant should reply with name of insurer, or the insurer should acknowledge.
Three months from acknowledging letter before claim	Defendant should have completed investigations. If liability is denied or if contributory negligence is alleged the defendant should provide documents on liability and reasons for the denial. Both parties should consider rehabilitation.
(Say) one month after denial	If contributory negligence has been alleged, the claimant should respond to these allegations.
(Say) one month after	Claimant sends defendant a Schedule of Special Damages defendant's letter and documents in support. This is particularly important where liability has been admitted.
At same time	Claimant sends defendant a list of suggested experts for each field of expertise. The letter should also state the basis of the proposed joint instructing of the necessary experts: that the expert will be sent a letter of instruction in accordance with the protocol, and that a copy of the report when obtained will be immediately sent to the other side.
14 days thereafter	Defendant has this time to raise any objections to the suggested experts.
Defendant objects to all suggested experts	Both parties are free to instruct their own experts. This may be penalised in costs later if either side has acted unreasonably.
Defendant does not object	Claimant selects an expert from those left, and sends a letter of instruction in accordance with the standard letter.
Receipt of report	Claimant's solicitor sends copies to client and defendant's insurer/solicitor.

Time	Comments
Ditto	Parties consider sending questions to clarify the report to the expert. The defendant should send its questions via the claimant's solicitors.
Ditto	Parties should consider sending Part 36 offers to the other side.
Ditto	Parties should consider whether mediation or ADR might be appropriate.
14 days before issue	Claimant should ask the defendant's insurers to nominate solicitors.
14 days after	Issue proceedings.

Figure 2.1   Table showing timetable laid down by the personal injury pre-action protocol

---

To: D. Stokes (Haulage) Limited, Defendant
Dear Sirs,

Our client:	Eleanor Jane Weldon
Our client's address:	47 Forest Road, London N10 4RS
Our client's employer:	Ellis Cuthbert Limited, Research Department, Manor Road, London N23 7PD

We are instructed by Eleanor Weldon to claim damages in connection with a road traffic accident on 27th November 2008 at the junction of Newlands Road and Waterfall Road, London N10.

Please confirm the identity of your insurers. Please note that the insurers will need to see this letter as soon as possible and it may affect your insurance cover and/or conduct of any subsequent proceedings if you do not send this letter to them.

The collision
The circumstances of the accident were that our client's car registration number YL06 PGE was stationary in Newlands Road waiting at its junction with Waterfall Road in order to turn right. Her right indicator was showing. Your van registration number XB51 YSJ driven by James Williams failed to stop as he approached the junction, and collided with the rear of our client's car.

Negligence
The reasons why we are alleging fault are that it was negligent not to slow down in time, or to see or take account of the presence of our client's car, and to collide with the rear of her stationary vehicle. You are vicariously liable for the negligence of your driver, Mr Williams.

Our client's injuries
A description of our client's injuries is as follows:
(a) whiplash injury to her cervical spine; and
(b) nervous reaction involving disturbance of sleep, flashbacks and panic attacks, particularly when travelling by car.
Our client received treatment for her injuries at the North London Hospital (hospital reference EJW 7469).
Our client is still suffering from the effects of her injury. We invite you to participate with us in addressing her immediate needs by the use of rehabilitation.

Loss of earnings
Our client is employed as a research assistant by Ellis Cuthbert Limited, Research Department, Manor Road, London N23 7PD, and had two weeks off work immediately following the accident. Her approximate net weekly income is £357.

Evidence

We are obtaining a police report and will let you have a copy of the same upon you undertaking to meet half the fee.

We have also sent a letter of claim to Mr Williams, and a copy of that letter is attached. At this stage of our enquiries we would expect the documents contained in Sections A and B of the RTA standard disclosure lists to be relevant to this claim.

Response

A copy of this letter is attached for you to send to your insurers. Finally we expect an acknowledgement of this letter within 21 days by yourselves or your insurers.

Yours faithfully,

Buchanan & Co

Figure 2.2   Letter before claim

Section A In all cases where liability is at issue—

(i)   Documents identifying the nature, extent and location of damage to the defendant's vehicle where there is any dispute about the point of impact.
(ii) MOT certificate where relevant.
(iii) Maintenance records where a vehicle defect is alleged or if it is alleged by the defendant that there was an unforeseen defect which caused or contributed to the accident.

Section B Accident involving commercial vehicle as potential defendant—

(i)   Tachograph charts or entry from individual control book.
(ii) Maintenance and repair records required for operator's licence where vehicle defect is alleged or it is alleged by defendants that there was an unforeseen defect which caused or contributed to the accident.

Section C Cases against local authorities where highway design defect is alleged—

(i)   Documents produced to comply with s 39 of the Road Traffic Act 1988 in respect of the duty designed to promote road safety to include studies into road accidents in the relevant area and documents relating to measures recommended to prevent accidents in the relevant area.

Figure 2.3   Standard disclosure list for road traffic accidents

2.5 Selection of experts under the protocol

The personal injuries protocol regards the joint selection of a single expert to be the norm. It therefore provides that before the claimant (or any other party) instructs an expert he or she should give the other party a list of the name(s) of one or more experts in the relevant speciality who are considered suitable to instruct. Within 14 days the defendant may indicate an objection to one or more of the listed experts. Provided the defendant does not object to all the proposed experts, the claimant should then instruct a mutually acceptable expert from those remaining from the original list.

If the defendant objects to all the listed experts, the parties may instruct experts of their own choice. It would be for the court to decide subsequently, if proceedings are issued, whether either party had acted unreasonably. This might be because all the claimant's listed experts are known to produce reports slanted in favour of the claimant, or it might be that the defendant does not have sustainable rational reasons for having objected to all the experts proposed by the claimant.

Some solicitors choose to obtain medical reports through medical agencies, rather than directly from a specific doctor or hospital. The defendant's prior consent to this being done should be sought, and if the defendant so requests, the agency should be asked to provide in advance the names of the doctor(s) whom they are considering instructing.

Where a medical expert is to be instructed the claimant's solicitor will organise access to the relevant medical records. A model form of letter of instruction can be seen in **Figure 2.4**. Any medical report obtained by agreement under the protocol should

---

Dear Sir,

Our client:	Eleanor Jane Weldon
Our client's address:	47 Forest Road, London N10 4RS
Our client's DoB:	14th July 1969
Telephone No.:	020 8764 9933
Date of accident:	27th November 2008

We are acting for Eleanor Weldon in connection with injuries received in a road traffic accident on 27th November 2008. The main injuries appear to have been a whiplash injury to her cervical spine and a nervous reaction involving disturbance of sleep, flashbacks and panic attacks, particularly when travelling by car.

We should be obliged if you would examine our client and let us have a full and detailed report dealing with any relevant pre-accident medical history, the injuries sustained, treatment received and present condition, dealing in particular with the capacity for work and giving a prognosis.

It is central to our assessment of the extent of our client's injuries to establish the extent and duration of any continuing disability. Accordingly, in the prognosis section we would ask you specifically to comment on any areas of continuing complaint or disability or impact on daily living. If there is such continuing disability you should comment upon the level of suffering or inconvenience caused and, if you are able, give your view as to when or if the complaint or disability is likely to resolve.

Please send our client an appointment direct for this purpose. Should you be able to offer a cancellation appointment please contact our client direct. We confirm we will be responsible for your reasonable fees.

We are obtaining the notes and records from our client's GP and hospitals attended, and will forward them to you when they are to hand.

In order to comply with Court Rules we would be grateful if you would address your report to 'The Court'. The report must refer to this letter and to any other written or oral instructions given, it must give details of your qualifications and of any literature or other materials used in compiling the report, and where there is a range of opinion it must summarise the range of opinion and give reasons for your opinion. At the end of the report you will need to include a statement that you understand your duty to the Court and have complied with it. Above your signature please include a statement in the following terms: 'I confirm that insofar as the facts stated in my report are within my own knowledge I have made clear which they are and believe them to be true, and that the opinions I have expressed represent my true and complete professional opinion.' In order to avoid further correspondence we can confirm that on the evidence we have there is no reason to suspect we may be pursuing a claim against the hospital or its staff.

We look forward to receiving your report within six weeks. If you will not be able to prepare your report within this period please telephone us upon receipt of these instructions. When acknowledging these instructions it would assist if you could give an estimate as to the likely time scale for the provision of your report and also an indication as to your fee. Yours faithfully,

Buchanan & Co

Figure 2.4   Model letter of instruction to medical expert

normally be disclosed to the other party. The claimant should delay issuing proceedings for 21 days from disclosure of the report, to enable the parties to consider whether the claim is capable of settlement.

Either party may send to the expert written questions on the report via the claimant's solicitors. The expert should send answers to the questions separately and directly to each party.

There is a distinction between jointly selecting an expert (such as by using the procedure in the first paragraph of this section) and jointly instructing an expert. A party instructing a jointly selected expert retains legal professional privilege in the expert's report, and can refuse to disclose it to the other side (*Carlson v Townsend* [2001] CPLR 405). Both parties are entitled to see a jointly instructed expert's report.

2.6 Compliance with the protocol with limitation approaching

If the claimant consults a solicitor close to the end of the limitation period, the solicitor should give as much notice to the defendant of the intention to commence proceedings as is practicable. The parties may invite the court to extend the time for service of supporting documents and/or service of the defence, alternatively, for a stay of proceedings pending completion of the steps required by the protocol. However, solicitors must ensure they issue proceedings before limitation expires.

2.7 Failure to comply

Obviously, there will be cases where either or both parties fail to comply with the requirements of a protocol. There may be a rational justification for doing so, and if this is accepted by the court there will be no adverse consequences. Where a failure to comply arises through slackness or deliberate flouting, a claimant may be justified in commencing proceedings without going through the rest of the procedures laid down in the protocol, and either party may find they are penalised by the court at a later stage. If, in the opinion of the court, non-compliance has led to the commencement of proceedings which might otherwise not have needed to be commenced, or has led to costs being incurred in the proceedings that might otherwise not have been incurred, by virtue of PD Pre-action conduct, para 4.6, the orders that the court may make include:

(a) staying the proceedings until steps which ought to have been taken are taken;

(b) an order that the party at fault pays the costs of the proceedings, or part of those costs, of the other party or parties;

(c) an order that the party at fault pays those costs on an indemnity basis;

(d) if the party at fault is a claimant in whose favour an order for the payment of damages or some specified sum is subsequently made, an order depriving that party of interest on such sum and in respect of such period as may be specified, and/or awarding interest at a lower rate than that at which interest would otherwise have been awarded;

(e) if the party at fault is a defendant and an order for the payment of damages or some specified sum is subsequently made in favour of the claimant, an order awarding interest on such sum and in respect of such period as may be specified

at a higher rate, not exceeding 10 per cent above base rate, rather than the rate at which interest would otherwise have been awarded.

The powers set out in (a) to (e) above are to be used to place the innocent party in no worse a position than he would have been in had the protocol been complied with.

Further, the court may make an order that the defaulting party should pay a sum of money into court if the default was without good reason (CPR, r 3.1(5)).

It is expressly provided that if the court has to consider the question of compliance, it will not be concerned with minor infringements, such as the failure by a short period to provide relevant information. A single minor breach will not exempt the 'innocent' party from complying with the protocol.

(1) Circumstances of the accident, to include:
  (a) Date of accident.
  (b) Where?
  (c) Who was involved?
  (d) Who is (are) the likely defendant(s)?
  (e) What happened?
  (f) Names and addresses of all witness known to the client.
(2) Did the police attend?
(3) Was there any other accident investigation?
(4) Were criminal proceedings brought as a result of the accident? If so, what was the result, and is a certificate of conviction available? Are notes of the hearing available?
(5) Nature of the injuries and treatment.
(6) Financial losses:
  (a) Employment.
  (b) Accident-related damage to car, clothes etc.
  (c) Out of pocket expenses to date, including prescriptions, travel costs, physiotherapy, medical appliances.
  (d) Nursing care (including from family): how many hours per week, did it vary over time?
  (e) DIY loss? Gardening loss? Decorating loss? Car maintenance loss?
(7) Have the documents in support of the financial losses been preserved? These should include:
  (a) Pay slips, preferably from about six months before the accident to date.
  (b) P60s and P45s.
  (c) Any employment contract or service contract or letter of appointment.
  (d) Any correspondence about job applications since the injury, and any advertisements for jobs applied for.
  (e) Receipts for out of pocket expenses.
  (f) Correspondence about matters such as pension rights, early retirement etc.
(8) The client's GP and hospital notes and records will need to be obtained.
(9) You will need the client's date of birth for the Particulars of Claim (this is often in the medical notes).
(10) The client's National Insurance number will be needed for the Compensation Recovery Unit certificate of recoupable benefits.

Figure 2.5   Checklist for information to be obtained from clients in personal injuries claims

2.8 Road traffic claims

Drivers are compulsorily required by the Road Traffic Act 1988 (RTA 1988) to be insured against liability for personal injuries and death in road accidents. Three matters connected with this are discussed below.

2.8.1   Recovery against insurer

At common law a person injured in a road accident had no cause of action against a negligent driver's insurer. However, since 19 January 2003 in most cases a claimant may recover damages direct from the driver's insurer pursuant to the European Communities (Rights against Insurers) Regulations 2002, SI 2002/2061. These Regulations apply to claims in tort arising out of accidents on roads or other public places caused by the use of insured vehicles. Insurance for this purpose means (broadly) insurance complying with RTA 1988, s 145, for compulsory motor insurance. Where the Regulations apply the insurer may be named as a defendant, and is liable, together with the driver, to the same extent as the driver (reg 3(2)).

In cases where the motor insurer is not named as a defendant, the motor insurer is in any event liable to pay any damages awarded to the claimant provided the claimant gives the insurer notice of the proceedings against the defendant driver before or within seven days after proceedings are commenced: RTA 1988, s 152. With regard to the form of notice, see *Desouza v Waterlow* The Independent, 27 October 1997, CA.

2.8.2   Uninsured drivers

The Motor Insurer's Bureau has been set up by the insurance industry to provide compensation to victims of road accidents who cannot bring effective proceedings in the usual way. To this end, two agreements have been made between the Motor Insurers' Bureau and the Minister for Transport.

Under the first agreement, provided the victim satisfies a number of conditions (including giving the Motor Insurers' Bureau notice of proceedings against the negligent driver within seven days of commencement), the Bureau will pay any award of damages against an uninsured driver in respect of compulsorily insurable risks if the judgment is not paid within seven days.

2.8.3   Untraced drivers

Under the second agreement, the Motor Insurers' Bureau will pay damages to road accident victims where the driver responsible is unidentified (eg a 'hit and run' driver). As there is no known defendant in such cases, claims are dealt with administratively. The Bureau considers the victim's injuries and the blame for the accident, reducing the compensation payable accordingly. The claimant can appeal from the assessment to an arbitrator, who is often a QC.

2.9   Other pre-action notices

For other types of proceedings notices of various sorts have to be sent before proceedings are issued. Examples are default notices in consumer credit cases, notice to quit and other statutory notices in landlord and tenant cases, demands in cases where money is payable on demand, and notice of assignment. These types of notices are laid down in the substantive law dealing with different causes of action.

2.10 Pre-action relief

The CPR allow parties to make applications before commencing the main proceedings in certain situations. The main ones are when the need for a court order arises in urgent circumstances such that there is no time to issue a claim form before having to go before the judge (a situation most frequently encountered when applying for injunctions), and in cases where it would be helpful to obtain evidence before commencing proceedings to check whether there is a good case against the proposed defendants. These situations will be considered further in **Chapters 10, 14–16** and **21**.

3 Commencement of proceedings

3.1 Introduction

Proceedings are commenced usually by issuing a claim form. There is a prescribed form for this document. There are some other methods of commencing proceedings, and they will be considered at the end of this chapter. Issuing involves the court sealing the claim form with its official seal. This is an important event, because it stops time running for limitation purposes, and starts time running for service. Generally, a claim form must be served within four months of being issued. In certain circumstances the four month period may be extended, which is a subject considered in **Chapter 25**. The main topics that will be considered in this chapter will be issuing and serving proceedings.

3.2 Which court?

Before issuing proceedings it is necessary to decide whether to use the High Court or the County Court. The High Court can generally be used in money claims with a value exceeding £25,000. A major exception is personal injuries cases, which may only be started in the High Court if they have a value exceeding £50,000. In claims where money is not the remedy being sought, it is a matter of professional judgement whether the importance and complexity of the case justifies using the High Court. These questions were considered in more detail at **1.3.2** above.

The second question is to decide on the location of the court to use. The High Court sits not only in London but also in a number of regional District Registries. There are also County Courts throughout the country. Essentially this is a question of convenience. Generally the claimant's solicitor is given the choice as to which local court to use, and as a practical matter will probably have the convenience of the claimant primarily in mind. However, if the case is defended the court will give primary consideration to the convenience of the defendant. A claimant wishing to avoid delay through the case being transferred may well decide to use the court most local to the defendant. Sometimes there is no choice. Proceedings seeking possession of residential property have to be commenced in the County Court serving the district where the property is situated.

3.3 The claim form

It is the responsibility of the claimant's solicitors to prepare the claim form before issue. For most proceedings there is a general purpose claim form (Form N1; see **Figure 3.1**) that should be used. To commence specialist proceedings, special claim forms as approved by any relevant Practice Direction should be used. A completed claim form will:

(a) set out the names and addresses of the respective parties;

(b) give a concise statement of the nature of the claim;

(c) state the remedy sought; and

(d) contain a statement of value where the claim is for money. This will be the amount sought if the claim can be specified, or, if not, whether it is expected the amount that will be recovered is no more than £5,000; between £5,000 and £25,000; or more than £25,000. In some cases all that can be said is that the amount cannot be stated. In personal injuries claims the amount expected for pain, suffering and loss of amenity must be stated as being either below or above £1,000.

Royal Arms   *Claim Form*   In the High Court of Justice
                                                Queen's Bench Division

                                                Claim No. 09Q 98744

Claimant
Shilton Machine Tools Limited
18 Rotherham Road,
Manchester
M36 3BJ   SEAL

Defendant
Banks Plastic Mouldings Limited

Brief details of claim
Price of goods sold and delivered, plus interest.

Value   £70,500

Defendant's name and address   £

                                      Amount claimed   70,500.00
Banks Plastic Mouldings Limited   Court fee   630.00
Registered office: Solicitor's costs   TBA
Unit 6,   Issue date   24.9.2009
Elland Trading Estate
Leeds LS8 3AN

The court office at The Royal Courts of Justice, Strand, London WC2A 2LL is open between 10 am and 4 pm Monday to Friday. When corresponding with the court, please address forms and letters to the Court Manager and quote the claim number.

                                                Claim No. 09Q 98744

Does, or will, your claim include any issues under
the Human Rights Act 1998?   ☐Yes   ☑ No

Particulars of claim (attached) (to follow)

1. By a contract contained in or evidenced by the Defendant's Order dated the 7 March 2008 the Claimant agreed to sell and deliver four plastic moulding machines to the Defendant for the sum of £60,000 plus VAT.

2. Despite delivering the machine tools to the Defendant and rendering an invoice number ST9922 dated the 12 May 2008 the Defendant has failed to pay all or any of the price of the machines.

PARTICULARS

Price of the machine tools	£60,000.00
VAT at 17.5%	£10,500.00
Total	£70,500.00

3. Payment was due 30 days after invoice. The Claimant is entitled to interest at the rate of 8% per annum pursuant to the Supreme Court Act 1981, section 35A on the sum of £70,500 from the 12 June 2008 to the 24 September 2009 amounting to £7,262.46, and continuing from the 25 September 2009 to judgment or earlier payment at the daily rate of £15.45.

AND the claimant claims:

1. The sum of £70,500.00.

2. Interest on the sum of £70,500 pursuant to the Supreme Court Act 1981, section 35A amounting to £7,262.46 to 24 September 2009, and continuing at the daily rate of £15.45.

Statement of Truth

(I believe) (The Claimant believes) that the facts stated in these particulars of claim are true.

I am duly authorised by the Claimant to sign this statement.

Full name

Name of claimants' solicitor's firm	Boardman, Phipps & Co
signed	position or office held
(Claimant) (Litigation friend) (Claimant's solicitor)	(if signing on behalf of firm or company)
delete as appropriate	
20 High Street, Manchester M15 9CZ	Claimant's or Claimant's solicitor's address to which documents should be sent if different from overleaf. If you are prepared to accept service by DX, fax or e-mail, please add details

Figure 3.1 Claim form

3.4 Jurisdictional indorsements

In cases that are to be issued in the High Court the claim form must, unless the claim is for a specified amount, be indorsed with:

(a) a statement that the claimant expects to recover more than £25,000 (or more than £50,000 in personal injuries claims); or

(b) a statement that a named enactment provides that the claim may only be commenced in the High Court; or

(c) a statement that the claim is for a named specialist High Court list, or the claim form must comply with the requirements laid down in a Practice Direction for one of the specialist lists.

Examples are:

- 'I expect to recover more than £25,000.'
- 'My claim includes a claim for personal injuries and the value of the claim is £50,000 or more.'

There is nothing to prevent a claimant stating a value below the full potential loss, even though the effect may be that a smaller fee will be payable when the claim is issued (*Khiaban v Beard* [2003] 1 WLR 1626).

3.5 Particulars of claim

Particulars of claim is the term used to describe the formal written statement setting out the nature of the claimant's case together with the nature of the relief or remedy sought from the defendant. It can be included in the claim form (on the reverse of the form), or be set out in a separate document. An example of a short form of particulars of claim in a debt recovery action can be seen on the claim form shown in **Figure 3.1**. If a separate document is used it must be served either with the claim form, or within 14 days after service of the claim form (CPR, r 7.4(1)), and in any event within the period of validity of the claim form (usually four months from issue; see r 7.4(2)). If contained in a separate document the claim form must state that the particulars are either attached or will follow (by deleting words at the top of the second page of the form). Further information regarding the contents of particulars of claim can be found in **Chapter 5**.

3.6 Issuing the claim form

3.6.1 The usual procedure

The claimant's solicitors will make sufficient copies of the claim form for themselves, the court and each defendant. They retain one, and send the others to the court office, together with the prescribed fee under cover of a letter asking for the claim to be issued. Alternatively, the claimant's solicitors may attend personally at the court office to ensure the claim is issued, which may be sensible if time is short. Technically, time stops running for limitation purposes when a claim is 'brought' (see the Limitation Act 1980) rather when the claim is issued (*Barnes v St Helens Borough Council (Practice Note)* [2007] 1 WLR 879). A claim is 'brought' when it is delivered to the court, whereas a claim is 'issued' when it is sealed by the court office. The date a claim form is sealed is often the best evidence of when it is brought. If the documents are sent by post, the court office stamps the covering letter when it is received. In such a case time stops running for limitation purposes on the date the covering letter is date stamped by the court (PD 7, paras 5.1, 5.2).

The court issues the claim by sealing the claim forms, and enters details of the claim in its records. On issuing the claim the court will allocate a claim number to the case, which it indorses on the claim forms. The court then sends a form called a notice of issue to the claimant's solicitors that tells them the claim number, date of issue, confirms receipt of the issue fee, and, if service is effected by the court, also confirms the date of service.

3.6.2 Money Claim Online

Most simple money claims with a value up to £100,000 can be issued electronically using a scheme known as 'Money Claim Online'. These claims are issued at Northampton County Court by sending an online claim form and paying the issue fee electronically.

The particulars of claim may be filed and served separately from the claim form, but, if indorsed on the claim form, must not exceed 1,080 characters. Service of the claim form is effected by the court, and is deemed to be effected on the fifth day after issue irrespective of whether that day is a business day or not (PD 7E, para 5.7). Defendants can respond either electronically or by using hard copies (para 7.1). If no response is obtained, judgment can be entered in default (see **Chapter 6**) by filing an electronic request (para 11). Electronic claims are transferred to the defendant's home court on various events, including the filing of a defence (para 12).

3.7 Service

Service on a defendant in England and Wales must be effected within four months of issue. The period of validity for service is six months if the defendant is to be served outside the jurisdiction (CPR, r 7.5(2)). Under the Civil Procedure Rules 1998 there are slightly different systems dealing with service of claim forms and service of other documents, with a third system dealing with service outside the jurisdiction (see **Chapter 11**). There is a fourth system dealing with service on companies at their registered offices. It is worth noting that 'service' deals with transmitting documents to the other side, and the related concept of 'filing' deals with providing documents to the court.

3.8 Service of the claim form

A 'claim form' for the purpose of the rules dealing with service of originating process includes a petition, any application to commence proceedings, and any pre-action application (CPR, r 6.2(c)).

3.8.1 Documents to be served

The documents to be served comprise the sealed claim form, particulars of claim (although this may follow), and a 'response pack'. The response pack consists of practice forms of acknowledgment of service, admission, defence, and counterclaim. Form N9 is a combined cover sheet for the response pack and tear-off acknowledgment of service form. The defence and counterclaim is also a combined form. There are two types of admission form and also two types of defence and counterclaim form. Forms N9A and N9B are for use in claims for specified amounts of money. Forms N9C and N9D are for use in claims for unspecified sums of money and in non-money claims.

In personal injuries claims the particulars of claim will have to be accompanied by a medical report and schedule of loss and expense, and these must be served with the claim form if the particulars of claim are served at the same time. In publicly funded cases a notice of issue of the funding certificate has to be served with the claim form. In cases funded under a conditional fee agreement the claim form must be accompanied by a notice giving information of the funding arrangement in Form N251.

3.8.2 Hierarchy of modes of service of claim forms

There is a hierarchy of methods of service and requirements of where claim forms must or may be served which are set out in CPR rr 6.3 to 6.13:

(a) If an enactment, a provision of the CPR or any PD or court order requires personal service, that method must be used (r 6.5(1)). Otherwise,

(b) If the defendant notifies the claimant in writing of the defendant's solicitor's address (in the jurisdiction) for service, or the defendant's solicitor notifies the claimant in writing the solicitor is instructed by the defendant to accept service, the claim form must be served at the address of the defendant's solicitor (r 6.7).

(c) If mandatory personal service (r 6.5) or mandatory service on the defendant's solicitor (r 6.7) do not apply, the claimant has the choice of serving a claim form either:

    (i) by personal service (r 6.5(2)); or

    (ii) at an address within the jurisdiction which the defendant has given for the purpose of service of the proceedings (r 6.8); or

    (iii) by a contractually agreed method of service (r 6.11); or

    (iv) where they apply, under the special rules dealing with service on the Crown (r 6.10), or in accordance with r 6.12 on an agent of a principal who is outside the jurisdiction, or in accordance with r 6.13 if the defendant is a child or protected party.

(d) If mandatory personal service (r 6.5) or mandatory service on the defendant's solicitor (r 6.7) do not apply, and the defendant has not given an address for service (r 6.8), the claim form may be served at the defendant's usual or last known address under r 6.9; see **3.8.3**.

3.8.3 Usual or last known address

The CPR, r 6.9, sets out in tabular form the appropriate places of service for different types of party (see **Figure 3.2**). For individuals it is their usual or last known residence. An address may be a defendant's last known address for this purpose even if the claimant knows or believes the defendant is no longer living there (*Cranfield v Bridgegrove Ltd* [2003] 1 WLR 2441), provided the claimant has taken reasonable steps to find the defendant's current address (r 6.9(3), *Mersey Docks Property Holdings v Kilgour* [2004] EWHC 1638 (TCC)). Where, having made reasonable inquiries, the claimant discovers the

Nature of defendant to be served	Place of service
Individual	Usual or last known residence.
Individual being sued in the name of a business	Usual or last known residence of the individual; or principal or last known place of business.
Individual being sued in the business name of a partnership	Usual or last known residence of the individual; or principal or last known place of business of the partnership.
Limited liability partnership	Principal office of the partnership; or any place of business of the partnership within the jurisdiction which has a real connection with the claim.
Corporation (other than a company) incorporated in England Wales	Principal office of the corporation; or any place within the jurisdiction where the corporation carries on its activities and which has a real connection with the claim.
Company registered in England and Wales	Principal office of the company; or any place of business of the company within the jurisdiction which has a real connection with the claim.
Any other company or corporation	Any place within the jurisdiction where the corporation carries on its activities; or any place of business of the company within the jurisdiction

Figure 3.2 Addresses for service for different kinds of party

defendant's current address, the claim form must be served at that address (r 6.9(4)(a)). If those inquiries point to some other address or method by which service could be effected, the claimant must make an application under r 6.15 (see **3.8.6**). It is only where these alternatives are not available that service may be effected at an address where the defendant no longer resides. An address where the defendant has never resided cannot be a 'last known' residence (*Collier v Williams* [2006] 1 WLR 1945). The address for a defendant who is a tenant of a room is the house address, not that of the room (*Akram v Adam* [2005] 1 WLR 2762).

3.8.4 Service within the jurisdiction

Service by these means (CPR, rr 6.3 to 6.13, other than service by a contractually agreed method) has to be effected within the jurisdiction (r 6.6(1)). This means personal service has to take place within the jurisdiction, and any address used for the other methods of service must be within the jurisdiction. Where the claim form is served at an address, it does not matter that the defendant was temporarily outside the jurisdiction at the time of deemed service (*City and Country Properties v Kamal* [2007] 1 WLR 1219).

3.8.5 Methods of service

Permissible methods of service are set out in CPR, r 6.3:

(1) *A claim form may be served by any of the following methods—*
   (a) *personal service, in accordance with r 6.5;*
   (b) *first class post, document exchange or other service which provides for delivery on the next business day, in accordance with [PD 6A];*
   (c) *leaving it at a place specified in rr 6.7, 6.8, 6.9 or 6.10;*
   (d) *fax or other means of electronic communication in accordance with [PD 6A]; or*
   (e) *any method authorised by the court under rule 6.15.*

3.8.5.1 Personal service

Personal service of a document is effected by leaving a copy of the document with the person to be served. If a person (whom it is intended to serve) has knowledge of the nature of the document and has been given a sufficient opportunity of possession to enable that person to exercise dominion over it for any period of time, however short, it will amount to 'leaving' for the purpose of this rule (*Nottingham Building Society v Peter Bennett and Co* The Times, 26 February 1997, CA).

Personal service on a company means service on a person in a senior position, which in turn means a director, treasurer, secretary, chief executive, manager or other officer (PD 6A, para 6.2).

Personal service on a partnership where partners are sued in the name of the partnership is effected by leaving the claim form with a partner or a person having the control or management of the partnership business at its principal place of business (CPR, r 6.5(3)(c)).

3.8.5.2 Postal service

Any postal service providing for next business day delivery can be used. Addresses have to include full postcodes (CPR, r 6.6(2)).

3.8.5.3 Document exchange (DX)

This is a system used by the great majority of solicitors and chambers, and a number of other businesses, for transporting documents between their offices. It only works between offices using the system. Members pay periodic lump sums for the service. Generally documents put into the document exchange system arrive the next business day, although there are occasional delays. It is permissible only where the defendant's address where they are to be served includes a DX number, or where the writing paper of the defendant or its solicitor includes a DX number, and the defendant or its solicitor has not stated they are unwilling to be served by DX (PD 6A, para 2.1).

3.8.5.4   Service by facsimile (fax)

As to fax, PD 6A, para 4.1, requires the defendant to have previously indicated in writing a willingness for service to be accepted in this way. Where the defendant is acting in person, the willingness to accept service by fax must be expressly stated in writing. Where the defendant is acting by a solicitor, such a willingness may be shown by including a fax number in the solicitor's writing paper or in a statement of case or a response to the claim (para 4.1(2)). Dispatching documents by fax without obtaining the defendant's prior agreement is more than a minor departure from the rules (*Kuenyehia v International Hospitals Group Ltd* The Times, 17 February 2006). There is no need to confirm service by fax by sending a second copy by post or DX (PD 6A, para 4.3).

3.8.5.5   Service by e-mail

Service may only be effected by e-mail where the recipient has previously expressly indicated a willingness to accept service in this way and provided an e-mail address. An e-mail address set out in the defendant's solicitor's writing paper which also states the e-mail address may be used for service, or inclusion of an e-mail address in a statement of case or response to a claim, is a sufficient indication for this purpose (PD 6A, para 4.1(2)(b), (c)).

3.8.5.6   Contractual service

Where a claim is brought under the terms of a contract, and that contract contains a term providing for court proceedings to be served by a specified method, the claim form may be validly served in accordance with that method (CPR, r 6.11). Many standard form contracts contain such terms. If the claim form has to be served outside the jurisdiction, the claimant must also comply with the rules regarding service outside the jurisdiction (discussed in **Chapter 11**).

3.8.5.7   Ad hoc agreement on service

Anderton v Clwyd County Council (No. 2) [2002] 1 WLR 3174 held that the only legitimate methods of service are those laid down by CPR, Part 6 (and the Companies Act 2006). *Cranfield v Bridgegrove Ltd* [2003] 1 WLR 2441 at [81], [85], however, approved *Kenneth Allison Ltd v AE Limehouse and Co.* [1992] 2 AC 105, which held that an ad hoc agreement between the parties about the method of service is effective.

3.8.6   Alternative service

Sometimes it is not possible to effect service using the various methods set out above, or the reasonable steps taken to find the defendant where the claimant has only a 'last known' address discloses some other means that could be used to bring the claim to the defendant's attention. The defendant may be evading service, or prove difficult to find. In such cases it is sometimes possible to persuade the court to allow service by an alternative method or at an alternative place under CPR, r 6.15. Such orders can be made prospectively (r 6.15(1)), or retrospectively to approve steps already taken in attempting to effect service (r 6.15(2)).

An application for such an order needs to be supported by written evidence which must:

- state the reason alternative service is sought;
- state the proposed alternative method or place of service; and
- explain why it is believed service will be effective if the alternative method or place is used.

Examples of possible methods of alternative service are by advertisement in a newspaper; service by text message; and service on the defendant at the address of his or her insurer. In *Abbey National plc v Frost* [1999] 1 WLR 1080, which involved a claim against a solicitor, it was held that an order to effect alternative service of proceedings upon the Solicitors' Indemnity Fund would be allowed. An order for alternative service at an address within the jurisdiction will not be made if its purpose is to evade the restrictions on serving defendants outside the jurisdiction (for which, see **Chapter 11**) (*Knauf UK GmbH v British Gypsum Ltd* [2002] 1 WLR 907).

3.8.7   Dispensing with service of the claim form

The court may dispense with service of the claim form if there are exceptional circumstances (CPR, r 6.16(1)). An application under this rule may be made at any time, may be made without notice, and must be supported by evidence (r 6.16(2)).

There may be an exceptional case where there has been a minor departure from the rules on service (*Cranfield v Bridgegrove Ltd* [2003] 1 WLR 2441). This power may be used where one of the translations of the claim form is omitted in a case where service has to be effected outside the jurisdiction (*Phillips v Symes (No 3)* [2008] 1 WLR 180, HL). Common errors, such as serving by fax when the defendant has not consented to such service, are not sufficiently exceptional (*Kuenyehia v International Hospitals Group Ltd* The Times, 17 February 2006).

3.9   Deadline for service of a claim form

Where a claim form is served within the jurisdiction, by CPR, r 7.5(1), the claimant must complete the step required for the method of service the claimant chooses to use by 12.00 midnight on the calendar day four months after the date of issue of the claim form. All the claimant has to do is to take the relevant step. Whether the deemed date of service (see **3.10**) takes place later, or the claim form never arrives, or is delayed in transmission, is irrelevant. **Figure 3.3** sets out the step the claimant is required to take for each method of service.

Method of service	Step required
First class post, DX, or other delivery service which provides for delivery on the next business day	Posting, leaving with, delivering to or collection by the relevant service provider
Delivery of the document to or leaving it at the relevant place	Delivering to or leaving the document at the relevant place
Personal service under r 6.5	Completing the relevant step required by r 6.5(3)
Fax	Completing the transmission of the fax
Other electronic method	Sending the e-mail or other electronic transmission

Figure 3.3   Step required for service under CPR, r 7.5(1)

3.10 Deemed date of service of the claim form

A claim form served in accordance with the above rules is deemed to be served on the second business day after completion of the step required by CPR, r 7.5 (see r 6.14). A 'business day' is any day except Saturday, Sunday, a bank holiday, Good Friday and Christmas Day (r 6.2(b)). Rule 6.14 creates an irrebuttable presumption of law, which means evidence to contradict the deemed date of service is inadmissible. See **3.12**.

3.11 Service of other documents

Service of documents other than the claim form within the jurisdiction is governed by CPR, rr 6.20 to 6.29. The normal rule is that the party has to serve the other side if it prepared the relevant document, and the court will do so if it prepared the document (r 6.21). In either case the court can order otherwise. The available methods of service are the same as for claim forms (r 6.20, and see **3.8**). While personal service must be used if this is prescribed (r 6.22, eg for orders with penal notices), generally documents other than claim forms are served at the address the party gives as their address where they may be served. Claimants do this by stating their address on the claim form, and defendants do likewise by stating their address on the acknowledgment of service or defence. Where the party has a solicitor acting for them, the address is that of their solicitor (r 6.23(2)). A litigant in person has to provide an address for service which must be within the United Kingdom (r 6.23(3)). Any change to these addresses has to be notified to the court and other parties as soon as it takes place (r 6.24).

The court also has powers to order service of non-claim form documents by alternative methods or at alternative places (r 6.27), and to dispense with service of such documents (r 6.28).

3.12 Deemed dates of service of documents other than the claim form

By CPR, r 6.26, documents other than the claim form are deemed to be served on the day shown in **Figure 3.4**.

The deemed dates of service set out in **Figure 3.4** take effect on proving one of the prescribed methods of service, and cannot be displaced by proving the actual date of receipt (*Godwin v Swindon Borough Council* [2002] 1 WLR 997). The deemed dates of service are calculated as ending on certain 'business days', which are defined by r 6.2(b) as excluding Saturdays, Sundays, bank holidays, Christmas Day and Good Friday. It will be seen from **Figure 3.4** that these calculations also include phrases like 'the second day' and 'that day'. These expressions mean calendar days (*Anderton v Clwyd County Council (No 2)* [2002] 1 WLR 3174), so are calculated including weekends and public holidays. *Anderton v Clwyd County Council (No 2)* makes it clear that this is so despite r 2.8, which excludes weekends and public holidays when calculating periods of less than five days (see **1.4.2.3**).

Method of service	Deemed day of service
First class post (and other delivery services providing for delivery on the next working day)	The second day after it was posted, left with, delivered to or collected by the relevant service provider provided that day is a business day; or if not, the next business day after that day
Document exchange	The second day after it was left with, delivered to or collected by the relevant service provider provided that day is a business day; or if not, the next business day after that day
Delivering the document or leaving it at a permitted address	If it is delivered to or left at the permitted address on a business day before 4.30 pm, on that day; or in any other case, on the next business day after that day
Fax	If the transmission of the fax is completed on a business day before 4.30 pm, on that day; or in any other case, on the next business day after the day on which it is transmitted
Other electronic method	If the e-mail or other electronic transmission is sent on a business day before 4.30 pm, on that day; or in any other case, on the next business day after the day on which it was sent
Personal service	If the document is served personally before 4.30 pm on a business day, on that day; or in any other case, on the next business day after that day

Figure 3.4   Deemed dates of service

3.13 Service on companies

Companies registered under the Companies Acts can be served using the CPR rules described above at their principal place of business or place of business having a real connection with the claim. Alternatively, such a company may be served at its registered office under the Companies Act 2006, s 1139. Unless CPR, r 6.3(2), brings service under s 1139 into the ambit of the CPR, service at the registered office will be governed by the Companies Act 2006. If so, service by post will be deemed to have been served in the ordinary course of posting (Interpretation Act 1978, s 7).

3.14 Certificate of service

A party effecting service is often required to file a certificate of service. For example, where the claimant serves the claim form, he must file a certificate of service within 21 days of service of the particulars of claim, unless all the defendants file acknowledgments of service within that time (CPR, r 6.17(2)). An example is shown in **Figure 3.5**.

3.15 Non-compliance with the rules on service

Where a claimant attempts to serve a claim form by a method not complying with CPR, Part 6, service will be set aside if an application is made by the defendant. If service cannot be effected within the period of validity of a claim form, the claimant may apply for an extension of the period of validity (see **Chapter 25**), but there are restrictions on extensions being granted (see CPR, r 7.6). The restrictions cannot be evaded by relying on the general powers to extend time and grant relief contained in Part 3 (see *Vinos v*

Certificate of service

In the High Court of Justice
Queen's Bench Division

Claim No. HQ 09 98744
Claimant Shilton Machine Tools Limited
Defendant Banks Plastic Mouldings Limited

On the 16th October 2009 the claim form and response pack a copy of which is attached to this notice was served on Banks Plastic Mouldings Limited

☐ by first class post   ☐ by Document Exchange
☐ by delivering to or leaving   ☐ by handling it to or leaving it with
☐ by fax machine (. . . . . time sent)
(you may want to enclose a copy of the transmission sheet)
☐ by other means *(please specify)*

at *(insert address where service*   Unit 6, Elland Trading Estate,
effected, including fax or DX number   Leeds LS8 3AN
or e-mail address)

being the defendant's:
      residence   registered office
      place of business   other *(please specify)*

The date of service is therefore deemed to be 20th October 2009 *(insert date — see over for guidance)*

Statement of truth I believe that the facts stated in this certificate of service are true.

Signed: Position or
            Claimant's Solicitor   office held
Date: 16th October 2009   *(if signing on behalf of firm or company)*

Figure 3.5   Certificate of service

Marks & Spencer plc [2001] 3 All ER 784). In exceptional cases the court may dispense with service (see **3.8.7**). The court may also be persuaded that the steps taken justify an alternative service order (see **3.8.6**).

Where a party purports to serve a claim form within its period of validity, but by an incorrect method, or at an incorrect address, the court has a discretion whether to grant relief under CPR, r 3.10 (for which, see **1.4.3**), which is exercised in accordance with the overriding objective. On an application for an order remedying such an error in procedure, the court will consider whether the claimant has taken all reasonable steps to put the matter right once the problem was discovered (*Nanglegan v Royal Free Hampstead NHS Trust* [2001] 3 All ER 793, where relief was refused).

3.16 Objecting to jurisdiction

A defendant who wishes to object to the court having jurisdiction over a claim should make an application pursuant to CPR, Part 11. The main provisions of Part 11 are as follows:

(1) *A defendant who wishes to—*
    (a) *dispute the court's jurisdiction to try the claim; or*
    (b) *argue that the court should not exercise its jurisdiction, may apply to the court for an order declaring that it has no such jurisdiction or should not exercise any jurisdiction which it may have.*

> (2) *A defendant who wishes to make such an application must first file an acknowledgment of service in accordance with Part 10.*
>
> (3) *A defendant who files an acknowledgment of service does not, by doing so, lose any right he may have to dispute the court's jurisdiction.*
>
> (4) *An application under this rule must—*
>
> > (a) *be made within 14 days after filing an acknowledgment of service; and*
> >
> > (b) *be supported by evidence.*
>
> (5) *If the defendant—*
>
> > (a) *files an acknowledgment of service; and*
> >
> > (b) *does not make such an application within the period specified in paragraph (4), he is to be treated as having accepted that the court has jurisdiction to try the claim.*
>
> . . .
>
> (9) *If a defendant makes an application under this rule, he must file and serve his written evidence in support with the application notice, but he need not before the hearing of the application file—*
>
> > (a) *in a Part 7 claim, a defence; or*
> >
> > (b) *in a Part 8 claim, any other written evidence.*

In the pre-CPR case of *Patel v Patel* [2000] QB 551, it was held that merely applying to set aside a default judgment did not amount to taking a step in the proceedings, and did not prevent the defendant from disputing the court's jurisdiction. Although the rule says the application must be made within 14 days after filing the acknowledgment of service, this period, like most others in the rules, may be extended under CPR, r 3.1(2)(a) (*USF Ltd v Aqua Technology Hanson NV/SA* (2001) LTL 31/1/2001).

3.17 Other types of originating process

There are a number of other forms used for commencing proceedings (these are called forms of originating process), two of the most common alternatives being:

(a) Part 8 claim forms, which are used in cases where there is no dispute of fact. These are discussed further at **3.18**; and

(b) Petitions, which are used in divorce proceedings, bankruptcy and winding up. The matrimonial and insolvency fields have their own detailed procedural rules, and will not be considered further in this manual. They are considered in the ***Family Law in Practice*** and ***Company Law in Practice*** manuals.

3.18 Part 8 claims

The main type of originating process under the CPR is the claim form previously discussed, and it is used for almost all types of proceedings where there is likely to be dispute of fact. As will be seen in **Chapter 5**, the issues raised in such claims are defined in written statements of case that have to be served and filed by each party. An alternative procedure for bringing a claim is that laid down in CPR, Part 8. A claim brought under Part 8 has its own 'Part 8 claim form' (form N 208). Part 8 claims are for use where there is no substantial dispute of fact (CPR, r 8.1(2)(a)). They perform a similar function to what used to be called a construction summons under the old rules, which was a type of originating process technically called an originating summons, often brought by a trustee or executor, seeking the court's ruling on the true meaning of a clause in a trust deed or will. In such cases the court is simply being asked to construe a document, and there should be no dispute of fact. A Part 8 claim can be used for some applications pursuant to statute/statutory instrument. For example, Part 8 claims are used for approval of children's settlements where proceedings have not been commenced (CPR, r 21.10(2)), and for applications made under various statutes listed in PD 8, Part B.

A Part 8 claim form must state that Part 8 applies, and must set out the question the claimant wants the court to decide or the remedy sought. If the claim is brought pursuant to statute the relevant statute must be stated (CPR, r 8.2). Otherwise, a Part 8 claim form looks very much like an ordinary claim form. Note, however, that under r 8.2A a Practice Direction may set out circumstances in which a Part 8 claim form may be used without naming a defendant. Where it appears to a court officer that a claim has been inappropriately issued using the Part 8 procedure, the claim may be referred to a judge to decide how the case should be dealt with (PD 8, para 3.4). A procedural judge may at any stage order the claim to continue as a Part 7 claim, and where this happens the court will issue directions and allocate the claim to a track (para 3.5).

Any evidence the claimant relies upon must be filed and served with the claim form (CPR, r 8.5(1), (2)). After the claim form has been issued and served, any defendants have 14 days to acknowledge service (r 8.3(1)). An acknowledgment should be on the official form, form N210 which includes a statement of truth (PD 8, para 5.2). Defendants must file their evidence when they acknowledge service. The claimant may file and serve evidence in reply within 14 days thereafter (r 8.5(5), (6)).

Part 8 claims are treated as allocated to the multi-track (CPR, r 8.9(c)), although the court may override this and allocate the claim to a track (PD 8, para 8.2). Directions may be given when the Part 8 claim is issued, or at a later stage either on the application by a party or by the court of its own initiative (para 6.1). If it appears there is unlikely to be a dispute, the court is likely to fix a hearing date when it issues the claim (para 6.1), which, depending on events, may be used for finally disposing of the claim or for giving directions (para 8.1). In more complex cases the court may postpone giving directions until after the defendant has acknowledged service (para 6.2), and may fix a directions hearing (para 6.4).

3.19 Specialist proceedings

The Rules and Practice Directions governing proceedings in the specialist courts (see **1.3.5**) often lay down different requirements for things such as acknowledging service (sometimes with acknowledgment being required after service of the claim form but before service of the claimant's statement of case), track allocation and directions.

In addition, there are special rules governing certain categories of proceedings. These include:

(a) defamation claims, which are governed by CPR, Part 53 and PD 53;

(b) claims for judicial review, which are governed by CPR, Part 54 and PD 54. Judicial review proceedings are considered in more detail in the **Remedies** manual, **Chapter 14**;

(c) landlord and tenant claims, which are governed by CPR, Parts 55 and 56. Residential landlord and tenant claims are considered in more detail in *Blackstone's Civil Practice*, chapters 84 to 91. Claims against trespassers are considered in more detail at **12.9** below; and

(d) probate claims, which are governed by CPR, Part 57.

3.20 Filing

Documents are filed by being delivered to the court. Some courts will accept documents filed electronically (see PD 5B). A court manager has no jurisdiction to refuse to accept a document (for example) on the ground it should have been filed in another County Court (*Gwynedd County Council v Grunshaw* (1999) 149 NLJ 1286). Filing takes effect immediately if documents are posted through the court's letter box, even if the court is closed at the time (*Van Aken v Camden London Borough Council* [2003] 1 WLR 684). If the court is closed on the final day for filing a document, filing will be in time if effected on the next day the court is open (*Aadan v Brent London Borough Council* The Times, 5 November 1999).

Responding to a claim

4.1 Introduction

Time only starts running against a defendant from service of the particulars of claim. A defendant served with a claim form without particulars of claim need do nothing, although once a claim form has been served it is fairly predictable that particulars of claim will follow in the near future. As mentioned earlier, in fact the particulars of claim should be served within 14 days of service of the claim form. Once the particulars of claim have been served the defendant has a limited time to decide what to do and to do it. Essentially the time available is 14 days from the date of service of the particulars of claim.

After service of the particulars of claim the defendant has a choice of:

- filing an admission;
- filing a defence, which may be combined with making a counterclaim; or
- filing an acknowledgment of service.

4.2 Admissions

A defendant who admits the claim is normally best advised to complete the admission form (N9A or N9C depending on whether the claim is for a specified sum of money) included in the response pack. The response pack form is illustrated at **Figure 4.1**, and the admission form N9A is illustrated at **Figure 4.2**. The admission form allows the defendant to admit either the whole claim or just a part. If the whole claim is admitted, the defendant needs to decide about payment. If the whole sum is paid within 14 days of service of the claim form, the defendant's liability for the claimant's costs will be limited to certain fixed sums laid down in the rules. This assists the defendant, because fixed costs are considerably lower than the sums recoverable in contested litigation. The admission form also allows a defendant who wants time to pay to make an offer to pay by instalments. If this is done the defendant must also complete a large number of questions set out in the form dealing with the defendant's personal and financial circumstances. The form will be returned to the claimant. The claimant will then consider the offer, and if it is acceptable will notify the court and a judgment will be entered for payment by the instalments offered by the defendant. If the claimant does not agree to the offer to pay by instalments, the rules make provision for the rate of payment to be determined by the court.

A defendant can also use the admission form to make a partial admission, denying the rest of the claim. The part that is denied has to be dealt with in a defence, which should be filed at court together with the admission form. Again, if this happens the claimant is asked whether the partial admission is acceptable, and if so a judgment will be entered in that sum.

4.3 Defences

A defendant disputing a claim must file a defence. Among the forms included in the response pack is a form of defence and counterclaim (N9B or N9D depending on whether the claim is for a specified sum of money), which has spaces where the defendant can set out the reasons why the claim is disputed, and also for details of any counterclaim. The defence and counterclaim form, N9B, is shown in **Figure 4.3**. Claims usually seen by counsel are sufficiently complicated to merit drafting a detailed defence which simply will not fit in the limited space available on the form in the response pack. This is recognised in the rules, which merely provide that a defence 'may' be set out in the response pack form (PD 15, para 1.3). A defence drafted by counsel will be properly laid out, with the full title to the claim including the claim number, court and parties' names, underneath which the word 'defence' appears in capitals and in tramlines, followed by the text of the defence. The contents of defences will be considered further in **Chapter 5**.

4.4 Acknowledgment of service

Acknowledgments of service are used if the defendant is unable to file a defence in the time limited, or if the defendant intends to dispute the court's jurisdiction. Acknowledging service delays the time within which the defence must be filed by an extra 14 days, so that the defence need not be served until 28 days after service of the particulars of claim (CPR, r 15.4(1)(b)).

As mentioned earlier, the acknowledgment of service form is combined with the cover sheet of the response pack (Form N9). It has a heading setting out the details of the court, parties and claim number. The defendants should write in their full names if they have been misnamed in the claim form. Defendants should also insert their address for service, which must be within the jurisdiction. If they are acting by a solicitor it will be their solicitor's address. If they are individuals, they must give their dates of birth. They then have to tick a single box saying whether they intend to defend the whole or part of the claim, or to contest the court's jurisdiction. The form is then signed and dated, and filed with the court. If two or more defendants acknowledge service through the same solicitors only a single acknowledgment of service need be used (PD 10, para 5.3).

Once an acknowledgment of service is received by the court it must notify the claimant in writing (CPR, r 10.4). This is normally done by sending a copy of the acknowledgment of service to the claimant.

Response pack

You should read the 'notes for defendant' attached to the claim form which will tell you when and where to send the forms

Included in this pack are:

- either **Admission Form N9A** (if the claim is for a specified amount)
- or **Admission Form N9C** (if the claim is for an unspecified amount or is not a claim for money)

- either **Defence and Counterclaim Form N9B** (if the claim is for a specified amount)
- or **Defence and Counterclaim Form N9D** (if the claim is for an unspecified amount or is not a claim for money)

- **Acknowledgment of service** (see below)

	Complete
If you admit the claim or the amount claimed and/or you want time to pay	the admission form
If you admit part of the claim	the admission form and the defence form
If you dispute the whole claim or wish to make a claim (a counterclaim) against the claimant	the defence form
If you need 28 days (rather than 14) from the date of service to prepare your defence, or wish to contest the court's jurisdiction	the acknowledgment of service
If you do nothing, judgment may be entered against you	

Acknowledgment of service

Defendant's full name if different from the name given on the claim form

Name of court High Court of Justice, Queen's Bench Division	
Claim No.	HQ09X98744
Claimant (including ref.)	Shilton Machine Tools Limited
Defendant	Banks Plastic Mouldings Limited

Address to which documents about this claim should be sent (including reference if appropriate)

	If applicable	
	Telephone no.	
	Fax no.	
	DX no.	
Postcode	Your ref.	

E-mail

Tick the appropriate box

1. I intend to defend all of this claim ☐
2. I intend to defend part of this claim ☐
3. I intend to contest jurisdiction ☐

(My) (Defendant's) date of birth is
☐☐ / ☐☐ / ☐☐☐☐

If you file an acknowledgment of service but do not file a defence within 28 days of the date of service of the claim form, or particulars of claim if served separately, judgment may be entered against you.

If you do not file an application to dispute the jurisdiction of the court within 14 days of the date of filing this acknowledgment of service, it will be assumed that you accept the court's jurisdiction and judgment may be entered against you.

If served outside the jurisdiction see CPR rule 6.35 and 6.37(5).

Signed

(Defendant) (Defendant's solicitor) (Litigation friend)

Position or office held (if signing on behalf of firm or company)

Date ☐☐ / ☐☐ / ☐☐☐☐

The court office at Royal Courts of Justice, Strand, London WC2A 2LL

is open between 10 am and 4 pm Monday to Friday. When corresponding with the court, please address forms or letters to the Court Manager and quote the claim number.

N9 Response pack (10.08)

© Crown copyright 2008

Figure 4.1 Response pack form N9

Admission (specified amount)

- You have a limited number of days to complete and return this form
- Before completing this form, please read the notes for guidance attached to the claim form

Name of court	
Claim No.	
Claimant (including ref.)	
Defendant	

When to fill in this form

Only fill in this form if:
- you are admitting all of the claim **and** you are asking for time to pay; or
- you are admitting part of the claim. (You should also complete form N9B)

How to fill in this form

- Tick the correct boxes and give as much information as you can. **Then sign and date the form.** If necessary provide details on a separate sheet, add the claim number and attach it to this form.
- Make your offer of payment in box 11 on the back of this form. **If you make no offer the claimant will decide how much and when you should pay.**
- If you are not an individual, you should ensure that you provide sufficient details about the assets and liabilities of your firm, company or corporation to support any offer of payment made in box 11.
- You can get help to complete this form at **any** county court office or Citizens Advice Bureau.

Where to send this form

- **If you admit the claim in full**
  Send the completed form to the address shown on the claim form as one to which documents should be sent.
- **If you admit only part of the claim**
  Send the form **to the court** at the address given on the claim form, together with the defence form (N9B).

How much of the claim do you admit?

- ☐ I admit the full amount claimed as shown on the claim form **or**
- ☐ I admit the amount of £ _____

1 Personal details

Surname _____

Forename _____

☐ Mr ☐ Mrs ☐ Miss ☐ Ms

☐ Married ☐ Single ☐ Other *(specify)* _____

Date of birth D D M M Y Y Y Y

Address _____

Postcode _____

Tel. no. _____

2 Dependants *(people you look after financially)*

Number of children in each age group

under 11 ☐   11-15 ☐   16-17 ☐   18 & over ☐

Other dependants *(give details)* _____

3 Employment

- ☐ **I am employed as a** _____
  My employer is _____
  Jobs other than main job *(give details)* _____

- ☐ **I am self employed as a** _____
  Annual turnover is............... £ _____
  - ☐ **I am not** in arrears with my national insurance contributions, income tax and VAT
  - ☐ **I am** in arrears and I owe........... £ _____

  Give details of:
  (a) contracts and other work in hand
  (b) any sums due for work done
  _____

- ☐ **I have been unemployed for** _____ years _____ months

- ☐ **I am a pensioner**

4 Bank account and savings

- ☐ **I have a bank account**
  - ☐ The account is in credit by........ £ _____
  - ☐ The account is overdrawn by.... £ _____
- ☐ **I have a savings or building society account**
  The amount in the account is.......... £ _____

5 Residence

I live in ☐ my own house ☐ lodgings
☐ my jointly owned house ☐ council accommodation
☐ rented accommodation

N9A Form of admission (specified amount) (04.06)   HMCS

Figure 4.2 Form of admission N9A

6 Income

My usual take home pay *(including overtime, commission, bonuses etc)*	£	per
Income support	£	per
Child benefit(s)	£	per
Other state benefit(s)	£	per
My pension(s)	£	per
Others living in my home give me	£	per
Other income *(give details below)*		
	£	per
	£	per
	£	per
Total income	**£**	**per**

8 Priority debts

(This section is for arrears only. Do not include regular expenses listed in box 7.)

Rent arrears	£	per
Mortgage arrears	£	per
Council tax/Community Charge arrears	£	per
Water charges arrears	£	per
Fuel debts: Gas	£	per
Electricity	£	per
Other	£	per
Maintenance arrears	£	per
Others *(give details below)*		
	£	per
	£	per
Total priority debts	**£**	**per**

7 Expenses

(Do not include any payments made by other members of the household out of their own income)

I have regular expenses as follows:

Mortgage *(including second mortgage)*	£	per
Rent	£	per
Council tax	£	per
Gas	£	per
Electricity	£	per
Water charges	£	per
TV rental and licence	£	per
HP repayments	£	per
Mail order	£	per
Housekeeping, food, school meals	£	per
Travelling expenses	£	per
Children's clothing	£	per
Maintenance payments	£	per
Others *(not court orders or credit debts listed in boxes 9 and 10)*		
	£	per
	£	per
	£	per
Total expenses	**£**	**per**

9 Court orders

Court	Claim No.	£	per

Total court order instalments	**£**	**per**

Of the payments above, I am behind with payments to *(please list)*

10 Credit debts

Loans and credit card debts *(please list)*

	£	per
	£	per
	£	per

Of the payments above, I am behind with payments to *(please list)*

11 Offer of payment

☐ I can pay the amount admitted on

or

☐ I can pay by monthly instalments of   £

If you cannot pay immediately, please give brief reasons below

12 Declaration

I declare that the details I have given above are true to the best of my knowledge

Signed

Position or office held *(if signing on behalf of firm or company)*

Date

Defence and Counterclaim
(specified amount)

- Fill in this form if you wish to dispute all or part of the claim and/or make a claim against the claimant (counterclaim).
- You have a limited number of days to complete and return this form to the court.
- Before completing this form, please read the notes for guidance attached to the claim form.
- Please ensure that all boxes at the top right of this form are completed. You can obtain the correct names and number from the claim form. The court cannot trace your case without this information.

How to fill in this form

- Complete sections 1 and 2. Tick the correct boxes and give the other details asked for.
- Set out your defence in section 3. If necessary continue on a separate piece of paper making sure that the claim number is clearly shown on it. In your defence you must state which allegations in the particulars of claim you deny and your reasons for doing so. **If you fail to deny an allegation it may be taken that you admit it.**
- If you dispute only some of the allegations you must
  - specify which you admit and which you deny; and
  - give your own version of events if different from the claimant's.

Name of court High Court of Justice Queen's Bench Division	
Claim No.	
Claimant (including ref.)	Shilton Machine Tools Limited
Defendant	Banks Plastic Mouldings Limited

- If you wish to make a claim against the claimant (a counterclaim) complete section 4.
- Complete and sign section 5 before sending this form to the court. Keep a copy of the claim form and this form.

Need help with your legal problems?
Community legal advice is a free confidential service, funded by legal aid. They can help you find the information and advice you need by putting you in touch with relevant agencies, helplines or local advice services. And if you are eligible for legal aid, the service can offer specialist legal advice over the telephone in cases involving: debt; housing; employment; benefits; and education.
Call **0845 345 4 345** or **www.communitylegaladvice.org.uk**

1. How much of the claim do you dispute?

☐ I dispute the full amount claimed as shown on the claim form.

or

☐ I admit the amount of £ _____

If you dispute only part of the claim you must **either:**

- pay the amount admitted to the person named at the address for payment on the claim form (see How to Pay in the notes on the back of, or attached to, the claim form). Then **send this defence to the court**

or

- complete the admission form **and this defence form and send them to the court.**

☐ I paid the amount admitted on __ / __ / ____

or

☐ I enclose the completed form of admission
(go to section 2)

2. Do you dispute this claim because you have already paid it? *Tick whichever applies*

☐ **No** *(go to section 3)*

☐ **Yes** I paid £ _____ to the claimant

on __ / __ / ____
(before the claim form was issued)

Give details of where and how you paid it in the box below *(then go to section 5)*

3. Defence (If you need to continue on a separate sheet put the claim number in the top right hand corner.)

(continue over the page)

Figure 4.3   Defence and counterclaim form N9B

Claim No.	

Defence (continued)

4. If you wish to make a claim against the claimant (a counterclaim)

- To start your counterclaim, you will have to pay a fee. Court staff can tell you how much you have to pay.
- You may not be able to make a counterclaim where the claimant is the Crown (e.g. a Government Department). Ask at your local county court office for further information.

If your claim is for a specific sum of money, how much are you claiming?   £

I enclose the counterclaim fee of   £

My claim is for *(please specify nature of claim)*

What are your reasons for making the counterclaim?
If you need to continue on a separate sheet put the claim number in the top right hand corner.

5. Signed - To be signed by you or by your solicitor or litigation friend.

*(I believe) (The defendant believes) that the facts stated in this form are true.
*I am duly authorised by the defendant to sign this statement.

delete as appropriate

Position or office held
(If signing on behalf of firm or company)

Date [ ] / [ ] / [   ]

Defendant's date of birth, if an individual [ ] / [ ] / [   ]

Give an address to which notices about this case can be sent to you

	If applicable
	Telephone no.
	Fax no.
Postcode [ ] [ ]	DX no.

E-mail

4.5 Agreed extensions

The parties may agree to extend the time for serving a defence, but any agreement can only be for a maximum of a further 28 days (CPR, r 15.5(1)). The defendant has to notify the court in writing of the agreed extension.

4.6 Transfer

Defended claims for specified sums of money against individuals are automatically transferred to the defendant's home court on receipt by the court of a defence (CPR, r 26.2). Transfers in other cases are governed by r 30.3(2), with criteria for deciding whether to transfer. These criteria include the financial value of the claim, whether it would be more convenient to try the case in another court and whether there is a real prospect of the court making a declaration of incompatibility under the Human Rights Act 1998. A court may transfer a claim to a county court even if the case is outside the jurisdictional limits of the county court (*National Westminster Bank plc v King* [2008] Ch 385).

Statements of case

5.1 Introduction

Statements of case are formal documents used in litigation to define what each party says about the case. The term 'statement of case' is defined by the CPR to include all the following documents:

- the claim form;
- particulars of claim where these are not included in a claim form;
- defence;
- counterclaim;
- additional claims under Part 20 (these will be considered further in **Chapter 9**);
- reply to defence; and
- further information given in relation to the above whether voluntarily or by court order (requests for further information are considered in **Chapter 22**).

Statements of case exceeding 25 pages must be accompanied by a short summary (PD 16, para 1.4).

Statements of case are usually the first documents that are served between the parties, other than the claim form and any acknowledgment of service. They are served in sequence, with the claimant serving particulars of claim first, followed by a defence from the defendant, then possibly a reply from the claimant. They are also often the first documents the judge will read when looking at the trial bundles, so the importance of having the client's case set out in a well-drafted document cannot be overemphasised.

The nature and content of statements of case are closely examined in the *Drafting* manual and what follows is a basic outline.

5.2 Purpose of statements of case

Statements of case serve two main purposes:

- To inform the other side of the case they will have to meet to ensure that they are not taken by surprise at the trial.
- To provide an outline of the contentions that will be put forward by the parties so that the trial judge can readily see what is in issue between the parties.

5.3   Particulars of claim

Particulars of claim will set out the facts that the claimant needs to prove in order to establish the cause of action. In short, the particulars of claim set out the material facts of the claim.

This means the document must set out the facts giving rise to the dispute, and must cover the facts which are the essential elements as a matter of law for the cause of action on which the case is based. For certain categories of action (such as personal injuries claims, fatal accidents and claims for the recovery of land) PD 16 sets out details that need to be included in the particulars of claim. If the claim is based on a written contract, the contractual documents must be attached to or served with the particulars of claim. In addition to setting out the cause of action relied upon, particulars of claim must include details of the remedies being claimed. Thus they must contain details of any claim for aggravated or exemplary damages; any claim for provisional damages; and any other remedy sought. They must also give full details of any interest claimed, including the rate, period covered, and the authority for claiming it. Often this will be the County Courts Act 1984, s 69, the Supreme Court Act 1981, s 35A, or the Late Payment of Commercial Debts (Interest) Act 1998.

For some classes of residential possession proceedings there are prescribed forms for particulars of claim; see PD 4 and, for example, N119, which is the form used for possession proceedings in respect of rented property.

Where a party seeks to raise a human rights point, the particulars of claim (and any other type of statement of case or appeal notice filed on behalf of that party) must set out precise details of the Convention right relied upon. It must also give details of the alleged infringement and it must state the relief sought (PD 16, para 15.1).

The claim form or particulars of claim must contain a signed statement of truth. This is a statement that its contents are believed to be true (CPR, r 22.1), and takes the form: 'I believe [the claimant believes] that the facts stated in these particulars of claim are true'. Any failure to include a statement of truth may result in an application for an unless order, with striking out as the sanction (PD 22, para 4.2).

Particulars of claim must be served within 14 days of service of the claim form. Additionally, service of the particulars of claim must be within the period of validity of the claim form (CPR, r 7.4(2)). If served separately from the claim form the claimant must file a copy within seven days of service (CPR, r 7.4(3)).

In personal injuries cases, the claimant must serve a medical report and statement of loss and expense with the particulars of claim. In contractual claims based on written contracts, the contractual documents must be served with the particulars of claim.

5.4   Defence

The defence answers the particulars of claim. It must state which of the allegations in the particulars of claim:

- are admitted, in which event it will no longer be in issue, or
- the defendant is unable to admit or deny, in which event the claimant will be put to strict proof, or

- are denied, in which event the defendant must state reasons for the denial, and must state any alternative version of events asserted by the defendant.

Any specific allegation that is not answered will be taken to be put in issue if the general nature of the defence on the issue appears from what is said in the defence. Otherwise the issue is deemed to be admitted (CPR, r 16.5(3), (5)). The amount of any money claim is deemed to be in dispute unless expressly admitted. If the claimant's statement of value is disputed, the defendant must say why and, if able to, give a counter-estimate.

Defendants who are individuals must state their dates of birth (PD 16, para 10.7). A defence may be set out on one of the forms included in the response pack, but it is usual for defences drafted by counsel to be typed on blank A4 paper. Like all other statements of case a defence must contain a statement of truth. It must be filed at court (CPR, r 15.2) and served on every other party (CPR, r 15.6) within 14 days of service of the particulars of claim, or 28 days if the defendant has acknowledged service.

5.5 Counterclaim

If the defendant has a cause of action against the claimant, this can be raised either by bringing separate proceedings or by way of counterclaim in the existing action. Assuming there is a defence, it is known as the defence and counterclaim.

It can be made using one of the forms included in the response pack. It must be verified by a statement of truth.

A counterclaim is treated as if it were a claim. A counterclaim may be made without permission if filed with the defence (CPR, r 20.4(2)(a)). An issue fee based on the full value of the counterclaim is payable.

5.6 Reply or defence to counterclaim

If the claimant wishes to deal with new matters raised in the defence, this is done in the reply. In a case where the defendant has counterclaimed, the claimant answers the counterclaim in the defence to counterclaim. Often, these are amalgamated into a reply and defence to counterclaim.

Replies must be filed within the time limited for filing allocation questionnaires, which is stated in the form and happens shortly after filing the defence. Like other statements of case the reply must be verified by a statement of truth.

5.7 Statement of truth

The usual rule is that every statement of case must be verified by a statement of truth signed by the party or their solicitor. This is to prevent parties relying on statements of case which they do not believe are true or which are not supported by evidence (*Clarke v Marlborough Fine Art (London) Ltd* [2002] 1 WLR 1731). A statement of case which is not verified remains effective unless it is struck out (CPR, r 22.2). When a statement of case is amended, the court may dispense with reverification (r 22.1(2)): this power may be exercised where a party relies, in the alternative, on facts asserted by the other side which are inconsistent with the facts he relies on for his primary case (*Binks v Securicor Omega Express Ltd* [2003] 1 WLR 2557).

5.8 False statement of truth

Proceedings for contempt of court may be brought by the Attorney-General (or by a party with the permission of the court) if a person makes, or causes to be made, a false statement in a document verified by a statement of truth without an honest belief in its truth (CPR, r 32.14). Permission to bring contempt proceedings is granted in flagrant cases where there has been an attempt to interfere with the course of justice (*Malgar Ltd v RE Leach Engineering Ltd* The Times, 17 February 2000). Permission was granted in *Kirk v Walton* [2008] EWHC 1780 (QB) where the evidence had been persisted in for a prolonged period of time, and there was strong prima facie evidence that it was false.

Although it is to be expected that such sanctions against solicitors signing statements of truth on behalf of their clients will be very rare, it is clearly important for solicitors to have statements of case approved by their clients before they are served. Counsel drafting statements of case should obviously bear this in mind, as a solicitor is unlikely to be very impressed if drafts settled by counsel result in difficulties over false statements of truth.

5.9 Striking out statements of case

The CPR, r 3.4, provides:

> (2) The court may strike out a statement of case if it appears to the court—
>   (a) that the statement of case discloses no reasonable grounds for bringing or defending the claim;
>   (b) that the statement of case is an abuse of the court's process or is otherwise likely to obstruct the just disposal of the proceedings; or
>   (c) that there has been a failure to comply with a rule, practice direction or a court order.

A Practice Direction supporting this rule provides that a claim may be struck out if it is incoherent or makes no sense, or if, even if the facts stated are true, they disclose no legally recognisable claim. It will also be struck out if it is vexatious, scurrilous or obviously ill-founded. Further, a defence may be struck out if it is a bare denial or otherwise fails to set out a coherent statement of facts amounting to a defence in law. If a statement of case is struck out, the judge may also make a declaration that it was totally devoid of merit. This can provide a foundation for making a vexatious litigant order or civil restraint order (see *Bhamjee v Forsdick* [2004] 1 WLR 88). These are orders which prevent litigants from misusing the right of access to the courts by requiring permission to be sought before the litigant can issue further proceedings or applications.

The same Practice Direction also refers to the power of the court to use this rule to strike out a claim or defence which is bound to fail, or to stay a claim which cannot proceed on the basis in which it is framed, and goes on to say the court may consider giving a party an opportunity of saving its statement of case by providing further information or documents. Even if a judge does not strike out under this power, the opposite party may still apply to strike out under r 3.4.

5.10 Interrelation with case management

Filing of the defence triggers the start of standard case management intervention by the court in the form of sending out of allocation questionnaires. This is the first step in the track allocation process, and leads also to the court making case management directions. These topics will be considered further in **Chapter 7**.

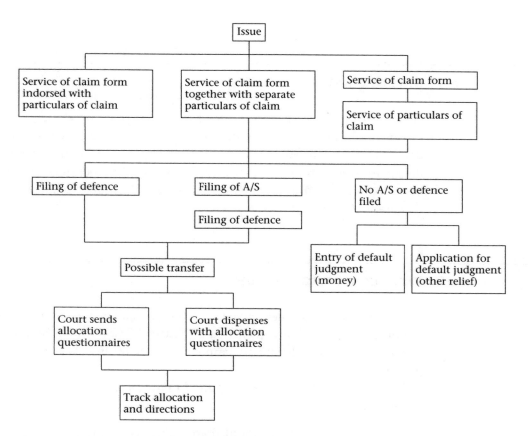

Figure 5.1   Flow diagram illustrating early stages in litigation

6

Judgment in default

6.1 Introduction

Where the defendant does not intend to contest the proceedings, it would be a waste of time and money, and very hard on the claimant, to proceed as if the claim were defended. Therefore, CPR, Part 12, allows a claimant to obtain early judgment against a defendant who fails to defend the claim. Usually, this does not even involve a hearing. In such cases, obtaining judgment is a purely administrative act, which is why one refers to 'entering' judgment.

6.2 What constitutes default?

A defendant who has been served with the particulars of claim has 14 days to make a response to a claim. Consequently, a defendant cannot be in default until that time has elapsed. Note that a defendant cannot be in default if a claim form is served without particulars of claim.

The CPR, r 12.3, allows a claimant to enter a default judgment in the following circumstances:

(a) if the defendant has not filed an acknowledgment of service or a defence to the claim (or any part of the claim) and 14 days has expired since service of the particulars of claim; or

(b) if the defendant has filed an acknowledgment of service but has not filed a defence, and 28 days has expired since service of the particulars of claim.

The CPR, r 12.3, provides:

(1) *The claimant may obtain judgment in default of an acknowledgment of service only if—*
   (a) *the defendant has not filed an acknowledgment of service or a defence to the claim (or any part of the claim); and*
   (b) *the relevant time for doing so has expired.*
(2) *Judgment in default of defence may be obtained only—*
   (a) *where an acknowledgment of service has been filed but a defence has not filed;*
   (b) *in a counterclaim made under rule 20.4, where a defence has not been filed, and, in either case, the relevant time limit for doing so has expired.*

6.3 Excluded cases

Default judgments are not available in a number of cases even if the defendant fails to respond to the claim. Excluded cases fall into two categories. In the first, the nature of the proceedings is a bar to obtaining a default judgment, and in the second some step taken by the defendant prevents the claimant entering judgment in default. Cases in the first category are summarised in PD 12, paras 1.2 and 1.3, as follows:

(a) claims which are brought using the alternative procedure in Part 8;

(b) claims for the delivery of goods subject to an agreement regulated by the Consumer Credit Act 1974;

(c) the rules governing certain specialist claims which do not include a requirement to file a defence or acknowledgment of service, or which provide special rules for obtaining default judgments. Cases falling into this sub-category are:

   (i)   admiralty proceedings;

   (ii) arbitration proceedings;

   (iii) contentious probate proceedings;

   (iv) claims for provisional damages; and

   (v)   possession claims.

Cases in the second category are set out in CPR, r 12.3(3), which provides:

> (3) *The claimant may not obtain a default judgment if—*
>   (a) *the defendant has applied—*
>   (i)   *to have the claimant's statement of case struck out under rule 3.4; or*
>   (ii) *for summary judgment under Part 24, and in either case that application has not been disposed of;*
>   (b) *the defendant has satisfied the whole claim (including any claim for costs) on which the claimant is seeking judgment; or*
>   (c) (i)   *the claimant is seeking judgment on a claim for money; and*
>   (ii) *the defendant has filed or served on the claimant an admission under rule 14.4 or 14.7 (admission of liability to pay all of the money claimed) together with a request for time to pay.*

6.4 Entering default judgment

6.4.1 By filing a request for judgment

In claims seeking to recover money and/or the delivery of goods, which are by far the most common types of cases, default judgments are available simply by filing a standard form request. In other words, entering judgment in undefended money claims is simply an administrative matter of posting forms to the court office, and a member of the court staff entering the judgment. There is no hearing, and no question of trying to persuade the court to enter judgment.

When proceedings are issued the court will send the claimant a notice of issue. There are three different forms of notice of issue, one for specified money claims, another for unspecified money claims, and the third for non-money claims. The two money claim notices include a tear-off section for the request for judgment. In the top part of the form the court staff enter the claim number, the date of issue, and the dates when the claim form was posted to the defendant, the deemed date of service, and the date by when the defendant has to respond. All the claimant has to do is wait until the time for responding has elapsed, then, if the claim is for a specified sum of money, tick a box saying the defendant has failed to respond, and enter details of the judgment sought. This involves calculating the amount owed together with interest and fixed costs (as set out in the CPR), and deciding whether to ask for the whole sum to be paid immediately or by stated instalments. The request form is then signed, dated and returned to the court. In claims for unspecified sums, all the claimant has to do, once the time for responding has elapsed, is to sign and date the request form, and return it to the court.

If the particulars of claim were served by the claimant, judgment in default cannot be obtained unless a certificate of service (see **Figure 3.5**) has been filed (CPR, r 6.17(2)(b)). There is no need for such a certificate if service is effected by the court.

As discussed at **3.10 and 3.12**, the deemed dates for service in rr 6.14 and 6.26 cannot be displaced by evidence showing that proceedings were in fact received on some other date (or were not in fact received at all). The judgments in *Godwin v Swindon Borough Council* [2002] 1 WLR 997, particularly at [49], are to the effect that a default judgment can be entered once the 14 days after deemed service of the particulars of claim have elapsed whether or not the defendant actually received the documents served.

6.4.2   By applying for judgment in default

Default judgments in non-money and non-recovery of goods claims (principally these will be cases where some form of equitable relief is sought, such as injunctions) have to be applied for. In other words, where equitable relief is sought and the defendant does not defend the claim, a judgment can only be obtained at a hearing before a District Judge or judge who will decide whether to exercise the court's discretion to grant the relief sought.

Within the context of claims seeking money or recovery of goods, there are a number of exceptional cases where default judgments cannot be entered by filing a request, but only by obtaining permission by making an application. These are:

(a) Where the claim form was served out of the jurisdiction without permission under the Brussels and Lugano Conventions or Jurisdiction Regulation on a defendant domiciled in a contracting State (essentially these are most countries in western Europe and across into eastern Europe) (see CPR, r 12.10(b)). Service outside the jurisdiction is considered further in **Chapter 11**. In these cases the Conventions prohibit the entry of judgment in default without the court checking that service complied with the relevant Convention. The claimant's evidence in support of the application for judgment must establish that the claim is one that the English court has power to hear and decide, that no other court has exclusive jurisdiction, and that the claim form has been properly served in accordance with the Convention (PD 12, para 4.3). The evidence in this particular case must be on affidavit (rather than the usual witness statement format) (PD 12, para 4.5).

(b) Where the defendant is a child or protected party (CPR, r 12.10(a)(i)). Before applying for judgment the claimant must apply for the appointment of a litigation friend to represent the person under disability. On the application for judgment the evidence must satisfy the court that the claimant is entitled to the judgment sought (PD 12, para 4.2).

(c) Where the claim is for or includes costs other than fixed costs (CPR, r 12.9).

(d) Where the claim is brought by one spouse against the other on a claim in tort (CPR, r 12.10(a)(ii)).

(e) Where the claim seeks delivery up of goods where the defendant is not to be allowed the alternative of paying their value. Relief in this form, as opposed to other types of delivery orders relating to claims relating to goods, is discretionary (see the Torts (Interference with Goods) Act 1977), which is why an application must be made. The evidence in support must identify the goods and say where the goods are believed to be kept and why the claimant says an order for specific delivery should be granted (PD 12, para 4.6). Usually this will have to be because of the rare or irreplaceable nature of the goods concerned.

Chapter 10 below describes how to make applications. Generally, the application will be made by issuing an application notice and must be supported by written evidence. The application notice must state the defendant's date of birth (if known) (CPR, r 12.4(2)). The evidence should include a certificate of service if the particulars of claim were served by the claimant. There is no need to serve the evidence in support on any defendant who did not acknowledge service (CPR, r 12.11(2)). This means that a defendant who acknowledged service but failed to file a defence has to be served with the evidence in support. Although the evidence in support in many cases does not need to be served on the defendant, the defendant should in all cases (other than service outside the jurisdiction, category (a) below) be given notice of the application itself by being served with the application notice (PD 12, para 5.1).

6.5 Final judgment and judgment for an amount to be decided

There are two main types of judgment obtainable in money claims. The best type is a final judgment, which will require the defendant to pay a set amount of money usually within 14 days. Apart from giving the defendant a limited amount of time to raise the money, this type of judgment allows the claimant to recover the whole sum straight away, or to apply to enforce if the defendant does not pay.

The other type is a judgment for damages to be decided by the court. There are variations on this form of judgment, such as judgments for the value of goods to be decided by the court and judgment for the amount of interest to be decided by the court. This type of judgment is sometimes called an 'interlocutory judgment', and the rules occasionally refer to this type of judgment as a 'relevant order'. This second type of judgment means that liability has been established and will not be considered any further, but all questions relating to the amount of damages or interest payable, or the value of the goods, have yet to be determined.

Final judgment will be entered in claims for specified sums (CPR, r 12.5), whereas judgment for damages to be decided will be entered in claims for unspecified amounts. There is some doubt as to what is meant by 'specified'. Options are specified by the claimant, or the same meaning as a liquidated demand. Liquidated demands are claims such as for the repayment of a loan or bank overdraft, or for the price of goods or services, or for rent. For each of these the amount claimed is fixed by the underlying agreement between the parties. This is so even though the amount may need to be calculated, such as the interest payable on the overdraft, or the rent payable over a period of time. Liquidated demands are usually contrasted with claims for unliquidated damages, such as for personal injuries or for the unsatisfactory quality of goods sold. The value of unliquidated claims requires an exercise of judicial judgment. Consequently, one school of thought takes the view that all damages claims are unspecified, and so default judgments in these cases should be for damages to be decided. However, the other school of thought takes the view that if the claimant spells out in the particulars of claim the amount of damages claimed the claim becomes one for a specified amount, so that a final judgment can be obtained.

6.6   Procedure for deciding the amount of damages

When the court enters a default judgment of the second type for damages or interest to be decided, or for the value of goods to be decided by the court, it will give any directions it considers appropriate. Further, if it thinks it appropriate it will also allocate the claim to a case management track (CPR, r 12.7). Alternatively, the court may list the matter for a disposal hearing, or will stay the action while the parties try to settle the case using ADR or other means.

The orders being considered here are described as 'relevant orders' by PD 26, para 12. In addition to being one of the possibilities on obtaining a default judgment, they may also be made on entry of judgment on an admission, on the striking out of a statement of case, on a summary judgment application, on the determination of a preliminary issue or on a split trial as to liability, or even by consent or at trial.

6.6.1   Disposal hearings

At a disposal hearing the court will either give directions or decide the amount payable (PD 26, para 12.4(2)). Relevant orders made by entry of default judgment without a hearing are usually dealt with in this way.

If the case is listed for a disposal hearing and the claim is worth less than £5,000 the court will usually allocate it to the small claims track (for costs purposes) and decide the amount payable there and then (PD 26, paras 12.3(1), 12.4(3)). If the financial value of the claim is more than £5,000 the court may still determine the amount payable at the disposal hearing, but in these cases the ordinary costs rules will apply. In cases determined at disposal hearings evidence may, unless the court otherwise directs, be adduced under CPR, r 32.6 (see PD 26, para 12.4(4)). This means that reliance may be placed on the matters set out in the particulars of claim (provided it is verified by a statement of truth) or by witness statement. The evidence relied upon must be served on the defendant at least three clear days before the disposal hearing.

6.6.2   Allocating relevant order cases to tracks

Allocating a case to the fast track or multi-track after a relevant order has been made should only happen if the amount payable is genuinely disputed on grounds that appear to be substantial (PD 26, para 12.3(2)). This topic is considered further in **Chapter 7**.

6.6.3   Hearing to assess damages

Generally, hearings to assess damages will be listed before Masters and District Judges irrespective of the amount in issue (PD 26, para 12.6), but the court may give directions specifying the level or type of judge who is to deal with the case (PD 26, para 12.2(2)). At the hearing the defendant can raise any point, such as mitigation of damages, which is not inconsistent with any issue settled by the judgment (*Pugh v Cantor Fitzgerald International* [2001] CPLR 271).

6.7   Setting aside default judgment

Because in most cases entering default judgment is an administrative process, there is no investigation of the merits of the claim. The court, therefore, retains wide powers to set aside or vary any such judgment (see CPR, Part 13). The court may exercise the power to set aside a judgment on an application by the defendant or of its own motion.

As Lord Atkin put it in *Evans v Bartlam* [1937] AC 480, HL:

The principle obviously is that unless and until the Court has pronounced a judgment upon the merits or by consent, it is to have the power to revoke the expression of its coercive power where that has only been obtained by a failure to follow any of the rules of procedure.

An application by a party is made by application notice to a Master or District Judge and must be supported by written evidence. Often a draft of the proposed defence is exhibited to the evidence in support.

6.7.1   Setting aside as of right

Setting aside is as of right if the default judgment was wrongly entered (CPR, r 13.2). There is a restrictive definition for this, limited to:

- situations where the essential conditions about failing to acknowledge service or defend, or the relevant time having elapsed, are not satisfied; or
- the claim was satisfied before judgment was entered; or
- the defendant had already applied for summary judgment; or
- the defendant had already filed an admission requesting time to pay.

Judgment was set aside as of right in *Credit Agricole Indosuez v Unicof Ltd* [2003] EWHC 77 (Comm), LTL 4/2/2003. The claimant purported to serve the claim form by leaving it with the defendant's company secretary in Kenya, whereas service in Kenya had to be by leaving the claim form at the company's registered office. As the claim form had not been served, the defendant was entitled to have the judgment set aside. Default judgment entered by the request method (see **6.4.1**) in circumstances where the application method had to be used (see **6.4.2**) will also be set aside as of right (*Intense Investments Ltd v Development Ventures Ltd* [2005] BLR 478).

6.7.2   Setting aside in the court's discretion

Otherwise, the court will only set aside or vary a default judgment if the defendant 'has real prospects of successfully defending the claim' or 'it appears . . . there is some other good reason why the defendant should . . . be allowed to defend the claim', taking into account any delay in applying (CPR, r 13.3). The question of whether the defence has real prospects of success is the same as in applications for summary judgment (see **12.7.1**). The only difference is that the burden of proof under r 13.3 rests on the defendant (*ED & F Man Liquid Products Ltd v Patel* [2003] CPLR 384).

Where a default judgment has been entered after the expiry of 14 days from the deemed date of service in a case where one of the prescribed methods of service in Part 6 has been used, but the defendant did not in fact receive the proceedings, setting aside is subject to the court's discretion rather than as of right (*Godwin v Swindon Borough Council* [2002] 1 WLR 997). Such a defendant will either have to show a defence with a real prospect of success, or rely on non-service as 'some other good reason' for setting aside the judgment. According to May LJ this may arise where a defendant would have paid instead of having an embarrassing judgment entered, and it may give rise to a different costs order (default judgments set aside on the merits usually result in the defendant being ordered to pay the costs thrown away; see **36.3**).

If there is a defence which carries some degree of conviction, the court will have a strong inclination to set aside a default judgment, even if strong criticism could be made of the defendant's conduct (*Citoma Trading Ltd v Federal Republic of Brazil* (CA, 29 July 1999), a case where judgment was set aside after seven and a half years). An application made several weeks after default judgment was entered was regarded as being 'prompt' within the meaning of r 13.3(2) where evidence for the application had to be obtained from overseas in *Shandong Chenming Paper Holding Ltd v Saga Forest Carriers Intl AS* [2008] EWHC 1055 (Comm).

In *Thorn plc v MacDonald* [1999] CPLR 660, the Court of Appeal approved the following principles:

- while the length of any delay by the defendant has to be taken into account, any pre-action delay is irrelevant;
- any failure by the defendant to provide a good explanation for the delay is a factor to be taken into account, but is not always a reason to refuse to set aside;
- the primary considerations are whether there is a defence with a real prospect of success, and that justice should be done; and
- prejudice (or the absence of it) to the claimant also has to be taken into account.

6.7.3   Conditions

Note, however, that when the court sets aside a default judgment which was regularly obtained, it may impose conditions (see CPR, r 3.1(3)). In most cases the court will order the defendant to pay the claimant's costs thrown away. In addition, the court may order the defendant to pay all or part of the disputed sum into court. Such terms will effectively amount to a precondition to allowing the defendant to contest the claim, ie, any failure to comply with the terms, and the claimant can proceed to enforce the default judgment. That being the case, the court should not impose a financial condition which the defendant cannot possibly meet, since that would be tantamount to giving judgment for the claimant. The onus, however, will be on the defendant to prove the impossibility of the condition. (See *MV Yorke Motors v Edwards* [1982] 1 WLR 444, a case on summary judgment, but applicable by analogy.)

6.8   Stay of undefended cases

If none of the defendants files an admission or defence, the claimant should generally enter judgment in default shortly after the time for doing so has elapsed, but in any event within six months of the period for filing the defence. Once the six months has elapsed, the claim is automatically stayed by virtue of CPR, r 15.11.

Any party may apply to lift the stay. They do so by making an application in accordance with the procedure discussed in **Chapter 10**, and must give the reason for the applicant's delay in proceeding with or responding to the claim (PD 15, para 3.4).

In considering whether to lift the stay the court will apply the criteria for granting relief from sanctions in r 3.9, which are discussed at **28.3.6** (see *Audergon v La Baguette Ltd* [2002] CPLR 192).

Track allocation

7.1 Introduction

It will be recalled from **1.4.1** above that the courts will seek to further the overriding objective of dealing with cases justly by active case management. In exercising their powers to manage cases, the courts will be seeking to ensure they are dealt with expeditiously and fairly. They will also try to allot to each case an appropriate share of the court's resources, and will endeavour to ensure they are dealt with proportionately bearing in mind factors such as the importance and complexities of the issues and the monetary value of the claim.

To assist with these aims defended claims are assigned to one of three case management 'tracks'. This happens shortly after the defendant files a defence, which is obviously quite early on in the litigation process. By this time the issues should have been defined by the parties in their statements of case. It is intended that procedural judges will be very willing to intervene during the early stages of proceedings, particularly at the track allocation stage, so as to ensure that the issues are narrowed, that cases are prepared economically and speedily, and disposed of fairly and without undue delay or expense.

The idea behind track allocation is that cases should be dealt with procedurally on a basis that is justifiable given the overall importance of each case. Difficult and important cases will be given Rolls Royce treatment, but cases which are simple and where not a great deal is at stake will be dealt with in a far more rough and ready way.

The smallest and simplest cases will therefore be assigned to the small claims track. These cases will usually be given an immediate date for hearing, with limited preparation being required, and the strict rules of evidence do not apply. Cases with a value in the range of £5,000 to £25,000 will usually be allocated to the fast track with standard directions and tight timetables of up to 30 weeks for completion of the preparatory stages before trial. Larger and more important cases will be assigned to the multi-track. The courts are given a great deal of flexibility in the way they can manage these cases, with a greater or lesser degree of intervention depending on how important the case is. Multi-track cases will mainly be dealt with at Civil Trial Centres (the larger court venues), and will usually be transferred to such locations as part of the case management process.

7.2 Allocation questionnaires

All defended cases will be allocated by the court to an appropriate track. On the defendant filing a defence the court will usually serve allocation questionnaires on all parties, although it does have a power to dispense with these questionnaires. Questionnaires may be dispensed with if there has already been an application, such as for summary judgment, which has been treated as an allocation hearing. If there are several defendants, the questionnaires are sent out after all the defendants have filed their defences, or when the time limited for them to do so has expired. An example of an allocation questionnaire is shown in **Figure 7.1**.

Before sending out allocation questionnaires the court will insert the date by which the forms must be returned, and must give the parties at least 14 days to do so. The date cannot be varied by agreement between the parties. The questionnaire asks for details as to whether the relevant pre-action protocol (if any) was complied with. It also asks whether a stay is sought for settlement; about possible transfer to another court; for the party's view on the appropriate track for the case; for details about expert and factual witnesses, and for details of any contemplated applications.

Parties may file additional information with their allocation questionnaires if this will assist the court in making its decisions regarding track allocation and case management. However, such additional information should only be filed if all the parties have agreed the information is correct and that it should be put before the court, or if the party intending to file the information confirms that copies have been delivered to all the other parties. The parties are encouraged to consult with one another and to cooperate in filling in their questionnaires. They are also encouraged to try to agree suggested directions, which may be sent to the court with the completed questionnaires. However, consulting between the parties should not be used as an excuse for late filing of the questionnaires.

When the parties return their completed questionnaires they should enclose a statement of their costs (an example is shown in **Figure 7.2**), and the claimant must pay a fee of £200 (the fee is £35 for small claims track cases, unless the claim does not exceed £1,500, when no fee is payable).

When the forms are returned or the time expires the court may order parties to provide further information about their cases, and may hold an allocation hearing. An example of such an order is shown on **Figure 7.3**.

7.3 Failing to file an allocation questionnaire

If a party fails to file an allocation questionnaire the court may give any direction it considers appropriate (CPR, r 26.5(5)). The court may allocate the claim if it considers it has enough information, or it may fix an allocation hearing and direct any of the parties to attend (PD 26, para 2.5(2)). If an allocation hearing takes place because of a failure to file an allocation questionnaire, the court will usually order the defaulting party to pay the costs of the other parties on the indemnity basis (para 6.6(2)). If the defaulting party fails to attend an allocation hearing, the court will usually make an order with sanctions (para 6.6(3)). If all the parties are in default, the file will be referred to the judge who will usually order that allocation questionnaires are to be filed within seven days from service of the order, failing which the claim and any counterclaim will be struck out without any further order from the court (para 2.5(1)).

Allocation questionnaire

To be completed by, or on behalf of,

Stephenson Hyperlinks Plc

Name of court
High Court of Justice
Queen's Bench Division

Claim No.	HCQ 87105

Last date for filing with court office	

who is [1ˢᵗ][2ⁿᵈ][3ʳᵈ][   ][Claimant][Defendant]
[Part 20 claimant] in this claim

Please read the notes on page six before completing the questionnaire.

You should note the date by which it must be returned and the name of the court it should be returned to since this may be different from the court where the proceedings were issued.

If you have settled this claim (or if you settle it on a future date) and do not need to have it heard or tried, you must let the court know immediately.

Have you sent a copy of this completed form to the other party(ies)?   ☑ Yes   ☐ No

---

A   Settlement

Under the Civil Procedure Rules parties should make every effort to settle their case before the hearing. This could be by discussion or negotiation (such as a roundtable meeting or settlement conference) or by a more formal process such as mediation. The court will want to know what steps have been taken. Settling the case early can save costs, including court hearing fees.

For legal representatives only

I confirm that I have explained to my client the need to try to settle; the options available; and the possibility of costs sanctions if they refuse to try to settle.   ☑

For all

Your answers to these questions may be considered by the court when it deals with the questions of costs: see Civil Procedure Rules Part 44.3 (4).

1. Given that the rules require you to try to settle the claim before the hearing, do you want to attempt to settle at this stage?   ☐ Yes   ☑ No

2. If Yes, do you want a one month stay?   ☐ Yes   ☑ No

3. Would you like the court to arrange a mediation appointment?   ☐ Yes   ☑ No

   (A fee will be payable to the mediation provider appointed by the National Mediation Helpline.)

4. If you answered 'No' to question 1, please state below the reasons why you consider it inappropriate to try to settle the claim at this stage.

Reasons:

There are a number of issues both on liability and quantum that require further investigation and clarification. The appropriate time to consider mediation further in this claim will be after inspection of documents following standard disclosure.

Figure 7.1   Allocation questionnaire

B Location of trial

Is there any reason why your claim needs to be heard at a particular court? ☐ Yes ☑ No

If Yes, say which court and why?

C Pre-action protocols

You are expected to comply with the relevant pre-action protocol.

Have you done so? ☑ Yes ☐ No

If No, explain why?

D Case management information

What amount of the claim is in dispute? £60,000.00

Applications

Have you made any application(s) in this claim? ☐ Yes ☑ No

If Yes, what for?   For hearing on
(e.g. summary judgment,
add another party)

Witnesses

So far as you know at this stage, what witnesses of fact do you intend to call at the trial or final hearing including, if appropriate, yourself?

Witness name	Witness to which facts
Mrs Lisa Stephenson Mr Vikesh Bharakhda Ms Suzanne Healey	Formation of contract, performance by Claimant Work done by the Claimant under the contract Cost of equipment and software incurred by the Claimant in performing the contract

Experts

Do you wish to use expert evidence at the trial or final hearing?   ☑ Yes   ☐ No

Have you already copied any experts' report(s) to the other party(ies)?

☑ None yet obtained
☐ Yes   ☐ No

Do you consider the case suitable for a single joint expert in any field?   ☑ Yes   ☐ No

Please list any single joint experts you propose to use and any other experts you wish to rely on.
Identify single joint experts with the initials 'SJ' after their name(s).

Expert's name	Field of expertise (eg. orthopaedic surgeon, surveyor, engineer)
Mr Jonathan Cousins	Computer Systems design

Do you want your expert(s) to give evidence orally at the trial or final hearing?   ☑ Yes   ☐ No

If Yes, give the reasons why you think oral evidence is necessary:

Tha claim raises difficult technical issues as to the nature of the equipment, software and services required under the contract, and the trial judge is likely to find it essential to have an independent technical expert available in court to assist in understanding these issues.

Track

Which track do you consider is most suitable for your claim? Tick one box

☐ small claims track
☐ fast track
☑ multi-track

If you have indicated a track which would not be the normal track for the claim,
please give brief reasons for your choice

E Trial or final hearing

How long do you estimate the trial or final hearing will take?

2 days	0 hours	0 minutes

Are there any days when you, an expert or an essential witness will not be able to attend court for the trial or final hearing?   ☑ Yes   ☐ No

If Yes, please give details

Name	Dates not available
Mr Jonathan Cousins	See attached list

F Proposed directions *(Parties should agree directions wherever possible)*

Have you attached a list of the directions you think appropriate for the management of the claim?   ☑ Yes   ☐ No

If Yes, have they been agreed with the other party(ies)?   ☐ Yes   ☑ No

G Costs

*Do **not** complete this section if you have suggested your case is suitable for the small claims track **or** you have suggested one of the other tracks and you do not have a solicitor acting for you.*

What is your estimate of your costs incurred to date?   £ 8,000.00

What do you estimate your overall costs are likely to be?   £ 30,000.00

In substantial cases these questions should be answered in compliance with CPR Part 43

H Fee

Have you attached the fee for filing this allocation questionnaire?   ☑ Yes   ☐ No

An allocation fee is payable if your claim or counterclaim exceeds £1,500.

Additional fees will be payable at further stages of the court process.

I   Other information

Have you attached documents to this questionnaire?	☑ Yes	☐ No
Have you sent these documents to the other party(ies)?	☐ Yes	☑ No

If Yes, when did they receive them?

Do you intend to make any applications in the immediate future?	☐ Yes	☑ No

If Yes, what for?

In the space below, set out any other information you consider will help the judge to manage the claim.

We are seeking to agree with the Defendant the appoinment of Mr Jonathan Cousins as a jointly instructed computer systems design expert.

Although documents were exchanged pursuant to paragraph 4 of Practice Direction Protocols before proceedings were issued, and some contractual documents were served with the particulars of claim, we consider that full standard disclosure should be ordered.

Signed

Date

[Counsel] [Solicitor] [for the][1st][2nd][3rd][   ]
[Claimant] [Defendant] [Part 20 claimant]

Please enter your name, reference number and full postal address including (if appropriate) details of telephone, DX, fax or e-mail

Smallwood & Co,	If applicable	
4 Market Place	Telephone no.	01562 384500
Corby	Fax no.	01562 384572
Northamptonshire	DX no.	87456 Corby
Postcode N N 1 7 6 A L	Your ref.	GS/89734

E-mail

IN THE HIGH COURT OF JUSTICE   Claim No. HQ 09 98744
QUEEN'S BENCH DIVISION
JUDGE/MASTER

BETWEEN:

                    SHILTON MACHINE TOOLS LIMITED   Claimant

                              and

                    BANKS PLASTIC MOULDINGS LIMITED   Defendant

                    ─────────────────────────────────

                    CLAIMANT'S STATEMENT OF COSTS
                        TO 23RD NOVEMBER 2009

                    ─────────────────────────────────

Claimant's statement of costs for the
hearing on   (interim application)

Description of Fee Earners

1.   Margaret Clements (MC) Grade A — £183 per hour
2.   Daniel Sprake (DS) Grade D — £101 per hour

Attendances on client
MC: 2.25 hours @ £183 per hour   £411.75

Attendances on opponents
MC: 1.5 hours @ £183 per hour   £274.50

Attendances on others
MC: 1.75 hours @ £183 per hour   £320.25
DS: 0.75 hours @ £101 per hour   £75.75

Site inspections etc.

Work done on negotiations

Other work not covered above

Work done on documents
MC: 4.5 hours @ £183 per hour   £823.50
DS: 3.5 hours @ £101 per hour   £353.50

Attendance at hearing

Counsel's fees
Ashley Bailey: advising in conference   £300.00

Other expenses:
Court fee   £630.00
Sub-Total   £3,189.25
VAT claimed on solicitor's and counsel's fees @ 17.5%   £447.86
Total   £3,637.11

The costs set out above do not exceed the costs which the claimant is liable to pay in
respect of the work

Dated the 23rd November 2009

Signed:

        Boardman, Phipps & Co
        Claimant's solicitor

Figure 7.2   Statement of costs

```
┌─────────────────────────────────────────────────────────────────────────┐
│ Order for Further Information      In the High Court of Justice           │
│ (allocation)                       Queen's Bench Division                 │
│                                                                           │
│                                    Claim No. HQ 09 98744                  │
│ To Claimant's solicitor            Claimant  Shilton Machine Tools Limited│
│                                    Defendant  Banks Plastic Mouldings     │
│                                              Limited                      │
│ Boardman Phipps & Co                                                      │
│ 20 High Street                                                            │
│ Manchester                                                                │
│ M15 9CZ                                                                   │
│                                                                           │
│                                    SEAL                                   │
│                                                                           │
│ Master Chesterfield has considered the statements of case and allocation │
│ question-naires filed and requires further information before making a   │
│ final decision about allocation.                                         │
│                                                                           │
│ The Master orders the claimant to provide information about:             │
│                                                                           │
│ 1.  The attempts made (if any) to agree the joint selection of expert    │
│     witnesses.                                                           │
│                                                                           │
│ 2.  The reasons (if any) for needing to call expert witnesses to give    │
│     oral evidence at trial.                                             │
│                                                                           │
│ 3.  The difficulties (if any) of obtaining a signed witness statement    │
│     from Mr Benetti before the 22nd February 2010.                       │
│                                                                           │
│ This information and any accompanying documents should be delivered to    │
│ the court and copies to the other parties on or before 14th December 2009.│
│                                                                           │
│ Note: Where an allocation hearing is necessary because a party does not   │
│ provide the information ordered above, the court may order that party to  │
│ pay the costs of any other party attending the hearing                   │
│                                                                           │
│ The court office at The Royal Courts of Justice, Strand, London WC2A 2LL  │
│ is open between 10 am and 4 pm Monday to Friday. Address all              │
│ communications to the Court Manager quoting the claim number.            │
└─────────────────────────────────────────────────────────────────────────┘
```

Figure 7.3   Order for further information

7.4 Failing to pay the allocation fee

If the claimant fails to pay the allocation fee the court will serve a notice (Form N173) on the claimant requiring payment within a stated period of time, failing which the claim will be struck out. If the claim is struck out for non-payment of the fee the claimant is also required to pay the defendant's costs, unless the court otherwise orders (CPR, r 3.7). Once the claim has been struck out the defendant is notified by the court so he or she can apply for his or her costs. Any injunction previously granted lapses after 14 days (r 25.11). The court retains a power to reinstate it (r 3.7(7)), and on such an application the court will apply the criteria set out in r 3.9 relating to applications for relief from sanctions (see **28.3.6**). However, any order for reinstatement will be made conditional on the fee being paid within two days of the order.

7.5 Track allocation

Generally, the court will allocate cases in accordance with their financial value. It may allocate a case to a higher track having regard to factors such as complexity, the value of any counterclaim, the amount of oral evidence and the importance of the case. It cannot allocate a case to a lower track than its financial value would indicate unless all the parties consent. Once it makes an allocation decision the court will send a notice of the decision to the parties, together with copies of the other parties' allocation questionnaires. An example of a notice of allocation can be seen at **Figure 7.5**. At the same time as it allocates the case to a track the court will usually also make case management directions.

Track allocation based on financial value results in the following basic position:

- claims with a value up to £5,000 will be allocated to the small claims track;
- claims between £5,000 and £25,000 will be allocated to the fast track; and
- claims exceeding £25,000 will be allocated to the multi-track.

However, there are some more detailed rules. For example, personal injury claims where the total claim does not exceed £5,000 will not normally be allocated to the small claims track unless the likely damages for pain, suffering and loss of amenity do not exceed £1,000 (CPR, r 26.6(1)).

In addition to the financial value of the claim (if it has one), the court is by CPR, r 26.8, required to have regard to the following factors when deciding which track to allocate the case to:

- the nature of the remedy sought;
- the likely complexity of the facts, law or evidence. Low value claims in emerging areas may be suitable for the multi-track (*Kearsley v Klarfeld* [2006] 2 All ER 303);
- the number of parties or likely parties;
- the value of any counterclaim or other additional claim under Part 20 and the complexity of any matters relating to those claims;
- the amount of oral evidence which may be required;
- the importance of the claim to persons who are not parties to the proceedings;
- the views expressed by the parties—these views will be regarded as important, but the court will not be bound by any agreement or common view expressed by the parties; and
- the circumstances of the parties.

7.6   Case management directions

The court will usually give directions at the track allocation stage. The court may (and usually will) give directions of its own initiative and without holding a hearing. However, particularly in multi-track cases, the court may convene a case management conference for the purpose of giving directions.

The idea behind giving directions is to provide a timetable pursuant to which the evidence needed to prove the claim or defence must be obtained and exchanged with the other side. In most cases the court is likely to insist on the necessary steps being taken within a relatively short period of time. **Figure 7.4** sets out the usual steps that are directed in fast track cases, with the periods of time usually set for taking those steps. The times referred to in **Figure 7.4** run from the date of allocation to the fast track.

Directions are not only given as part of the track allocation procedure. The rules provide that the court will consider giving directions at the end of any hearing, such as an application for an interim injunction or for summary judgment (if the claim is to proceed). If directions have already been given at an application made in the very early stages of the

Step		Time from allocation
1.	Disclosure of documents by serving lists of documents	4 weeks
2.	Exchange of witness statements	10 weeks
3.	Exchange of experts' reports	14 weeks
4.	Sending pre-trial checklists to the parties by the court	20 weeks
5.	Returning pre-trial checklists to the court	22 weeks
6.	Trial	30 weeks

Figure 7.4   Typical directions timetable for fast track cases

proceedings there may be little or no need for the court to give further directions at the track allocation stage. Directions may also be given at later stages in the litigation, long after track allocation has been dealt with. The court may do this at a specially convened directions hearing, such as a case management conference or pre-trial review, or on an application made by one of the parties (such as an application to extend the directions timetable, or to enforce compliance with the timetable by the other side), or after any other type of interim application, such as an application for an interim payment.

7.7   ADR and Stay for settlement

One of the court's case management functions is to help the parties to settle the whole or part of the case (CPR, r 1.4(2)(f)), and another is to encourage the parties to use alternative dispute resolution (ADR) procedures if appropriate, and to facilitate the use of such procedures (r 1.4(2)(e)). It is with these objectives in mind that the rules provide for the court ordering a stay of proceedings to allow for settlement of the case.

There are many forms of ADR available. Arbitration involves the appointment of an arbitrator by the parties or through a mechanism agreed by the parties. There are many forms of procedure that may be followed in arbitrations, from the reasonably informal through to procedures often more complicated than litigation (and see the Arbitration Act 1996). This reflects the range of disputes that maybe arbitrated, from simple matters through to complex commercial cases. Ultimately, an arbitrator's function is to consider the evidence available and reach a decision binding on the parties. A similar role is played by adjudicators in building disputes under the Housing Grants, Construction and Regeneration Act 1996. Mediation, on the other hand, involves the appointment of a mediator whose main function is to facilitate channels of communication between the parties, seeking common ground, and encouraging the parties to find agreement where possible. A mediator does not make rulings on matters in dispute between the parties. If the parties cannot agree, they are free to walk away from a mediation. In addition, there are numerous complaints and grievance handling procedures operated by public bodies and trade associations which can be successful in avoiding the need to go to litigation.

One of the headings in the allocation questionnaire allows a party to include a request for the proceedings to be stayed while the parties try to settle the case. If all the parties make such a request, or if the court on its own initiative considers that such a stay would be appropriate, a direction will be made staying the proceedings for one month or such specified time as the court considers appropriate. The court has power to extend the stay

---

Notice of Allocation to
Multi-track

In the High Court of Justice
Queen's Bench Division

Claim No. HQ 09 98744
Claimant Shilton Machine Tools Limited
Defendant Banks Plastic Mouldings Limited

To Claimant's solicitor

Boardman, Phipps & Co
20 High Street
Manchester
M15 9CZ

SEAL

Master Chesterfield has considered the statements of case and allocation questionnaires filed and allocated the claim to the **multi-track**.

The Master has ordered that:

1.   Disclosure shall take place as follows:

Each party shall give standard disclosure to every other party by list. The latest date for delivery of the lists is 12th January 2010.

The latest date for service of any request to inspect or for a copy of a document is 19th January 2010.

2.   Further directions will be given at a case management conference to be heard at 10.30 am on Monday 8th February 2010.

3.   Costs in the case.

[The claim is being transferred to the [Civil Trial Centre at   County Court]
[Division of the Royal Courts of Justice] where all future applications, correspondence and so on will be dealt with.]

The reason[s] the judge has given for allocation to this track [is] [are] that:

The claim has a value exceeding £25,000 and neither party has consented to it being dealt with other than on the multi-track.

Notes:

• You and the other party, or parties, may agree to extend the time periods given in the directions above provided this does not affect the date given for any case management conference, for returning the listing questionnaire, for any pre-trial review or the date of the trial or trial period.

• If you do not comply with these directions, any other party to the claim will be entitled to apply to the court for an order that your statement of case (claim or defence) be struck out.

• Leaflets explaining more about what happens when your case is allocated to the multi-track are available from the court office.

The court office at The Royal Courts of Justice, Strand, London WC2A 2LL is open between 10 am and 4 pm Monday to Friday. Address all communications to the Court Manager quoting the claim number.

Figure 7.5   Notice of allocation to the multi-track

for such specified periods as it thinks appropriate. Periods of extension can be sought simply by writing to the court. During the period of such a stay the claimant is under a duty to inform the court if a settlement is reached (CPR, r 26.4(4)). If, by the end of the defined period of the stay, the claimant has not told the court that the case has been settled, the court will give such directions for the management of the case as it considers appropriate, including allocating it to an appropriate track.

As encouraging the use of ADR is part of the overriding objective, sometimes parties who lose at trial argue that an opponent's failure to try ADR procedures should result in an order depriving the opponent of its costs. In such applications, the burden is on the unsuccessful party to establish that the usual rule that costs follow the event should be departed from (*Halsey v Milton Keynes General NHS Trust* [2004] 1 WLR 3002). Factors relevant to the question of whether a refusal to agree to ADR was unreasonable include:

1. the nature of the dispute and circumstances of the case;
2. the merits of the case (it may not be reasonable for a party with a weak case to insist on the use of ADR);
3. the extent to which other settlement methods had been attempted; and
4. the costs and delays involved in using ADR.

7.8 Trial in the Royal Courts of Justice

One of the questions that will be considered in claims brought in the High Court is whether a case should be managed and tried in the Royal Courts of Justice as opposed to another Civil Trial Centre. The idea is that only the most important cases justify use of the resources of the Royal Courts of Justice. Accordingly, generally cases with an estimated value of less than £50,000 will be transferred out of the Royal Courts of Justice to a County Court at the track allocation stage (PD 29, para 2.2). Exceptions where claims worth less than £50,000 may be retained in the Royal Courts of Justice are:

- cases which are required by an enactment to be tried in the High Court;
- cases falling within any of the specialist lists;
- professional negligence claims;
- Fatal Accident Act claims;
- fraud and undue influence claims;
- defamation claims;
- claims for malicious prosecution and false imprisonment; and
- claims against the police.

7.9 Changing tracks

The court may make a subsequent order re-allocating a claim to a different track (CPR, r 26.10). Where a claim was initially allocated to the small claims track, and is later reallocated to another track, the small claims costs restrictions cease to apply from the date of reallocation (CPR, r 27.15).

A party who is dissatisfied with an allocation decision may challenge the decision either by appealing up to the next higher court or by making an application back to the judge who made the initial decision. Applications should be used where the decision was made without a hearing of which he was given due notice or if there has been a material change of circumstances. If the party was present, represented or given due notice of the hearing where the decision was made the only appropriate route is by way of appeal (PD 26, paras 11.1(2) and 11.2).

In cases where an additional claim under Part 20 has been issued (see **Chapter 9**) there may need to be a redetermination as to the most suitable track for the proceedings. Mere issue of an additional claim will not have this effect, but where a defence to the additional claim has been filed the proceedings will be reconsidered by the procedural judge to determine whether the claim should remain on its existing track (particularly in cases on the small claims and fast tracks), and whether there needs to be any adjustment to the timetable. At the same time the procedural judge will consider whether the additional claim should be dealt with separately from the main action.

There needs to be a good reason for re-allocating a claim to a different track. If the financial value of a claim is substantially increased on an amendment to the statement of case the claim will usually be re-allocated. However, permission to amend may be refused if re-allocating will involve aborting a trial where a fast track claim is being tried by a district judge, and the amendment will bring the claim into the multi-track (*Maguire v Molin* [2003] 1 WLR 644).

7.10 Allocation in specialist proceedings

Each specialist court has its own procedure dealing with case management at the allocation stage. Some types of specialist proceedings are automatically allocated to the multi-track (see, for example, CPR, r 60.6, for claims in the TCC). Allocation questionnaires are not, in general, used in specialist cases which are automatically allocated to the multi-track. In the Commercial Court, after service of the defence, the legal representatives for each party must liaise for the purpose of preparing a short case memorandum and for the purpose of preparing an agreed list of important issues (with a separate section dealing with matters which are common ground between all or some of the parties), and the claimant's solicitors must prepare a case management bundle (Commercial Court Guide, paras D5.1, D6.1 and D7.1). A case management conference will be held as soon as practicable (CPR, r 58.13(3)), which the claimant must apply for within 14 days after service of the last defence (PD 58, para 10.2). Seven days before the case management conference each party must file a completed case management information sheet, in the form set out in the Commercial Court Guide, appendix 6, and it is this form that takes the place of the allocation questionnaire (para D8.5). On the other hand, allocation questionnaires are used in ChD cases despite the fact they are automatically allocated to the multi-track.

Parties and joinder

8.1 Introduction

Prior to the Judicature Acts of 1873 and 1875 any failure in bringing the correct parties before the court would have been fatal to civil proceedings. Nowadays the rules in this area are far more liberal. The general policy stated in SCA 1981, s 49(2), is that the court

. . . shall so exercise its jurisdiction in every cause or matter before it as to secure that, as far as possible, all matters in dispute between the parties are completely and finally determined, and all multiplicity of legal proceedings with respect to any of those matters is avoided.

Nevertheless, it remains of great importance that all necessary parties, and no others, are named in proceedings when they are commenced, and that each party be correctly named. Any failure in these matters is likely to delay the ultimate resolution of the litigation and will almost certainly be penalised in costs. Any delay may prejudice the eventual resolution of the litigation either through evidence becoming stale or lost, or by the passing of a limitation period.

This chapter will first consider the rules relating to particular classes of party. It will then look at the rules governing joinder of parties and causes of action. Finally, it will consider representative proceedings, consolidation of actions, intervening and interpleading.

8.2 Parties

8.2.1 Children

8.2.1.1 General

A person attains full age at 18. Until then an individual is under disability. In the past the terms 'infant' and 'minor' were used, but the Civil Procedure Rules 1998 use the terms 'child' and 'children'.

A child must sue or be sued by his or her 'litigation friend' (CPR, r 21.2). However, the court may make an order to permit a child to conduct proceedings without a litigation friend. It is desirable that the person appointed as the litigation friend should be someone who can fairly and competently conduct the proceedings on behalf of the child, and have no interest in the claim adverse to the child. Further, where the child is a claimant (but not if a defendant), the litigation friend must undertake to pay any costs which the child may be ordered to pay, subject to any right of repayment from the child. The litigation friend must file a written certificate in the appropriate court office. An example of a certificate of suitability is shown in **Figure 8.1**.

If a child has no litigation friend, an application can be made for a suitable person to be appointed by the court.

Certificate of suitability of litigation friend

If you are acting
- **for a child**, you must serve a copy of the completed form on a parent or guardian of the child, or if there is no parent or guardian, the carer or the person with whom the child lives
- **for a protected party**, you must serve a copy of the completed form on one of the following persons with authority in relation to the protected party as: (1) the attorney under a registered enduring power of attorney (2) the donee of the lasting power of attorney; (3) the deputy appointed by the Court of Protection; or if there is no such person, an adult with whom the protected party resides or in whose care the protected party is. You must also complete a certificate of service (obtainable from the court office)

You should send the completed form to the court with the claim form (if acting for the claimant) or when you take the first step on the defendant's behalf in the claim together with the certificate of service (if applicable).

Name of court	
Birmingham County Court	
Claim No.	9BM 732776
Claimant (including ref.)	Miss Kay Metcalf (a child by Mrs Joyce Metcalf her litigation friend)
Defendant (including ref.)	Ms Alison Grainger

You do not need to complete this form if you are a deputy appointed by the Court of Protection with power to conduct proceedings on behalf of the protected party.

I consent to act as litigation friend for <u>Kay Metcalf</u>
(claimant)(defendant)

I believe that the above named person is a

[✓] child   [ ] protected party *(give your reasons overleaf and attach a copy of any medical evidence in support)*

I am able to conduct proceedings on behalf of the above named person competently and fairly and I have no interests adverse to those of the above named person.

*
delete if you are acting for the defendant

*I undertake to pay any costs which the above named claimant may be ordered to pay in these proceedings subject to any right I may have to be repaid from the assets of the claimant.

Please write your name in capital letters

[ ] Mr   [✓] Mrs   [ ] Miss   Surname   METCALF

[ ] Ms   [ ] Other _____   Forenames JOYCE

Address to which documents in this case are to be sent.

Hutchinson & Brayhead 45 Church Street, Birmingham B3 7YS

I certify that the information given in this form is correct

Signed _____

Date   12.10.2009

The court office at 33 Bull Street, Birminham B4 6DS

is open between 10 am and 4 pm Monday to Friday. When corresponding with the court, please address forms or letters to the Court Manager and quote the claim number.

N235 Certificate of suitability of litigation friend (10.07)   ©Crown copyright 2007

Figure 8.1   Certificate of suitability of litigation friend

8.2.1.2   Title

A child acting by a litigation friend should be referred to in the title to the proceedings as, eg, 'Miss JANET SMITH (a child by Mrs LUCY SMITH her litigation friend)'. A child acting without a litigation friend is referred to as 'Miss JANET SMITH (a child)'.

8.2.1.3   Child attaining 18 years

When a child who is a party to proceedings reaches full age he or she must serve on the other parties and file at court a notice stating that he or she is now over 18 and that the litigation friend's appointment has ceased, giving an address for service, and stating whether or not he or she intends to carry on being a party. If the child is to carry on, he or she will be described from that point on as, eg, 'Miss JANET SMITH (formerly a child but now of full age)'. If the child (now of full age) fails to serve such a notice, the litigation friend can serve a notice to the effect that the child has reached full age and the appointment as litigation friend has ceased. A child claimant's litigation friend's liability in costs continues until notice is given to the other parties.

8.2.1.4   Children's settlements

When a claim brought on behalf of a child is settled, two main problems arise. First, it is necessary to protect the child, who might otherwise be pressured into accepting a disadvantageous settlement. Secondly, as a child will not be bound by an out-of-court settlement unless it is proved to have been for his or her benefit, it is necessary to find means for providing the defendant with a valid discharge for the money paid in settlement. It is to meet these two problems that Rules of Court have been made to provide for the approval by the court of children's settlements (see CPR, r 21.10).

If a claim is settled before proceedings are commenced the parties may (and would be well advised to) make an application under Part 8 for approval of the settlement by the court. If approved, the child will be bound by the settlement. After proceedings have been commenced any settlement will only be valid if it is approved, approval being sought by making an application under Part 23 (see **Chapter 10**). Whether court approval is obligatory or not, a proposed settlement involving a child is not binding, and either party can resile from it, until it is approved by the court (*Drinkall v Whitwood* [2004] 1 WLR 462). CPR, r 21.10, provides:

1. *Where a claim is made—*
   (a)   *by or on behalf of a child or protected party; or*
   (b)   *against a child or protected party no settlement, compromise or payment and no acceptance of money paid into court shall be valid, so far as it relates to the claim by, on behalf of or against the child or protected party, without the approval of the court.*
2. *Where—*
   (a)   *before proceedings in which a claim is made by or on behalf of, or against, a child or protected party (whether alone or with any other person) are begun, an agreement is reached for the settlement of the claim; and*
   (b)   *the sole purpose of proceedings on that claim is to obtain the approval of the court to settlement or compromise of the claim, the claim must—*
      (i)   *be made using the procedure set out in Part 8 (alternative procedure for claims); and*
      (ii)   *include a request to the court for approval of the settlement or compromise.*

Approval is sought from a Master or District Judge sitting in private, but the decision will be pronounced in public (in accordance with the European Convention on Human Rights, art 6(1)). Often the court will prefer a parent to attend. In difficult cases written evidence may be required, but usually the documents required are the application and statements of case, any police reports and witness statements, both sides' medical reports, a schedule of special damages, counsel's opinion on liability and quantum, and (if in the High Court) the appropriate Court Funds office forms. If a Part 8 claim is used, the claim form must set out details of the claim and also the terms of the settlement or compromise, or must have attached to it a draft consent order. Information to be provided at the hearing includes whether and to what extent the defendant admits liability, the age and any occupation of the child, the litigation friend's approval of the proposed settlement, and details of any relevant prosecution. If liability has not been admitted the court considers the child's prospects of success, and decides whether in the light of the medical evidence the proposed settlement is a reasonable one and for the child's benefit. If not, the Master adjourns to give the parties an opportunity to renegotiate and gives directions as to the future conduct of the litigation. If the settlement is approved, the Master gives directions as to how the money shall be dealt with.

8.2.1.5 Investment of money recovered for persons under disability

Money recovered for children is administered on their behalf by the High Court, whereas money recovered for protected parties is administered by the Court of Protection. Fees are charged by the Court of Protection, which should be included in any award of damages. If the sum is very small the court may order it to be paid to the litigation friend for it to be put into a building society account.

The courts act on the principle that money awarded to a person under disability should be applied for the purpose for which it was awarded. Decisions have to be taken as to what it should be spent on, how much should be invested for the future, and what sorts of investments should be made. From time to time, applications may be made for the release of more funds for various purchases. Money in court must be paid out to the child when he or she reaches full age.

8.2.1.6 Limitation

Time does not run against a child for limitation purposes until the child ceases to be under disability: see LA 1980, s 28.

8.2.2 Protected parties

A protected party is a person who lacks capacity to conduct proceedings (Mental Capacity Act 2005, s 2). This applies where a person has an impairment of the mind or brain which is such as to prevent that person from making decisions in relation to a matter. There is a presumption of full capacity, which will be displaced where an individual has an impairment in the functioning of their mind or brain which prevents them from being able to make decisions in the litigation (Mental Capacity Act 2005, s 3 and *Masterman-Lister v Brutton and Co (Nos 1 and 2)* [2003] 1 WLR 1511). Protected parties must act in proceedings through a litigation friend, who may be a deputy appointed under the Mental Capacity Act 2005, s 16(2).

Time will not run against a protected party for limitation purposes if the protected party was under disability when the cause of action accrued: LA 1980, s 28(1). Thus, if a cause of action accrued at a time when the claimant was of full capacity, time will continue running during a subsequent period of disability through mental incapacity.

8.2.3 Partners

8.2.3.1 General

A partnership exists where a number of people carry on a business in common with a view of profit (Partnership Act 1890, s 1(1)). Partnerships typically trade under a firm name, which may (but does not have to) consist of the surnames of each of the partners. Every partner is an agent for the firm (s 5). In most situations a partnership will be bound by acts done on behalf of the firm (ss 6 and 10), and the individual partners will also be personally liable, either jointly or jointly and severally (ss 9 and 12). The partners who will be liable are those who were partners at the time of the relevant event.

By PD 7, para 5A.3, where a partnership has a name, unless it is inappropriate to do so, any claim must be brought in or against the name under which the partnership carried on business at the time the cause of action accrued.

8.2.3.2 Title

The fact that a party is a partnership is disclosed in the title by adding the words '(a firm)' after its name.

8.2.3.3 Service

Service on partners was considered in **Chapter 3**. As mentioned in **Figure 3.2**, the address for service of an individual suing or being sued in the name of a partnership is that person's usual or last known place of residence, or his or her place of business or last known place of business. As mentioned at **3.8.5.1**, personal service on a partnership may be effected on the manager of its principal place of business.

8.2.3.4 Acknowledgment of service

PD 10, para 4.4 provides that where a claim is brought against a partnership:

(a) service must be acknowledged in the name of the partnership on behalf of all persons who were partners at the time when the cause of action accrued; and

(b) the acknowledgment of service may be signed by any of those partners, or by any person authorised by any of those partners to sign it.

8.2.3.5 Disclosure of partners' names

Any party to a claim may make a request to the firm, stating the date when the relevant cause of action accrued, seeking details of the partners at that time. The partners are obliged to provide a 'partnership membership statement' within 14 days of receipt of such a request. This is a written statement of the names and last known places of residence of all the persons who were partners at the time the cause of action accrued (PD 7, paras 5B.1 to 5B.3).

8.2.3.6 Enforcement

A judgment obtained against a partnership may be enforced against any partnership property within the jurisdiction (PD 70, para 6A.1). It may also be enforced against a partner who acknowledged service as a partner, or if certain other conditions are satisfied, for example a finding by the court that the person in question was a partner at the relevant time (PD 70, paras 6A.2 to 6A.4).

8.2.4 Sole traders

8.2.4.1 General

A sole trader, even if trading under an artificial business name, must be distinguished from a partnership. Such a person must sue in his or her own name, but *may* be sued in the business name: PD 7, para 5C.2.

8.2.4.2 Title

If the claimant does not know the defendant's own name, the defendant may be described, eg, 'SPEEDY MOTORS (a trading name)'. If both names are known, the description becomes, eg, 'Mr HENRY WILLIAMS, trading as SPEEDY MOTORS'.

8.2.5 Companies

8.2.5.1 Name

Companies must sue and be sued in their full registered name. The words 'public limited company' or 'limited' are part of a limited liability company's name, and must be included. If its true legal description is not apparent from a company's name, the description should be stated in the title, eg 'a company limited by guarantee'.

8.2.5.2 Service

The Companies Act 2006, s 1139(1), provides 'A document may be served on a company by leaving it at, or sending it by post to the company's registered office'. Alternatives provided for by the CPR are set out in **Figure 3.2** and at **3.8.5.1** above.

Service by post on a company is deemed to be effected in the ordinary course of posting (Interpretation Act 1978, s 7).

8.2.5.3 Representation of companies

Companies are artificial bodies. They therefore need to act through directors or other duly authorised individuals. Where a director or some other individual appears for a company at a hearing, a written statement must be completed giving the company's full name, its registered number, the status of the representative within the company (such as being a director), and the date and form by which the representative was authorised to act for the company. For example: '16th October 2009: Board resolution dated 16th October 2009'. See PD 39, para 5.2.

8.2.6 Unincorporated associations

These have no separate legal personality, and so generally cannot sue or be sued in their own names. A proprietary club may be construed as a partnership, in which event it may be sued in the way described at **8.2.3**, or it may be a sole trader, company or registered industrial society. If all the members of a members' club have the same interest in a dispute, one or more of their members may sue on behalf of them all in representative proceedings: CPR, r 19.6 (see **8.4**).

8.2.7 Gender

An individual must be described by the appropriate prefix in the title of the proceedings, eg, 'Mr', 'Miss', 'Ms' or 'Mrs'. This can be of assistance for the purposes of service and enforcement.

Where a woman changes her name on marriage, a notice of the change must be filed in the court office and served on the other parties. The title becomes, eg, 'Mrs ANN SMITH (formerly Ms ANN JONES)'.

8.2.8 Bankrupts

Generally, when a person becomes bankrupt, all causes of action other than for personal injuries and defamation vest in the trustee in bankruptcy. A single cause of action giving rise to heads of damage in respect of loss of earnings and also for pain, suffering and loss of amenity will vest in the trustee in bankruptcy, but the trustee will be required to account as a constructive trustee to the bankrupt for the general damages (see *Ord v Upton* [2000] Ch 352). The official name of the trustee is 'the trustee of the estate of Mr JOHN JONES a Bankrupt'. The trustee need not disclose his or her own name (see Insolvency Act 1986, s 305(4)).

If a claimant becomes bankrupt during the currency of proceedings, the trustee in bankruptcy may continue the proceedings, but must obtain an order for substitution under CPR, r 19.2(2). If a defendant becomes bankrupt during the currency of proceedings the claim may be stayed or allowed to continue on terms: Insolvency Act 1986, s 285.

8.2.9 Death during proceedings

A claim will only abate on the death of the claimant if the cause of action is a personal one, such as a claim in libel. Otherwise, the executors or administrators of a claimant who dies during proceedings may obtain an order for substitution under CPR, r 19.2(2). On the death of a defendant, a claimant may apply for an order to continue the proceedings against the defendant's personal representatives.

8.2.10 Estates

Where a cause of action survives for the benefit of or against the estate of a deceased person, all the deceased's executors or administrators must be named as parties to the claim. If the deceased has no personal representatives, proceedings may still be commenced against the estate, describing the defendant as, eg, 'the estate of Mr DAVID WILLIAMS deceased'. During the four month period of validity the claimant should seek an order for the appointment of someone to represent the estate of the deceased: PD 7, para 4.5.

If a claim is brought against someone who was in fact dead when the claim was issued, it will be treated as if it was brought against the estate of the deceased (CPR, r 19.8(3)(b)). By way of exception to these general rules, in a claim where one of the persons having an interest in the claim has died and has no personal representatives, it is possible for any of the parties to apply to the court for an order that the claim may proceed in the absence of a person to represent the estate of the deceased (see r 19.8(1)(a)). If such an order is made any judgment or order made in the claim will still bind the estate of the deceased (r 19.8(5)).

8.2.11 Trusts

Claims in respect of trust property may be brought by or against the trustees without joining the beneficiaries, and any judgment will bind the beneficiaries unless the court orders otherwise: CPR, r 19.7A.

8.2.12 Charities

In Part 8 claims where questions arise as to the validity of charitable bequests to an established charity, the trustees are the proper parties. Where the questioned bequest could be construed as being charitable, but is not to an existing charity, the Attorney-General must be joined to represent the interests of charity.

If proceedings are brought against a charity, logic would indicate that the trustees should be named as the defendants. The practice, however, is to name an official of the charity, such as the clerk, treasurer or secretary who is sued '. . . on behalf of the [name of charity]'.

8.2.13   Relator actions

Actions to restrain an interference with a public right, or to abate a public nuisance, or to compel the performance of a public duty, were until May 2000 brought in the name of the Attorney-General as he is the only person recognised by public law as entitled to represent the public in a court of law. The current position in these cases is uncertain, as the old rule dealing with this (RSC Ord 15, r 11) has been revoked but not replaced.

8.2.14   The Crown

Proceedings by and against the Crown are governed by the Crown Proceedings Act 1947. CPR, Part 66, regulates proceedings involving the Crown, the basic effect of which is to give the Crown a number of privileges not enjoyed by other litigants. Periodically the Minister for the Civil Service publishes a list of authorised government departments and their solicitors for service. If a department does not appear on the list (eg, Foreign and Commonwealth Office) it must sue and be sued in the name of the Attorney-General.

There are numerous quasi-governmental public bodies which are not formal departments of State. These bodies will usually have an implicit power to bring proceedings to protect their special interests in the performance of their functions (*Broadmoor Special Hospital Authority v R* [2000] QB 775, where it was held the hospital authority had a power to bring proceedings seeking an injunction to restrain a patient from publishing a book about how he had killed someone, although the order was refused).

8.2.15   Persons unknown

In exceptional cases it is permissible to issue a claim against 'persons unknown'. There is an express rule to this effect where the claim is for possession of land against trespassers (see **12.9.3**). In other cases this may be permitted where the unknown defendants can be identified clearly enough, such as where an unknown person was seeking to sell unauthorised rights in breach of the claimant's copyright (see *Bloomsbury Publishing Group Ltd v News Group Newspapers Ltd* [2003] 1 WLR 1633; *South Cambridgeshire District Council v Persons Unknown* The Times, 11 November 2004).

8.3   Joinder

The main rules dealing with joinder are:

7.3 The claimant may use a single claim form to start all claims which can be conveniently disposed of in the same proceedings.

19.1 Any number of claimants or defendants may be joined as parties to a claim.

It is therefore for the claimant to decide whether to join a number of causes of action in a single claim. For example, it may well be convenient to join causes of action where they are simply alternative ways of formulating a single claim, such as in negligence, or breach of statutory duty, or in occupier's liability. Claims joined under r 7.3 could give rise to separate remedies, such as a creditor who joins claims for two or more separate debts in a single claim against a defendant. Regarding joinder of parties, it could be that two claimants have a joint right, such as where they are joint contractors suing the other party to the contract. Joint claimants could be suing in the alternative, such as where there may be some doubt whether a contract was entered into by one of them as an agent for the other, or as a principal. Co-defendants may be sued in a single claim where they are both liable (such as where the second defendant is alleged to be vicariously liable for the negligence of the first defendant), or where they may be liable in the alternative, such as in cases where an injured employee sues his employer, a sub-contractor, and the site owner. In the last example, it is probable that different causes of action will be alleged against the different co-defendants, but joinder is still likely to be convenient.

This wide discretion given to claimants to decide what and who to include in a single claim is cut down in relation to joint (as opposed to several) rights, where CPR, r 19.3, provides that all persons jointly entitled to the remedy must be parties, unless the court otherwise orders. If anyone does not agree to being a claimant, that person must be made a defendant, again unless the court otherwise orders.

Once causes of action or parties have been joined together in a single claim, the court retains the power to separate them if it regards the joinder as inconvenient. This may be because the joinder may make the claim unnecessarily complicated, and cause delays or an increase in costs that would be avoided if the parties had been sued or if claims had been brought separately. Case management powers available to the court to deal with this include directing separate trials, deciding on the order in which issues are to be tried, and striking out part of the claim if it is likely to obstruct the just disposal of the proceedings (see CPR, rr 3.1(2) and 3.4(2)(b)).

8.4 Representative proceedings

The CPR, r 19.6(1), provides:

Where more than one person has the same interest in a claim—

   (a) the claim may be begun; or
   (b) the court may order that the claim be continued, by or against one or more persons who have the same interest as representatives of any other persons who have that interest

By CPR, r 19.6(4), unless the court otherwise directs, any judgment or order made in representative proceedings is binding on all persons represented in the claim, but may only be enforced by or against such a person with the permission of the court.

Representative proceedings are comparatively rare, but contribute a convenient way of litigating a dispute where otherwise a large number of persons would have to be named in the proceedings. The rule requires the persons represented to have 'the same interest'. According to Lord Macnaghten in *Duke of Bedford v Ellis* [1901] AC 1, at p 8, this has three elements:

Given a common interest and a common grievance, a representative suit is in order if the relief sought is in its nature beneficial to all whom the [claimant] proposes to represent.

An example is *Smith v Cardiff Corporation* [1954] QB 210. The defendants had more than 13,000 tenants. They gave notice to each tenant of a scheme to increase their rents on a differential basis according to the income of each tenant. The four claimants commenced proceedings, purporting to represent all the council's tenants, claiming a declaration that the scheme was ultra vires. It was held by the Court of Appeal that the tenants did not have a common grievance and that the relief claimed was not in its nature beneficial to all the tenants. Under the scheme the more affluent tenants were, in effect, to subsidise the less affluent. Therefore the tenants fell into two classes whose interests were in conflict.

8.5 Representation of unascertained interested persons

In Part 8 claims to construe wills and deeds, and proceedings concerning the estates of deceased persons or trust property, the court may appoint one or more persons to represent any unascertained or unborn persons (or persons who cannot be found) who may be interested in the proceedings if it is expedient to do so: CPR, r 19.7. Any judgment will then bind the persons represented, and the court's approval is required for any settlement. Although such an order may be made on an interim application, the order is most frequently made at the hearing.

8.6 Consolidation

The CPR, r 3.1(2)(g), gives the court power to consolidate proceedings. This involves ordering two or more separate claims to continue together, with one of the claims being nominated as the lead claim. Nothing is said in the rule about the circumstances where this might be appropriate. It is likely to be just to make such an order, in accordance with the overriding objective, where the various claims have a strong link with each other. This may be because they all involve the same allegation of negligence against a common defendant, or the claims may all arise out of the same incident.

8.7 Intervening

8.7.1 Jurisdiction

By CPR, r 19.2(2), someone who is not a party to a claim as originally constituted may be ordered to be added as a party if either:

(a) the presence of the intervener is desirable to ensure the court can resolve all matters in dispute; or

(b) it would be desirable to determine a question or issue relating to the relief already claimed between the intervener and an existing party at the same time as determining the existing action.

8.7.2 Who may intervene?

The court has a discretion whether to allow a non-party to intervene. It may be appropriate for the court to exercise its discretion in the following situations:

(a) Where the claim will directly affect the intervener's proprietary or pecuniary rights. This includes cases where the intervener will be bound to pay any damages awarded, such as the Motor Insurers Bureau where the defendant in a motor vehicle personal injuries case is uninsured (*Gurtner v Circuit* [1968] 2 QB 587). Another common situation is where the Legal Services Commission may be ordered to pay an unassisted defendant's costs under the Access to Justice Act 1999, s 11(4)(d) (see **35.7.9**).

(b) Where the claim involves public policy or may affect the prerogative of the Crown. In such cases the Attorney-General may intervene.

(c) Where a claimant claims to represent a class, a member of the class may be allowed to intervene to dispute the claimant's entitlement to represent the class (see CPR, r 19.6(3)).

8.7.3 Intervention in human rights claims

The court may not make a declaration of incompatibility under the Human Rights Act 1998, s 4, unless 21 days' notice has been given to the Crown (CPR, r 19.4A(1)). Directions requiring notice to be given will usually be made at a case management conference (PD 19, para 6.2). In these cases a Minister, or other person permitted by the Human Rights Act 1998, is entitled to be joined as a party on giving notice to the court (r 19.4A(2)).

In claims for damages in respect of a judicial act the claim must be stated in the statement of case, notice given to the Crown (usually the Lord Chancellor), and the appropriate Minister may be joined either on application by the Minister or by direction of the court (r 19.4A(3), (4)).

8.8 Interpleader

There are occasions when a person, with no personal interest in property or a debt he or she is holding, receives rival claims to that property or debt from two or more other persons. Interpleader is a procedure whereby such a stakeholder can gain protection by calling upon the rival claimants to claim against each other.

For example, Tom leaves a table with a storage company under a contract of bailment. Janet then writes to the storage company claiming the table belongs to her. Another, and more frequently recurring, situation is where the enforcement officer or bailiff seizes goods in execution, and subsequently some third party, such as a finance company or a member of the judgment debtor's family, claims the goods belong to them. Neither the storage company nor the enforcement officer or bailiff have a personal claim to the disputed property, and they can therefore interplead so that the title to the property can be decided.

Interpleader proceedings can be taken where the stakeholder either is being, or expects to be, sued by the rival claimants.

8.8.1 Procedure

In the County Court, special forms of summons are prescribed (Forms N88 and N89). In the High Court, by RSC Ord 17, r 3 (preserved by CPR, Sch 1), if proceedings have not yet been commenced against the stakeholder the application is made by issuing a claim form and if proceedings have already been issued, by ordinary application notice.

In each case the application must be supported by evidence stating:

- that the stakeholder claims no interest in the disputed property other than for charges and costs;
- that the stakeholder is not colluding with any of the claimants; and
- that the stakeholder is willing to transfer the property as the court may direct.

8.8.2   The hearing

On the return day the court may:

- if proceedings have already been issued, order that the other claimant(s) be made defendants in substitution for or in addition to the stakeholder; or
- order that an issue be stated and tried, with a direction as to who should be the claimants and defendants; or
- if all the parties consent or the facts are not in dispute, summarily determine any question of law or the dispute; or
- if a claimant fails to attend, order that they be completely debarred from prosecuting their claim against the stakeholder.

8.9   Group litigation

Where a number of claims give rise to common or related issues of fact or law, the court may make a group litigation order (a 'GLO'); see CPR, rr 19.10 and 19.11. A GLO can only be made with the consent of a senior judge (Lord Chief Justice for QBD claims; Vice-Chancellor for ChD claims; and Head of Civil Justice for County Courts) (PD 19B, para 3.3). These orders are most likely to be made where a number of claims are made arising out of a disaster (such as a serious public transport accident) or where a number of claims are made against a manufacturer having a common cause (such as claims arising out of the side effects of a medication). If a GLO is made it will:

- contain directions about maintaining a group register of the claims governed by the GLO;
- specify the GLO issues to be dealt with under the group litigation and identify the claims which can be managed under the GLO;
- specify the court that will manage the group litigation.

Further directions made under a GLO include directing that group claims must be transferred to the management court; that certain details must be included in the particulars of claim to show that the criteria for entry of the claim on that group register have been met; that future claims raising GLO issues must be commenced in the management court; that one or more of the claims shall proceed as test cases; and that the others shall be stayed until further order. Documents disclosed (see **Chapter 20**) in a GLO claim are treated as disclosed to all the parties on the group register (CPR, r 19.12(4)), unless the court otherwise orders. Any judgment or order made in a claim on the group register is binding on the parties to all the other claims, unless the court otherwise orders (r 19.12(1)(a)). The court may give directions as to the extent that an order or judgment shall bind the parties to claims added to the group register after the order or judgment was made or given (r 19.12(1)(b)).

Additional claims under Part 20

9.1 Introduction

A claimant or number of claimants commencing civil proceedings have, in accordance with the rules on joinder (see **8.3**), a wide scope for choosing who will be the initial parties. In most cases the defendant or defendants simply accept the choice made by the claimant(s). However, in a number of situations a defendant may wish to make a claim of their own against the claimant, a co-defendant, or a third party (ie a person not yet a party to the proceedings). These situations are described as 'additional claims' in the CPR. Technically, an additional claim under Part 20 is any claim for a remedy made in existing proceedings other than a claim made by a claimant against a defendant (r 20.2(1)).

A defendant with an additional claim may be seeking to do one or both of the following:

(a) Blame another person (a co-defendant or a third party) for the case being brought by the claimant, and seek to pass on any liability the claimant may establish against the defendant to that other person. The defendant may be able to do this by claiming a contribution or indemnity from the other person, or by claiming damages for breach of a contract between the defendant and that other person which has resulted in the defendant being in breach of some obligation owed by the defendant to the claimant (category (a)).

(b) Sue someone (the claimant, a co-defendant, or a third party) for damage suffered by the defendant which the defendant alleges was caused by some breach of obligation that person owed to the defendant (category (b)).

Going beyond these two categories, there are also cases where a claim made in the original proceedings raises an issue which is identical to an issue that would arise if the defendant were to sue a third party. For example, a claimant may sue a defendant for non-delivery of goods. The defendant may allege that he did not deliver because his supplier, the third party, failed to deliver to him. There may be a common issue both in the original claim and in the defendant's claim against the third party as to whether some defence (such as frustration or illegality) applies. It may be convenient for that issue to be determined not only between the claimant and the defendant, but also between the defendant and the third party (category (c)).

9.1.1 Options for bringing additional claims

(a) A defendant with an additional claim in category (a) above should do one of the following:

(i) if the additional claim is against a co-defendant, issue a contribution notice under r 20.6 (see **9.3**);

(ii)   if the claim is against a third party, issue an additional claim under Part 20 against the third party (often called a third party notice) (see **9.4**); or

(iii) in either case, issue a separate claim in the usual way.

(b) A defendant with an additional claim in category (b) above should do one of the following:

(iv)   if the additional claim is against a claimant, serve a counterclaim—this is usually done by serving a combined defence and counterclaim (see **9.2**);

(v)   if the additional claim is against a co-defendant, issue a contribution notice;

(vi)   if the additional claim is against a third party, issue a claim form under Part 20; or

(vii) in any of the three situations in (iv) to (vi), issue a separate claim in the usual way.

(c) A defendant with a connected issue in category (c) above should do one of the following:

(viii) raise the issue in a contribution notice or an additional claim under Part 20 against the third party;

(ix)   seek permission from the court to have the third party joined to the original claim under r 19.2(2)(b); or

(x)   have the issue determined twice, once in the original claim and secondly in the separate proceedings against the third party. This runs the risk of irreconcilable judgments, as well as incurring the costs of determining the same issue twice.

9.1.2 Remedies available in additional claims under Part 20

In a counterclaim, a defendant can seek any remedy, including interest, that could have been sought if the additional claim had been brought by way of separate proceedings.

A defendant issuing a contribution notice or additional claim under Part 20 against a third party can, by CPR, r 20.2(1)(b), claim a contribution (a percentage towards any liability the defendant owes to the claimant), an indemnity (full reimbursement), or some other remedy. The latter covers all the remedies available in civil litigation, but in practice tends to be restricted to claims brought by defendants which are connected to the claim brought by the claimant in the original proceedings. See the discussion on discretion at **9.4.4**.

9.2 Counterclaims

The rules on counterclaims are to be found in Part 20 of the Civil Procedure Rules 1998, but they are treated very differently from true third party claims. The straightforward situation of a defendant counterclaiming against a claimant has already been considered at **5.5**. A rather more complex situation is where the defendant wants to make a counterclaim against someone other than the claimant (usually in addition to the claimant). Before making such a counterclaim the defendant must obtain an order from the court adding the new party to the proceedings as a defendant to the counterclaim: CPR, r 20.5.

An application for such an order may be made without notice, and a draft of the proposed statement of case must be filed with the application notice (PD 20, para 1.2). The evidence in support of the application has to set out the stage reached in the main claim, the nature of the claim against the new party, and a summary of the facts on which that claim is based.

If an order is made adding the new party, the court will also give directions for managing the case. These are likely to include provision for service of all statements of case on the new party together with a response pack and a time for responding to the counter-claim, the role the new party can play at trial, as well as the usual matters such as disclosure of documents, witness statements etc. In the title to the proceedings the various parties are described as follows:

Mr ALAN BEST	<u>Claimant</u>
Mr COLIN DOWN	<u>Defendants</u>
Mrs EDNA FORBES	<u>Third Party</u>

As with other counterclaims, a counterclaim against a new party needs to be issued and an issue fee must be paid (together with a fee for adding the new party).

9.3 Contribution notice

A contribution notice is the old fashioned term describing an additional claim made by one co-defendant against another. They are used to claim indemnities or contributions against the co-defendant (CPR, r 20.6). However, where the defendant simply wants a contribution under the Civil Liability (Contribution) Act 1978 towards any damages that may be awarded, the accepted practice is to dispense with the service of contribution notices, and simply to ask the judge at trial to make the necessary apportionment of liability between the defendants, thereby saving the costs of the Notice.

This relaxation should not be relied on where there is some reason for having the issues between the defendant and the co-defendant defined, and so, in the following circumstances, contribution notices should be served, even though the defendant is seeking a contribution, namely where:

- the claim for the contribution is contractual rather than under the 1978 Act; or
- the defendant wants to combine the claim for a contribution with a claim for some related relief or remedy, or the determination of a related question or issue;
- the defendant needs to seek disclosure of documents or further information from the other party (the entitlement to which can only be decided when the issues have been defined).

A defendant must, by r 20.6(2), obtain permission to file and serve a contribution notice unless this is done either:

- with that defendant's defence; or
- if the claim for the contribution or indemnity is against a defendant added to the claim after the original defence was filed, within 28 days after the new defendant filed its defence.

9.4 Claims against third parties

9.4.1 Additional claim form under Part 20

An example of an additional claim form under Part 20 appears as **Figure 9.1**. Note the following points, however:

(a) The claim against the third party should specify the different heads of claim being made—eg if a claim is being made for indemnity under a contract, and also for a contribution under statute, these should be separately mentioned. The same applies if there are distinct claims for debt and damages, or if different questions are to be resolved.

(b) The particulars of the additional claim can be set out either in the additional claim form or in a separate particulars of claim attached to the claim form.

(c) The description of an additional claim (traditionally set out in tramlines beneath the names of the parties in the title) must reflect the nature of the document and its relation to the parties. Thus:

- a 'defendant's additional claim against third party' is an additional claim brought by the defendant against a single additional party, the third party;

- a 'third party's defence to defendant's additional claim' would be the defence filed by the third party in the previous example.

(d) Claimants and defendants in the original claim should be described as such, a position that does not change even if they acquire an additional procedural status (PD 20, para 7.3). The first party added under Part 20 is called the 'third party', the next is the 'fourth party' etc (para 7.4). If an additional party ceases to be a party, all the remaining parties retain their existing status (para 7.9).

(e) If an additional claim is brought against more than one party jointly, they are known as the 'first named third party' and 'second named third party' (etc) (para 7.5).

(f) It is normal to use names or abbreviations when referring to fourth and subsequent parties in the particulars of claim.

(g) The contents of an additional claim must be verified by a statement of truth.

9.4.2 Indemnity and contribution

An indemnity is an obligation to reimburse someone. Put another way, it is a claim for the fulfilment of an obligation, not for damages for breach of one. A right to an indemnity can arise in the following ways:

- Under a contractual promise to indemnify someone.

- Under certain relationships, eg between principal and agent.

- By statute, eg the LPA 1925, s 76(1)(D), and Sch 2, Pt IV, which implies a covenant to indemnify a mortgagee in a conveyance by way of mortgage of freehold property subject to a rent or of leasehold property.

A contribution can, broadly speaking, be defined as a partial indemnity. A right to a contribution can arise as between joint debtors or contractors, or joint wrongdoers or by statute. Under the Civil Liability (Contribution) Act 1978, where two or more persons are liable to the same claimant for the same damage, each may claim contribution towards the joint liability against the others. For example, in a two-vehicle accident the passenger in one of the vehicles may commence proceedings claiming damages for personal injuries against the driver of the other vehicle as the sole defendant. The defendant may then issue an additional claim against the driver of the claimant's car seeking a contribution towards any damages the claimant might be awarded based on their relative blameworthiness for the collision. However, the defendant can only recover a contribution under the Act if the third party is 'liable for the same damage' as the defendant. The 'damage' referred to is damage suffered by the claimant. Note also that the word used is 'damage' rather than 'damages' (see *Birse Construction Ltd v Haiste Ltd* [1996] 1 WLR 675). The 1978 Act extends the reach of the contribution principle to cover cases whatever the legal basis of the liability, whether in tort, breach of contract, breach of trust or otherwise (see s 6(1)).

In deciding whether the defendant and the third party are 'liable for the same damage', the words from s 1(1) must be given their natural and ordinary meaning, without any restrictive or expansive gloss (*Royal Brompton Hospital NHS Trust v Hammond* [2002] 1 WLR 1397, HL). The words do not cover damage which is merely substantially or materially similar (per Lord Steyn). The defendants in *Royal Brompton Hospital* were architects who were sued by the hospital for negligently issuing certificates to building contractors, the effect of which was to give the contractors a defence to a claim the hospital had against the contractors for breach of contract for delays in completing building work. It was held that the hospital's claims against the contractors and against the architects were different, so the architects could not claim a contribution against the contractors. In *Charter plc v City Index Ltd* [2008] Ch 313 it was held that, while a contribution could be claimed for breach of trust to make good the claimant's loss, a claim for an account of profits arising out of a breach of trust falls outside s 1(1). If the third party has no liability to the claimant, such as through a term in a contract absolving the third party from liability, the defendant cannot claim contribution from the third party (*Cooperative Retail Services Ltd v Taylor Young Partnership Ltd* [2002] 1 WLR 1419).

9.4.3   Some other remedy

An example would be where a passenger involved in a two-car collision brings proceedings against one of the other drivers as a sole defendant claiming damages for personal injuries. The defendant could issue an additional claim under Part 20 against the other driver seeking a contribution (see **9.4.2**), and also for damages for his or her own personal injuries and other damage sustained in the collision, being a claim for a remedy arising out of the same facts as the claim.

9.4.4   Discretion

If an additional claim is technically within r 20.2, the court still retains a discretion whether to allow the additional claim to proceed. In *Chatsworth Investments Ltd v Amoco (UK) Ltd* [1968] 1 Ch 665, Russell LJ said that the court, in exercising its discretion under the old rules, had to take a wide approach, and ask whether the third party claim accorded with the general functions of third party proceedings. In *Barclays Bank Ltd v Tom* [1923] 1 KB 221, Scrutton LJ identified these functions as safeguarding against differing results, ensuring the third party is bound by the decision between the claimant and the defendant, ensuring the additional claim is decided as close in time to the proceedings commenced by the claimant, and saving the expense of having two trials.

These ideas are largely reflected in CPR, r 20.9(2), which provides that in deciding whether to grant permission to allow an additional claim to be made (where permission is needed, see **9.4.5.2** below), or to dismiss an additional claim at a later stage, the matters the court will take into account include:

- the degree of connection between the additional claim and the main claim;
- whether the defendant is seeking substantially the same remedy on the additional claim as is being claimed by the claimant;
- whether the additional claim raises any question connected with the subject matter of the main claim.

9.4.5 Issuing an additional claim

9.4.5.1 Issuing without permission

A defendant can issue an additional claim form *without* seeking permission if it is issued before or at the same time as filing his or her defence (CPR, r 20.7(3)).

9.4.5.2 Issuing with permission

Permission to issue an additional claim will be required if the additional claim form was not issued before filing of the defence. Permission is usually sought without giving notice to any of the existing parties or anyone else (CPR, r 20.7(5)). The application notice has to be supported by evidence setting out the stage the main claim has reached together with a timetable of the action to date; the nature of the additional claim; the facts on which it is based; and the name and address of the proposed third party (PD 20, para 2.1). Where delay has been a factor an explanation for the delay should be included. Permission to bring an additional claim was refused in *Borealis AB v Stargas Ltd* (2002) LTL 9/5/2002 where the application was made four months before trial and where there was no adequate explanation for protracted delay in making the application. If the court grants permission it will at the same time give directions as to service of the additional claim form (CPR, r 20.8(3)).

9.4.5.3 Procedural effects of issuing an additional claim

An additional claim form is issued and served in the same way as an ordinary claim form (CPR, r 20.3). Rule 20.7(2) says that an additional claim is made when the court issues the additional claim form. This was intended to fix when the claim is brought for limitation purposes, but almost certainly fails to do so. The word used in the Limitation Act 1980 is when a claim is 'brought', whereas r 20.7(2) uses the word 'made'. As held in *Barnes v St Helens Metropolitan Borough Council (Practice Note)* [2007] 1 WLR 879, a claim is 'brought' for the purposes of the Limitation Act 1980 when the claimant delivers the relevant documents to the court office.

Service must be effected within 14 days after the additional claim is issued (r 20.8(1)(b)). It must be served with a response pack of forms for acknowledging service, admitting and defending the claim. It must also be served with copies of all the statements of case already served in the proceedings (r 20.12). A copy of the additional claim form must also be served on all other existing parties. The third party becomes a party to the proceedings once they are served with the additional claim form (r 20.10).

After being served with an additional claim, a third party can, in turn, issue an additional claim against a fourth party (without permission if the third party's additional claim is issued at the same time as or before the third party's defence to the additional claim is filed).

9.4.6 Responding to an additional claim

The time for filing a defence acknowledging service by a third party who is not already a party to the claim, is identical to that for an ordinary claim.

The general rules set out in the Civil Procedure Rules 1998 apply to additional claims, and these include the provisions relating to default judgments (discussed in **Chapter 11**).

If a third party fails to file a defence or acknowledge service within the 14 day period, the defendant may obtain a default judgment. If the additional claim seeks an indemnity or a contribution, this is done simply by filing a request for judgment, and the third party will be deemed to admit the additional claim and will be bound by any judgment or decision in the main proceedings which may be relevant to the additional claim. If the additional claim seeks some other remedy against the third party the defendant will have to make an application for judgment, although the application may be made without notice (CPR, r 20.11).

9.4.7 Directions

If the third party files a defence the court must consider the future conduct of the proceedings and give appropriate directions. So far as practicable the court will seek to manage the main proceedings and the additional claim together (CPR, r 20.13).

In addition to the usual directions laying down a timetable to trial, the court may direct that 'the third party be at liberty to appear at the trial and take such part as the judge should direct', and that his liability be determined 'at the trial, but subsequent thereto'. Other orders may be made, eg to add or substitute a third party as a defendant.

It is important to realise that the various interim remedies available between claimant and defendant (or vice versa) are also available as between defendant and third party (or vice versa). Thus, for example, the defendant may claim summary judgment against the third party.

9.4.8 Interrelation with main proceedings

An additional claim is a separate claim, and in many ways has a life of its own independent of the main action. The fact the main claim is settled, dismissed, stayed or struck out does not necessarily terminate the defendant's additional claim. If the defendant is claiming additional relief the issues it raises will still be live and the additional claim will continue so that they can be determined despite the fact the main claim has been settled, dismissed, stayed or struck out.

However, if the defendant is seeking an indemnity or a contribution, the additional claim is dependent on the claimant's claim as the defendant in these situations is seeking to pass on to the third party the liability to the claimant, and if the claimant's claim fails there is nothing to pass on. Therefore, in indemnity and contribution claims a distinction must be drawn between cases:

(a) where the claimant's claim is settled, because in these cases there will still be a live issue as to whether the third party should contribute towards the settlement, and if so, to what extent. In these cases the additional claim will continue (see *Stott v West Yorkshire Road Car Co Ltd* [1972] 2 QB 651); and

(b) where the claimant in effect loses (as when the claim is dismissed or struck out), after which there is nothing to litigate between the defendant and the third party (other than costs).

9.4.9 Hearing the additional claim

At the beginning of the trial, the judge will usually consider the part that the third party should play. That will usually include cross-examination, and may include calling witnesses. The claimant, on the other hand, will not normally be interested in the hearing of the additional claim (except possibly on the question of costs). Therefore, the judge will decide the most convenient procedure, which will depend on the facts of the particular case.

Claim Form (Additional claims- CPR Part 20)	**In the** High Court of Justice Queen's Bench Division
	Claim No. HQ 09 873547

Claimant(s)   Whiteside Properties Limited

Defendant(s)   Edmund Bailey Construction Plc

(SEAL)

Part 20 Claimant(s)   Edmund Bailey Construction Plc

Part 20 Defendant(s)   Fastbuck Builders Plc

Brief details of claim

A contribution, alternatively an indemnity, against the Claimant's claim for damages and interest against the Defendant based on alleged delay in construction works at Pembridge House, Maplethorpe Road, Peterborough PE4 9SY, and specific performance of a sub-contract between the Defendant and the Third Party under which the Third Party agreed to carry out construction works at Pembridge House, and damages and interest for breach of the sub-contract in the alternative to specific performance.

Value

More than £15,000

Defendant's name and address

(Third Party)
Fastbuck Builders Plc,
Fastbuck House,
Norwich,
NR1 8DP

	£
Amount claimed	exceeding £300,000
Court fee	1,530.00
Solicitors costs	TBA
Total amount	
Issue date	

The court office at

is open between 10 am and 4 pm Monday to Friday. When corresponding with the court, please address forms or letters to the Court Manager and quote the claim number.

N211 - w3 Claim Form (CPR Part 20 - additional claims)(4.99)   *Printed on behalf of The Court Service*

Figure 9.1   Claim form (additional claims – CPR Part 20)

	Claim No.	HQ 09 873547

Particulars of Claim (attached)

1. This claim has been brought by the Claimant against the Defendant. In it the Claimant claims liquidated damages and interest arising from alleged delay in construction works at Pembridge House, Maplethorpe Road, Peterborough, PE4 8SY ("Pembridge House") which the Claimant alleges was caused by the breach of contract on the part of the Defendant, as appears from the Particulars of Claim, a copy of which is served with this claim form.

2. The Defendant denies it is liable to the Claimant on the grounds set out in its Defence, a copy of which is also served with his claim form. These Particulars of Claim set out the Defendant's claim against the Third Party.

3. At all material times the Defendant and the Third Party were building construction companies, and the Third Party held itself out to the Defendant as a construction company specialising in large construction projects.

4. By a contract in writing dated 1 June 2007, a true copy of which is served with these Particulars of Claim, the Claimant engaged the Defendant to construct and oversee all the building works at Pembridge House ("the main works"). The main works involved the construction of office space using the facade of the former building on the Pembridge House site, which, on completion, was to be let by the Claimant on commercial leases

[Continue as in full particulars of Claim]

Statement of Truth
*(I believe)(The Part 20 Claimant believes) that the facts stated in these particulars of claim are true.
* I am duly authorised by the Part 20 claimant to sign this statement

Full name ___Helen Phipps_____

Name of Part 20 claimant's solicitor's firm __Boardman, Phipps & Co_____

signed_____ position or office held_Partner_____
*(Part 20 Claimant)('s solicitor)(Litigation friend)   (if signing on behalf of firm or company)
*delete as appropriate

Boardman, Phipps & Co
20 High Street,
Peterborough,
PE5 9CZ

Part 20 Claimant ('s solicitor's) address to which documents or payments should be sent if different from overleaf. If you are prepared to accept service by DX, fax or e-mail, please add details.

10

Interim applications

10.1 Introduction

Interim applications are made when a party to proceedings seeks an order or directions from the court prior to the substantive hearing of the claim. When the application should be made depends on the nature of the case. In urgent cases, the application may be made even before the originating process has been issued. More usually the application will be heard shortly after filing of the defence. There is a general obligation to apply early, although the court can deal with applications up to trial (and even beyond trial).

Parties seeking interim orders or directions in general have to issue an application notice on Form N244, pay the court fee, and often have to provide written evidence in support. The application must in general be served at least three clear days before the date given by the court for the hearing.

The major sub-division of interim applications is into those made in the absence of the other side ('without notice'), and those made on notice. These two categories will be considered after discussing the form of evidence used in interim applications.

10.2 Evidence

10.2.1 General

Although the court has power to hear witnesses for the purposes of interim applications (see CPR, r 32.2), oral testimony is very much the exception to the rule. The almost universal rule is that, if evidence is required, it is given in writing. Whether or not written evidence is required depends on the nature of the application. Many of the Rules of Court governing particular kinds of interim application specifically require evidence in support. Examples are applications for summary judgment and for service by alternative methods. Further there is a general requirement for evidence in support if the application is for an interim remedy (CPR, r 25.3(2)) as opposed to applications of a case management nature. In most other cases where the Rules are silent on the matter, evidence is still required in practice in order to establish the merits of the application. Even so, there remain a number of cases where evidence in support is unnecessary. These fall into two main categories. In the first, all the relevant matters to be considered in the application can be ascertained from the face of the statements of case, for example, on an application for security for costs on the ground that the claimant is stated in the claim form to be ordinarily resident out of the jurisdiction (see CPR, r 25.13(2)(a)), or on an application to strike out on the ground that the statement of case discloses no reasonable cause of action. The second category covers orders and directions which are made or given almost as a matter of course. Examples would include orders for standard disclosure and directions to list for trial.

10.2.2 Format of evidence in support

There are four options available regarding the format of the evidence to be used in support of an interim application. They are:

(a) To provide sufficiently full factual information in support of the application in the application notice itself, and sign the statement of truth in the notice.

(b) To rely on the facts stated in a statement of case filed in the proceedings, provided it contains a statement of truth.

(c) To rely on a witness statement with a statement of truth signed by the witness, which must be served with the application. The general rule is that any fact that needs to be proved at any hearing other than the trial should be proved by the evidence of witnesses in writing, and at hearings other than the trial evidence is to be by witness statement unless the court, a Practice Direction or any other enactment requires otherwise. Consequently, evidence by witness statement is to be expected to be the primary means of adducing evidence at interim hearings.

(d) To rely on affidavit evidence. However, using affidavits may result in the loss of the additional costs over and above the cost of using an ordinary witness statement. There are some situations where affidavit evidence is required, such as in applications for search orders, freezing injunctions, applications for contempt of court, and applications for judgment in default in Jurisdiction Regulation cases.

10.2.3 Form of affidavits

See generally PD32. The top right-hand corner and backsheet of the affidavit must be marked with the party on whose behalf it is filed, the initials and surname of the deponent, the number of the affidavit in relation to the deponent, the reference numbers of any exhibits, and the date it is sworn (for example: 2nd Dft: S.M. Hall: 4th: SMH3-SMH5: 14.9.09). There then follows the title of the claim, then the commencement. If it is sworn, the commencement may read 'I, Sara May Hall of 2 Tower Side, London E1, state on oath as follows:—'. If the document is affirmed it is called an affirmation (rather than an affidavit), and instead of making oath the commencement will state '. . . do solemnly and sincerely affirm . . .'. The address stated may be a work address if the affidavit is sworn in the deponent's business, etc capacity.

If the deponent is, or is employed by, a party, that must be stated. The affidavit must also state the deponent's occupation or description (eg 'unemployed').

The affidavit sets out the facts in numbered paragraphs, and is expressed in the first person. Dates, sums and other numbers are expressed in figures rather than in words. The text of an affidavit must indicate which of the facts stated are known to the deponent personally and those based on hearsay. Material based on information or belief must be supported by stating the sources and grounds for such belief. The source or grounds of such belief need not be an original source of evidence which would be admissible at trial, especially where the application is of an urgent nature where a deponent may not have the time to trace or identify evidence which would be admissible (*Deutsche Ruckversicherung AG v Walbrook Insurance Co Ltd* [1995] 1 WLR 1017). Clearly, original sources will normally carry much more weight than intermediate sources. Where original sources *are* known they should be identified.

Very often, documents or physical items are referred to in affidavits, and where this is so, they must be exhibited to the affidavit. This is done by identifying the exhibit in the text of the affidavit (eg 'SMH1', 'SMH2', etc) and clearly marking the documents or items in the same way. Documents of a similar nature such as a series of letters and replies should be bundled together in date sequence with the earliest on top, and paginated at centre bottom. Where a number of documents are collected in one exhibit, a front page must be attached listing its contents. If copies are used, care must be taken that all the pages are clearly legible.

The affidavit itself must be written or typed leaving a 3.5 cm margin and using just one side of the paper. It must, if possible, be securely bound (traditionally with green ribbon, but not with anything, such as plastic strips, which will make it more bulky than it needs to be). If the pages are left loose, each page should bear the claim number and the initials of the deponent and the person before whom it was sworn. It must be sworn or affirmed before a proper officer, usually a solicitor or commissioner for oaths, and signed by the deponent. The jurat (stating where and before whom the affidavit was sworn) must be completed and signed by the person before whom it was sworn, who must also initial any alterations.

10.2.4 Witness statements

Witness statements take much the same form as affidavits and affirmations, except they are not sworn or affirmed, and instead contain a simple statement of truth. Consequently, all the formalities required for affidavits, such as corner markings, and the rules on paragraphing, exhibits etc, have to be complied with. However, a witness statement will not have a commencement, and it will not have a jurat. Also, because it is not sworn there will be a saving of the fees payable for swearing an affidavit (£10 for the affidavit plus £2 per exhibit). The statement of truth at the end of a witness statement takes the form: 'I believe the facts stated in this witness statement are true.'

An example of a witness statement for use in an interim application is shown in **Figure 10.1**.

1. I am Brian Parkes, of Unit 6, Elland Trading Estate, Leeds LS8 3AN. I am a director of the Defendant company. I have full knowledge of the facts of this case and I am duly authorised to make this statement on behalf of the Defendant in support of its application to set aside a default judgment entered on 4 November 2009. Insofar as the contents of this statement are within my personal knowledge they are true, otherwise they are true to the best of my knowledge, information and belief.

2. The Defendant has a trading account with the Claimant, and it is true that it ordered 4 moulding machines from the Claimant on 10 March 2009 at a price of £60,000 plus VAT. Although the machines were delivered, they have been the subject of repeated breakdowns and have suffered a number of faults. The main problem with 2 of the machines is that despite a number of site attendances by the Claimant's engineers they have proved incapable of producing mouldings to industry standards. I have been advised by Mr Edward Knight, a consulting engineer of 36 Harrogate Road, Leeds LS3 8DQ, that these 2 machines are so badly designed that it will be impossible to put them right.

3. As a result of the problems with all 4 machines the Defendant has suffered a substantial loss of business. In particular, it has lost a contract with United Plastic Containers Plc, under which the Defendant was producing goods valued at between £10,000 and £20,000 per month. There is now shown to me marked '**BP1**' a bundle containing true copies of the Defendant's contractual documentation with United Plastic Containers Plc, monthly invoices, and recent correspondence in which the termination of the contract is explained. I have been advised by the Defendant's solicitors and believe that it has a substantial counterclaim with a value significantly above the value of the claim.

4. As soon as I received the court papers in this action I raised the matter with Mrs Elaine Stepney, the finance director of the Claimant. A true copy of my letter to her dated 19 October 2009 is at page 1 of the bundle of correspondence now shown to me marked '**BP2**'. Her reply, at page 2, says she will look into the matter. Nevertheless, judgment was entered on 4 November 2009.

5. For the reasons set out above, I ask that this judgment be set aside on the merits. There is now shown to me marked '**BP3**' a draft defence and counterclaim which the Defendant intends to file if judgment is set aside, and I confirm the truth of the contents of the draft defence and counterclaim.

6. If judgment is set aside and the case allowed to continue, I respectfully ask that the claim be transferred to the Leeds County Court, the local court of the Defendant.

Statement of truth

I believe the facts stated in this witness statement are true.

Signed:

Dated: 16th November 2009.

Figure 10.1   Witness statement seeking to set aside a judgment in default and transfer of claim

10.2.5   Other materials

In any application the court may, of course, wish to see the claim form and statements of case, and earlier orders. All these documents should be on the court file, which will be available for the judge. In addition, letters from the other side consenting to orders being made are frequently placed before the court.

10.3   Applications without notice

10.3.1   General

Applications made in the absence of the other side used to be called *ex parte* applications. They are exceptions to the general rule that applications must be made on notice to other parties (CPR, r 23.4(1)). Such an application can only be made if there is some sufficient reason. Sufficient reasons are:

- where there is no other party on the record (for example, on an application for permission to serve process outside the jurisdiction under CPR, r 6.36); or
- where no other party is affected (for example, to correct an accidental slip in a Master's order: CPR, r 40.12); or
- where there is real urgency; or
- where secrecy prior to the application is essential for the order to be efficacious.

Applications without notice can be made either with or without an oral hearing. An applicant who is disappointed with an order made without a hearing can renew the application (at a hearing before a judge at the same level as the one who dealt with the application on the papers), and does not have to appeal (*Collier v Williams* [2006] 1 WLR 1945).

10.3.2 Full and frank disclosure

It is the duty of a party seeking an order without notice to give full and frank disclosure to the court of all material facts, including those that go against the application. This is a continuing duty. Any failure in observing this duty may result in any order obtained being set aside (*R v Kensington Income Tax Commissioners, ex p Polignac* [1917] 1 KB 486. See also **15.6.1.3**).

The amount of detail required in order to discharge this duty depends on the nature of the relief sought and the conditions for granting that relief. Thus, in applications for search orders (see **Chapter 16**) it is necessary to show an extremely strong prima facie case on the merits. The applicant for such an order must disclose any known weaknesses in the cause of action against the defendant and any known defences, including any such matters which could have been discovered on making reasonable inquiries. When in doubt, the applicant must err on the side of excessive disclosure. To take a different example, on an application to extend the validity of a claim form (see **Chapter 25**) the main consideration is the reason for not having served the claim form. The merits of the case are not in issue, so the applicant is not required to give a detailed analysis of its strengths and weaknesses.

10.3.3 Nature of orders made without notice

Generally, orders made without notice are provisional. If the respondent objects to such an order, the correct procedure is to apply to set it aside (CPR, r 23.10(1)), rather than entering an appeal. Applications to set aside are made to the court that made the original order. Where an order made without notice will affect other parties, it must contain a statement explaining that it is possible to apply to set aside or vary the order, and that such an application must be made within seven days of service of the order (rr 23.9(3) and 23.10(2)).

10.3.4 Procedure on making an application without notice

Even in applications made without notice to the other parties, the applicant must in general issue an application notice in Form N244 (CPR, r 23.3(1)) and pay a court fee. As explained at **10.2** above, usually the application will need to be supported by written evidence. Sometimes, a party will decide to make an application at a hearing that has already been fixed, but there is insufficient time to serve an application notice. In cases of this sort the applicant should inform the other parties and the court (preferably in writing) as soon as possible of the nature of the application, the reason for it, and then make the application orally at the hearing (PD 23, para 2.10).

10.3.5 Application notice and evidence in support

The application notice must state the order being sought and the reasons for seeking the order (CPR, r 23.6). The application notice must be signed, and include the title of the claim, its reference number, and the full name of the applicant. If the applicant is not already a party it should also give his or her address for service. If the applicant wants a hearing, that too must be stated. The nature of any evidence in support must be identified in the notice. In an application made without notice, the supporting evidence must state the reasons why notice was not given, in addition to setting out the evidence in support of the relief sought (r 25.3(3)). An example of an application notice is shown in **Figure 10.2**.

10.3.6 Urgent applications

The court has a power to dispense with the need to have issued an application notice (CPR, r 23.3), which may be appropriate if the application is sufficiently urgent. In applications arising in urgent circumstances, where there is no practical possibility of giving the required minimum of three clear days' notice to the other side, informal notification should be given to the other parties unless the circumstances require secrecy (PD 23, para 4.2). Giving only one hour's notice for no good reason, combined with a failure to give full and frank disclosure, resulted in an interim injunction being discharged in *Kulkarni v Milton Keynes Hospital NHS Trust* [2008] LS Law Medical 494.

Generally, applications can only be brought after a claim form has been issued. However, if an application is sufficiently urgent, or if otherwise it would be in the interests of justice, the court has power to consider an application before the main proceedings have been commenced (CPR, r 25.2). Usually, if the court entertains an application before proceedings have been issued, it will give directions requiring a claim to be issued.

10.3.7 Urgent injunction hearings

Cases where injunctions are needed occasionally have to be dealt with by the court more or less straight away, or else the harm that the applicant wants to avoid will be done. Examples are where an allegedly libellous article is going to be published within the next few hours, or if a proposed defendant is about to remove assets from the jurisdiction.

If the court is approached during the working day while the court is still sitting, the hearing will take place in court as soon as the circumstances permit. This means that generally such applications are heard before any other matters already listed as soon as the court sits in the morning, or immediately after lunch. The necessary arrangements must be made with the court staff, who will invariably do all they can to ensure urgent applications are dealt with at the first available opportunity. Solicitors should therefore contact the court by telephone as soon as they know they will need an urgent appointment so as to allow the court time to make the necessary arrangements. Sometimes urgent applications arise during the course of the morning or afternoon in circumstances where it is not possible to wait for the beginning of the next session. If the case is sufficiently urgent the court will interrupt whatever it is doing at a convenient moment so that it can hear the application.

On other occasions the need for a pre-action interim injunction arises at a time when it is not possible to wait until the next occasion when the court will be sitting. If the application is of extreme urgency it may be dealt with by telephone (PD 25, para 4.2). Telephone hearings, however, are only available if the applicant is acting by solicitors or counsel (PD 25, para 4.5(5)). If the problem has arisen during business hours, but in circumstances where it will not be possible to go before a judge before the close of business, initially it is necessary to telephone the court asking to be put in touch with a High

Application notice

For help in completing this form please read
the notes for guidance form N244Notes.

Name of court High Court of Justice Queen's Bench Division	
Claim no.	HQ 09 98744
Warrant no. (if applicable)	
Claimant's name (including ref.)	Shilton Machine Tools Limited
Defendant's name (including ref.)	Banks Plastic Mouldings Limited
Date	

1. What is your name or, if you are a solicitor, the name of your firm?

Messrs Davis, Hendry & Co

2. Are you a   ☐ Claimant   ☐ Defendant   ☑ Solicitor

   ☐ Other *(please specify)*

   If you are a solicitor whom do you represent?   Defendant

3. What order are you asking the court to make and why?

(a) That the judgment entered on 4 November 2009 be set aside.
(b) That the costs of this application be provided for.
On the ground that there is a defence on the merits of the claim, and judgment was entered at a time when the
Claimant's representative said that she would look into the points raised on behalf of the Defendant as to why it was
not liable on the claim.

4. Have you attached a draft of the order you are applying for?   ☐ Yes   ☑ No

5. How do you want to have this application dealt with?   ☑ at a hearing   ☐ without a hearing

   ☐ at a telephone hearing

6. How long do you think the hearing will last?   [0] Hours   [30] Minutes

   Is this time estimate agreed by all parties?   ☐ Yes   ☑ No

7. Give details of any fixed trial date or period   N/A

8. What level of Judge does your hearing need?   Master

9. Who should be served with this application?   Claimant

N244 Application notice (05.08)   1   © Crown copyright 2008

Figure 10.2   Application notice

10. What information will you be relying on, in support of your application?

☑ the attached witness statement

☐ the statement of case

☐ the evidence set out in the box below

If necessary, please continue on a separate sheet.

Statement of Truth

(I believe) (The applicant believes) that the facts stated in this section (and any continuation sheets) are true.

Signed _____ Dated _____
Applicant('s Solicitor)('s litigation friend)

Full name _____

Name of applicant's solicitor's firm _____

Position or office held _____
(if signing on behalf of firm or company)

11. Signature and address details

Signed _____ Dated 12.10.2009 _____
Applicant('s Solicitor)('s litigation friend)

Position or office held _____
(if signing on behalf of firm or company)

Applicant's address to which documents about this application should be sent

Boardman, Phipps & Co 20 High Street, Manchester,	If applicable	
	Phone no.	0161 855 9217
	Fax no.	0161 855 7034
Postcode	DX no.	5442 Manchester 1
M 1 5 9 C Z	Ref no.	RFL/4895

E-mail address	ghoward@boardphipps.com.uk

Court judge of the appropriate Division or County Court judge available to deal with an emergency application (PD 25 Interim Injunctions, para 4.5(1)).

If the problem has arisen outside office hours the applicant should telephone either the High Court (on the same number as above) asking to be put in touch with the clerk to the appropriate duty judge (or the appropriate area Circuit judge where known), or should telephone the urgent court business officer of the appropriate Circuit, who will contact the local duty judge.

If the facilities are available a draft of the order sought will usually be required to be sent by fax to the duty judge who will be dealing with the application.

Counsel have a duty to take a full note on any without notice hearing, which should be provided to other persons affected by the order (*Cinpres Gas Injection Ltd v Melea Ltd* The Times, 21 December 2005).

10.4 Applications on notice

As mentioned above, the general rule is that applications must be made on notice (see CPR, r 23.4(1)), and should normally be made by filing an application notice stating the order being sought and the reasons for seeking the order: CPR, r 23.3(1) and r 23.6 (see **10.3.5** above). On receipt of the application notice the court may either notify the parties of the time and date of the hearing, or may notify them that it proposes to consider the application without a hearing (PD 23, para 2.4).

The normal rule is that it is the applicant who must serve the application notice and documents in support, unless the court orders otherwise (r 6.21(1)). When the court is to effect service, the applicant must file with the court copies of the evidence in support for service on the respondents and a copy of any draft order prepared on behalf of the applicant.

Service must be effected as soon as possible after the application is issued, and in any event not less than three days before it is to be heard (CPR, r 23.7(1)). In accordance with the general rules on computing time, this means clear days (excluding the date of effective service and the date of the hearing), and, because the period is less than five days, also excluding weekends, bank holidays, Christmas Day and Good Friday. Thus, take for example a hearing which is listed for Wednesday 14 October 2009. Assume the solicitor for the applicant decides to serve the application and evidence in support by document exchange. The three clear days before the hearing are 9 (Friday), 12 (Monday) and 13 October 2009 (Tuesday). The documents must arrive on Thursday 8 October, and given the deeming provision in CPR, r 6.26, that documents transmitted by DX are deemed to be served on the second day after being left at the document exchange, the latest the documents could be left at the document exchange would be Tuesday 6 October 2009.

10.5 Disposal without a hearing

One of the ways stated for furthering the overriding objective is that the court may save costs by dealing with cases without the parties needing to attend court (CPR, r 1.4(2)(j)). As part of this objective the CPR, r 23.8, says the court may deal with an interim application without a hearing if either:

(a) the parties agree that the court should dispose of the application without a hearing. The applicant's view on whether there should be a hearing should be stated in the application notice; or

(b) the court does not consider that a hearing would be appropriate.

A party dissatisfied with any order or direction made without a hearing is able to apply to have it set aside, varied or stayed (CPR, r 3.3(5)(a)). Such an application must be made within seven days after service of the order, and the right to make such an application must be stated in the order (CPR, rr 3.3(5)(b) and 3.3(6)).

10.6   Hearing by telephone

Active case management in accordance with the overriding objective includes dealing with cases without the parties needing to attend court, and by making use of technology (CPR, r 1.4(2)(j) and (k)). Both may be achieved by dealing with some applications by telephone conference calls, which is specifically provided for by r 3.1(2)(d). The rule enables the court to hold a hearing by telephone or any other method of direct oral communication, so other means of electronic communication may be used as technology develops. Telephone hearings are most commonly used in 'telephone conference enabled courts', and are most commonly used for interim hearings estimated to take up to an hour and for case management hearings (PD 23, paras 6.1 to 6.12).

10.7   Orders made on the court's own initiative

As part of the ethos of active case management, the courts can exercise their powers on their own initiative where this is appropriate. This power may be exercised for the purpose of managing the case and furthering the overriding objective. Orders made in this way must, by virtue of CPR, rr 3.3(5)(b) and (6), include a statement that parties who are affected may apply within seven days (or such other period as the court may specify) after service for the order to be set aside, varied or stayed.

There is a related power enabling the court to make orders on its own initiative after giving the parties an opportunity of making representations on the matter. Where the court proposes to make such an order it will specify a time within which the representations must be made (r 3.3(2)).

10.8   Court hearing

The general rule is that hearings on interim applications will be in public (CPR, r 39.2). There are exceptions, including hearings where publicity would defeat their object, and in matters involving national security.

At the hearing the applicant should bring a draft order, unless the application is particularly simple. If the order is unusually long or complex the draft should be supplied on disk as well as on hard copy (PD 23, para 12.1). In all but the most simple applications it is usual for counsel to exchange and file skeleton arguments in advance of the hearing. See **33.8** below and the ***Advocacy*** and ***Drafting*** manuals for skeleton arguments. It is also usual to have paginated application bundles prepared by the solicitors for the applicant for all but the most simple applications. For guidance on how applications are argued in court, see the ***Advocacy*** manual. Disputed questions of fact in interim applications are as a general rule decided by asking whether the applicant has established a good arguable case on the matter (*Re H (Minors) (Sexual Abuse: Standard of Proof)* [1996] AC 563, per Lord Nicholls of Birkenhead). This is intended to encapsulate the principle that the court must be as satisfied as it can be, given the limitations inherent in a hearing based on written evidence and the need to avoid mini-trials over interim matters (*WPP Holdings Italy SRL v Benatti* [2007] 1 WLR 2316). While this is the general rule, different formulations have developed for the standard of proof for different types of application, which are mentioned in the relevant chapters of this manual. Disputed evidence is considered further in relation to summary judgment applications at **12.6.4** below.

In addition to dealing with the specific application that has been made, the court may wish to review the conduct of the case as a whole and give any necessary case management directions. The parties will therefore have to be prepared for this and be able to answer any questions the court may ask (para 2.9). The procedural judge will keep, either by way of a note or a tape recording, brief details of all proceedings before him or her, including a short statement of the decision taken at each hearing (para 8).

10.9   Summary determination of interim costs

Where an interim application is disposed of in less than a day (which will cover the vast majority of such applications), the court may well make a summary assessment of the costs of the application immediately after making its order: PD Costs, para 13.2(2). To assist the judge in assessing costs the parties are required to file and serve not less than 24 hours before the interim hearing signed statements of their costs for the interim hearing (**Figure 7.2**). The court must not, however, make a summary assessment of the costs of a publicly funded party (para 13.9), or of a party under a disability unless the solicitor waives the right to further costs (para 13.11(1)). However, the court can make a summary assessment of the costs payable by an assisted party (para 13.10) or by a person under a disability (para 13.11(2)).

Any failure to file or serve a statement of costs, without reasonable excuse, will be taken into account in deciding the costs order to be made on the application (see **36.3.1**).

Immediate summary assessment of costs will only be appropriate where the court decides to order costs in any event. Where the interim costs are to be in the case, assessment of the costs will be left to the conclusion of the case.

10.10   General powers regarding interim relief and orders

The CPR, r 3.1(2), sets out a non-exhaustive list of orders that may be made for the purpose of managing cases, and CPR, r 25.1(1), sets out a non-exhaustive list of interim remedies that may be granted by the court. These various powers include:

- extending or shortening time for compliance with rules and orders (see **1.4.2.5** and **28.3**);
- adjourning or bringing forward hearing dates (see **33.10**);
- requiring a party or a legal representative to attend court;
- dealing with part of a case as a preliminary issue (see **33.3**);
- consolidating two or more claims (see **8.6**);
- deciding the order in which issues are to be tried;
- excluding an issue from consideration;
- granting interim injunctions (see **Chapter 14**);
- making freezing injunctions and search orders (see **Chapters 15** and **16**); and
- granting interim payments (see **Chapter 13**).

Service outside the jurisdiction

11.1 Introduction

11.1.1 Problems that arise

When intending litigants live in different countries, a number of problems arise. These include:

(a) In which country should proceedings be commenced?

(b) Which system of law should govern the dispute?

(c) If proceedings are commenced in one country, how can documents be served in another?

(d) If proceedings are commenced over the same dispute in different countries, which takes precedence, or will they be permitted to proceed in competition with each other?

(e) If proceedings are issued in one country and served in another, how can the defendant contest the jurisdiction of the issuing courts to determine the dispute?

Item (b) above is resolved by the principles pertaining to the conflict of laws, and is outside the scope of this manual. Answers to the other questions will be attempted in this chapter.

11.1.2 Defendants outside the jurisdiction

Usually proceedings in England and Wales must be served on a defendant within the jurisdiction. If the defendant is outside the jurisdiction it is sometimes possible to obtain permission under CPR, r 6.20, to serve proceedings outside the jurisdiction (see **11.3**). Where the proposed litigation has a European flavour, it may, however, be possible to issue proceedings in England and Wales for service abroad without the permission of the court, and this will be considered at **11.2**.

11.2 Service without permission

11.2.1 Conventions and Regulations on jurisdiction

Until 28 February 2002 there were two international conventions, the Brussels Convention between member States of the EU, and the Lugano Convention between member States of the European Free Trade Association and the EU, which were designed to allocate jurisdiction in civil litigation involving parties in more than one member State. These Conventions were given the force of law in this country by the Civil Jurisdiction and Judgments Acts 1982 and 1991 (the CJJA 1982 and the CJJA 1991). On 1 March 2002, Council Regulation (EC) No. 44/2001 (the Jurisdiction Regulation) on jurisdiction and the recognition and enforcement of judgments in civil and commercial matters came into force. The Jurisdiction Regulation covers all member States of the EU. The CJJA 1982 has been amended by the Civil Jurisdiction and Judgments Order 2001, SI 2001/3929, making the amendments necessary to give effect to the Jurisdiction Regulation. The UK itself is divided into 'parts' (England and Wales, Scotland and Northern Ireland), and a separate modified Jurisdiction Regulation, set out in the CJJA 1982, Sch 4, allocates jurisdiction between the courts of each part. The modified Regulation does not apply to the Channel Islands etc (which will not be considered further here). The countries admitted to the EU in recent years are governed by the Jurisdiction Regulation. The current position, regarding service outside the jurisdiction and reciprocal enforcement, is set out in **Figure 11.1**:

Lugano Convention	Iceland, Norway and Switzerland
Jurisdiction Regulation	Austria, Belgium, Bulgaria, Cyprus, Czech Republic, Denmark, Estonia, Finland, France, Germany, Greece, Hungary, Ireland, Italy, Latvia, Lithuania, Luxembourg, Malta, Netherlands, Poland, Portugal, Romania, Slovakia, Slovenia, Spain, Sweden, and the UK
CJJA 1982, Sch 4	Other 'parts' of the UK

Figure 11.1   European jurisdiction and reciprocal enforcement system

The Brussels and Lugano Conventions, and also the Jurisdiction Regulation and CJJA, Sch 4, are in substantially the same terms (but with some numbering and other small variations). They apply to all civil and commercial matters, with certain exceptions, such as revenue, customs, administrative, matrimonial, probate, insolvency, and social security matters. In this chapter all references will be to the Jurisdiction Regulation, as it is the most important of these instruments, but it should be kept in mind that cases decided under the Brussels Convention will refer to the old article numbers.

11.2.2   Conditions

Three conditions must be satisfied for service of proceedings out of the jurisdiction without permission (CPR, r 6.33), the third being capable of being fulfilled in three alternative ways:

(a) the court must be given power to determine each claim made against the defendant in the claim form under the Jurisdiction Regulation (see **11.2.3** and **11.2.5**); and

(b) there are no other pending proceedings concerning the same claim in the UK or any other Regulation State (see **11.2.6**); and

(c) either

(i) the defendant is domiciled in a Regulation State (see **11.2.4**); or

(ii) art 22 confers exclusive jurisdiction to the courts of England and Wales (see **11.2.7.1**); or

(iii) one of the parties is domiciled in a Regulation State and they have conferred jurisdiction on the courts of England and Wales by agreement (art 23) (see **11.2.7.2**).

11.2.3 General rule

Article 2 provides:

Subject to this Regulation, persons domiciled in a Member State shall, whatever their nationality, be sued in the courts of that Member State.

By art 3(2), jurisdiction cannot be founded on service on the defendant while temporarily present in the UK in respect of defendants domiciled in other member States.

11.2.4 Domicile

By art 59, domicile is determined by the law of the courts seised of the matter. The CJJA 1982, ss 41–46, define domicile in terms approximating to genuine residence. By s 41(2):

an individual is domiciled in the UK if and only if—

(a) he is resident in the United Kingdom; and

(b) the nature and circumstances of his residence indicate that he has a substantial connection with the United Kingdom.

By s 41(6), 'substantial connection' is presumed by three months' residence, unless the contrary is proved. Residence is established if an individual has a settled or usual place of abode within the jurisdiction (*Bank of Dubai Ltd v Abbas* [1997] IL Pr 308).

By art 60, a corporation is domiciled where it has its 'seat', central administration or principal place of business. A company's 'seat' is its registered office or, if it does not have one, the place where it was incorporated. Domicile can also be established in the country of a company's principal place of business, which is where it is controlled and managed (*Ministry of Defence and Support for the Armed Forces for the Islamic Republic of Iran v FAZ Aviation Ltd* [2008] 1 All ER (Comm) 372).

11.2.5 Special jurisdiction

11.2.5.1 Special jurisdiction

Article 5 specifies seven types of claim where a person domiciled in one Regulation State may be sued in another. The most important are:

(1) (a) in matters relating to a contract, in the courts for the place of performance of the obligation in question;

(b) for the purpose of this provision, and unless otherwise agreed, the place of performance of the obligation in question shall be:

– in the case of the sale of goods, the place in a Member State where, under the contract, the goods were delivered or should have been delivered,

– in the case of the provision of services, the place in a Member State where, under the contract, the services were provided or should have been provided;

> *(3) in matters relating to tort . . ., in the courts for the place where the harmful event occurred or may occur;*
>
> *(6) as settlor, trustee or beneficiary of a trust created by the operation of a statute, or by a written instrument, or created orally and evidenced in writing, in the courts of the Member State in which the trust is domiciled.*

11.2.5.2   Contract

A dispute as to the existence of a contract does not deprive a national court of the jurisdiction it would otherwise have under art 5(1) (*EfferSpa v Kantner* [1982] ECR 825, ECJ). However, the bare assertion of the existence of a contract is not enough. If there is no serious question to be tried or good arguable case on whether there was a contract, the defendant will be entitled to apply to set aside service of the claim (*Tesam Distribution Ltd v Shuh Mode Team Gmbh* [1990] ILPr 149, CA, and *Boss Group Ltd v Boss France SA* [1996] 4 All ER 970, CA). Whether art 5(1) applies to a transaction which is void *ab initio* was referred to the ECJ (*Barclays Bank plc v Glasgow City Council* [1994] QB 404, CA). The ECJ would not make a ruling as the question arose under the Modified Convention. The case eventually went to the House of Lords where it was held that a claim to recover money paid under a contract which was *ultra vires* and void *ab initio* did not come within art 5(1) or 5(3) (*Kleinwort Benson Ltd v Glasgow City Council* [1999] 1 AC 153, HL).

Jurisdiction is given under art 5(1), however, where the only connection with this country is an alleged non-disclosure or misrepresentation in relation to the making of a contract, these being matters 'relating to a contract' (*Agnew v Lansförsäkringsbolagens AB* [2001] 1 AC 223, HL).

Individual contracts of employment are not governed by the usual rule in art 5(1). By virtue of the EC Contractual Obligations Convention 1980, art 6, which was implemented in the UK by the Contracts (Applicable Law) Act 1990, proceedings should be commenced in the country where the employee habitually carries out his or her work (*Roger Ivenel v Helmut Schwab* [1982] ECR 1891 (ECJ)). This exception applies only when there is a relationship of employer and employee of a personal nature. It does not apply to contracts of commercial agency (*Mercury Publicity Ltd v Wolfgang Loerke GmbH* The Times, 21 October 1991, CA).

For most contracts the question under art 5(1)(a) is simply to determine where the contractual obligation giving rise to the claim was to be performed. The claimant may then bring proceedings in that country under art 5(1)(a), or in the country of the defendant's domicile under art 2. In more complex disputes involving a number of obligations arising under a single contract, the country where the principal obligation is to be performed has jurisdiction (*Shenevai v Kreischer* [1987] ECR 239, ECJ and *Union Transport Group plc v Continental Lines SA* [1992] 1 WLR 15, HL). In a claim based on the sale of goods, jurisdiction is given by art 5(1)(b) to the country where the goods were delivered or should have been delivered. If goods are to be delivered to a number of locations, it is the principal place of delivery that matters (*Color Drack GmbH v Lexx International Vertriebs GmbH* (case C-386/05) [2008] 1 All ER (Comm) 168).

11.2.5.3   Tort

Obviously, the law of tort differs considerably between the Contracting States. In order to ensure consistency in the application of the Brussels Convention it seems the courts must give the term 'tort' an 'independent' interpretation broadly consistent with what is common between the laws of the Contracting States (*Netherlands v Ruffer* [1980] ECR 3807, ECJ).

The expression '. . . place where the harmful event occurred' in art 5(3) gives the claimant the option of commencing proceedings either at the place where the wrongful act or omission took place or at the place where the damage occurred (*Handelskwekerij GJ Bier BV v Mines de Potasse dAlsace SA* [1976] ECR 1735, ECJ). However, the place where the damage occurred is not the place where the damage was quantified or where steps are taken to mitigate damage caused by the wrongful act or omission (*Netherlands v Ruffer* [1980] ECR 3807).

The claimants in *Shevill v Presse Alliance SA* [1995] 2 AC 18, ECJ, [1996] AC 959, HL, complained of a libel in a French newspaper. The newspaper had a daily circulation of 200,000 copies in France, and about 250 in England. The amended statement of claim relied solely on publication in England. It was held that English proceedings had been validly served without permission. The claimants could rely on the common law presumption of damage to show that the 'harmful event' in art 5(3) occurred in England provided they restricted their claim to the harm caused in England, even if the substance of their original complaint was the publication in France.

In the case of a negligent misstatement, the harmful event takes place where the misstatement is made rather than where it is received (*Domicrest Ltd v Swiss Bank Corporation* [1999] QB 548).

11.2.5.4   Jurisdiction in insurance and consumer contracts

Special rules allocate jurisdiction in insurance matters (arts 8-14) and proceedings concerning consumer contracts (arts 15-17). Broadly:

- insurers may be sued in their own country or in the policyholder's country (art 9);

- insurers may only sue in the defendant's country (art 12);

- consumers (non-traders who buy goods on credit or who contract with a person pursuing commercial or professional activities) may be sued only in their own country (arts 15, 16(2)). A contract having a mixed consumer and business purpose is treated as a consumer contract only if the business purpose is negligible (*Gruber v Bay Wa AG* [2006] QB 204, ECJ);

- consumers may bring proceedings in their own country or where the defendant is domiciled (art 16(1)).

11.2.5.5   Multiple parties and cross-claims

Article 6 provides:

A person domiciled in a Member State may also be sued:

1. *Where he is one of a number of defendants, in the courts for the place where any one of them is domiciled, provided the claims are so closely connected that it is expedient to hear and determine them together to avoid the risk of irreconcilable judgments resulting from separate proceedings;*
2. *As a third party . . . in the court seised of the original proceedings, unless these were instituted solely with the object of removing him from the jurisdiction of the court which would be competent in his case;*
3. *On a counterclaim arising from the same contract or facts on which the original claim was based, in the court in which the original claim is pending. . .*

These exceptions must not be extended beyond their proper limits so as to derogate from the general requirement in art 2 that defendants should be sued in the courts of the country where they are domiciled (*Gascoine v Pyrah* The Times, 26 November 1991).

The time for judging whether there is a defendant domiciled within the jurisdiction for the purposes of art 6 is the date of issue, not the date of service (*Canada Trust Co v Stolzenberg (No. 2)* [2002] 1 AC 1, HL). In *Kinnear v Falconfilms NV* [1994] 3 All ER 42, a claim was brought in England by the administrators of an actor's estate against a film company claiming damages arising out of an incident when the actor fell from a horse while shooting a film in Spain. The defendant issued an additional claim seeking an indemnity or a contribution (see **Chapter 9**) against the Spanish hospital that treated the actor, alleging that the actor's death was caused by the negligence of the hospital. The hospital's application to strike out the additional claim was dismissed, because the nexus required for bringing additional claims was in practical terms sufficient to satisfy the special jurisdiction granted by art 6(2) and to confer jurisdiction on the English Court.

11.2.6 No other pending proceedings

The second condition in CPR, r 6.33(2)(a), is that there must be no proceedings concerning the same claim pending in another Regulation State. There are a number of procedural safeguards to ensure such a conflict does not arise.

11.2.6.1 Statement of grounds for bringing claim

A claimant intending to issue a claim form for service on a defendant outside the jurisdiction without permission under CPR, r 6.33, is required to file a notice with the claim form containing a statement of the grounds on which the claimant is entitled to serve the claim form outside the jurisdiction (r 6.34(1)(a)). Form N 510 is used for this purpose (PD 6B, para 2.1 and r 6.34(1)(b)).

11.2.6.2 Conflicting proceedings

If for any reason proceedings involving the same cause of action are pending in more than one country, any court other than the court first seised must decline jurisdiction of its own motion (arts 27 and 29). If actions are related rather than involving the same cause of action, the later actions may be stayed rather than jurisdiction being declined (art 28). For the purposes of art 28, actions are deemed to be related where they are so closely connected that it is expedient to hear and determine them together to avoid the risk of irreconcilable judgments resulting from separate proceedings.

The Courts in England and Wales become 'seised' of the proceedings for the purposes of these Articles when the claim form (or other originating process) is lodged at court for issue, provided the claimant does not subsequently fail to effect service (art 30(1)). Where there is an attempt to serve English proceedings, but the attempt is defective (such as through not including all the correct documents in the package sent to the defendant), CPR, r 6.16 (the power to dispense with service) or r 3.10 (the power to cure irregularities), can be used to regularise the position even if the effect is to allow the English courts to gain priority as the courts first seised (*Phillips v Symes (No 3)* [2008] 1 WLR 180). If it is not clear whether a competing foreign court became seised of its proceedings before an English court, it may be appropriate to adjourn the English proceedings pending a ruling by the foreign court of the date it became seised (*Polly Peck International Ltd v Citibank NA* The Times, 20 October 1993).

A defendant to proceedings in one Regulation State is not permitted to bring proceedings in another Regulation State to challenge the jurisdiction of the courts of the first Regulation State (*Overseas Union Insurance Ltd v New Hampshire Insurance Co* [1992] 1 QB 434, ECJ). The court in one Regulation State is not permitted to grant an injunction to restrain proceedings in another Regulation State, even if those other proceedings are brought in bad faith with a view to frustrating proceedings in the first state (*Turner v Grovit* [2005] 1 AC 101, ECJ). Likewise, it is contrary to the Jurisdiction Regulation to seek an injunction from the courts of a second Regulation State to restrain a person from commencing or continuing court proceedings in the first Regulation State on the ground that the proceedings in the first Regulation State would be contrary to an arbitration agreement (*West Tankers Inc v Riunione Adriatica di Sicurta SpA* (case C-185/07) [2009] 1 All ER (Comm) 435).

11.2.6.3 *Forum non conveniens*

CJJA 1982, s 49, provides that nothing in the Act prevents the court from staying proceedings on the ground of *forum non conveniens* (see **11.3.2.2** and **11.3.2.3**), 'where to do so is not inconsistent with the 1968 Convention'. It is implicit in this that the court cannot stay proceedings on this ground where to do so would be inconsistent with the Convention (*Re Harrods (Buenos Aires) Ltd* [1992] Ch 72, CA per Dillion LJ).

11.2.7 Defendant domiciled, etc

The usual way of fulfilling the third condition in CPR, r 6.33(2)(b), is by the proposed defendant being domiciled in another Regulation State. However, art 22 gives certain courts exclusive jurisdiction over certain matters, and art 23 gives effect to jurisdiction agreements.

11.2.7.1 Exclusive jurisdiction

Article 22 gives exclusive jurisdiction to the courts of the State where the relevant land or register is situated in the following cases:

- rights in and tenancies of land;
- the validity of various company matters;
- the validity of entries in public registers; and
- the registration or validity of patents and other registrable industrial property rights.

Exclusive jurisdiction is only conferred by art 22 if the relevant matter is the principal subject matter of the action.

11.2.7.2 Jurisdiction agreements

By art 23, provided one of the parties, whether the claimant or defendant, is domiciled in a Regulation State, they may by agreement in writing confer jurisdiction on the courts of their choice. Such an agreement will not displace:

- art 22 cases; or
- insurance contracts being enforced by the insured or consumer contracts being enforced by the consumer or employment contracts being enforced by the employee.

Where there are conflicting proceedings involving the same cause of action (see **11.2.6.2**), and it is alleged the court second seised has exclusive jurisdiction under a jurisdiction agreement, the court second seised must stay its proceedings under art 27 until the court first seised has determined whether it has jurisdiction (*Erich Gasser GmbH v MISATSrl* [2005] QB 1, ECJ).

In *Kurz v Stella Musical Veranstaltungs GmbH* [1992] Ch 196, Hoffmann J held that art 23 is to be interpreted so as to allow the parties to confer jurisdiction on the courts of more than one country, thereby giving themselves a choice of venue.

Also by art 23, if a jurisdiction agreement is concluded by parties neither of whom is domiciled in a Regulation State, the rule is that the courts of other States shall have no jurisdiction unless the chosen courts decline jurisdiction.

11.3 Service with permission

11.3.1 Introduction

This section considers the more traditional jurisdiction of the courts in England and Wales to grant permission to serve proceedings abroad, which still governs cases where the defendant is abroad in a non-EU country.

11.3.2 When will permission be granted?

The principles to be applied when the court is considering an application for permission to allow service out of the jurisdiction were restated by the House of Lords in *Seaconsar Far East Ltd v Bank Markazi Jomhouri Islami Iran* [1994] 1 AC 438 as altered by what is now the CPR, r 6.37. There are three matters that the intending claimant must establish:

(a) There must be a good arguable case that the court has jurisdiction within one of the 20 grounds set out in PD 6B, para 3.1 (see **11.3.2.1**).

(b) There must be a reasonable prospect of success on the merits. This formulation was introduced on 2 May 2000 by amendment of the CPR (now r 6.37(1)(b)). Since *Seaconsar*, this second limb had been satisfied by showing a 'serious issue to be tried', which was the same test as that applied in applications for interim injunctions under the *American Cyanamid* principles (for which, see **14.3.1.1**). Before *Seaconsar*, the accepted test had been one of showing a 'good arguable case' on the merits.

(c) The court must be satisfied that England and Wales is the proper place in which to bring the claim (CPR, r 6.37(3)). This requirement is considered further at **11.3.2.2** and **11.3.2.3**.

11.3.2.1 What are the grounds for granting permission?

PD 6B, para 3.1, giving effect to CPR, r 3.36, lists 20 grounds on which service out of the jurisdiction is permissible. These grounds include cases where:

(3) *A claim is made against a person ('the defendant') on whom the claim form has been or will be served (otherwise than in reliance on this paragraph) and—*
   (a) *there is between the claimant and the defendant a real issue which it is reasonable for the court to try; and*
   (b) *the claimant wishes to serve the claim form on another person who is a necessary or proper party to that claim.*
   . . .
(5) *A claim is made for an interim remedy under section 25 (1) of the Civil Jurisdiction and Judgments Act 1982.*
(6) *A claim is made in respect of a contract where the contract—*
   (a) *was made within the jurisdiction;*
   (b) *was made by or through an agent trading or residing within the jurisdiction;*

    (c) *is governed by English law; or*

    (d) *contains a term to the effect that the court shall have jurisdiction to determine any claim in respect of the contract.*

  (7) *A claim is made in respect of a breach of contract committed within the jurisdiction.*

  (8) *A claim is made for a declaration that no contract exists where, if the contract was found to exist, it would comply with the conditions set out in paragraph (6).*

  (9) *A claim is made in tort where—*

    (a) *damage was sustained within the jurisdiction; or*

    (b) *the damage sustained resulted from an act committed within the jurisdiction.*

It has been held that the intending claimant may choose which ground to rely on. Generally, the grounds are to be read disjunctively. However, the case must fall within the spirit, as well as the letter, of the rule (*Johnson v Taylor Bros and Co* [1920] AC 144). There is a large body of case law dealing in detail with the various paragraphs of this rule, but which is beyond the scope of the civil litigation component of this course.

11.3.2.2 What is a 'proper case'? The doctrine of *forum conveniens*

The third requirement from *Seaconsar* (see **11.3.2**) gives the court an overriding discretion to refuse permission. The court applies what is often called 'the doctrine of *forum conveniens'* and will grant permission only if satisfied that England is the most appropriate forum for the trial of the claim. This means that England must be the place where the case can be tried most suitably for the interests of all parties and the ends of justice. The tag of *forum conveniens* is somewhat inapt, in that the question is not one of convenience but of appropriateness.

The intending claimant has the burden of proving that England is clearly the appropriate forum for the trial.

11.3.2.3 Factors which the court will take into consideration in determining the appropriate forum

The court will consider any factors which point towards another forum being more appropriate than England. These include the availability of witnesses (including experts), local knowledge, the places where the parties reside and carry on business, the law governing the relevant transaction, and whether justice can only be obtained elsewhere at excessive cost, delay or inconvenience.

Sometimes the intending claimant will have some legitimate personal or juridical advantage in bringing proceedings in England. Recurring examples relate to disclosure, limitation periods, and damages. Usually this should not be a factor in considering permission: the claimant's advantage will ordinarily be the defendant's disadvantage. However, there may be cases where, provided the claimant has not acted unreasonably, it may be appropriate in order to secure the ends of justice to allow the claimant to take advantage of, for example, a longer limitation period in England.

In *Spiliada Maritime Corp v Cansulex Ltd* [1986] AC 460, Lord Templeman said:

The factors which the court is entitled to take into account in considering whether one forum is more appropriate are legion. The authorities do not, perhaps cannot, give any clear guidance as to how these factors are to be weighed in any particular case.

Lord Goff, in the same case, said:

It is also significant to observe that the circumstances specified in [what is now PD 6B, para 3.1], as those in which the court may exercise its discretion to grant leave to serve proceedings on the defendant outside the jurisdiction, are of great variety, ranging from cases where, one would have thought, the discretion would normally be exercised in favour of granting leave (eg where the relief sought is an injunction ordering the defendant to do or refrain from doing something within the jurisdiction) to cases where the grant of leave is far more problematical. In addition, the importance to be attached to any particular ground invoked by the plaintiff may vary from case to case.

11.3.3 Procedure

Permission is sought by issuing an application notice supported by written evidence, and is dealt with by a Master or District Judge without a hearing and without giving notice.

CPR, r 6.37(1) and (2), provide:

> (1) An application for permission under rule 6.36 must set out—
>   (a) which ground in paragraph 3.1 of [PD 6B] is relied on;
>   (b) that the claimant believes that the claim has a reasonable prospect of success; and
>   (c) the defendant's address or, if not known, in what place or country the defendant is, or likely, to be found.
> (2) Where the application is made in respect of a claim referred to paragraph 3.1(3) of [PD 6B], the application must also state the grounds on which the claimant believes that there is between the claimant and the defendant a real issue which it is reasonable for the court to try.

The application is made without notice so the claimant has the usual duty of giving full and frank disclosure in the evidence in support. While permission should be sought before the claim is served, it is possible to grant retrospective permission (*Nesheim v Kosa* LTL 4/10/2006).

11.4 Submission to the jurisdiction

Even in cases outside the scope of CPR, rr 6.34 and 6.36, the defendant may submit to the jurisdiction of the courts of England and Wales. This may be by agreement after the dispute has arisen, or by a failure to dispute the jurisdiction after acknowledging service (*SMAY Investments Ltd v Sachdev* [2003] 1 WLR 1973). However, in cases governed by the Jurisdiction Regulation, a defendant cannot submit to the jurisdiction where exclusive jurisdiction is given to another court by art 22 (see art 24).

11.5 Service abroad

11.5.1 Acknowledgment of service

The claim form and acknowledgment of service forms must be amended to give the defendant an enhanced period to acknowledge. For States governed by the Jurisdiction Regulation the period is 21 days. The periods for other countries are set out in a table to PD 6B, eg USA is 22 days, India 23 days, Vanuatu 29 days.

11.5.2 Effecting service

The general rule is that service must be in accordance with the law of the country where the defendant is to be served. Depending on the status of the country where the defendant resides, and on whether that country is a member of the Hague Convention 1965 or any other Civil Procedure Convention, one or other of the following methods of service should be used, namely through:

- use of the Service Regulation (Council Regulation (EC) No. 1348/2000) in relation to service in member States;
- the government of the defendant's country;
- the British consular authority;
- the judicial authorities of the defendant's country;
- the authority designated under the Hague Convention; and
- instructing local agents to effect service according to local law.

11.6 Period of validity

Where a claim form is to be served within the jurisdiction, it is initially valid for four months. If the claim form is to be served out of the jurisdiction it is valid initially for six months (CPR, r 7.5(2)).

11.7 Objecting to service abroad

A defendant who wishes to dispute the jurisdiction of the court after being served abroad must first acknowledge service, then apply to set aside service or discharge the order giving permission.

11.8 Judgment in default

By CPR, r 12.10(b)(i), judgment cannot be entered in default of giving notice of intention to defend (see **Chapter 6**) without permission where the claim form was served abroad without permission under the Jurisdiction Regulation. Applications for permission under CPR, r 12.10(b)(i), are made without notice by an affidavit stating that the deponent believes each claim made by the claim form is one which, by virtue of the CJJA 1982, the court has power to hear and determine, that no other court has exclusive jurisdiction under art 22, and that service satisfied the relevant rules.

Summary judgment

12.1 Introduction

In cases where the defendant fails to defend it is usually possible to enter a default judgment (see **Chapter 6**). Entering summary judgment is a related procedure, and is used where it is felt that a purported defence filed by a defendant can be shown to have no real prospects of success.

Summary judgment is not limited to use by claimants against defendants. It can also be used by defendants to attack weak claims brought by claimants. Further, summary judgment can be used by the court of its own initiative to perform the important function of stopping weak cases from proceeding. The procedure can also be used to attack the weaker parts of cases, thereby reducing complexity and costs. It should be noted:

(a) that the procedure is available not only to claimants against defendants, but also to defendants who can use it to knock out the whole or part of the claim;

(b) the procedure supplements the power to strike out, and allows the court summarily to dispose of cases on points of law; and

(c) that the procedure may be invoked by the court of its own initiative.

Summary judgment is closely related to the power to strike out under CPR, r 3.4 (discussed at **5.9** and **28.2**). Both powers are used to achieve the active case management aim of summarily disposing of issues that do not need full investigation at trial (CPR, r 1.4(2)(c)). It is very common for parties to make applications in suitable cases for striking out and summary judgment in the alternative. Striking out under r 3.4 is primarily aimed at cases and issues that are weak in the way in which they are set out in the relevant statement of case, whereas summary judgment is primarily aimed at cases that are weak on the facts, so that they can be said to have no real prospect of success (see CPR, r 24.2(a)). There is an inevitable overlap between the two concepts. On an application to strike out, the court has the power to treat the application as one for summary judgment (*Three Rivers District Council v Bank of England (No. 3)* [2003] 2 AC 1).

An application for summary judgment is decided applying the test of whether the respondent has a case with a real prospect of success, which is considered having regard to the overriding objective of dealing with the case justly. This has been said to be consistent with the need to have a fair trial under Article 6(1) of the European Convention on Human Rights (*Three Rivers District Council v Bank of England (No. 3)*).

12.2 Time at which the application may be made

A claimant may only apply for summary judgment after the defendant has filed either an acknowledgment of service or a defence, unless the court gives permission (CPR, r 24.4(1)). If the defendant fails to do either of these within the time limited by the Civil Procedure Rules 1998, the claimant may enter a default judgment, either with or without the court's permission, depending on the nature of the claim. By analogy with CPR, r 25.2(2)(c), a defendant likewise can only apply for summary judgment after either filing an acknowledgment of service or a defence. Where the claimant has failed to comply with a relevant pre-action protocol, an application for summary judgment will only be entertained after the period for filing a defence has expired (PD 24, para 2(6)).

It is normally appropriate to make the application early on in the litigation process, if possible very shortly after the acknowledgment or defence, because if the other side have no realistic prospects of success entering summary judgment early prevents unnecessary costs being incurred. The application should be made before or when the applicant files the allocation questionnaire (PD 26, para 5.3(1)).

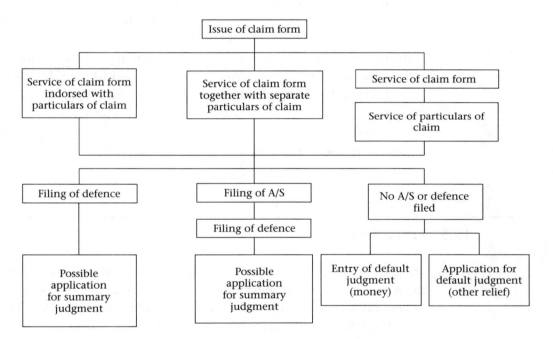

Figure 12.1   Flow diagram showing stages for applying for default and summary judgments

12.3 Excluded proceedings

Under CPR, r 24.3(2), the only excluded proceedings in cases where the application is brought by the claimant are residential possession proceedings (whether brought against a tenant, mortgagee or a person holding over at the end of a tenancy), and admiralty claims *in rem*. Summary judgment will not be granted in a libel claim where there is a material issue of fact between the parties, because such issues must be decided by the jury (Supreme Court Act 1981, s 69, and *Safeway Stores plc v Tate* [2001] QB 1120).

However, where the evidence, taken at its highest, is such that no properly directed jury could reach a verdict contended for by one of the parties, summary judgment is available (*Alexander v Arts Council of Wales* [2001] 1 WLR 1840). Summary judgment will almost always be inappropriate where there are allegations of deceitful, dishonest or unlawful conduct (*Espirit Telecoms UK Ltd v Fashion Gossip Ltd* (2000) LTL 27/7/2000). In applications against claimants there are no excluded types of proceedings (CPR, r 24.3(1)).

12.4   Effect of making an application for summary judgment

There are three procedural effects of having a pending application for summary judgment:

(a) If the application is made after filing an acknowledgment of service but before filing of the defence, there is no need to file a defence before the hearing (CPR, r 24.4(2)). At that stage the court will give directions, which will include providing a date for filing the defence. The permissive wording of the rule confirms *Natural Resources Inc v Origin Clothing Ltd* [1995] FSR 280, which held that there is nothing to prevent a defendant from serving a defence in the period before the hearing if the defendant chooses to do so.

(b) Where a party makes a summary judgment application before a claim has been allocated to a case management track, the court will not allocate the claim before hearing the summary judgment application (PD 26, paras 5.3(2) and 12.3).

(c) Where a defendant has applied for summary judgment against a claimant, the claimant cannot obtain a default judgment until the summary judgment application has been disposed of (CPR, r 12.3(3)(a)).

12.5   Procedure

The general rules on making interim applications (see **Chapter 10**) apply on making an application for summary judgment, with certain refinements. The application is made by application notice, which must be supported by evidence (CPR, r 25.3(2)). The facts supporting the claim will have been verified by a statement of truth included in the particulars of claim. It is risky to rely solely on a statement of case (*Korea National Insurance Corporation v Allianz Global Corporate and Specialty AG* [2007] 2 CLC 748). It is more usual to rely on evidence set out in the application notice (in simple cases) or witness statements (all but simple cases). The evidence in support of an application by a claimant will have to state a belief that there is no defence with a reasonable prospect of success. It may be prudent to go further and to give details of the background facts and to exhibit relevant documentation to show there is no reasonable defence. On an application by the defendant there may or may not be a filed defence. If not, clearly the evidence will have to explain why the claim is unlikely to succeed, and will probably have to go into the background in some detail.

The rules specifically mention that the court may fix a summary judgment hearing of its own initiative (CPR, r 24.4(3)). If the court is minded to make use of this power, it is most likely to do so on the initial scrutiny at the track allocation stage shortly after filing of the defence. If the court uses the power it will not allocate the case to a track, but instead it will fix a hearing, giving the parties 14 days' notice and informing them of the issues it proposes to decide (PD 26, para 5.4).

While the court can enter summary judgment or dismiss a claim against an applicant on the applicant's own application for summary judgment against the other side, such a reversal should not take place unless the court has given fair notice to the applicant that it is minded to consider taking this course (*P & O Nedlloyd BV v Arab Metals Co (No 2)* [2007] 1 WLR 2288).

Instead of the usual notice period of three clear days which applies to most types of interim application, the notice period in applications for summary judgment is 14 clear days (CPR, r 24.4(3)). The 14-day period of notice has been shortened to four clear days for specific performance claims (see **12.8**).

The respondent must file and serve any evidence in reply at least seven clear days before the hearing (CPR, r 24.5(1)). The application notice must inform the respondent of this time limit (PD 24, para 2(5)). If the applicant wishes to respond to the respondent's evidence, the further evidence must be served and filed at least three clear days before the hearing of the application (CPR, r 24.5(2)).

In cases where the hearing is fixed by the court on its own initiative, all parties must file and serve their evidence at least seven clear days before the return day, and if they want to respond to their opponents' evidence, that must be done at least three clear days before the return day (CPR, r 24.5(3)).

In the time-honoured phrase, the evidence in reply must 'condescend to particulars'. For example, it should deal with the specific allegations in the particulars of claim, and state the nature of and facts in support of the defence.

12.6   The hearing

12.6.1   Defendant fails to attend

In such cases the Master is almost bound to make the order, unless the particulars of claim for some reason give cause for concern. By CPR, r 23.11, and PD 24, para 8, 'judgment given against a party who does not attend may be set aside or varied'. On such an application, the onus is on the defendant to satisfy the court as to:

- the merits of the defence; and
- the reasons for the non-attendance.

12.6.2   No notice of defendant's evidence in response

Sometimes, the defendant attends on the return day with written evidence in support of a defence, having failed to give the claimant the necessary seven days' notice. In such cases, the Master usually adjourns to give the claimant time to serve evidence in reply. The costs thrown away are usually ordered against the defendant.

12.6.3   Effective return day

Where both parties attend, the claimant mentions the nature of the application and refers to the evidence in support. The defendant refers the Master to his or her evidence setting out the reasons against entering summary judgment. The claimant then argues that there is no defence to the claim, referring to the evidence in reply, if any. The defendant then argues that there is a defence or some other reason for a trial, and that the application should be dismissed. (See the *Advocacy* manual.)

12.6.4   Going behind the written evidence

An application for summary judgment is not a trial of the veracity of the written evidence. Generally, the court must act on the undisputed evidence and the respondent's version of any disputed facts (*HRH Prince of Wales v Associated Newspapers Ltd* [2008] Ch 57). There are limits. As Lord Lindley said in *Codd v Delap* (1905) 92 LT 810, HL, the respondent's evidence may be rejected 'if it is obviously frivolous and practically moonshine'.

In *Banque de Paris et des Pays-Bas (Suisse) SA v de Naray* [1984] 1 Lloyd's Rep 21, Ackner LJ said:

> It is of course trite law that [summary judgment] proceedings are not decided by weighing the two affidavits. It is also trite that the mere assertion in an affidavit of a given situation which is to be the basis of a defence does not, *ipso facto*, provide leave to defend; the court must look at the whole situation and ask itself whether the defendant has satisfied the court that there is a fair or reasonable probability of the defendants' having a real or bona fide defence.

A slightly different formulation, approved in *National Westminster Bank plc v Daniel* [1993] 1 WLR 1, CA, was: 'Is what the defendant says credible?' If it is not, there is no fair or reasonable probability of the defendant being able to set up a defence. The rigid formulation of categories where it is appropriate to go behind the defendant's evidence, as attempted by Webster J in *Paclantic Financing Co Inc v Moscow Narodny Bank Ltd* [1983] 1 WLR 1063, was deprecated in *National Westminster Bank plc v Daniel* as too narrow. However, Webster J's categories are still useful examples. They are where:

- the defendant's evidence is inherently unreliable through being self-contradictory; or
- the defendant's evidence is inadmissible; or
- the defendant's evidence is irrelevant; or
- there is affirmative evidence which is either admitted or unchallengeable by the defendant which is unequivocally inconsistent with the written evidence, there being no plausible explanation for the inconsistency.

12.6.5   Amendment at hearing

There are many cases where the defective nature of one side's statement of case becomes clear at a hearing of an application for summary judgment. If the defect is one of how the case is put rather than of substance, the court has a wide power to allow an amendment to correct the problem, which can be exercised at the hearing (*Stewart v Engel* [2000] 1 WLR 2268).

12.7   Possible orders

The orders available to the court are:

- judgment on the claim;
- striking out or dismissal of the claim;

- dismissal of the application; and
- a conditional order.

It is possible to combine these orders. Thus, if the claimant claims £50,000, and there is a reasonable defence in the sum of £30,000, the order should be judgment in favour of the claimant in the sum of £20,000, with the application dismissed as to the balance.

12.7.1 Entering summary judgment

The CPR, r 24.2, provides:

The court may give summary judgment against a claimant or defendant on the whole of a claim or on a particular issue if—

    (a) it considers that—
        (i)   that claimant has no real prospect of succeeding on the claim or issue; or
        (ii)   that defendant has no real prospect of successfully defending the claim or issue; and
    (b) there is no other compelling reason why the case or issue should be disposed of at a trial.

The 'real prospect of success' formula is the same as that applied on an application to set aside a judgment in default. The only difference is that it is for the applicant to show that the respondent's case has no real prospect of success (*ED & F Man Liquid Products Ltd v Patel* [2003] CPLR 384). In *Swain v Hillman* [2001] 1 All ER 91, Lord Woolf MR said that 'real prospect of success' did not need any amplification as the words spoke for themselves. The word 'real' directed the court to the need to see whether there was a realistic, as opposed to a fanciful, prospect of success. The phrase does not mean 'real and substantial' prospects of success. Nor does it mean that summary judgment will only be granted if the claim or defence is 'bound to be dismissed at trial'.

A claim may be fanciful where it is entirely without substance, or where it is clear beyond question that the statement of case is contradicted by all the documents or other material on which it is based (*Three Rivers District Council v Bank of England (No. 3)* [2003] 2 AC 1). Conversely, there is no rule of practice that summary judgment cannot be given if a case is weak despite there being some documentary evidence in support (*Miller v Garton Shires* [2006] EWCA Civ 1386). In *Swain v Hillman* the Master of the Rolls went on to say that summary judgment applications have to be kept within their proper role. They are not meant to dispense with the need for a trial where there are issues which should be considered at trial. Further, summary judgment hearings should not be mini-trials. They are simply summary hearings to dispose of cases where there is no real prospect of success.

Where the defence put forward is in the realm of being a mere (and distinctly improbable) possibility, the court should enter summary judgment (*Akinleye v East Sussex Hospitals NHS Trust* [2008] LS Law Med 216). It is similar where there are no primary facts to support the alleged defence (*P & S Amusements Ltd v Valley House Leisure Ltd* [2006] EWHC 1510 (Ch)). There may be no real prospect of success if the defence consists entirely of admissions and bare denials (*Broderick v Centaur Tipping Services Ltd* LTL 22/8/2006). In *Penningtons v Abedi* (1999) LTL 13/8/99, there had been ongoing litigation in which the defendant had advanced a series of defences which had each been shown to be false. An application was made for summary judgment, and it was held that the defendant's conduct of the litigation was such that there was no realistic prospect of her successfully defending the claim. In *Public Trustee v Williams* (2000) LTL 10/2/2000, the Public Trustee, as executor of a deceased's estate, sought to recover the sum of £74,000 which was received by one of the defendants and used by her to buy a house. The evidence of the recipient filed in response to an application for summary judgment was at its best unclear and at its worst confusing as to where she thought the money had come from. However, there was no clear evidence that the money had come from the estate, and it was held that it was not a suitable case for summary judgment. In *ED & F Man Liquid Products Ltd v Patel* [2003] CPLR 384, a defence that might have had a real prospect of success was destroyed by clear, written, admissions made by the defendant before proceedings were issued.

The claimant is entitled to judgment where the respondent's only suggested claim or defence is a point of law which is clearly misconceived, or which can be shown to be unsustainable after relatively short argument. Note that some judges do on occasion allow summary judgment applications which take (say) two or three days to argue. Complex claims are unlikely to be suitable for summary judgment (*Three Rivers District Council v Bank of England (No. 3)* [2003] 2 AC 1), as are cases raising issues in developing fields of law (*Brooks v Commissioner of Police of the Metropolis* [2005] 1 WLR 1495, HL at [3]).

Where a case raises difficult questions of law which call for detailed argument and mature consideration, there is a real prospect of success, and summary judgment is inappropriate (*Home and Overseas Insurance Co Ltd v Mentor Insurance Co (UK) Ltd* [1990] 1 WLR 153, CA). Likewise, where the background facts need further investigation, such as through disclosure of documents (**Chapter 20**), summary judgment may be refused (*Groveholt Ltd v Hughes* [2008] EWHC 1358 (Ch)).

A dispute of facts will usually produce a real prospect of success. For this reason it is unusual to obtain summary judgment in personal injuries cases, which often turn on disputed facts. However, there is no rule to this effect, and in *Dummer v Brown* [1953] 1 QB 710 summary judgment was given in a personal injuries case in favour of a passenger in a coach where the coach driver had previously pleaded guilty to dangerous driving. Even if there is a conviction, summary judgment may be refused if there are good reasons for believing the conviction was erroneous (*McCauley v Vine* [1999] 1 WLR 1977, CA).

Although CPR, r 24.2, expressly says that the court can give summary judgment on particular issues, the court may consider that, where there are connected issues, some of which should go to trial, summary judgment should be refused on the others as well (*Redevco Properties v Mount Cook Land Ltd* (2002) LTL 30/7/2002).

12.7.2 Conditional orders

PD 24, para 4, provides:

Where it appears to the court possible that a claim or defence may succeed but improbable that it will do so, the court may make a conditional order . . .

PD 24, para 5.2, provides:

A conditional order is an order which requires a party:

1. *to pay a sum of money into court, or*
2. *to take a specified step in relation to his claim or defence, as the case may be, and provides that that party's claim will be dismissed or his statement of case will be struck out if he does not comply. (Note—the court will not follow its former practice of granting leave to a defendant to defend a claim, whether conditionally or unconditionally.)*

Conditional orders are appropriate for cases in the grey area between granting judgment and dismissing the application. For example, in *Homebase Ltd v LSS Services Ltd* (2004) LTL 28/6/2004 the claim was for licence fees for occupying land. The defendant agreed it was occupying the land, but argued that it had orally agreed with the claimant that no fees would be payable until the claimant obtained consent from the claimant's landlord to assign the land to the defendant. The court did not think the defence was incredible (in which event judgment would have been entered), but the unlikely nature of the alleged agreement combined with a lack of any contemporaneous documentation meant there were justifiable doubts, and a conditional order was made.

If money is paid into court pursuant to a conditional order, the claimant is protected against the defendant's bankruptcy. The claim must still be proved in the insolvency, but the claimant has security for the sum paid into court (*Re Ford* [1900] 2 QB 211).

In *Yorke (MV) Motors v Edwards* [1982] 1 WLR 444, HL, a condition of payment of £12,000 into court within 28 days had been ordered by the judge, who was 'sceptical' about Mr Edwards' defence to the £23,000 claim. He appealed against the condition. He was unemployed, living with his father, and had legal aid with a nil contribution. Lord Diplock endorsed the following principles:

(a) A defendant seeking to limit a financial condition must make full and frank disclosure and must put sufficient and proper evidence of his or her impecuniosity before the court. The defendant should be given an opportunity to produce evidence of means. A claimant may need to give advance notice that such an order is to be sought if summary judgment is not ordered, or an adjournment may be necessary (*Anglo-Eastern Trust Ltd v Kermanshahchi* [2002] EWCA Civ 198).

(b) Reliance on a public funding certificate is not sufficient.

(c) The test of the appropriateness or otherwise of the condition is whether it will be impossible for the defendant to fulfil it, as this would be equivalent to giving judgment. However, merely finding the condition difficult to fulfil is no ground for complaint.

On the facts the House of Lords substituted a condition for bringing £3,000 into court.

12.7.3 Set-off

If a cross-claim is for a sum of money and it amounts to a defence it is called a set-off. (A set-off is pleaded in any defence and is usually also pleaded as a counterclaim.) As a set-off is a defence it will justify dismissing the application up to the amount of the set-off claimed. The following are established set-off situations:

(a) Mutual debts. Under statute, if the claimant and defendant both owe each other liquidated sums, even if unconnected, the defendant's debt should be set-off against the debt to the claimant.

(b) Sale of Goods Act 1979, s 53(1). Where the seller sues for the price of goods sold and delivered the buyer can set-off a claim for damages for breach of the statutory implied terms (such as the goods being not of satisfactory quality, not fit for their purpose, or not corresponding to description).

(c) On a claim for the price of services, the defendant can set-off a counterclaim for damages for poor workmanship (*Basten v Butler* (1806) 7 East 4710).

(d) Equitable set-off. Although it is clear that an equitable set-off is a defence, the ambit of the doctrine is less certain. Lord Wilberforce in *The Aries* [1977] 1 WLR 185, HL, at 405 said 'One thing is clear—there must be some equity, some ground for equitable intervention, beyond the mere existence of a cross-claim.' In *Hanak v Green* [1958] 2 QB 9, CA, the claimant sued her builder for breach of contract for failing to complete, or complete properly, certain building works on her house. The defendant counterclaimed by way of set-off:

(i)   a quantum meruit for extra work done outside the contract;

(ii)   losses sustained by the claimant's refusal to admit his workmen; and

(iii) damages for trespass to his tools.

It was held that all three heads were equitable set-offs, because a court of equity before the Judicature Acts would have required that either side should take the other side's claims into account before insisting on its own claims.

It is clear that the mere existence of a cross-claim is not enough. Even where the claim and cross-claim arose out of the same contract or transaction, there would only be a set-off if the two claims were so inseparably connected that the one ought not to be enforced without taking the other into account (*Dole Dried Fruit and Nut Company v Trustin Kerwood Ltd* [1990] 2 Lloyd's Rep 309, CA). Putting the matter slightly differently, it must be manifestly unjust to allow one party to enforce payment without taking into account the cross-claim (*Insituform (Ireland) Ltd v Insituform Group Ltd* The Times, 27 November 1990, CA).

A classic example of an equitable set-off is that a tenant is allowed to set-off a counterclaim for damages for breach of covenant in the lease in respect of which the landlord is claiming arrears of rent (*British Anzani (Felixstowe) Ltd v International Marine Management (UK) Ltd* [1980] QB 137 (QBD)).

12.7.4   The cheque rule

It is an old rule that a cheque, bill of exchange or promissory note is given and taken as so much cash (*Jackson v Murphy* (1887) 4 TLR 92). The so-called 'cheque rule' is that where *inter alia* goods or services are paid for by a cheque which is subsequently dishonoured, the payee is entitled to summary judgment on the cheque and the defendant cannot set-off against that claim any cross-claim for damages allegedly due under the contract of sale or services. The doctrine goes as far as laying down that the defendant will not even get a stay of execution pending resolution of a counterclaim. It was held in *Esso Petroleum Co Ltd v Milton* [1997] 1 WLR 938, CA, that the same rule applies to payments by direct debit. It also applies to letters of credit (*SAFA Ltd v Banque du Caire* [2000] 2 All ER (Comm) 567) and to performance bonds (*Solo Industries UK Ltd v Canara Bank* [2001] 1 WLR 1800).

There is both a commercial and a legal justification for the rule. Commercial people regard cheques as almost equivalent to cash, and expect payment at the end of the usual clearing period. In legal terms there are two contracts: the underlying contract of sale or services; and the independent contract on the bill of exchange itself. It is because the claimant is suing on the independent cheque contract that cross-claims on the sale contract will not be entertained.

A number of limited defences have been recognised to cheque actions, namely:

(a) fraud;

(b) invalidity;

(c) illegality;

(d) duress;

(e) total failure of consideration;

(f) as a partial defence, ascertained and liquidated partial failure of consideration; and

(g) a misrepresentation made to induce the defendant to give a cheque will be a defence to a claim on the cheque (*SAFA Ltd v Banque du Caire* [2000] 2 All ER (Comm) 567), but an allegation that the claimant made a misrepresentation about the quality of the subject matter of the underlying contract (such as the goods in a sale of goods) will not be a defence to a claim on a cheque given in payment of the contract price (see also *Solo Industries UK Ltd v Canara Bank* [2001] 1 WLR 1800).

12.7.5 Some other compelling reason for a trial

Even if there is no claim or defence with a real prospect of success, summary judgment should not be given if there is some other compelling reason for a trial. Other reasons include:

(a) Where the defendant has been unable to contact an important witness who may provide material for a defence.

(b) Where the applicant has acted harshly or unconscionably, so it would be desirable to ensure that judgment is obtained only in the full light of publicity.

12.8 Specific performance, rescission and forfeiture in property cases

An even speedier process for obtaining summary judgment is available by virtue of PD 24, para 7, in claims for specific performance and similar claims arising out of mortgage and tenancy agreements. Again the test is whether there is a defence with a realistic prospect of success (*North East Lincolnshire Borough Council v Millennium Park (Grimsby) Ltd* The Times, 31 October 2002). Summary judgment in these cases can be sought at any time after the claim is served, rather than having to wait until after acknowledgment or defence, and the application can be made even in the absence of particulars of claim. The application notice, evidence in support, and a draft order must be served no less than four clear days before the hearing.

12.9 Claims against trespassers and possession claims

12.9.1 Police

There are occasions when trespassers enter onto land and refuse to leave. A person entitled to possession who attempts to turn trespassers off the land without the sanction of a court order risks a breach of the peace and may incur civil or criminal liability for doing so. A court order is not needed, however, if the person entitled to the land can make use of the Criminal Law Act 1977, s 7, as substituted by the Criminal Justice and Public Order Act 1994, s 73. This makes it an offence for any person who is on premises as a trespasser to fail to leave on being required to do so by the residential occupier or a protected occupier. A constable in uniform may arrest such a person without a warrant. The section only applies to residential property, and not to commercial property or open land.

12.9.2   Possession claims against trespassers

Possession claims against trespassers are claims for the recovery of land which is alleged to be occupied by persons who entered or remained on the land without the consent of a person entitled to possession of the land. They do not include claims against tenants or sub-tenants, whether the defendant's tenancy has terminated or not. These claims can include claims against licensees who remain in occupation after the termination of their licences.

12.9.3   Procedure on possession claims against trespassers

These claims must normally be started in the County Court for the district in which the land is situated (CPR, r 55.3(1)). There are special forms for the claim form and defence. Where the claimant does not know the names of all the occupiers, the claim is brought against 'persons unknown' in addition to any named defendants. Particulars of claim and witness statements in support must be filed when the claim is issued (rr 55.4 and 55.8(5)). When the claim is issued the court will fix a date for the hearing, which will usually be just a few days after issue. Where the claim is against named defendants the normal rules on service apply (see **Chapter 3**). Where the claim is against persons unknown, in addition to serving the named defendants in the normal way, the documents must be served by:

(a) attaching copies to the main door or some other part of the land so they are clearly visible, and by inserting another set of the documents through the letter box in a sealed transparent envelope addressed to 'the occupiers'; or

(b) attaching copies contained in sealed transparent envelopes addressed to 'the occupiers' to stakes placed in the land in places where they are clearly visible. This method is used where the trespassers are on open land.

Service must be effected not less than five days before the hearing in the case of residential property, and not less than two days before the hearing in respect of commercial property and open land (r 55.5(2)).

12.9.4   Hearing in claims against trespassers

Unless the court orders otherwise, the facts are placed before the court at the hearing by relying on the evidence in the witness statements served with the claim form (CPR, r 55.8(3)). The fact of service is proved by producing a certificate of service (r 55.8(6)). The procedure is only appropriate where the defendants have no real defence. If the defendants attend and adduce evidence showing a substantial defence the claim is usually converted into an ordinary possession claim. If an order is made a warrant of possession can only be issued without permission within the next three months (CCR Ord 24, r 6, in CPR, Sch 2).

12.9.5   Interim possession orders

Under CPR, rr 55.20-55.28, a claimant may secure an interim possession order where premises (not open land) are in wrongful occupation. The application must be made within 28 days of the claimant discovering about the wrongful occupation. If an order is made, the defendant is required to vacate within 24 hours after service of the order, failing which the defendant will be committing an offence under the Criminal Justice and Public Order Act 1994, s 76. Thereafter the case is considered a second time, when the court will consider whether to make a final possession order.

12.9.6 Ordinary possession claims

These are also governed by CPR, Part 55, but the court has the power to allocate these claims to the fast track or multi-track (r 55.8(2)), may give case management directions, and may require the facts to be proved by calling witnesses at the trial.

12.9.7 Accelerated procedure for assured shorthold tenancies

The CPR, r 55.11 to 55.19, set out an accelerated procedure for obtaining possession orders to recover possession of residential properties previously let under assured short-hold tenancies. There are prescribed claim forms and defence forms, and the papers are referred to a District Judge or judge who may strike out the claim if it discloses no reasonable grounds (r 55.16(1)(c)), or may make an order for possession without requiring the attendance of the parties (r 55.17). Although an application can be made to set aside such an order (r 55.19), the procedure is intended to provide a speedy and inexpensive means of obtaining possession orders in cases where there is unlikely to be any defence.

13

Interim payments and provisional damages

13.1 Interim payments

13.1.1 Reason for introducing interim payments

Regrettably but inevitably, the administration of justice takes time. There are often occasions when it is clear for one reason or another that the claimant will recover damages at the end of the day, even though the exact amount may be uncertain. In such cases, the system of interim payments has been devised to prevent the claimant from being 'kept out of his money' for an indecently long period.

13.1.2 Interim payments in general

Interim payments can be defined as payments on account of any damages, debt or other sum which a party to a claim may be held liable to pay to another party if a final judgment is given in favour of that party. An interim payment will be ordered where it is clear that the claimant will be at least partially successful and it would be unjust to delay immediate payment of that entitlement.

Interest, but not costs, may be included in an interim payment.

Interim payments may be ordered in respect of counterclaims and in additional claims under Part 20.

13.2 Qualification for an interim payment

13.2.1 Jurisdiction

The circumstances in which an interim payment may be ordered are set out in CPR, r 25.7, which provides:

> (1) The court may only make an order for an interim payment where any of the following conditions are satisfied—
>
>   (a) the defendant against whom the order is sought has admitted liability to pay damages or some other sum of money to the claimant;
>
>   (b) the claimant has obtained judgment against that defendant for damages to be assessed or for a sum of money (other than costs) to be assessed;
>
>   (c) it is satisfied that, if the claim went to trial, the claimant would obtain judgment for a substantial amount of money (other than costs) against the defendant from whom he is seeking

> *an order for an interim payment whether or not that defendant is the only defendant or one of a number of defendants to the claim;*
>
> (d) *the following conditions are satisfied—*
>> (i) *the claimant is seeking an order for possession of land (whether or not any other order is also sought); and*
>> (ii) *the court is satisfied that, if the case went to trial, the defendant would be held liable (even if the claim for possession fails) to pay the claimant a sum of money for the defendant's occupation and use of the land while the claim for possession was pending; or*
>
> (e) *in a claim in which there are two or more defendants and the order is sought against any one or more of those defendants, the following conditions are satisfied—*
>> (i) *the court is satisfied that, if the claim went to trial, the claimant would obtain judgment for a substantial amount of money (other than costs) against at least one of the defendants (but the court cannot determine which); and*
>> (ii) *all the defendants are either—*
>>> (a) *a defendant that is insured in respect of the claim;*
>>> (b) *a defendant whose liability will be met by an insurer under section 151 of the Road Traffic Act 1988 or an insurer acting under the Motor Insurers Bureau Agreement, or the Motor Insurers Bureau where it is acting itself; or*
>>> (c) *a defendant that is a public body.*

13.2.2 Standard of proof

The CPR, r 25.7(1)(c), (d) and (e), provide that before it can order an interim payment the court must be 'satisfied' the claimant would obtain judgment or the defendant 'would be held liable' if the claim went to trial. This means that the claimant must satisfy the court on a balance of probabilities, but to a high standard within the range (*Shearson Lehman Bros Inc v Maclaine Watson and Co Ltd* [1987] 1 WLR 480, CA).

13.2.3 Cross-claims and defences

Where the application is under ground (c), obviously any defence available to the defendant has to be fully taken into account before the court can be satisfied that the claimant will obtain judgment at any trial. Where a cross-claim amounts to a set-off (and hence a defence), it must be taken into account both in considering whether the claimant would obtain judgment and in deciding whether to make an order and its amount (*Shanning International Ltd v George Wimpey International Ltd* [1989] 1 WLR 981, CA). General cross-claims or counterclaims not amounting to defences must be taken into account in all cases at the second stage of the court's determination, namely in deciding whether to make an order, and in what amount. Where a counterclaim is worth less than the claim, even where the value of the claim is unclear, it may be appropriate to make an interim payment order (*O2 (UK) Ltd v Dimension Data Network Services Ltd* (2007) LTL 8/11/2007).

13.2.4 Multiple defendants

As ground (c) makes clear, in cases where there are a number of defendants, an interim payment can be ordered against any specific defendant, provided the court is satisfied to the relevant standard that that specific defendant will be found liable for a substantial sum of money if the case went to trial. If the claimant can satisfy the court that a specific defendant will lose, subject to the court's discretion whether to make the order, there are no other conditions and the court can order an interim payment.

There are many cases where a claimant has a strong case against alternative defendants, but cannot say in advance of trial which of the defendants will lose. In such cases there is jurisdiction to make an interim payment order under ground (e), but the claimant also has to satisfy the additional condition laid down by r 25.7(1)(e)(ii) that all the defendants are insured, public bodies etc. The point behind this additional requirement is that if the court orders the 'wrong' defendant to make an interim payment, as all the defendants have to be backed by substantial financial resources, it should be possible to make effective post-judgment adjustment orders (see **13.6**).

13.2.5 Relationship with summary judgment

It is quite common to combine applications for summary judgment with applications for interim payments. Summary judgment is available where the defence has no real prospect of success, and interim payments are available where the claimant can show liability will be established. Obviously these are similar concepts. Further, on the summary judgment application the court may make a 'relevant order' entering judgment for damages to be assessed, which would itself provide grounds for making an order for an interim payment. Another possibility is that the court may make a conditional order on the summary judgment application, and the court may be invited to make an interim payment order as the condition. Under the old rules there were a number of reported cases that considered the question of whether it was possible to make an interim payment order if a summary judgment application was unsuccessful. The better view under the old rules was that an interim payment order should not be made in such cases, although it was possible to make an interim payment order if conditional leave to defend (the old equivalent to a conditional order) was granted. With the increased availability of summary judgment under the CPR, there can be no doubt that if summary judgment is refused it would be inconsistent for the court to then decide that the claimant 'would' succeed so as to give grounds for an interim payment. There may even be a little doubt about whether making an interim payment order can be consistent with making a conditional order, again because of the change in the test for summary judgment. If the defence is on the border of having a real prospect of success (the situation where conditional orders are appropriate), how can the court simultaneously find that the claimant will win for the purposes of making an interim payment order?

13.3 Restrictions on awards of interim payments

13.3.1 Amount

13.3.1.1 Reasonable proportion of final award

It is important that the court should not order an interim payment greater than the amount ultimately awarded at the trial, since there may be difficulty in recovering an overpayment. In other words, the court will wish to be fairly certain that the amount ultimately awarded will exceed the interim payment it is preparing to award.

An interim payment must not exceed 'a reasonable proportion' of the likely damages, taking into account any contributory negligence, set-off or counterclaim. The judge is obliged to assess the likely amount of the final judgment, and is not permitted to take short-cuts such as basing the assessment on offers made by the defendant (*Eeles v Cobham Hire Services Ltd* [2009] EWCA Civ 204). A reasonable proportion may well be a high proportion, provided the assessment of the likely final award is conservative. The objective is to avoid making an overpayment.

There is a standard interim payment of £50,000 in mesothelioma cases where the defendant fails to show cause on all issues (PD 3D, paras 2 and 6.7).

13.3.1.2 Need for the interim payment

As a general rule, when one of the jurisdictional conditions in CPR, r 25.7(1), is met, the court will usually order the defendant to make an interim payment, and will not consider what the claimant intends to do with the money or whether the claimant has a need for the money which cannot wait until trial (*Stringman v McArdle* [1994] 1 WLR 1653). Where the interim payment is limited to an advance payment out of the damages alleged to have been suffered to the date of the application (*Schott Kem Ltd v Bentley* [1991] 1 QB 61; *Eeles v Cobham Hire Services Ltd* [2009] EWCA Civ 204) the judge should not be influenced by how the claimant may intend to spend any interim payment. In *Tinsley v Sarkar* (2004) LTL 23/7/2004 it was held that, although *Stringman v McArdle* states the general rule, it is not to be applied in a mechanistic manner. The desirability of the proposed expenditure may be relevant in persuading the court for or against ordering the interim payment.

One particular factor is whether the claimant wants to use the money in a way intended to prejudge an issue that has to be decided at the trial. Where the interim payment is sought to cover future expenses, it becomes essential to establish a real need for the money, and an award will be made only if the judge can confidently predict the trial judge will wish to award a capital sum greater than past special damages and damages for pain, suffering, and loss of amenity (*Eeles v Cobham Hire Services Ltd*).

13.3.1.3 Defendant's resources

The defendant's lack of resources is a very relevant factor to be taken into account when fixing the amount of any interim payment (*British and Commonwealth Holdings plc v Quadrex Holdings Inc* [1989] QB 842, CA).

13.4 How to apply for an interim payment

13.4.1 Procedure

Applications for interim payments are made on notice, and must be served at least 14 clear days before the hearing of the application. The evidence in support should set out all relevant matters including:

(a) the amount sought by way of interim payment;

(b) what the money will be used for;

(c) the likely amount of money that will be awarded;

(d) the reasons for believing a relevant ground (see above) is satisfied;

(e) in a personal injuries claim, details of special damages and past and future loss; and

(f) in a claim under the Fatal Accidents Act 1976, details of the persons on whose behalf the claim is made and the nature of the claim.

All relevant documents in support should be exhibited. In personal injuries claims these will include the medical reports.

Respondents wishing to rely on evidence in reply must file and serve their witness statements at least seven clear days before the hearing. If the applicant wants to respond to the respondent's evidence, any further evidence must be filed and served at least three clear days before the hearing. In personal injuries claims the defendant will need to obtain a certificate of recoverable benefits from the Secretary of State under the Social Security (Recovery of Benefits) Act 1997. A copy of the certificate should be filed at the hearing, and any order made must set out the amount by which the payment to be made to the claimant has been reduced in accordance with the Act and the Social Security (Recovery of Benefits) Regulations 1997.

13.4.2 Second or further applications

Second or further applications may be made upon cause being shown. This might be, for example, because the proceedings have been delayed longer than originally envisaged by the parties, or if, in the case of an action for damages for personal injury, the claimant has had to undergo additional private treatment, or has suffered additional hardship.

13.5 Main trial

As with Part 36 offers (see **27.10**), an interim payment must not be disclosed to the court until all issues of liability and quantum have been decided, unless the defendant agrees. There may be occasions, however, where the public interest requires that an interim payment should be ordered in open court rather than in private, for example, where the amount is large and two public companies are involved, to ensure that a false market is not created (*British and Commonwealth Holdings plc v Quadrex Holdings Inc (No. 2)* The Times, 8 December 1988, CA).

13.6 Adjustments after judgment

On making its final order the court will, upon the interim payment being revealed, make whatever consequential adjustments are necessary. In particular, the court may order repayment by the claimant and adjustments between defendants (CPR, r 25.8). Any repayment may be ordered with interest. There are detailed provisions about how the judgment drawn up by the court should be formulated where there has been an interim payment in PD 25, paras 5.1 to 5.6.

13.7 Provisional damages

Under general principles, an award of damages in a personal injuries case is a once-and-for-all payment. This is far from ideal where there is a danger of the claimant's condition deteriorating some time in the future. It was to remedy this situation that the courts were given power to make awards of provisional damages.

13.7.1   Jurisdiction

The SCA 1981, s 32A, applies to personal injuries cases where there '. . . is proved or admitted to be a chance that at some definite or indefinite time in the future the [plaintiff] will . . . develop some serious disease or suffer some serious deterioration in his physical or mental condition'.

In such cases the section empowers the court to make an award of provisional damages, namely:

- immediate damages, which are assessed on the assumption that the claimant will not develop the disease or suffer the deterioration; and
- an entitlement to apply for further damages in the future if the disease develops or deterioration is suffered.

The section contemplates such an order being made in favour of a living claimant. There is jurisdiction, however, where a claimant has been awarded provisional damages, for the claimant's dependants, in the event of later injury-related death, to recover further damages under the FAA 1976: Damages Act 1996, s 3.

The County Court has a similar power under CCA 1984, s 51.

13.7.2   Conditions

There are three conditions:

- the claim for provisional damages must be set out in the particulars of claim;
- the possible future disease or deterioration must be 'serious' in nature; and
- it must be 'proved or admitted' that there is a 'chance' of the future development or deterioration.

13.7.2.1   'Serious' disease or deterioration

According to Scott Baker J in *Willson v Ministry of Defence* [1991] 1 All ER 638, 'serious' means something beyond ordinary deterioration. The effect on the particular claimant, eg a hand injury on a concert pianist, is one of the relevant factors. Osteoarthritis is a commonly occurring sequela in personal injuries cases. Scott Baker J took the view that arthritic deterioration to the point that it required surgery or a change in the claimant's employment would not qualify as being serious. This view is consistent with that of Michael Davies J in *Allott v Central Electricity Generating Board* (19 December 1988).

13.7.2.2   A 'chance' of future deterioration

This is rather easier to establish. It must be measurable rather than fanciful (*Willson v Ministry of Defence* [1991] 1 All ER 638). In *Patterson v Ministry of Defence* [1987] CLY 1194, Simon Brown J assessed the claimant's chances of developing further pleural thickening in the region of five per cent, but regarded the chance of this occurring as 'plain'.

13.7.2.3   Subsequent injury

It seems to have been held in *Hughes v Cheshire County Council* (2 March 1989) that a subsequent injury caused as a result of the injury for which the defendant is responsible may be a 'deterioration' within SCA 1981, s 32A. This appears to have been doubted in *Willson v Ministry of Defence* [1991] 1 All ER 638.

13.7.2.4 Discretion

Where the basic conditions are satisfied, the court retains a discretion whether to make a provisional damages award rather than a conventional damages award. The following factors were identified by Scott Baker J in *Willson v Ministry of Defence* [1991] 1 All ER 638:

(a) Diseases which by their nature follow a developing pattern are not suitable for provisional damages awards.

(b) If the claimant can point to some clear-cut future event, provisional damages may be appropriate.

(c) The greater the degree of risk of future deterioration the more likely an award will be made.

(d) The possibility of doing better justice by reserving the claimant's right to return to court.

13.7.3 Procedure

Whether provisional damages are agreed or ordered after trial, PD 41 sets out the form of order and for the lodgement in court of a case file of relevant documents. These include the order or judgment, medical reports, statements of case, and any transcript of the judgment and of the claimant's evidence as the judge may consider necessary.

Hurditch v Sheffield Health Authority [1989] QB 562, CA was an asbestosis case. The parties agreed to a provisional damages award. However, there was some conflict between the two sides' medical reports on the question of future deterioration, and some dispute on the drafted statement of facts. The defendants resiled from the agreement. The Court of Appeal held that the presence of a few 'loose ends' did not prevent the court making a provisional damages order. The purpose of the case file is to provide material to assist the court in the event of the claimant applying for further damages in the future. If the disputes over the documents were limited, the papers filed could be restricted to what was agreed. If the disputes were more serious, the Master could order a trial of the outstanding issues.

13.7.4 The order

By CPR, r 41.2, the order must specify the disease or diseases or type of deterioration which will entitle the claimant to apply for further damages, and will specify the period (or an indefinite period) within which the application may be made. The period may be extended, but only one application for further damages may be made in respect of each disease or type of deterioration specified in the order. An application to extend the period for making an application for further damages is made by application notice supported by evidence which should include a current medical report.

An application for further damages is made after giving the defendant and the defendant's insurers 28 days' notice of the intention to make the application. This is necessary because it may be several years since the case was last considered, and the defendant will need to retrieve its file from storage. The subsequent procedure is the same as that for applying for an interim payment, with the application being made on notice, and being served at least 14 clear days before the hearing of the application. The defendant must file and serve any evidence in reply at least seven clear days before the hearing. If the claimant wants to respond to the respondent's evidence, any further evidence must be filed and served at least three clear days before the hearing. Causation of any further damages within the scope of the provisional damages order is determined when the application for further damages is made.

Interim injunctions

14.1 Introduction

If a defendant's alleged wrongdoing will cause the claimant irreparable continuing damage pending trial, or if the damage may have already been done by the time the case comes on for trial, it is appropriate for the courts to have power to make orders to avoid the potential injustice that would otherwise arise. To meet this need the courts have jurisdiction to grant interim injunctions to regulate the position between the parties pending the trial. A number of special terms are used in this area, and the following definitions may be of assistance:

Perpetual injunction	Final judgment for an injunction normally granted at trial.
Interim injunction	Provisional order made before trial.
Mandatory injunction	Order requiring specific acts to be done. It is the substance of the order that makes it mandatory, not its positive wording.
Prohibitory injunction	Order to refrain from doing specific acts.
Quia timet injunction	Order to prevent an apprehended legal wrong, where none has been committed at the date of the application.

14.2 Jurisdiction

14.2.1 High Court

Jurisdiction to grant interim injunctions in the High Court derives from the SCA 1981, s 37, which provides:

(1) The High Court may by order (whether interlocutory or final) grant an injunction or appoint a receiver in all cases in which it appears to the court to be just and convenient to do so.

(2) Any such order may be made either unconditionally or on such terms and conditions as the court thinks just.

With the introduction of the Human Rights Act 1998, the test to be applied may be whether granting relief is just and proportionate rather than just and convenient (*South Bucks District Council v Porter* [2003] 2 AC 558).

14.2.2 County Court

County Court jurisdiction to grant interim injunctions derives from the CCA 1984, s 38(1), which allows the court to make any order which could be made by the High

Court if the proceedings were in the High Court. The only restrictions are in relation to search orders and freezing injunctions (see **1.2.1.2**).

14.2.3 Cause of action

In *Siskina v Distos Compania Naviera SA* [1979] AC 210 at 256, Lord Diplock said:

A right to obtain an interlocutory injunction is not a cause of action. It cannot stand on its own. It is dependent on there being a pre-existing cause of action against the defendant arising out of the invasion, actual or threatened, by him of a legal or equitable right of the plaintiff for the enforcement of which the defendant is amenable to the jurisdiction of the Court. The right to obtain an injunction is merely ancillary and incidental to the pre-existing cause of action.

In this particular case, a freezing injunction was refused because there was no dispute justiciable in the courts of England and Wales at all. The actual result has been reversed by the CJJA 1982, s 25 (see **15.3.1**). In other cases, injunctions have been refused because the claimant's allegations do not amount to a cause of action.

The correctness of the *Siskina* principle was confirmed by the Privy Council in *Mercedes-Benz AG v Leiduck* [1996] 1 AC 284. However, in *Morris v Murjani* [1996] 2 All ER 384, the Court of Appeal while not disputing that *Siskina* and *Mercedes-Benz v Leiduck* correctly stated the position regarding litigation affecting the private rights of litigants distinguished the position in respect of cases where a public duty was involved. In such circumstances even though there may be no pre-existing cause of action there was still a 'substantive right' which could be protected by an interim injunction.

Therefore, in most ordinary disputes which will relate to private rights, a pre-existing cause of action is necessary, but in cases involving public duties the court may not insist on a pre-existing cause of action as a prerequisite to the granting of an interim injunction.

14.3 Principles

14.3.1 American Cyanamid guidelines

Interim injunctive relief is both temporary and discretionary. Guidelines on how that discretion should be exercised were laid down by the House of Lords in the leading case of *American Cyanamid Co v Ethicon Ltd* [1975] AC 396. The facts were that Ethicon, the defendants, manufactured absorbable catgut sutures. Cyanamid patented a synthetic absorbable suture, and started eating into Ethicon's market. Ethicon then produced its own synthetic suture with a slightly different chemical composition from Cyanamid's. Cyanamid issued proceedings, and applied for an interim injunction to restrain Ethicon's sales. Ethicon said their suture was different from that patented by Cyanamid, or alternatively that the patent was invalid. Voluminous affidavits and exhibits were filed by both parties on the interim application. The following paragraphs set out the principles stated by Lord Diplock.

14.3.1.1 Serious question to be tried

It is no part of the court's function at this stage of the litigation to try to resolve conflicts of evidence on affidavits as to facts on which the claims of either party may ultimately depend nor to decide difficult questions of law which call for detailed argument and mature consideration. (p 407H)

The purpose sought to be achieved by giving the court discretion to grant such injunctions would be stultified if the discretion were clogged by a technical rule forbidding its exercise if upon that incomplete untested evidence the court evaluated the chances of the plaintiff's ultimate success in the action at 50 per cent or less, but permitting its exercise if the court evaluated his chances at more than 50 per cent. (p 406G)

The court no doubt must be satisfied that the claim is not frivolous or vexatious; in other words, that there is a serious question to be tried. (p 407G)

This initial hurdle is fairly easily satisfied. However, the condition will not be satisfied where the claimant relies on a cause of action unknown to the law, or if the cause of action is unarguable on the facts. Seriously flawed evidence as to the likelihood of customers being deceived by a rival product in a passing off action was not regarded as being so weak that there was no serious issue to be tried in *Dalgety Spillers Foods Ltd v Food Brokers Ltd* [1994] FSR 504. Weakness on the facts was the problem in *Morning Star Co-operative Society Ltd v Express Newspapers Ltd* [1979] FSR 113 where the claimants alleged the defendants were proposing to pass off the soon to be released *'Daily Star'* as the *'Morning Star'*. Given the differences between the publications, Foster J was inclined to the view that there was no serious question to be tried, as 'Only a moron in a hurry would be misled.'

Unless the material available to the court fails to disclose that the plaintiff has any real prospect of succeeding in his claim at trial, the court should go on to consider the balance of convenience. (p 408B)

Therefore, if a serious issue is disclosed the court will proceed to consider the balance of convenience in its wide sense (see **14.3.1.2** to **14.3.1.7**).

14.3.1.2   Adequacy of damages to the claimant

. . . the court should first consider whether, if the plaintiff were to succeed at the trial in establishing his right to a permanent injunction, he would be adequately compensated by an award of damages for the loss he would have sustained as a result of the defendant's continuing to do what was sought to be enjoined between the time of the application and the time of the trial. If damages in the measure recoverable at common law would be an adequate remedy and the defendant would be in a financial position to pay them, no interlocutory injunction should normally be granted, however strong the plaintiff's claim appeared to be at that stage. (p 408C)

Damages will not be adequate if:

- the defendant is or is likely to be unable to pay;
- the wrong is irreparable, eg loss of the right to vote;
- the damage is not pecuniary, eg many nuisances;
- damages would be difficult to assess, eg loss of business reputation, disruption to business.

14.3.1.3   Adequacy of the undertaking in damages as protection for the defendant

If . . . damages would not provide an adequate remedy for the plaintiff in the event of his succeeding at the trial, the court should then consider whether, on the contrary hypothesis that the defendant were to succeed at the trial in establishing his right to do that which was sought to be enjoined, he would be adequately compensated under the plaintiff's undertaking as to damages for the loss he would have sustained by being prevented from doing so between the time of the application and the time of the trial. If damages in the measure recoverable under such an undertaking would be an adequate remedy and the plaintiff would be in a position to pay them, there would be no reason upon this ground to refuse an interlocutory injunction. (p 408D, E)

Undertakings given by claimants on the grant of interim injunctions to pay damages to defendants who may suffer unjustifiable loss where it transpires the injunction should not have been granted are considered at **14.5**. One of the reasons for introducing such undertakings was that '. . . it aided the court in doing that which was its great object, viz. abstaining from expressing any opinion on the merits of the case until the hearing' (*Wakefield v Duke of Buccleugh* (1865) 12 LT 628). There are limited circumstances in which an undertaking in damages will not be required (see **14.5.2**).

If the undertaking does adequately protect the defendant, there is 'no reason' for refusing the injunction at this stage, and the court should consider the balance of convenience (narrow sense). If the claimant is not in a financial position to honour the undertaking and appreciable damage to the defendant is likely, it was said, obiter, in *Morning Star Co-operative Society Ltd v Express Newspapers Ltd* [1979] FSR 113 that the injunction should be refused. In this case the likely damage to the defendants if the launch of their newspaper was restrained was unquantifiable, and the financial evidence showed that the claimant was unlikely to be able to pay on the undertaking.

14.3.1.4   Narrow balance of convenience

It is where there is doubt as to the adequacy of the respective remedies in damages available to either party or to both, that the question of balance of convenience arises. It would be unwise to attempt even to list all the various matters which may need to be taken into consideration in deciding where the balance lies, let alone to suggest the relative weight to be attached to them. These will vary from case to case. (p 408F)

The extent to which the disadvantages to each party would be incapable of being compensated in damages in the event of his succeeding at the trial is always a significant factor in assessing where the balance of convenience lies. (p 409B)

On the facts in *American Cyanamid*, the balance of convenience tended to favour the claimants. Ethicon's new sutures were not at that time on the market. Granting the injunction would not close factories or cause unemployment. If refused, Cyanamid may have failed to increase its growing market and effectively lost the benefit of its patent.

The following cases are other examples of the operation of the balance of convenience:

Fellowes and Son v Fisher [1976] QB 122, CA. Solicitors sued their former clerk for breach of a covenant in restraint of trade. The interim injunction was refused because the defendant would otherwise have been deprived of his job, and that was likely to be more serious to him than the harm to the claimants through his continuing to work for a rival firm.

Hubbard v Pitt [1976] QB 142, CA. An interim injunction was granted to the claimant estate agents to restrain the defendants picketing their office. The claimant was likely to suffer irreparable damage, whereas the defendants could press their views elsewhere.

Potters-Ballotini Ltd v Weston-Baker [1977] RPC 202, CA. An interim injunction to prevent the defendants manufacturing products allegedly in breach of covenant was refused, because it would have been catastrophic to compel the defendants to close their factory.

Wake Forest University Health Sciences v Smith and Nephew plc [2009] EWHC 45 (Pat). An important factor is the length of time to trial. A relatively short time to trial favours granting the injunction.

Dalgety Spillers Foods Ltd v Food Brokers Ltd [1994] FSR 504. Factors influencing the court in refusing an interim injunction in a passing off action were that the defendant had undertaken to maintain accurate records of sales of the products in question, and the fact the claimant had not responded to a letter from the defendant frankly stating its plans for its new product and enclosing sample containers.

14.3.1.5 Status quo

As part of the balance of convenience,

> Where other factors appear to be evenly balanced it is a counsel of prudence to take such measures as are calculated to preserve the status quo. (p 408G)

In *Garden Cottage Foods Ltd v Milk Marketing Board* [1984] AC 130, HL, it was held that the status quo means the state of affairs immediately before the issue of the claim form, ignoring minimal periods of time, unless the claimant is guilty of unreasonable delay. If the claimant has delayed, the status quo will be the state of affairs immediately before the application. Delay, therefore, tends to benefit the defendant.

14.3.1.6 Special factors

Also as part of the balance of convenience,

> . . . there may be many other special factors to be taken into consideration in the particular circumstances of individual cases. (p 409D)

A special factor identified in *American Cyanamid* was that, once doctors and patients had got used to Ethicon's suture in the period prior to trial, it might well have become commercially impracticable for Cyanamid to insist after trial that it be withdrawn. Therefore, the interim injunction was granted.

14.3.1.7 The merits of the case

If other factors do not differ widely,

> . . . it may not be improper to take into account in tipping the balance the relative strength of each party's case as revealed by the affidavit evidence adduced on the hearing of the application. This, however, should be done only where it is apparent upon the facts disclosed by evidence as to which there is no credible dispute that the strength of one party's case is disproportionate to that of the other party. The court is not justified in embarking upon anything resembling a trial of the action upon conflicting affidavits in order to evaluate the strength of either party's case. (p 409B, C)

14.3.2 *American Cyanamid* in practice

The impact of *American Cyanamid* was to remove the need to show a prima facie case on the merits before an interim injunction would be granted. The extent to which the merits of the case could be looked at were considered by Lord Diplock in his comments at **14.3.1.1** and **14.3.1.7**. In most cases, once a serious issue is shown the court should not embark further upon an examination of the claimant's prospects of success (unless the court reaches the stage described at **14.3.1.7**).

In *Series 5 Software Ltd v Clarke* [1996] 1 All ER 853, a decision at first instance, Laddie J considered that Lord Diplock did not intend to exclude consideration of the strength of the case, merely that the court should not attempt to resolve difficult issues of fact or law. If the court was able to come to a clear view as to the strength of each party's case on credible evidence, then it could do so, and it would be a factor the court could bear in mind when deciding whether or nor to grant an interim injunction.

This appears to be a radical departure from the traditional interpretation of the *American Cyanamid* decision, and tends to be an exceptional approach which is only occasionally adopted.

It is clear, however, that the principles stated by Lord Diplock must not be read as if they were statutory provisions. The remedy is always discretionary, and the *American Cyanamid* principles are applied with some degree of flexibility.

14.3.3   Exceptional cases

In a number of fairly well-defined areas, the courts do not adopt a strict *American Cyanamid* approach to the granting of interim injunctions. It is sometimes said that these cases can be explained by the 'special factors' referred to by Lord Diplock (**14.3.1.6**). It is also said that *American Cyanamid* is restricted to '. . . cases where the legal rights of the parties depend upon facts that are in dispute . . .' (p 406H). In other cases it is said that *American Cyanamid* was decided on the assumption there would be a trial (eg 'these are matters to be dealt with at the trial', p 407H), and, if there will be no trial, Lord Diplock's principles do not apply. Whether these are strictly exceptions to, or particular applications of, the *American Cyanamid* principles has little practical importance.

14.3.3.1   Interim injunction would finally dispose of the claim

In *NWL Ltd v Woods* [1979] 1 WLR 1294, 1306, Lord Diplock said '*American Cyanamid v Ethicon Ltd* . . . was not dealing with a case in which the grant or refusal of an injunction at that stage would, in effect, dispose of the action finally in favour of whichever party was successful in the application, because there would be nothing left on which it was in the unsuccessful party's interest to proceed to trial.' In such cases, Lord Diplock said, '. . . the degree of likelihood that the plaintiff would have succeeded in establishing his right to an injunction if the action had gone to trial is a factor to be brought into the balance by the judge in weighing the risks that injustice may result from his deciding the application one way rather than the other.'

In *Cayne v Global Natural Resources plc* [1984] 1 All ER 225, CA, the claimants, who were shareholders in the defendant company, sought interim injunctions to restrain the company from:

- implementing a merger transaction; and
- issuing or allotting any shares to one of the parties to the proposed merger;

without first obtaining the approval of the company in general meeting. The alleged purpose of the deals was to maintain the directors in office. The claimants' evidence supported the case they presented. The company's evidence, if true, completely destroyed the claimants' case. If the relief claimed by the claimants were to be granted, the injunction would have lasted until the next annual general meeting of the company. By the time of trial, that meeting would already have taken place. If the injunction was refused, the deals would have been implemented and there would be no point in seeking an injunction. Therefore there was no realistic prospect of a trial.

It was held that the *American Cyanamid* principles on balance of convenience did not apply. The court was to apply the broad principle of doing its best to avoid injustice. An interim injunction could only properly be granted if the claimants' case on the merits was overwhelming. Here it was not, and the injunction was accordingly refused. As Eveleigh LJ said, '. . . it would be wrong to run the risk of causing an injustice to a defendant who is being denied the right to trial where the defence put forward has been substantiated by affidavits and a number of exhibits.'

In *Lansing Linde Ltd v Kerr* [1991] 1 All ER 418, CA, however, a restraint of trade case where the court considered the merits as the granting or refusal of an interim injunction may have finally determined the issue, Staughton LJ said that in the circumstances of the case justice simply required '. . . some assessment of the merits . . . more than merely a serious issue to be tried'.

It was also made clear in *Lansing* that the claimant's assertion that it would in any event wish to proceed to trial to recover damages could in appropriate circumstances be disregarded as unlikely.

14.3.3.2 Negative covenants

Where the defendant is in breach of a valid express negative covenant a perpetual injunction has been held to issue 'as of course' (*Doherty v Allman* (1878) 3 App Cas 709, HL). The same principle applies to interim injunctions (*A-G v Barker* [1990] 3 All ER 257, CA).

14.3.3.3 No defence

In *Official Custodian for Charities v Mackay* [1985] Ch 168, Scott J said:

> I do not . . . think that this is a case to which the *Cyanamid* principles can be applied. Those principles are not, in my view, applicable to a case where there is no arguable defence to the plaintiff's claim.

The effect, in such cases, is that, prima facie, the claimant is entitled to interim relief. As James LJ said in *Stocker v Planet Building Society* (1879) 27 WR 877, CA, 'Balance of convenience has nothing to do with a case of this kind; it can only be considered where there is some question which must be decided at the hearing.' Alternatively, it may be appropriate in such cases to apply immediately for final relief by way of summary judgment (*World Wide Fund for Nature v World Wrestling Federation Entertainment Inc.* The Times, 14 March 2002, CA).

14.3.3.4 Defamation claims

Since the nineteenth century (*Bonnard v Perryman* [1891] 2 Ch 269) it has been held that, generally, interim injunctions will not be granted in defamation actions, or will be discharged if granted without notice, if the defendant intends to plead justification. In *Greene v Associated Newspapers Ltd* [2005] QB 972, it was held that this rule is unaltered by the Human Rights Act 1998, ss 6 or 12(3). There are two conditions:

- the defendant must state in his or her witness statement an intention to set up justification; and
- the alleged libel must not be obviously untruthful.

In *Holley v Smyth* [1998] QB 726, CA, it was held that the defendant's motive in seeking to publish material, alleged to be defamatory by the claimant, was irrelevant in deciding whether the threatened publication ought to be restrained.

Woodward v Hutchins [1977] 1 WLR 760 extended the rule in that the claimants claimed articles in a national newspaper were libellous and also written in breach of confidence. The defendants intended to justify, and it was held that the added possible breach of confidence made no difference, and the injunction was refused. The defamation rule does not, however, apply to trade mark infringement cases, even where the trade mark is used in comparative advertising (*Boehringer Ingelheim Ltd v Vetplus Ltd* [2007] FSR 29).

14.3.3.5 Respect for private and family life and freedom of expression

Article 8(1) of the European Convention on Human Rights provides that everyone has the right to respect for his private and family life, his home and correspondence. Article 10(1) provides that everyone has the right to freedom of expression. Neither right is absolute (see arts 8(2) and 10(2)). The right to freedom of expression is subject to various restrictions, such as for the protection of the reputation of others (art 10(2)).

Proceedings to restrain newspapers from publishing articles that are alleged to invade the claimant's privacy often bring both arts 8 and 10 into play. There is no cause of action for breach of privacy as such, whether at common law or based on the European Convention on Human Rights, art 8 (*Wainwright v Home Office* [2004] 2 AC 406). These cases therefore have to be framed in breach of confidentiality. Newspapers typically rely on art 10(1) to justify publication. The court has to balance the competing interests in protecting private and family life under art 8(1), and the freedom of expression in art 10(1) (*Campbell v Mirror Group Newspapers plc* [2004] 2 AC 457).

Interim injunctions in these cases should normally be governed by *American Cyanamid*, as adapted by the Human Rights Act 1998, s 12(3). This provides that no relief to restrain publication before trial which might affect the art 10(1) right is to be allowed '. . . unless the court is satisfied that the applicant is likely to establish that the publication should not be allowed.' In *Cream Holdings Ltd v Banerjee* [2005] 1 AC 253, it was held that in most cases s 12(3) means that an interim injunction will be refused unless the applicant establishes on the balance of probabilities a case which is likely to succeed at trial. Lord Nicholls recognised that this would not always achieve the legislative aim of s 12(3), and that there would be exceptional cases where an injunction could be granted even if the applicant did not have such a strong claim. An example would be where there would be particularly grave consequences if an injunction were not granted. Damage to reputation is not in itself sufficiently exceptional, otherwise the exceptions would be so wide that s 12(3) would be meaningless (*Boehringer Ingelheim Ltd v Vetplus Ltd* [2007] FSR 29). In *McKennitt v Ash* [2008] QB 73, Buxton LJ said there were two questions:

(a) whether the information is private in the sense that it is in principle protected by art 8. In most cases any duty of confidence arises out of a transaction or relationship between the parties. For example, an employee may have expressly agreed to maintain an employer's confidences, or sensitive information may have been communicated in a letter marked 'private and confidential' (see *HRH Prince of Wales v Associated Newspapers Ltd* [2008] Ch 57). There may also be a reasonable expectation of privacy depending on the circumstances (*Murray v Express Newspapers plc* [2008] 3 WLR 1360, photographs of child in a public place). If the information is not private, there is no case; and

(b) whether in all the circumstances the interest of the owner of the private information should yield to the right of freedom of expression conferred on the publisher by art 10. Much depends on whether there is a breach of confidence (*HRH Prince of Wales v Associated Newspapers Ltd*). Where there is no breach of confidence, the balance between arts 8 and 10 usually involves weighing the nature and consequences of the breach of privacy against the public interest, if any, in the disclosure of the information. In cases where there is a breach of confidence, that is in itself a factor capable of justifying restrictions on freedom of expression under art 10(2). The court has to consider whether a fetter on the right of freedom of expression is in the particular circumstances necessary in a democratic society. This includes weighing the importance attached in a democratic society to upholding duties of confidence, as well as considering the nature of the information and the nature of the relationship giving rise to the duty of confidentiality.

In *Douglas v Hello! Ltd* [2001] QB 967, an interim injunction to restrain a magazine from publishing wedding photographs alleged to infringe the first two claimants' rights of privacy was refused. If the event had been more intimate and private the court would have been more willing to assist, but the first two claimants had already sold the rights to their wedding photographs to the third claimant, and the third claimant was adequately protected by an award of damages. It was held in *McKennitt v Ash* [2008] QB 73 that it is no defence to prove that the information to be published was untrue.

14.3.3.6 Industrial disputes

By the Trade Union and Labour Relations (Consolidation) Act 1992, s 221(2), where an interim injunction is sought against a union which claims it

. . . acted in contemplation of a trade dispute, the court shall, in exercising its discretion whether or not to grant the injunction, have regard to the likelihood of that party's succeeding at the trial of the action in establishing any matter which would afford a defence to the action under [sections 219 or 220].

Although views differ as to the precise effect of this section, it seems that there are three matters the court must consider (*NWL Ltd v Woods* [1979] 1 WLR 1294, HL, per Lord Scarman):

- whether there is a serious question to be tried;
- the balance of convenience; and
- the likelihood of establishing the statutory defence.

14.3.4 Covenants in restraint of trade

Care needs to be taken in deciding the appropriate principles to be applied in applications for interim injunctions in cases involving covenants in restraint of trade.

In *Office Overload Ltd v Gunn* [1977] FSR 39, CA, the defendant was the claimant's branch manager at its Croydon agency. In his contract of employment he covenanted that he would not work for or set up a competing business in the Croydon area for one year after ceasing to work for the claimant. The defendant gave notice and immediately started competing. The claimant applied for an interim injunction. Lord Denning MR said 'Covenants in restraint of trade are in a special category . . . if they are prima facie valid and there is an infringement the courts will grant the injunction.' Bridge LJ pointed out that often the trial would be some years after issuing the claim form. If the merits of the case were not considered, and the injunction refused, the effect would be to deprive the claimant completely of the benefit of his covenant. Therefore, if:

- all the facts are before the court; and
- there is no substantial question of law, ie the covenant is prima facie reasonable in duration, area and ambit of business;

the injunction should be granted in the usual case unless there are good reasons for not doing so in any individual case.

In *Lawrence David Ltd v Ashton* [1991] 1 All ER 385, CA, however, Balcombe LJ stated at p 393 'it should now be firmly stated that the principles of the *American Cyanamid* case apply as well in cases in interim injunctions in restraint of trade as in other cases.' The Court of Appeal made it clear in that case, however, that if there is no serious issue to be tried because the case is an open and shut one then it is a case where an interim injunction should be granted without further consideration of the balance of convenience.

Office Overload Ltd v Gunn can, therefore, be explained as a case where there was no serious issue to be tried as the covenant was clearly valid and is thus akin to the general category of cases where there is no defence (see **14.3.3.3**). *Lawrence David* itself was not an open and shut case. The claimants had dismissed the defendant from their employment, and it was in issue whether this amounted to a repudiatory breach. Regarding the covenant, Balcombe LJ described it as impossible to say it was obviously bad. In those circumstances it was entirely appropriate to apply *American Cyanamid*.

If the action in respect of the covenant in restraint of trade cannot be tried before the period of restraint has expired or has run a large part of its course, so that the grant of an interim injunction would effectively dispose of the action, the case will fall within the exception to the rule in *American Cyanamid* considered in *NWL Ltd v Woods* (see **14.3.3.1**; *Lawrence David Ltd v Ashton*).

Applications for interim injunctions to prevent the misuse of confidential information when employees leave the claimant's employment and join a competing business, where there is no covenant in restraint of trade, are governed by the principles in *American Cyanamid Co v Ethicon Ltd* [1975] AC 396, HL (see *Lock International plc v Beswick* [1989] 1 WLR 1268, Hoffmann J).

14.3.5   Mandatory interim injunctions

The court is far more reluctant to grant an interim mandatory injunction than to grant an equivalent prohibitory injunction. In *Shepherd Homes Ltd v Sandham* [1971] Ch 340, 351, Megarry J said that 'In a normal case' the court must feel a 'high degree of assurance' that at trial an injunction would be granted. This formulation was approved by the Court of Appeal in *Locabail International Finance Ltd v Agroexport* [1986] 1 WLR 657 in refusing a mandatory injunction for the payment of money.

However, there are different approaches. So, for example, Pumfrey J in *Incasep Ltd v Jones* (2001) LTL 26/10/2001 said that the *American Cyanamid* guidelines had to be applied, but having regard to the fact that a mandatory order is a very strong step and the potential injustice that such injunctions could cause.

14.3.6   Defences

Any of the following matters may be raised in defence to an application for an interim injunction:

(a) Delay or laches. There is authority for saying that the court will more readily refuse an interim injunction on the ground of delay than a perpetual injunction (*Johnson v Wyatt* (1863) 2 De G J & S 18).

(b) Acquiescence. Again, acquiescence is more readily established as a defence at the interim stage. Further, a failure to apply for an interim injunction may be a factor in establishing acquiescence at trial (*Shaw v Applegate* [1977] 1 WLR 970).

(c) Hardship. An injunction may be refused if granting it would inflict a hardship on the defendant (*Shell UK Ltd v Lostock Garage Ltd* [1976] 1 WLR 1187, 1202 per Ormrod LJ). At the interim stage this will usually be considered as part of the balance of convenience.

(d) Inequitable conduct by the claimant. 'He who comes to equity must come with clean hands' in relation to the subject matter of the dispute.

(e) Incapable of being effectively enforced. On this ground injunctions are rarely granted against children (*G v Harrow London Borough Council* (2004) LTL 23/1/2004).

14.4 Procedure

14.4.1 General

An application for an interim injunction may be made by any party to an action or matter, and whether or not a claim for the injunction was included in the originating process. Such applications must generally be made to a Judge, and not a District Judge or Master. Exceptional cases where a County Court District Judge can grant interim injunctions include claims with a value below £25,000. Exceptional cases where a Master can grant interim injunctions include where it is in the terms agreed by the parties or it is ancillary or incidental to a charging order or the appointment of a receiver by way of equitable execution.

14.4.2 Urgent cases

Applications for interim injunctions can be made before the issue of the originating process in urgent cases or where it is otherwise in the interests of justice. The test on whether notice should be given to the other side is whether there has been a true impossibility in giving notice to the other side (*Bates v Lord Hailsham of St Marylebone* [1972] 1 WLR 1373). If the impossibility in giving the three clear days' notice has arisen through delay on the part of the claimant, or is otherwise insufficiently explained, the application may be refused (unless, perhaps, the case is overwhelming on the merits) on this ground alone (see **10.3.7** for further information on urgent applications).

14.4.3 Paperwork

In County Court cases there is a prescribed form of application for interim injunctions (Form N16A), which, among other things, requires the applicant to set out the terms of the injunctions sought. Evidence in support is required, usually by witness statement. The documents required in High Court cases are:

- an application notice;
- the claim form and any statements of case;
- copies of the witness statements and exhibits in support of the application;
- draft order;
- skeleton argument (in all but the simplest cases).

The draft order should, in the absence of good reason to the contrary, be in the standard form set out in PF 39CH (for injunctions sought before proceedings are issued) or PF 40CH (for interim injunctions sought after proceedings are issued). A computer disk containing the draft order should also be made available to the court.

The evidence in support of an application for an interim injunction should contain a clear and concise statement of the following matters (see PD 25 Interim Injunctions):

- the facts giving rise to the cause of action against the defendant;
- the facts giving rise to the claim for injunctive relief;
- the precise relief sought.

Further, if the application is made without notice it should also contain:

- the facts relied on as justifying the application being made without notice, including details of any notice given to the defendant, or, if none has been given, the reasons for giving none;
- any answer asserted by the defendant, or which it is thought is likely to be asserted, either to the claim or to the interim relief; and
- any facts known to the claimant which might lead the court to refuse the interim relief.

14.5 Undertakings

14.5.1 Undertakings on applications without notice

As appropriate, the claimant may be required to undertake to issue and/or serve proceedings, serve and file the evidence in support, and to serve the order, usually 'on the same or the next working day'. The undertakings are incorporated into the order when it is drawn up.

14.5.2 Undertaking in damages

If an interim injunction is granted against a defendant, but no perpetual order is obtained at trial, in effect the defendant will have been unjustifiably restrained from doing whatever the injunction prohibited while it was in force. To safeguard the defendant against such an eventuality, the claimant is invariably required to give an undertaking in damages on being granted an interim injunction. The court should consider whether to extend the undertaking so that it also covers third parties who may suffer loss caused by the order (PD 25, para 5.1A). It requires the applicant to pay compensation to the defendant (or third party) for any loss in fact incurred as a result of the injunction.

The court may dispense with an undertaking in favour of a government department or a local authority seeking to enforce the general law (*Hoffmann-La Roche (F) and Co AG v Secretary of State for Trade and Industry* [1975] AC 295; *Kirklees Borough Council v Wickes Building Supplies Ltd* [1993] AC 227, HL).

Where the claimant is of limited means, so that the undertaking is of little value, the injunction may still be granted in a proper case (*Allen v Jambo Holdings Ltd* [1980] 1 WLR 1252, CA). In such cases the undertaking may be dispensed with. An impecunious claimant may be required to fortify the undertaking by providing security or paying money into court.

14.5.3   Inquiry as to damages

Where, after the grant of an interim injunction, the claimant fails to obtain a perpetual injunction at trial, or it is established before trial that the injunction should not have been granted, the defendant or third party affected by the injunction may apply for an order for an inquiry as to damages. The application is made to the trial judge or to the judge dealing with the interim application during which it becomes clear that the injunction should not have been granted.

When an interim injunction is discharged before trial the court has four options (see *Cheltenham and Gloucester Building Society v Ricketts* [1993] 1 WLR 1545, CA):

- to order that the undertaking in damages shall be enforced, and to assess the damages immediately. This is only appropriate if all the relevant evidence on damage is available;
- to direct an inquiry as to damages. The inquiry is usually conducted by a Master, who will determine all issues of causation and quantum;
- to adjourn the application until trial; and
- to refuse the application for an inquiry as to damages.

The order is not penal; it is simply to compensate the defendant or third party for damage suffered during the currency of the injunction. If it is likely that there has been no provable damage, the inquiry may be refused (*McDonald's Hamburgers Ltd v Burger King UK Ltd* [1987] FSR 112). In most circumstances evidence is required to support an award for general damages; damages for emotional distress are only recoverable in exceptional circumstances; and aggravated/exemplary damages are only available under the second (and not the first) sentence of the standard search order undertaking (and not under other types of standard injunction undertakings) (*Al-Rawas v Pegasus Energy Ltd* [2009] 1 All ER (Comm) 393).

Ordinary principles of the law of contract are applied both as to causation and quantum (*Hoffmann-La Roche (F) and Co AG v Secretary of State for Trade and Industry* [1975] AC 295, HL).

14.5.4   Defendants' undertakings in lieu of an injunction

Instead of contesting an application for an interim injunction, the defendant may give undertakings in terms similar to the injunction sought by the claimant. The defendant will then be bound in the same way as if an injunction had been granted, and the claimant will be required to enter into a cross undertaking in damages to safeguard the defendant and third parties. In some cases undertakings given by a defendant will be construed as having contractual effect (*Independiente Ltd v Music Trading On-Line (HK) Ltd* [2008] 1 WLR 608).

14.5.5   Consequences of not applying for interim relief

Sometimes a claimant may commence proceedings but avoid making an application for an interim injunction where one might be obtained, simply to avoid the potential liability under the undertaking in damages. This may provide grounds for awarding damages in lieu of a final injunction at trial (*Jaggard v Sawyer* [1995] 1 WLR 269), although it should not bar the granting of an injunction where the claimant has made clear his objection to the defendant's conduct (*Mortimer v Bailey* (2004) LTL 29/10/2004).

14.6 Discharge

Interim injunctions are invariably granted subject to later discharge. For example, injunctions made on notice are usually granted 'until trial or further order'. A defendant seeking discharge of an interim injunction will often find that the application is heard by the same judge who granted the initial injunction. Grounds for discharge include:

- Material non-disclosure on an application made without notice.
- Failure by the claimant to comply with the terms on which the injunction was granted.
- That the facts do not justify interim injunctive relief.
- The oppressive effect of the injunction (though this may justify a variation of its terms).
- A material change in the circumstances of the parties or in the law since the injunction was granted.
- Failure by the claimant to prosecute the substantive claim with due speed.
- That the injunction interferes with the rights of innocent third parties.

14.7 Breach of an injunction

Disobedience of the terms of an injunction is a contempt of court. When the injunction is drawn up it will contain a penal notice warning the defendant of this fact. The serious consequences of breach are such that the terms of the order should be sufficiently precise so the defendant knows exactly what it is that must or must not be done. Sequestration of assets and committal to prison for up to two years are possible sanctions if contempt proceedings are brought (see **38.12**).

Freezing injunctions

15.1 Introduction

In certain circumstances, a claimant, who has a very strong case against a defendant, may feel that there is a serious risk that the defendant will dispose of his or her assets before the case proceeds to trial, thereby preventing the claimant, if successful at the trial, from being able to execute judgment, as there may no longer be any assets available which would realise the value of the judgment debt.

The freezing injunction is a form of interim injunction designed to guard against this, and has the effect of restraining defendants from disposing of, or dissipating, their assets so as to frustrate any judgment which the claimant may obtain against them.

Freezing injunctions have for many years been called *'Mareva'* injunctions. This name stems from the decision of the Court of Appeal in *Mareva Compania Naviera SA v International Bulk Carriers SA* [1980] 1 All ER 213. In this case the claimants were shipowners and the defendants voyage charterers. The defendants failed to pay the hire charges due to the claimants. The defendants had received money from their sub-charterers, which had been paid into a bank account in London. The court refused to consider itself bound by *Lister & Co v Stubbs* (1890) 45 ChD 1, CA, which had held that a defendant could not be compelled to give security before judgment, relying on the wide discretion conferred by what is now SCA 1981, s 37. This was held to be a proper case for granting an injunction restraining the defendants from removing or disposing out of the jurisdiction the moneys in the London bank.

15.2 Jurisdiction

We have already seen that SCA 1981, s 37(1), which is extracted at **14.2.1**, enables the High Court to grant interim injunctions if it is 'just and convenient to do so'. Specific statutory confirmation of the *Mareva* jurisdiction is contained in s 37(3), which provides:

The power of the High Court . . . to grant an interlocutory injunction restraining a party to any proceedings from removing from the jurisdiction of the High Court, or otherwise dealing with, assets located within that jurisdiction shall be exercisable in cases where that party is, as well as in cases where he is not, domiciled, resident or present within that jurisdiction.

As we have seen at **1.2.1.2**, the County Courts have limited powers to grant freezing injunctions.

15.3 Principles

There are four requirements:

- A cause of action justiciable in England and Wales.
- A good arguable case.
- The defendant having assets within the jurisdiction.
- A real risk that the defendant may dispose of or dissipate those assets before judgment can be enforced.

These four requirements will now be considered, together with the exception to the third requirement in the case of so-called 'worldwide' freezing injunctions.

15.3.1 Justiciable in England and Wales

Traditionally it has been said that a freezing injunction can only be granted if the claim is justiciable in England and Wales (*Siskina v Distos Compania Naviera SA* [1979] AC 210, HL). Restrictions in this regard have been almost entirely removed by the CJJA 1982, s 25, which empowers the English courts to grant interim relief, including freezing injunctions, where proceedings have been or are to be commenced in an overseas jurisdiction. The only restriction is s 25(2), which provides that the court may refuse relief if the fact the court has no jurisdiction other than under s 25 makes it inexpedient to grant the relief sought. The result is that the key question under this heading is whether the applicant can formulate a claim for substantive relief (either here or in an overseas jurisdiction) against the defendant (*Fourie v Le Roux* [2007] 1 WLR 320).

15.3.2 Good arguable case

The claimant's affidavit must disclose a good arguable case as regards the merits of the substantive claim against the defendant (*The Niedersachsen* [1983] 2 Lloyd's Rep 600, 605). This imposes a stricter standard than the 'serious issue to be tried' test in the *American Cyanamid* guidelines (*Fiona Trust Holding Corporation v Privalov* (2007) LTL 30/5/2007). Anticipation that the defendant will in the future be in breach of contract is insufficient (*Veracruz Transportation Inc v VC Shipping Co Inc* [1992] 1 Lloyd's Rep 353, CA; *Zucker v Tyndall Holdings plc* [1993] 1 All ER 124, CA).

15.3.3 Assets

15.3.3.1 General

It is usually the case that the claimant has to show that the defendant has some assets within the jurisdiction. 'Assets' for this purpose is given a wide meaning, and includes chattels such as motor vehicles, jewellery, objets d'art, and choses in action (*CBS UK Ltd v Lambert* [1983] Ch 37, 42 per Lawton LJ) as well as money. The assets must be owned in the same capacity as that in which the defendant is being sued. Assets held by a defendant as a bare trustee will not be covered by the order (*Federal Bank of the Middle East v Hadkinson* [2000] 1 WLR 1695, CA).

15.3.3.2 Bank accounts

If the defendant has a bank account in England, the court is likely to infer the presence of assets within the jurisdiction even if that account is in fact overdrawn.

If the defendant holds a bank account jointly with someone who is not a party to the action, that account may none the less be frozen by a *Mareva* (*SCF Finance Co Ltd v Masri* [1985] 1 WLR 876).

If the order is to be made against a bank account, the claimant must give the best possible particulars of that account (eg branch and account number, if known).

15.3.3.3 Land

Land can be the subject of a freezing injunction. However, the order is not 'made for the purpose of enforcing a judgment' and so cannot be registered as a land charge under Land Charges Act 1972, s 6(1)(a) (*Stockler v Fourways Estates Ltd* [1984] 1 WLR 25 (Kilner Brown J)). Nevertheless, it can be registered as a caution.

15.3.3.4 Related companies

In two decisions, *Atlas Maritime Co SA v Avalon Maritime Ltd (No. 3)* [1991] 1 WLR 917, CA, and *TSB Private Bank International SA v Chabra* [1992] 1 WLR 231, the courts were prepared to look beyond the corporate structure adopted by the defendants in order to give the claimants *Mareva* relief. In the *TSB* case it was clear the claimant had a good cause of action against Mr Chabra, the first defendant, and equally clear that there was no independent cause of action against the second defendant, a company owned by Mr Chabra and/or his wife. A freezing injunction was unlikely to be effective against Mr Chabra. As there was credible evidence that assets apparently owned by the second defendant in fact belonged to Mr Chabra, Mummery J granted a freezing injunction against the second defendant on the ground that it was ancillary and incidental to the claim against Mr Chabra.

15.3.3.5 Worldwide freezing injunctions

A freezing injunction will not normally extend to assets outside the jurisdiction. However, in an exceptional case, the court may make an order affecting assets both here and abroad. A worldwide freezing injunction may be made in support of foreign proceedings, but only if the defendant or the dispute has a sufficiently strong link with this country, or if there is some other factor justifying the English court's intervention despite the lack of such a link (*Mobil Cerro Negro Ltd v Petroleos de Venezuela SA* [2008] 1 Lloyd's Rep 684). In *Derby v Weldon (No. 2)* [1989] 1 All ER1002, CA, it was held that the court may make an order affecting assets abroad even if there are no assets in England.

Such an order will be rare. It will certainly not be made where there are sufficient assets within the jurisdiction to satisfy any judgment which the claimant may obtain (*Derby v Weldon (No. 1)* [1990] Ch 48, CA).

To avoid the problem of the court trying to assume an exorbitant jurisdiction over third parties outside the jurisdiction, the terms of the order should state that it shall not affect third parties unless, and to the extent that, it may be enforced by the courts of the State where the assets are located (*Derby v Weldon (No. 2)* [1989] 1 All ER 1002, CA; *Babanaft International Co SA v Bassatne* [1990] Ch 13, CA). For the principles applied when seeking permission to enforce a worldwide freezing order outside the jurisdiction, see *Dadourian Group International Inc v Simms* [2006] 1 WLR 2499, discussed in *Blackstone's Civil Practice 2010* at para 38.11.

15.3.4 Risk of disposal

In order to obtain a freezing injunction, the claimant must show that there is a risk that the defendant will remove assets from the jurisdiction, or dispose of them, or dissipate them, or hide them. There has to be 'solid evidence' of this risk (*Dean and Dean v Grinina*

[2008] EWHC 927 (QB)). The SCA 1981, s 37(3), which is extracted at **15.2**, makes it clear that a freezing injunction may be granted whether the defendant is or is not resident within the jurisdiction. However, the court is likely to infer the risk of disposal of assets more readily if the defendant is resident overseas, or is a company based overseas. However, as Kerr LJ said in *Z v A–Z* [1982] 1 QB 558, at 585, an order should not be made against someone who has substantial links with England, such as persons who are 'established within the jurisdiction in the sense of having assets here which they could not, or would not wish to, dissipate merely to avoid some judgment which seems likely to be given against them'.

In *Montecchi v Shimco Ltd* [1979] 1 WLR 1180, CA, it was held that the fact that the judgment of the English court is enforceable overseas by virtue of reciprocal enforcement provisions is a relevant factor to take into account in deciding whether or not to grant a freezing injunction. An order will only be made in such a case if there is good reason to apprehend that without an order, the judgment creditor would not be able to enforce any judgment that is obtained. So the claimant will have to show grounds for believing that, despite the reciprocal enforcement provisions, the defendant will be able to evade satisfying the judgment. This will of course be particularly relevant in the case of EU defendants, by virtue of the Civil Jurisdiction and Judgments Act 1982.

In *Customs and Excise Commissioners v Anchor Foods Ltd* [1999] 1 WLR 1139, it was said that the court would be slow to prevent a bona fide transaction in the ordinary course of business by granting a freezing injunction, especially where the price payable accorded with a professional valuation. However, in this case there was conflicting valuation evidence provided by the claimant's experts, and a freezing injunction was continued (but with additional safeguards for the defendants).

15.3.5   Discretion

Under SCA 1981, s 37(1), the court has a power to grant freezing injunctions where it is 'just and convenient'. In deciding whether or not to grant a freezing injunction, a factor the court will consider is the value of the defendant's assets from the claimant's point of view, namely their resale value in the light of the amount which the claimant is claiming in the action. In other words, would these assets in fact assist the claimant in a material way to satisfy any judgment that may be obtained?

For example, in *Rasu Maritima SA v Perusahaan Pertambangan Minyak Dan Gas Bumi Negara* [1978] QB 644, CA, the claimant was a Liberian company and the defendant an Indonesian state-owned company. The claim was for very substantial damages for a breach of charterparty. The assets in respect of which the claimant sought a freezing injunction comprised part of a fertiliser plant to be built in Indonesia. Its value as such was some $12 million; but its scrap value was only about $350,000. Lord Denning MR described that (at p 663) as a 'drop in the ocean' compared to the immense claim which was being made. His Lordship said that 'this amount is so trifling in the circumstances that it does not seem proper to interfere with the construction work on this fertiliser plant to secure it'.

15.4   Procedure

As it would defeat the purpose of the order if the defendant were to be warned of the application, applications for freezing injunctions are made without notice to the defendant. Giving advance notice to the defendant may be a ground for refusing a freezing injunction, because once alerted the defendant is likely to remove its assets from the jurisdiction (*Oaktree Financial Services Ltd v Higham* (2004) LTL 11/5/2004). The application is heard by a judge, and may be made at any stage in the proceedings, even before a claim form has been issued (if the application is urgent), or after judgment in aid of execution.

The applicant will need to issue an application notice setting out the nature of the order sought. The application needs to be supported by evidence, and this is one of the rare occasions where the evidence must be in the form of affidavits (PD 25, para 3.1). Whenever possible a draft of the order sought should be filed with the application notice, together with a disk containing the draft (para 2.4).

15.5 The order

15.5.1 Form of the order

A standard form of freezing injunction is laid down in the Annex to PD 25. This is a combined worldwide and domestic order. The form indicates which provisions are relevant if the order is to have a worldwide effect, these provisions being deleted if not needed. The standard form was drafted with considerable care, based on the experience of numerous appellate decisions. It must be used save to the extent that the judge considers there to be a good reason for adopting a different form. The full wording of the standard form can be found in the Annex to PD 25. The operative words of the order are in clause 5, which provides:

Until the return date or further order of the court, the respondent must not remove from England and Wales or in any way dispose of, or deal with or diminish the value of any of his assets which are in England and Wales up to the value of £   .

At clause 3 the order provides for a return date, which is usually a few days after the without-notice hearing, when the court will reconsider the position after the defendant has been served with the order. By clause 12 the costs of the without-notice application are reserved to the return date. It will be noticed that clause 5 restrains the respondent until the return date 'or further order'. This latter expression means (if the order continues beyond the return day) that the order continues until any further order relating to the freezing injunction. Unless the court discharges the injunction, it will continue after any judgment is obtained on the substantive claim (*Cantor Index Ltd v Lister* (2001) LTL 23/11/2001). Clause 13 allows the defendant or any third party affected by the injunction to apply to the court to vary or discharge the order on simply giving prior notice to the applicant's solicitor.

15.5.2 Undertakings

The claimant has to give the following undertakings, which are incorporated into the order:

(a) The usual undertaking as to damages. This should normally be supported by a bank guarantee, for a fixed amount, which the claimant undertakes to obtain within a certain period of time. This undertaking is usually dispensed with in favour of regulatory authorities pursuing claims for the general benefit of the public (*United States Securities and Exchange Commission v Manterfield* [2009] EWCA Civ 27).

(b) Because the application is without notice, to notify the defendant forthwith of the order and to serve on the defendant a copy of the affidavit used in support of the application, together with the claim form (unless it has already been served) and the order.

(c) To inform affected third parties of their right to apply to the court for directions or for variation of the order.

(d) To indemnify any third party in respect of expenses incurred in complying with the order. For example, where the claimant seeks an order which affects the defendant's bank account, an undertaking is required to indemnify the bank against any costs which it reasonably incurs in complying with the order (*Searose Ltd v Seatrain UK Ltd* [1981] 1 Lloyd's Rep 556).

15.5.3   Publicly funded claimant

In *Allen v Jambo Holdings Ltd* [1980] 1 WLR 1252, CA, the claimant, who was legally aided, made a claim under the Fatal Accidents Acts in respect of the death of her husband. She obtained a freezing injunction preventing the defendant from removing a propeller engined aeroplane from the jurisdiction. The Court of Appeal continued the injunction despite the fact Mrs Allen could not give a valuable undertaking in damages. The defendants had sworn incredible evidence on the application to discharge, and could obtain a release of their aeroplane if they provided security. It was therefore just and convenient to continue the order.

15.5.4   Terms of the order

The amount frozen by the order should not exceed the maximum amount of the claimant's claim against the defendant (including interest and costs), leaving the defendant free to deal with the balance as desired.

If, at the time the order is granted, the defendant does not have sufficient assets to meet the claimant's claim, the order need not state a maximum sum (*Z Ltd v A-Z* [1982] 1 QB 558 at 576, per Lord Denning MR). The order will then cover assets which are acquired by the defendant between the granting of the injunction and the execution of any judgment obtained in the claim (*TDK Tape Distributor (UK) Ltd v Videochoice Ltd* [1986] 1 WLR 141, 145, Skinner J).

15.5.5   Purpose of the order

There are two points:

- The object of a freezing injunction is not to give the claimant priority over the defendant's other creditors.
- The effect of the freezing injunction should not be such as to place undue pressure on the defendant to settle the claim on terms unduly favourable to the claimant.

To ensure the just operation of the *Mareva* jurisdiction, certain provisos must be incorporated into each freezing injunction order.

15.5.6   Provisos

15.5.6.1   Banks

'To safeguard the bank, the order will expressly state that it does not prevent the bank from exercising any right of set-off it may have in respect of facilities afforded by it to the defendant before the date of the order. Once the order has been served, the bank should recall any cheque card previously issued to the defendant' (*Z Ltd v A-Z* [1982] 1 QB 558 at 591 per Kerr LJ).

15.5.6.2 Living/business expenses and legal costs

The order should make provision for the defendant's ordinary living expenses if the defendant is an individual. In assessing what constitutes ordinary living expenses, the court takes account of the defendant's lifestyle (*PCW (Underwriting Agencies) Ltd v Dixon* [1983] 2 All ER 697, CA). The order often allows the defendant to pay the ordinary costs of the present litigation if no other funds are available. Quite a lot of latitude is given to a defendant in allowing expenditure on legal expenses in formulating its defence (*Furylong Ltd v Masterpiece Technology* (2004) LTL 13/7/2004).

It is a breach of the order to spend sums allocated to ordinary living expenses under the order for extraordinary purposes, such as the payment of Queen's Counsel's fees in unrelated litigation or the purchase of an expensive motor car, even if there are unused 'living expenses' funds in the defendant's account (*TDK Tape Distributor (UK) Ltd v Videochoice Ltd* [1986] 1 WLR 141, Skinner J).

If the defendant is a trader or company, the order should make provision for the defendant's ordinary and proper business expenses.

15.5.6.3 Trade debts

If the defendant is a trader or a company, the order should make provision for legitimate dealing or disposal of assets in the ordinary course of trading (even if the defendant has to use assets within those otherwise frozen by the court). Trade debts may be defined as payments which are made in good faith in the ordinary course of business (*Iraqi Ministry of Defence v Arcepy Shipping Co SA* [1981] QB 65).

15.5.7 Ancillary orders

The court will usually order disclosure of documents and/or the provisions of information on affidavit designed to enable the claimant to ascertain the whereabouts of the defendant's assets. This is done by clauses 9 and 10 of the standard form freezing injunction order, and see CPR, r 25.1(1)(g). A defendant will normally be required to provide this information even if there is a pending application to set aside the freezing injunction (*Motorola Credit Corporation v Uzan* [2002] 2 All ER (Comm) 945). There is no freestanding power under r 25.1(1)(g) to order the disclosure of information which might be of assistance in seeking a freezing injunction if the applicant has no material at present justifying an application for a freezing injunction (*Parker v CS Structured Credit Fund Ltd* The Times, 10 March 2003). Similar problems arise as with search orders regarding the privilege against self-incrimination (see **16.5.3.5**).

Even if the defendant swears an affidavit as to his or her assets, it may be that the claimant feels that the information given is evasive or incomplete. In such a case the claimant may apply for an order for cross-examination on the affidavit. Such an order would be an exceptional measure (*Yukong Line Ltd of Korea v Rendsburg Investments Corp. of Liberia* The Times, 22 October 1996). If an order is made, the cross-examination is generally to be conducted before a Master.

15.5.8 Effect of the order

The order is addressed to the defendant, but it also binds third parties with knowledge of it. A person with knowledge of the order who assists in the disposal of enjoined assets is therefore in contempt of court (*Z Ltd v A-Z* [1982] 1 QB 558, 572 per Lord Denning MR).

If an order is made against a bank account, it operates to freeze the account up to the amount of the order as soon as the bank has notice of the grant of the order. Technically, the bank does not owe a duty of care in tort to the claimant not to pay money out to the defendant (*Customs and Excise Commissioners v Barclays Bank plc* [2007] 1 AC 181). However, it would be in contempt of court if it honoured cheques drawn on the account after being notified of the terms of the order. The order should therefore be served on the bank and then on the defendant.

15.6 Discharge or variation

15.6.1 Grounds for discharge

15.6.1.1 Not an appropriate case

An application to discharge the order may be made where the defendant can show that the claimant does not have a good arguable case on the merits or by showing that there is insufficient risk that the assets will be dissipated.

15.6.1.2 Defendant providing security

The defendant may also obtain discharge of the order by providing security for the claimant's claim instead. This may take the form of creating a charge over the defendant's property, paying money into a bank account in the joint names of the solicitors acting for the claimant and the defendant, or even paying the sum claimed into court. The standard security provision in a freezing injunction only gives 'security' against the risk of dissipation of assets. It does not provide security against the defendant's other creditors (*Technocrats International Inc v Fredic Ltd* [2005] 1 BCLC 467).

15.6.1.3 Claimant guilty of material non-disclosure

The claimant is under a strict duty to make full and frank disclosure in the affidavit of all facts and matters which are or which reasonably should be within his or her knowledge. This means that as well as stating what is in fact known, the claimant is also under a duty to make reasonable inquiries. The claimant's duty of disclosure includes fairly stating any points which could be made against the claim. The judge should be informed of any counterclaim or defence which the defendant may have to the substantive claim and any facts known to the claimant as regards the defendant's financial standing (*Third Chandris Shipping Corp v Unimarine SA* [1979] QB 645, 688 (Lord Denning MR)). Whether a fact is material is often difficult to judge. In *Indicii Salus Ltd v Chandrasekaran* [2008] EWCA Civ 67, the company's accountants' reservations about the claimant's ability to pay their fees was regarded as non-material.

Material facts must appear in the affidavit in support itself. It is not sufficient if they appear in exhibited documents (*National Bank of Sharjah v Dellborg* The Times, 24 December 1992, CA). Nor is it enough for counsel to refer to an affidavit prepared earlier in the claim which sets out the alleged defence: it is part of counsel's duty to the court to attempt to persuade the judge to read it (*Art Corporation v Schuppan* The Times, 20 January 1994). Any shortcomings in the claimant's own financial standing, which is relevant to the adequacy of the undertaking in damages, must also be disclosed. A breach of an advocate's duty to the court may result in sanctions being imposed against the client (*Memory Corporation v Sidhu (No. 2)* [2000] 1 WLR 1443, CA).

In deciding what should be the consequences of any breach of duty, it is necessary to take into account all the relevant circumstances, including the gravity of the breach, the excuse or explanation offered, the severity and duration of any prejudice occasioned, and whether the consequences of the breach were remediable and had been remedied. The court must also apply the overriding objective and the need for proportionality (*Memory Corporation v Sidhu (No. 2)*). It is important that the rule against material non-disclosure does not itself become an instrument of injustice (*Brink's Mat Ltd v Elcombe* [1988] 1 WLR 1350).

When the injunction has been set aside for material non-disclosure, the question then arises as to whether, on the full facts, a second injunction should be granted in its place. A fresh order will only be granted if:

- the non-disclosure was innocent (ie there was no deliberate attempt to mislead the court); and

- on the whole of the facts, including the fact of the original non-disclosure, a freezing injunction could properly be granted.

Note, however, that the court will do its best to do justice between the parties. For example, in *Behbehani v Salem* [1989] 1 WLR 723, CA, discharge was upheld upon the defendant giving an undertaking not to dispose of property within the jurisdiction without giving reasonable notice to the claimant.

15.6.2 Grounds for variation

If the order does not make provision for ordinary living expenses or legitimate trade debts, or freezes an amount in excess of the claimant's claim against the defendant, the defendant may apply for the order to be varied so as to remedy these defects.

Where the application is for living expenses or trade debts, the defendant has to show that there are no other assets out of which payment could reasonably be made (*A v C (No. 2)* [1981] QB 961).

A change in the management of a company defendant, eg by the appointment of an administrative receiver by a debenture holder (see *Company Law in Practice* manual) may remove the risk of dissipation of the company's assets and give grounds for varying or even discharging a freezing injunction (*Capital Cameras Ltd v Harold Lines Ltd* [1991] 1 WLR 54).

15.7 Change of circumstances

In *Commercial Bank of the Near East plc v A* [1989] 2 Lloyd's Rep 319, Saville J said that in the period up to the first hearing on notice, it is the claimant's duty to bring to the attention of the court any material changes in the circumstances which occur after the freezing injunction is granted. After the first hearing on notice, there is a continuing duty to disclose material changes in the applicant's financial circumstances (*Staines v Walsh* The Times, 1 August 2003).

Search orders

16.1 Introduction

Search orders are a form of interim injunctive relief that were originally known as *Anton Piller* orders. This name came from *Anton Piller KG v Manufacturing Processes Ltd* [1976] Ch 55, CA. The claimants were German manufacturers of electric motors and generators. One of their products was a frequency converter for use in computers. The defendants were the claimants' UK agents. Two 'defectors' employed by the defendants flew to Germany and informed the claimants that the defendants had been secretly negotiating with the claimants' competitors with the object of supplying the competitors with manuals, drawings and other confidential information which would allow the competitors to copy the claimants' products and ruin their market. The 'defectors' had documentary evidence in support of their claims.

The claimants were worried that if the defendants were given notice of court proceedings they would destroy or remove any incriminating evidence. So, before they had time even to issue the contemplated proceedings, their solicitors applied without notice and obtained an order requiring the defendants to permit them to enter their premises for the purposes of searching for and seizing relevant documents and other evidence.

The jurisdiction to grant search orders was placed on a statutory basis by the Civil Procedure Act 1997, s 7.

16.2 Relief of last resort

The search order, involving the violation of the defendant's home and business premises, is recognised as a draconian measure. The reason, according to Dillon LJ in *Booker McConnell plc v Plascow* [1985] RPC 425, CA, is that '. . . the courts have always proceeded . . . on the basis that the overwhelming majority of people in this country will comply with the court's order.' The fact that someone is a tortfeasor or is in breach of contract, and hence can be sued, does not necessarily mean they will disobey an order of the court. In many cases it may be enough to apply for some less drastic form of interlocutory relief. Examples are:

- An application on notice under CPR, r 25.1, to enter the defendant's premises and inspect property.
- An application on notice for negative injunctions with orders to deliver up documents or material belonging to the claimant.
- An order on notice that the defendant delivers up documents to his or her own solicitor.

- An order on notice that the defendant allows the claimant's solicitor to make copies of documents.
- Awaiting disclosure of documents in the usual way.

16.3 Principles

In *Anton Piller KG v Manufacturing Processes Ltd* [1976] Ch 55, Ormrod LJ identified three basic requirements that must be satisfied before the court may grant a search order (although it could be said that the third requirement can be subdivided in two). Each of the requirements must be substantiated in the affidavit in support. Note that even if the three requirements are made out, the granting of a search order remains in the discretion of the court. The three requirements are:

- There must be an extremely strong prima facie case on the merits.
- The defendant's activities must cause very serious potential or actual harm to the claimant's interests.
- There must be clear evidence that incriminating documents or things are in the defendant's possession and that there is a real possibility that such material may be destroyed before any application on notice can be made.

For a period in the 1980s it was thought that the conditions for the grant of *Anton Piller* orders had been relaxed by two Court of Appeal decisions (*Yousif v Salama* [1980] 1 WLR 1540 and *Dunlop Holdings Ltd v Staravia Ltd* [1982] Com LR 3).

However, since *Booker McConnell plc v Plascow* [1985] RPC 425, CA, the courts have insisted on the strict observance of the conditions laid down by Ormrod LJ in *Anton Piller KG v Manufacturing Processes Ltd* [1976] Ch 55. The importance of strict compliance with the conditions was emphasised in *Columbia Picture Industries Inc v Robinson* [1987] Ch 38 by Scott J, who said the effect of a search order is often to close down the defendant's business. The defendant's business records and, in many cases, the whole stock-in-trade will be removed. If the order is combined with a freezing injunction it will be served on the defendant's bankers who will almost certainly decline any further credit. Even if the defendant's business is not closed down, a search order plainly carries the suggestion that the defendant is not to be trusted, and may result in people being reluctant to carry on business with the defendant in the ordinary way.

An example of the present practice is *Lock International plc v Beswick* [1989] 1 WLR 1268. The defendants had held key posts with the claimant, which manufactured metal detectors. They became dissatisfied with the management of the company, and joined a new company which was intended to compete in the metal detector business. The claimant apprehended that the defendants were making use of its trade secrets and confidential information, and obtained and executed a search order. On the defendants' application to discharge the order, Hoffmann J said:

The evidence [on the application without notice] came nowhere near disclosing an 'extremely strong prima facie case' or 'clear evidence that the defendants [had] in their possession incriminating documents or things' or that there was a 'grave danger' or 'real possibility' that the defendants might destroy evidence. The lack of specificity in the [claimant's] affidavit was such that I have some doubt whether it could be said to have raised a triable issue. Furthermore, these defendants were no fly-by-night video pirates. They were former long-service employees with families and mortgages, who had openly said that they were entering into competition and whom the [claimant] knew to be financed by highly respectable institutions.

16.4 Procedure on application for search order

Applications for search orders are made by issuing an application notice with a draft order (and a copy on disk), supported by evidence on affidavit (rather than witness statement).

Secrecy is essential if the order is to be effective. The application is therefore made without notice, and in ChD cases the court sits in private rather than in open court. Usually the application is made after issue but before service of the claim form, although in urgent cases the application can be made before issue.

As the application is made without notice, the claimant has the usual duty of swearing an affidavit giving full and frank disclosure of all material facts. This is especially important in applications for search orders, and the claimant should err on the side of excessive disclosure.

16.5 Form of the order

A standard form of search order can be found in the Annex to PD 25. This standard form should be used save in so far as the judge considers there are good reasons for adopting a different form.

16.5.1 Claimant's undertakings

The claimant is required to provide certain safeguards for the defendant in the form of undertakings incorporated into the search order. The undertakings are divided into two categories: those entered into by the claimant personally; and those entered into by the claimant's solicitors. Commonly, the claimant will personally undertake:

- If the application was of an urgent nature, to issue process, and to swear and file affidavits forthwith as appropriate.
- To serve the search order by a solicitor together with copies of the affidavits, photocopiable exhibits in support, and an application for a hearing a few days after service.
- To serve the defendant with a written report on the carrying out of the order to be prepared by the supervising solicitor. This will be considered by the court on the return day.
- To abide by any order as to damages.
- Not to inform any third party of the proceedings until the return day.
- Not to use items seized other than for the purposes of the claim without the court's leave.
- To insure items removed from the defendant's premises.

The claimant's solicitors will normally undertake:

- To retain all documents and articles seized in safe custody.
- Within two working days, to deliver the originals of the documents and articles seized to the defendant or defendant's solicitors except original documents belonging to the claimant.

16.5.2 Implied undertaking

An undertaking not to use items seized for collateral purposes will also be implied against the claimant (*Crest Homes plc v Marks* [1987] AC 829, HL). The reason is that a search order operates as an order for disclosure in advance of the usual directions given as part of judicial case management. In proper cases permission can be given to use the material disclosed in related civil proceedings (*Crest Homes plc v Marks*) or criminal prosecutions (*A-G for Gibraltar v May* [1999] 1 WLR 998, CA).

16.5.3 The order

16.5.3.1 The operative provision

The order is that the defendant 'must permit' the supervising solicitor and the claimant's solicitor together with a limited number of other persons to enter his or her premises. An order that the claimant's representatives 'be entitled to enter' is defective (*Manor Electronics Ltd v Dickson* [1988] RPC 618, Scott J). The order is not a civil search warrant, and reasonable force may not be used to gain entry. The wording of the standard order is as follows:

6. The Respondent must permit the following persons: (a) Mr/Mrs/Miss _____ ('the Supervising Solicitor'); (b) _____ a solicitor in the firm of _____ the Applicant's solicitors; and (c) up to _____ other persons being [their identity or capacity] accompanying them (together 'the search party'), to enter the premises mentioned in Schedule A to this Order and any other premises of the Respondent disclosed under paragraph 18 below and any vehicles under the Respondent's control on or around the premises ('the premises') so that they can search for, inspect, photograph or photocopy, and deliver into the safekeeping of the Applicant's solicitors all the documents and articles which are listed in Schedule B to this Order ('the listed items').

7. Having permitted the search party to enter the premises, the Respondent must allow the search party to remain on the premises until the search is complete. In the event that it becomes necessary for any of those persons to leave the premises before the search is complete, the Respondent must allow them to re-enter the premises immediately upon their seeking re-entry on the same or the following day in order to complete the search.

16.5.3.2 Safeguards for the defendant

The courts are anxious to prevent the oppressive use of the *Anton Piller* jurisdiction. A number of safeguards must therefore be incorporated into the terms of the order. These include:

(a) That the order must be served, and its execution must be supervised, by a named solicitor other than a member of the firm acting for the claimant. The supervising solicitor must be an experienced solicitor with familiarity with the workings of search orders. The affidavit in support of the application for the order must give details of the proposed supervising solicitor's experience.

(b) That the order must be served on a weekday between 9.30 am and 5.30 pm. This is to give the defendant a realistic prospect of seeking legal advice (see (g) below).

(c) That if the defendant is a woman living alone, that a woman must accompany those executing the order.

(d) That, even in the case of business premises, the order must only be executed in the presence of a responsible representative of the defendant.

(e) Restricting the number of people who may seek entry under the order.

(f) That the supervising solicitor must explain the meaning and effect of the order to the defendant in everyday language.

(g) That the supervising solicitor must advise the defendant that he may avail himself of legal professional privilege and the privilege against self-incrimination and of the right to seek legal advice before complying with the order, provided such advice is sought at once.

(h) That, unless it is impracticable to do so, eg if the defendant may get violent, a list of the items removed must be prepared on the premises before they are removed, and the defendant must be given an opportunity to check it. This is intended to reduce the risk of disputes as to what has been removed.

It is most important that the order is drawn so as to extend no further than the minimum extent necessary to preserve the documents or articles which may otherwise be destroyed or concealed (*Columbia Picture Industries Inc v Robinson* [1987] Ch 38, Scott J). The order will expressly give the defendant liberty to apply to discharge or vary the order on short notice and will provide in the order for a return date for a hearing on notice.

16.5.3.3 Provisions to assist execution

The defendant will commonly be ordered to do a number of things to facilitate the execution of the order. These include:

- Where it is anticipated that evidence is stored on computer, an order that the defendant print out material in legible or computer readable form.
- An order that the defendant open locked drawers, safes, etc on the premises.
- An order that the defendant provide washing and toilet facilities for the claimant's representatives.

16.5.3.4 Ancillary orders

It is common to augment the main search order with a number of ancillary orders. Examples are:

- To deliver to the claimant any documents or articles covered by the search order but which are at addresses other than those stated in the order.
- To deliver within, say, 48 hours to the claimant any relevant documents coming into the defendant's possession after service of the order.
- To swear an affidavit verifying that all relevant documents have been delivered up to the claimant.
- To disclose addresses not covered by the order where relevant documents are stored.

- To restrain the defendant from warning other persons of the existence of the proceedings.

- To disclose, and verify on affidavit, the names and addresses of persons who have been involved in the defendant's activities.

16.5.3.5 Privilege against self-incrimination

The last of the ancillary orders in **16.5.3.4**, for the disclosure of other persons against whom the claimant may have causes of action, is especially useful in cassette and video pirating cases. The decision of the House of Lords in *Rank Film Distributors Ltd v Video Information Centre* [1982] AC 380 threatened to destroy its utility by holding that where a criminal charge was more than a contrived, fanciful or remote possibility the defendant could refuse to provide the information, relying on the privilege against selfincrimination. In pirating cases, conspiracy to defraud was an appropriate description of the defendant's activities. The privilege does not cover free-standing evidence that may be found on a search, such as photographs stored on a computer (*C plc v P* [2008] Ch 1). While it will cover those parts of a search order which require a defendant to produce and verify documents and information (*Tate Access Floors Inc v Boswell* [1991] Ch 512), following *C plc v P* it is doubtful whether entry and the search itself are also covered (despite the contrary view in *Tate Access Floors Inc v Boswell*).

Following *Rank Film Distributors Ltd v Video Information Centre* Parliament intervened by enacting SCA 1981, s 72, which removed the privilege in intellectual property and passing off cases, subject to the defendant's answers being inadmissible in subsequent criminal proceedings. A similar position has been reached where the defendant alleges that disclosure may lead to a prosecution for a substantive crime under the Theft Act (see Theft Act 1968, s 31(1)) or the Fraud Act (see Fraud Act 2006, s 13).

If the risk of the information obtained under the search order being used against the defendant in subsequent criminal proceedings can be removed then the right of the defendant to avoid the impact of a search order by raising the privilege against self-incrimination can be avoided. This can be achieved by securing the written agreement of the Crown Prosecution Service that they do not wish to make use of such information, and by inserting a suitable clause in the search order itself (*AT and T Istel Ltd v Tulley* [1993] AC 45, HL). The clause approved in *AT and T Istel* was to the effect that no disclosure made in compliance with the order shall be used as evidence in the prosecution of any offence alleged to have been committed by the defendant or the defendant's spouse. Unless the prosecuting authorities do agree in writing, an *AT and T Istel* clause will not be included in an order (*United Norwest Co-operatives Ltd v Johnstone* The Times, 24 February 1994, CA).

When such a clause cannot be used, the search order should not be executed until after the defendant has had his right to claim privilege explained to him in everyday language, and has expressly declined to claim privilege (*IBM United Kingdom Ltd v Prima Data International Ltd* [1994] 4 All ER 748).

It is not permissible to include in a search order a requirement that the defendant must hand potentially self-incriminating material to the supervising solicitor, even simply for safekeeping (*Den Norske Bank ASA v Antonatos* [1999] QB 271, CA). Nor should the defendant be required to answer questions to discover whether the claimant has additional claims (*International Fund for Agricultural Development v Jazayeri* (2001) LTL 8/3/2001).

16.6 Execution of the order

The concept of having a supervising solicitor to serve and execute *Anton Piller* orders was introduced by Sir Donald Nicholls V-C in *Universal Thermosensors Ltd v Hibben* [1992] 1 WLR 840. Before then the practice was for the claimant's own solicitor to serve the order on the defendant. Decisions before 1992 must therefore be read with this change of practice in mind.

Execution of the order needs to be properly planned. If there are several addresses covered by the order, it is important that execution is simultaneous. The police are often informed beforehand if there is any anticipation of a breach of the peace.

The order is not a search warrant, and the solicitors cannot use force to gain entry. After the supervising solicitor has explained the effect of the order, it may well be that the defendant will claim that various items are privileged. The usual procedure is for the defendant to ask the supervising solicitor to assess whether the materials are privileged. If they are, they will be excluded from the search. If the supervising solicitor feels they may be privileged, the supervising solicitor excludes them from the search, but retains them pending further order from the court (clause 11 of the standard order).

There is a heavy duty on the applicant's solicitors to comply strictly with the terms as to the addresses covered and the goods and documents to be seized. The claimant's solicitor retains the articles seized, not the claimant, and must comply with the undertakings as to listing items removed and duly returning them to the defendant after they are copied. It is important that neither the claimant nor the claimant's employees be allowed to conduct searches of documents belonging to a trade competitor, even if the competitor is the defendant to the action.

16.7 Non-compliance by the defendant

There are two sanctions:

- The claimant can bring contempt proceedings, which may result in the defendant being committed to prison.
- 'The refusal to comply may be the most damning evidence against the defendant at the subsequent trial', per Ormrod LJ in *Anton Piller KG v Manufacturing Processes Ltd* [1976] Ch 55, CA.

The standard search order requires the supervising solicitor to inform the defendants that they are not obliged to comply with the order until they have sought legal advice, which must be sought within two hours. While the defendant is seeking legal advice the supervising solicitor must be admitted to the premises. Other people named in the order may be excluded in this period. Although the supervising solicitor may be inside the premises, the search will not be started until the defendant has obtained legal advice (or the two hours has elapsed). Once that time has expired, the defendant will be at risk of committal proceedings. While it stands, an order must be obeyed. That is so even if an application is successfully made shortly thereafter for the order to be discharged or varied (*Wardle Fabrics Ltd v G Myristis Ltd* [1984] FSR 263). However, the bare fact of a refusal of entry, and hence breach of the order, does not mean that the breach was contumacious or that it requires punishment. Important factors are whether the application to discharge is merely a device to postpone the search and whether there is evidence of impropriety in respect of any relevant materials during the period of the delay (*Bhimji v Chatwani* [1991] 1 WLR 989).

16.8 Material changes before execution

If a material change takes place between the granting of a search order and its execution, it is the claimant's duty to return to the court so that the court can reconsider the application in the light of the new facts (*O'Regan v Iambic Productions Ltd* (1989) 139 NLJ 1378, Sir Peter Pain).

16.9 Application to discharge

16.9.1 The application

The order itself will contain express liberty for the defendant to apply to vary or discharge on short notice. The application to discharge or vary is made on notice usually to the judge who granted the original order. Evidence in support will be given on affidavit.

16.9.2 Grounds for discharge

Grounds upon which a search order may be discharged include:

- One or more of the basic conditions not being satisfied.
- Material non-disclosure on the application without notice.

Misstatements as to the claimant's means have occurred in several cases. This is usually material because it affects the value of the claimant's undertaking in damages. The usual penalty for any material non-disclosure is the discharge of the order. However, if the non-disclosure is inadvertent and no injustice is caused to the defendants, the court has a discretion to maintain the order.

A search order was discharged in *Gadget Shop Ltd v Bug.Com Ltd* The Times, 28 June 2000 for multiple breaches of procedure. Small variations in the standard form of order had not been drawn to the attention of the judge on the initial application; the lack of experience of the supervising solicitor had not been adequately explained in the evidence in support; and the evidence in support did not give adequate full and frank disclosure, for example, that some of the allegedly confidential material said to have been taken by the defendants had been published on the applicant's own web site.

16.9.3 Order for discharge

Once a search order has been executed there is a strong argument that it should not be discharged, even if there are grounds for doing so. Discharging the order is always a matter in the court's discretion, and discharge can be little more than an empty gesture, enforcing the undertaking in damages being a matter which can wait until trial.

However, there are cases where justice requires the immediate discharge of an executed search order:

(a) If the ground is material non-disclosure, the argument in favour of immediate discharge is stronger (and, usually, irresistible) if the non-disclosure is not concerned with the merits of the cause of action, because such a question would not usually be investigated at trial.

(b) If the ground is material non-disclosure as to the claimant's solvency, the justice of the case may point towards the defendant being able to recover on the claimant's undertaking in damages immediately rather than being on risk pending trial.

(c) The continuing stigma of having a search order hanging over the defendant may be interfering with the defendant's business.

See *Dormeuil Freres SA v Nicolian International (Textiles) Ltd* [1988] 1 WLR 1362, as interpreted by *Tate Access Floors Inc v Boswell* [1991] Ch 512. See also *Network Multimedia Television Ltd v Jobserve Ltd* The Times, 25 January 2001, on whether an application to discharge should be listed for the same time as an application to continue the order.

16.9.4 Variation

The usual ground for varying a search order is that it has been drawn too widely. The safeguards established by the courts may not have been incorporated into the order, for example, the claimant may have been allowed to retain the defendant's documents for more than a reasonable period, or the classes of documents covered by the order may be wider than necessary.

16.10 Misconduct by the claimant

The solicitor executing a search order in *VDU Installations Ltd v Integrated Computer Systems and Cybernetics Ltd* The Times, 13 August 1988, negligently failed to explain the effect of the order to the defendant in a fair and accurate manner. Knox J held the solicitor to be in contempt of court.

If the order is executed in an excessive or oppressive manner, the claimant may become liable under the undertaking in damages. 'Excessive' means simply beyond the terms of the order, such as by seizing more documents than those listed in the order. In such circumstances the defendant may be entitled to aggravated and, perhaps, exemplary damages (*Columbia Picture Industries Inc v Robinson* [1987] Ch 38).

It is incumbent on a claimant who has obtained and executed a search order to press on with the main action without delay. In *Hytrac Conveyors Ltd v Conveyors International Ltd* [1982] 1 WLR 44, CA, a search order was executed on 30 April 1982. Over 10 weeks after the defendants had given notice of intention to defend the claimant had still not served particulars of claim. Lawton LJ said that claimants 'must not use *Anton Piller* orders as a means of finding out what sort of charges they can make', and refused the claimant's application for permission to appeal against the judge's order dismissing the claim.

Small claims track

17.1 Introduction

In accordance with the ideas set out in the overriding objective that cases should be dealt with proportionately to the amount at stake and to the importance of the case, the Civil Procedure Rules 1998 provide for the allocation of claims with a limited financial value to what is known as the small claims track. This is intended to provide a streamlined procedure with limited pre-trial preparation, very restricted rules on the recovery of costs from the losing party, and with the strict rules of evidence not applying to the hearing. It is appropriate for the most straightforward types of cases, such as consumer disputes, accident claims where the injuries suffered are not very serious, disputes about the ownership of goods, and landlord and tenant cases other than claims for possession.

As discussed in **Chapter 7**, track allocation is considered by the court (usually a District Judge) in defended cases after receipt of allocation questionnaires from the parties. These questionnaires are sent to the parties after receipt of the defence, so allocation occurs usually a few weeks after the proceedings were served.

Regulation (EC) No. 861/2007 of 11 July 2007 established a European Small Claims Procedure. The Regulation applies to cross-border cases in civil and commercial matters where the value of the claim does not exceed 2,000 euros. Procedural rules for European Small Claims can be found in CPR, Part 78.

17.2 Allocation to the small claims track

This is the normal track for defended claims with a value not exceeding £5,000 (CPR, r 26.6(3)). Although most claims up to £5,000 will be dealt with on the small claims track, the following types of claim will not normally be allocated there even if they have a value up to £5,000:

- personal injuries cases where the value of the claim for pain, suffering, and loss of amenity exceeds £1,000 (CPR, r 26.6(1)(a) and (2));
- claims by tenants of residential premises seeking orders that their landlords should carry out repairs or other works to the premises where the value of the claim exceeds £1,000 (CPR, r 26.6(1)(b));
- claims by residential tenants seeking damages against their landlords for harassment or unlawful eviction (CPR, r 26.7(4)); and
- claims involving a disputed allegation of dishonesty.

Even if the claim is worth less than £5,000 there may be other reasons why it should not be allocated to the small claims track. One relates to expert evidence, which is not allowed in small claims track cases, either by calling an expert at the hearing or simply relying on an expert's report, unless the court gives permission: CPR, r 27.5. Although permission may be granted, there are also severe restrictions on the costs recoverable for expert evidence in small claims track cases, including a limit of £200 for experts' fees (PD 27, para 7.3(2)), which may make it unjust for a small case which requires expert evidence to be allocated to this track.

If the claim is worth more than £5,000 the parties may consent to it being allocated to the small claims track: CPR, r 26.7(3). However, the court retains control, and may refuse to allocate the case in accordance with the parties' wishes if it feels the case is not suitable for the small claims track. For example, it is unlikely to agree to a case being allocated to the small claims track if the hearing is likely to take more than a day. If the court agrees with the parties and allocates the case to the small claims track, the case is treated for the purposes of costs as a small claims track case, unless the parties agree that the fast track costs rules are to apply: CPR, r 27.14(5).

17.3 Provisions of the Civil Procedure Rules 1998 that do not apply

The idea behind having a small claims track is to provide a relatively inexpensive means of resolving disputes having a limited financial value. Some of the more sophisticated procedures available for larger claims are therefore inappropriate for cases on the small claims track, and do not apply once a case has been allocated to the small claims track. These include:

- most interim remedies, except interim injunctions;
- standard disclosure of documents (a more limited form of disclosure applies; see below);
- several of the rules on experts;
- requests for further information can be made only by the court on its own initiative (CPR, r 27.2(3)), and cannot be made by the parties; and
- Part 36 offers to settle (because this would interfere with the no costs rule; see below). However, in a suitable case the court can treat a refusal of a Part 36 offer as 'unreasonable behaviour' within the meaning of r 27.14(2)(g), and in such a case would have consequences on costs (r 27.14(3)).

17.4 Standard directions

Once a case has been allocated to the small claims track the court will give directions, which are usually set out in the notice telling the parties that the case has been allocated to this track.

There are a number of options available to the court, but it is most likely that the court will give what are described as standard directions. Different forms of standard directions apply to different categories of small claims. However, the general form of standard directions provides for:

- the parties to serve on the other side copies of the documents they intend to rely upon no later than 14 days before the hearing;
- the original documents to be brought to the hearing;
- notice of the hearing date and the length of the hearing;
- encouraging the parties to contact each other with a view to settling the claim or narrowing the issues; and
- an obligation on the parties to inform the court if they settle the case by agreement.

17.5 Special directions

A District Judge allocating a claim to the small claims track may decide that standard directions will not ensure the case is properly prepared, and may instead formulate special directions specifically for the case in hand. At the same time the District Judge may fix the date for the final hearing, or may list the matter for further directions. Alternatively, if the District Judge takes the view that it will be necessary to have a hearing with the parties present in court to ensure they understand what they must do to prepare the case, or if the District Judge is minded to consider whether the claim should be struck out or summarily disposed of, the case will be listed for a preliminary hearing where these matters can be dealt with.

In most small claim cases witness statements are not exchanged, as this adds to the costs and formality. A District Judge nevertheless has the power to make a direction for the exchange of witness statements. Whether such a direction will be made depends on the amount in dispute, the complexity of the case, and the need to avoid formality (PD 27, para 2.5).

The general rule in small claims track cases is that no expert evidence is allowed, whether oral or in the form of a report. If a party regards expert evidence as necessary, a special direction will be required, and this should be mentioned in the allocation questionnaire.

Where witness statements and expert reports are used in small claims cases, they do not have to comply with the strict rules on format discussed in **Chapters 10** (witness statements) and **29** (experts), because the relevant provisions of the CPR are excluded from small claims cases by r 27.2(1).

17.6 Determination without a hearing

If all the parties agree, a small claim can be determined by the District Judge on the papers without a hearing: CPR, r 27.10.

17.7 Final hearings

Final hearings in small claims track cases are usually dealt with by County Court District Judges. Hearings are generally conducted in the judge's room rather than in one of the court rooms. The normal rule is that hearings will be in public, but there are several exceptions, such as the parties agreeing to the hearing being in private.

Small claims hearings are informal, and the strict rules of evidence do not apply. The informality in small claims proceedings was stressed by the Court of Appeal in *Bandegani v Norwich Union Fire Insurance Ltd* (1999) LTL 20/5/99 when allowing an appeal against a decision to dismiss a claim after a submission of no case to answer. The submission had been based on the claimant's failure to produce expert evidence for the value of his car, which had been damaged in an accident. The Court of Appeal also made the point that permission to call expert evidence in small claims cases ought not to be encouraged for reasons of proportionality.

The District Judge may proceed in any way that is considered fair. The District Judge may ask the witnesses questions before allowing the parties to do so, may refuse to allow cross-examination until all the witnesses have given evidence-in-chief, and may impose limits on the scope of cross-examination. Unless the District Judge intervenes in one of these ways, the usual sequence of events is for the claimant's representative to make a short opening (just a few sentences), and then to call their evidence. Everyone will be sitting around the District Judge's table, so no one leaves their seat when this is being done. Each witness is questioned first on behalf of the claimant, then on behalf of the defendant. The District Judge makes a note of the evidence as it is given, and will ask questions as appropriate. There may be scope for some re-examination. Once all the claimant's evidence has been introduced, the claimant's representative says that is the case for the claimant. It is then the defendant's opportunity to call its evidence. Once the defendant's evidence has been introduced, the defendant's representative will make some closing remarks. The claimant's representative's closing submissions come last.

The District Judge will usually give a short reasoned judgment there and then. The judgment is likely to be as short and simple as the nature of the case will allow. After giving judgment the form of the order to be made and costs are considered.

17.8 Costs

Claims allocated to the small claims track are subject to severe costs restrictions. The rule is that no costs will be ordered between the parties except:

- the fixed costs relating to issuing the claim;
- court fees (these are likely to include the issue fee; an allocation fee if the claim is worth more than £1,500, and a hearing fee);
- witness expenses reasonably incurred for travel and subsistence;
- loss of earnings or loss of leave up to £50 per day;
- expert's fees, up to £200 per expert; and
- in cases involving a claim for an injunction or specific performance, the cost of legal advice and assistance up to £260.

The above restrictions apply in the vast majority of small claims cases. There is however an exception if the court finds that one of the parties has behaved unreasonably. In such cases the court may make a summary assessment of costs in favour of the innocent party.

17.9 Rehearings

A party who did not attend the final hearing may apply to set aside the order made in his or her absence and for an order that the claim be reheard. An application for a rehearing must be made within 14 days of the absent party being notified of the judgment. A rehearing will be allowed only if there is a good reason for the absence and if the absent party has a reasonable prospect of success at a reconvened hearing.

18

Fast track

18.1 Introduction

The fast track is intended for medium sized cases that require more careful preparation than small claims track cases, but still do not justify the detailed and meticulous preparation appropriate for complex and important cases. The full range of interim remedies and orders are available in fast track cases. However, procedure on the fast track steers a middle course between the extremes of simple preparation on the small claims track, and the often time consuming and expensive procedures appropriate for the important cases on the multi-track. The reason it is called the fast track is that at the same time as a case is allocated to this case management track the court will give directions laying down a timetable for all the stages up to and including trial, but with the trial date or window no more than 30 weeks after the track allocation decision. It is intended that the timetable will be sufficient for the parties to undertake the work necessary for preparing the case for trial, but sufficiently tight to discourage elaboration. Discouraging elaboration is seen as important, as one of the aims is to prevent costs in fast track cases spiralling out of control.

The majority of defended claims within the £5,000 to £25,000 monetary band will be allocated to the fast track. Non-monetary claims such as injunctions, declarations and claims for specific performance which are unsuitable for the small claims track and do not require the more complex treatment of the multi-track will also be dealt with on the fast track.

18.2 Allocation to the fast track

The fast track is the normal track for cases broadly falling into the £5,000 to £25,000 bracket, and which can be disposed of by a trial which will not exceed a day. The value criterion is a little more complicated than this broad position, and technically the following cases will normally be allocated to the fast track:

- personal injuries cases with a value between £5,000 and £25,000;
- personal injuries cases with an overall value under £5,000, but where the damages for pain, suffering, and loss of amenity are likely to exceed £1,000;
- claims by residential tenants for orders requiring their landlords to carry out repairs or other work to the premises where the value of the claim is between £1,000 and £25,000;

- claims by residential tenants for damages against their landlords for harassment or unlawful eviction where the value of the claim does not exceed £25,000; and

- other categories of cases, where the value of the claim is between £5,000 and £25,000.

18.3 Directions

When it allocates a case to the fast track, the court will send an allocation notice to the parties which will include case management directions given by the District Judge which set a timetable for the steps to be taken from that point through to trial. An example of a notice of allocation (in fact to the multi-track, but the fast track form is very similar) was illustrated in **Figure 7.5**. The directions given will be designed to ensure the issues are identified and the necessary evidence is prepared and disclosed. Usually the court will give directions of its own initiative without a hearing, but will take into account the respective statements of case, the allocation questionnaires, and any further information provided by the parties. If any direction or order is required that has not been provided for, it is the duty of the parties to make an application as soon as possible so as to avoid undue interference with the overall timetable: PD 28, para 2.8. If a directions hearing becomes necessary because of the default of any of the parties the court will usually impose a sanction: PD 28, para 2.3.

Figure 7.4 sets out the usual main provisions of fast track directions, together with typical periods for compliance. Each direction actually made will state a date (and time) by which it must be completed. Model form directions are set out in the Appendix to the Fast Track Practice Direction (PD 28), and provide for matters such as:

- service and filing of further statements of case, such as replies;
- requests for further information arising out of the statements of case;
- disclosure and inspection of documents;
- service of witness statements from witnesses as to fact;
- expert evidence, including instruction of experts, exchange of reports, and whether experts will be allowed at trial or whether their evidence should be admitted simply in the form of their reports;
- without prejudice meetings between experts;
- written questions put to experts for the purpose of clarifying their reports;
- requests for further information arising out of disclosure of documents, and the exchange of witness statements and experts' reports;
- filing of pre-trial checklists;
- trial bundles;
- trial.

Fast track directions will be tailored to the circumstances of each case. For example, if the parties have already given full disclosure of documents there will be no need for any directions dealing with this. It may be that the court takes the view that no expert evidence is required. Alternatively, it may be that the court decides that expert evidence is necessary, but that a single jointly instructed expert will suffice. Yet alternatively, it may decide that each party should be allowed to instruct their own experts on an issue, that there should be mutual exchange of experts' reports, and perhaps that there should be a without prejudice discussion between the experts to seek to narrow the expert issues. Further, the court may decide that the parties should be given an opportunity to put written questions to the experts in order to clarify technical points in the reports.

18.4 Time limits set out in the rules

In addition to the requirements of the express directions made by the court at the allocation stage, there are a number of time limits for taking procedural steps set out in the rules. These include time limits relating to service of hearsay notices under the Civil Evidence Act 1995, service of notices to admit, and the requirements relating to preparation of trial bundles. The result is that the specific directions given in a case are not the only time limits that have to be complied with. Details will obviously vary from case to case depending on the actual directions that have been made, but **Figure 18.1** sets out a chronology of typical events in a fast track case from issue of proceedings through to trial. It will be seen that the process may take less than 40 weeks, or about 10 months.

Week	Step in the proceedings	Time limit
1	(a) Issue of proceedings	Usual limitation period
	(b) Service (takes effect on second day after posting)	4 months from issue (6 months if outside the jurisdiction)
2	Acknowledgment of service or filing of defence	14 days after deemed service of the particulars of claim
(Say) 5	(a) Service of allocation questionnaires (may be dispensed with)	Not before all defendants have filed defences, or expiry of time for filing defences
7	(b) Possible transfer to defendant's home court	On filing defence
7	Return of allocation questionnaires	Not less than 14 days after service of the questionnaire
(Say) 9	Allocation decision and directions given by the procedural judge	After return of questionnaires
13	Disclosure of documents by lists	Usually 4 weeks after allocation
14	Inspection of documents	Usually 7 days after lists
19	(a) Exchange of witness statements	Usually 10 weeks after allocation
	(b) Service of hearsay notices	With witness statements
23	Experts' reports	Usually 14 weeks after allocation
29	Service of pre-trial checklists (may be dispensed with)	Usually 20 weeks after allocation
31	Return of pre-trial checklists	Usually 22 weeks after allocation
(Say) 33	(a) Any directions arising out of the pre-trial checklists	Optional
	(b) Hearing if pre-trial checklists not returned	Only if parties in default

Week	Step in the proceedings	Time limit
36	(a) Confirmation of trial date	3 weeks before trial
	(b) Service of notice to admit	21 days before trial
38	Lodging trial bundle	3 to 7 days before trial
39	Service and filing of statements of costs	Not less than 24 hours before the hearing
39	Trial	30 weeks after allocation

Figure 18.1   Progress of fast track case to trial

18.5   Experts in fast track claims

One of the powers available to the court is that of directing that the evidence on particular issues may be given by a single expert jointly instructed by the opposing parties: CPR, r 35.7. In order to keep down costs and to reduce the length of fast track trials, it will be usual for the court to make directions for the joint instruction of a single expert unless there is good reason for doing something else: PD 28, para 3.9(4). In addition, in fast track cases the court will not direct an expert to attend at trial unless it is necessary to do so in the interests of justice: CPR, r 35.5(2).

Normally expert evidence should be prepared and be ready for exchange about 14 weeks after the order giving directions: PD 28, para 3.12. However, there are a number of options, including:

(a) Sequential service of experts' reports. Normally it will be the claimant who will serve first.

(b) Simultaneous exchange of reports on some issues, with sequential service on the others.

(c) Holding of a discussion between experts in cases where the other side's reports cannot be agreed within a short time (usually 14 days) after service. This form of direction provides for a specified calendar date by which the discussion must take place, and the filing of a joint statement of the agreed issues and those in dispute (with reasons for the lack of agreement) by another specified date (which will often be close to the date for filing listing questionnaires).

(d) That expert evidence is not necessary and no party has permission to call or rely on expert evidence at the trial.

(e) That the parties may rely on experts' reports at trial, but cannot call oral expert evidence.

(f) That the parties may rely on expert reports, and the court will reconsider whether there is any need for experts to be called when the claim is listed for trial.

18.6   Pre-trial checklists

At least eight weeks before the trial date the parties must (unless dispensed with by the court) file pre-trial checklists at the court. An example is shown in **Figure 18.2**. These forms are similar to allocation questionnaires, and are designed to check whether the parties have complied with the directions made at the allocation stage and whether the case is ready for trial. At the same time the claimant must pay a non-returnable fee of £100, and a hearing fee of £500. The hearing fee is refundable in whole or part if the court is notified at least seven days before trial that the case has settled. Further, both parties must file statements of costs (see **Figure 7.2**).

18.7 Pre-trial directions

The court may hold a hearing under CPR, r 28.5(4), after which it will confirm the trial date and may give further directions. However, in most cases it will not feel the need to have such a hearing, and will simply confirm or alter the trial date as appropriate, and may make further directions. The court will give the parties at least three weeks' notice of the date of the trial unless, in exceptional circumstances, the court directs that shorter notice will be given: CPR, r 28.6(2).

18.7.1 Trial bundles

Standard pre-trial directions will provide that an indexed, paginated, bundle of documents contained in a ring binder must be lodged with the court not more than seven days or less than three days before the trial. The parties must seek to agree the contents of the trial bundle a reasonable time in advance, which in practical terms means no later than 14 days before the trial. Responsibility for lodging the bundle is that of the claimant. Lodging the bundle at court is required so that the trial judge can read the case papers in advance of the trial. Judges generally take a very dim view if the bundle is not lodged in time. Identical bundles will be needed for each of the parties, with an additional bundle for the witness box.

18.7.2 Case summary

Standard pre-trial directions give the procedural judge the option of directing that a case summary should be included in the trial bundle. This document should be no more than 250 words, and should outline the matters in issue, referring where appropriate to the relevant documents in the trial bundle. Again, responsibility for this rests with the claimant and, if possible, it should be agreed with the other side.

18.7.3 Trial timetable

The court may, if it considers that it is appropriate to do so, and in consultation with the parties, set a timetable for the trial. Setting a timetable is discretionary (CPR, r 28.6(1)(b)), but if it decides to do so, it must consult with the parties (CPR, r 39.4). The timetable contemplated is not the same as the directions timetable, but will define how much time the court will allow at trial for the various stages of the trial itself. A suitable direction may limit the time to be spent by each party in calling its evidence and in addressing the court in closing submissions. More sophisticated timetables will define how much time will be allowed for each witness, or even for cross-examination and re-examination.

Listing questionnaire
(Pre-trial checklist)

To be completed by, or on behalf of,

who is [1ˢᵗ][2ⁿᵈ][3ʳᵈ][   ][Claimant][Defendant]
[Part 20 claimant][Part 20 defendant] in this claim

In the	
Claim No.	
Last date for filing with court office	
Date(s) fixed for trial or trial period	

This form must be **completed** and **returned** to the court no later than the date given above. If not, your statement of case may be struck out or some other sanction imposed.	If the claim has settled, or settles before the trial date, you must let the court know immediately.	**Legal representatives only:** You must **attach** estimates of costs incurred to date, and of your likely overall costs. In substantial cases, these should be provided in compliance with CPR Part 43.	For multi-track claims only, you must also **attach** a proposed timetable for the trial itself.

A Confirmation of compliance with directions

1. I confirm that I have complied with those directions
   already given which require action by me.   ☐Yes ☐No

   If you are unable to give confirmation, state which directions you have
   still to comply with and the date by which this will be done.

Directions	Date

2. I believe that additional directions are necessary before the trial takes place. ☐Yes ☐No

   If Yes, you should attach an application and a draft order.

   *Include in your application all directions needed to enable the claim **to be tried on the date, or within the trial period, already fixed.** These should include any issues relating to experts and their evidence, and any orders needed in respect of directions still requiring action by any other party.*

3. Have you agreed the additional directions you are seeking with the
   other party(ies)?   ☐Yes ☐No

B Witnesses

1. How many witnesses (including yourself) will be giving evidence on
   your behalf at the trial? *(Do not include experts - see Section C)* ☐

Continued over ↵

Figure 18.2 Listing questionnaire

Witnesses continued

2. If the trial date is not yet fixed, are there any days within the trial period you or your witnesses would wish to avoid if possible? *(Do not include experts - see Section C)*

Please give details

Name of witness	Dates to be avoided, if possible	Reason

Please specify any special facilities or arrangements needed at court for the party or any witness (e.g. witness with a disability).

3. Will you be providing an interpreter for any of your witnesses?   ☐ Yes ☐ No

C Experts

You are reminded that you may not use an expert's report or have your expert give oral evidence unless the court has given permission. If you do not have permission, you must make an application (see section A2 above)

1. Please give the information requested for your expert(s)

Name	Field of expertise	Joint expert?	Is report agreed?	Has permission been given for oral evidence?
		☐ Yes ☐ No	☐ Yes ☐ No	☐ Yes ☐ No
		☐ Yes ☐ No	☐ Yes ☐ No	☐ Yes ☐ No
		☐ Yes ☐ No	☐ Yes ☐ No	☐ Yes ☐ No

2. Has there been discussion between experts?   ☐ Yes ☐ No

3. Have the experts signed a joint statement?   ☐ Yes ☐ No

4. If your expert is giving oral evidence and the trial date is not yet fixed, is there any day within the trial period which the expert would wish to avoid, if possible?   ☐ Yes ☐ No

If Yes, please give details

Name	Dates to be avoided, if possible	Reason

D Legal representation

1. Who will be presenting your case at the trial?　　　☐ You　☐ Solicitor　☐ Counsel

2. If the trial date is not yet fixed, is there any day within the trial
   period that the person presenting your case would wish to avoid,
   if possible?　　　☐ Yes　☐ No

   If Yes, please give details

Name	Dates to be avoided, if possible	Reason

E The trial

1. Has the estimate of the time needed for trial changed?　　　☐ Yes　☐ No

   If Yes, say how long you estimate the whole trial will take, including
   both parties' cross-examination and closing arguments　　　☐ days　☐ hours　☐ minutes

2. If different from original estimate have you agreed with the other
   party(ies) that this is now the **total** time needed?　　　☐ Yes　☐ No

3. Is the timetable for trial you have attached agreed with the
   other party(ies)?　　　☐ Yes　☐ No

Fast track cases only
The court will normally give you 3 weeks notice of the date fixed for a fast track trial unless, in
exceptional circumstances, the court directs that shorter notice will be given.

Would you be prepared to accept shorter notice of the date
fixed for trial?　　　☐ Yes　☐ No

F Document and fee checklist

Tick as appropriate

I attach to this questionnaire -

☐ An application and fee for additional directions　　　☐ A proposed timetable for trial

☐ A draft order　　　☐ An estimate of costs

☐ Listing fee

Signed	Please enter your [firm's] name, reference number and full postal address including (if appropriate) details of DX, fax or e-mail
[Counsel][Solicitor][for the][1ˢᵗ][2ⁿᵈ][3ʳᵈ][ ] [Claimant][Defendant] [Part 20 claimant][Part 20 defendant]	
Date	Postcode

Tel. no.		DX no.		E-mail	
Fax no.		Ref. no.			

18.8   Failing to pay the pre-trial fee

If the claimant fails to pay the fees payable with the pre-trial checklist the court will serve a notice (Form N173) on the claimant requiring payment within a stated period of time, failing which the claim will be struck out. If the claim is struck out for non-payment the claimant is also required to pay the defendant's costs, unless the court otherwise orders (CPR, r 3.7). Once the claim has been struck out the court retains a power to reinstate it (CPR, r 3.7(7)), and on such an application the court will apply the criteria set out in r 3.9 relating to applications for relief from sanctions (see **Chapter 28**). However, any order for reinstatement will be made conditional on the fee being paid within two days of the order.

18.9   Varying the directions timetable

The parties may agree to vary the timetables set by the court at the allocation and pre-trial checklist stages (or at other times). However, they cannot between themselves agree to change the dates for returning allocation questionnaires, pre-trial checklists or the trial: CPR, rr 26.3(6A) and 28.4(2). If a party cannot complete the necessary preparation in time, or if there are other difficulties, it is possible to make an application to break the trial date.

PD 28, para 5, makes it clear that variations involving loss of the trial date on account of any failure to comply with case management directions will be considered matters of last resort. However, it is recognised there will be cases where it will become necessary to vary the date for trial. Examples include cases where there are significant problems with the evidence, where there is a change of solicitor, where proceedings are issued at the very end of the limitation period, and in personal injuries cases where the prognosis is uncertain. Any necessary postponement will be for the shortest possible time, and the court will give directions for taking the necessary steps outstanding as rapidly as possible. In some of these cases the best course may be to have split trials of liability and quantum, or to proceed only on those issues that are ready. Where this happens the court may disallow the costs of the remaining issues, or order them to be paid by the party in default in any event.

18.10   Fast track trials

Trials will usually take place in the County Court where they are proceeding, but may take place in a Civil Trial Centre or any other court if it is appropriate because of listing difficulties, the needs of the parties, or for other reasons. The judge (who will often be a District Judge) will generally have read the trial bundle and may well dispense with opening speeches. Unless the trial judge otherwise directs, the trial will be conducted in accordance with any order previously made laying down a trial timetable (see **18.7.3** above). This means the judge is free to set a different trial timetable: PD 28, para 8.3. Given the time constraints and the need for proportionality, it is likely the trial judge will exercise the power (see **Chapter 30**) to order witness statements to stand as their evidence in chief, and otherwise control the evidence to be presented. If a trial is not concluded on the day it is listed, the judge will normally sit on the following day to complete it: PD 28, para 8.6.

18.11 Fast track costs

The normal rule is that costs in fast track cases will be dealt with by the trial judge by way of summary assessment at the end of the trial. This means that the judge will decide there and then how much the loser will have to pay towards the winner's costs of the entire proceedings. To assist with this process, each party is required to file and serve a statement of costs (see **Figure 7.2**) at least 24 hours before the hearing.

There are also rules on fixed trial costs for fast track cases. The basic rules for trial costs (ie the costs of the day of the trial, which are in addition to the general costs of the claim, discussed in the previous paragraph) provide that advocates' fees in fast track cases are:

Awards up to £3,000	£485
Awards between £3,000 and £10,000	£690
Claims for non-money remedies	£690
Awards over £10,000 and up to £15,000	£1,035
Awards over £15,000	£1,650
Additional fee for solicitor attending trial with counsel	£345

For the purpose of quantifying the amount of the claim, for a successful claimant it is the amount of the judgment excluding interests, costs and any reduction for contributory negligence, whereas for a successful defendant it is the amount the claimant specified on the claim form (or the maximum amount that could have been recovered on the pleaded case): CPR, r 46.2(3). If there is a counterclaim and both parties succeed, the relevant amount is the difference (if any) between the trial costs recoverable given the value of the two claims: r 46.3(6). If there is a counterclaim with a greater value than the claim, and the claimant succeeds on the claim and defeats the counterclaim, the relevant amount is the value of the counterclaim: r 46.2(6). There are detailed rules dealing with cases where there are several claimants or several defendants, including whether more than one party can be awarded fast track trial costs, which are set out in r 46.4. For claims for non-monetary remedies the court has a discretion to make some other order: r 46.2(4).

The additional allowance for a solicitor attending with counsel is provided by r 46.3. The solicitor's attendance fee will only be payable if the court awards fast track trial costs and if the court considers that it was necessary for a legal representative to attend to assist counsel: r 46.3(2).

If a fast track claim settles before the start of the trial, costs may be allowed in respect of the advocate preparing for trial, but the amount allowed cannot be more than the above figures: r 44.10. In deciding the amount to be allowed for the abortive preparation, the court will take into account when the claim was settled and when the court was notified of that fact.

If there are split trials, such as on liability and quantum, it is possible to be awarded a second tranche of fast track trial costs, but the second award should not exceed two-thirds of the amount payable under the first award, subject to a minimum award of £485: r 46.3(3), (4).

A successful party may, by r 46.3(7), be awarded less than the above fixed fast track trial costs for unreasonable or improper behaviour during the trial, and the losing party may be ordered to pay an additional amount if it is guilty of behaving improperly during the trial: r 46.3(8).

Multi-track

19.1 Introduction

The multi-track is intended for the more complex and important cases. However, there will be a great variety of cases on this track, and efficient case management dictates that they will have to be dealt with in different ways dependent on each case's own particular circumstances. In fact, any case not allocated to either the small claims track or fast track will be dealt with on the multi-track, and so will any case commenced using the alternative procedure in the Civil Procedure Rules 1998, Part 8, and most specialist proceedings. Cases on the multi-track will range from simple contractual disputes involving just over the £25,000 threshold, through to complex commercial cases involving difficult issues of fact and law with values of several million pounds. Case management on the multi-track is intended to reflect this. Simpler cases should be given standard directions not very different from those given in fast track cases without the need for hearings, and the parties will be expected to comply with those directions without complicating or delaying matters. At the other end of the scale, the courts will adopt a far more active approach, possibly with several directions hearings in the form of case management conferences and pre-trial reviews. The courts are expected to adopt a flexible approach to ensure that each case is dealt with in an appropriate way.

19.2 Directions on allocation

As already mentioned earlier in the manual, when a case is allocated to the multi-track the court will send the parties a notice telling them of the allocation decision. An example of such a notice was illustrated at **Figure 7.5**. At the same time as allocating the case the procedural judge will decide whether to give directions or to fix a case management conference or pre-trial review (or both a case management conference and a pre-trial review and such other directions as are thought fit). The court will seek to make directions suitable to the needs of the case, and the steps the parties have already taken to prepare it for trial. It will also take into account the extent to which the parties have complied with any pre-action protocol (see **Chapter 2**). The court's concern will be to ensure the issues between the parties are identified, and that the evidence required for the trial is prepared and disclosed.

Similar things will be dealt with in multi-track directions as are dealt with in fast track cases. They will deal with disclosure of documents, exchange of witness statements, expert evidence, and arrangements for trial. However, because many multi-track cases are rather complex it is recognised that the time required for each step may be considerably longer than that allowed in fast track claims. Moreover, difficulties encountered at any of the stages, such as disclosure of documents, may impact the subsequent stages. It is for this reason that allocation directions may be quite limited, and why directions hearings in the form of case management conferences and pre-trial reviews are often held in multi-track cases.

19.2.1 Inadequate information

There will be cases allocated to the multi-track where the parties provide little or no information other than that contained in their statements of case. In such cases the court could call a case management conference, and it could order the parties to provide further information, with sanctions in default. However, it is perhaps more likely that it will simply impose directions giving a tight timetable for trial: PD 29, para 4.10. Doing so will put enormous pressure on the parties. They will either have to comply, or will find themselves in considerable difficulty unless they apply promptly for tailored directions. This is because the court will assume for the purposes of any later application (in the absence of any appeal or application within 14 days to vary) that the parties were content that the directions were correct in the circumstances then existing: PD 29, para 6.2(2).

The general approach in these cases where there is inadequate information is for directions along the following lines to be made by the court of its own initiative:

(a) filing and service of any further information required to clarify either party's case;

(b) standard disclosure (for further details on which, see **Chapter 20**) between the parties;

(c) simultaneous exchange of witness statements;

(d) for the appointment of a single expert unless there is good reason for not doing so;

(e) simultaneous exchange of experts' reports in cases or on issues where single expert directions have not been given (unless expert evidence is required on both liability and quantum, in which event the direction may be for simultaneous exchange on the liability issues, but sequential exchange on quantum issues);

(f) if experts' reports are not agreed, that there be a discussion between the experts for the purpose of identifying the expert evidence issues, and, if possible, reaching agreement between the experts, and the preparation of a statement setting out the issues on which they are agreed and a summary of their reasons on the issues where they disagree;

(g) listing a case management conference after the final date in the above directions;

(h) specifying a trial period; and

(i) for the parties to consider ADR.

19.2.2 Agreed directions

If the parties in a case likely to be allocated to the multi-track agree proposals for the management of the case and the court considers that the proposals are suitable, the court may simply approve them without the need for a directions hearing: PD 29, paras 4.6, 4.7. This is encouraged by the Civil Procedure Rules 1998, as it obviously saves costs and court time. In order to obtain the court's approval the agreed directions must:

(a) if appropriate, include a direction regarding the filing of a reply;

(b) if appropriate, provide for amending any statement of case;

(c) include provision about the disclosure of documents;

(d) include provision about both factual and expert evidence (the provision about expert evidence may be to the effect that no expert evidence is required);

(e) if appropriate, include dates for service of requests for further information and/or questions to experts, and when they should be answered;

(f) include a date or a period when it is proposed the trial will take place; and

(g) if appropriate, a date for a case management conference.

It will be seen that only items (c), (d) and (f) are obligatory in all cases, although the others will frequently arise in practice. Proposed agreed directions must lay down a timetable by reference to calendar dates. The court will scrutinise the timetable carefully, with particular attention to the proposals for the trial and case management conference, and will be astute to ensure these are no later than is reasonably necessary.

The provision in any agreed directions relating to disclosure may:

(a) limit disclosure to standard disclosure, or less than that; and/or

(b) direct that disclosure will take place by the supply of copy documents without a list of documents, but if so, it must say either that the parties must serve a disclosure statement with the copies, or that they have agreed to disclose in this way without a disclosure statement.

The provision regarding factual and expert evidence should, if appropriate, deal with:

- whether the evidence should be disclosed simultaneously or sequentially;
- the use of a single expert; and
- without prejudice discussions between the experts if a single expert is not going to be instructed.

The court is free to reject directions that have been agreed between the parties, but will take them into account when making its own directions (either without a hearing or on a case management conference).

19.3 Case management conferences

Case management conferences are an integral part of the system of active case management by the courts. They are not simply directions hearings, but are intended to ensure that the real issues between the parties are identified. Side issues will be dispensed with either by agreement between the parties with due encouragement from the judge, or by means of summary or striking out determinations at an early stage. Case management conferences may be held immediately after a case is allocated to the multi-track or at any time thereafter through to the listing stage. They can be used as the vehicle for laying down directions at the allocation stage, or may be used later in order to assess how the case is progressing when the initial directions on allocation should have been completed. Normally the court has a discretion whether to call a case management conference. However, where it is contemplated that an order may be made either for the evidence on a particular issue to be given by a single expert, or that an assessor should be appointed, PD 29, para 4.13, provides that a case management conference must be held unless the parties have consented to the order in writing.

Case management conferences will also be called in cases where the court feels it cannot properly give directions on its own initiative, and where no agreed directions have been filed which it feels can be approved: PD 29, para 4.12.

By encouraging the parties to settle their dispute or resolve it outside the court system, and by forcing the parties into identifying the real issues at an early stage, case management conferences are intended to be a means of using court time to save more time.

19.3.1 Listing of case management conferences

The minimum period of notice the court will give to the parties of the date for the case management conference is three clear days: CPR, r 3.3(3) and PD 29, para 3.7.

19.3.2 Attendance at case management conferences

If a party has a legal representative, someone familiar with the case must attend the case management conference: CPR, r 29.3(2). The person attending will have to be the fee-earner concerned, or someone (possibly counsel) who is fully familiar with the file, the issues, and the proposed evidence. They must be able to field the questions that are likely to be covered at the hearing, and have the authority to agree and/or make representations on the matters reasonably to be expected to arise. Where the inadequacy of the person attending or his instructions leads to the adjournment of the hearing, it will be normal for a wasted costs order to be made: PD 29, para 5.2(3).

In the ChD, whenever possible the advocates instructed or expected to appear at trial should attend case management conferences and other case management hearings: Chancery Guide, para 3.7. In the Commercial Court, case management conferences should be attended on behalf of each party both by the fee earner with conduct of the case and by at least one of the advocates retained (Commercial Court Guide, para D8.2). This is because case management conferences in the Commercial Court are regarded as particularly significant stages in the litigation, and are conducted by a judge who will usually form part of the two-judge team that will manage the case, one of whom will usually subsequently be the trial judge: paras D4.1 and D4.2.

19.3.3 Issues to be dealt with at case management conferences

At a case management conference the court will:

- make a thorough review of the steps the parties have taken to date in preparing the case for trial;
- consider the extent to which they have complied with any previous orders and directions;
- decide on the directions needed to progress the action in accordance with the overriding objective;
- ensure that reasonable agreements are made between the parties about the matters in issue and the future conduct of the action; and
- record all such agreements.

To assist the court the legal representatives for all parties should ensure that all documents (and in particular witness statements and expert reports) the court is likely to ask to see are brought to court. They should also consider whether the parties themselves should attend, and consider in advance what orders and directions may be appropriate.

19.3.4 Control of evidence

The CPR, r 32.1, provides that the court may control the evidence to be adduced in the course of proceedings, which may involve excluding evidence that would otherwise be admissible, by giving directions as to:

- the issues on which it requires evidence;
- the nature of the evidence which it requires to decide those issues; and
- the way in which the evidence is to be placed before the court.

This power is exercised in accordance with the overriding objective. It has a particular relevance regarding expert evidence, which is often expensive and time intensive. The power may be used to save expense, to ensure cases are dealt with proportionately, and to ensure that the real issues are addressed at trial.

The court can use its power to control evidence to prevent the parties calling unnecessary expert evidence at trial. This is particularly important, because professional experts are entitled to charge fees at commercial rates for the time they are engaged on a case, and these can often run to well over £1,000 per day. It has been held that apparently one-sided expert directions are permissible if they accord with the overriding objective. Thus, in *Baron v Lovell* [1999] CPLR 630, CA, the court felt there was not a great deal of difference between the two sides' medical reports, and directed that the medical evidence be limited to the claimant's medical reports. It is becoming increasingly common in fast track cases where the injuries are not too severe for directions to be made for the medical evidence to be restricted to the report served by the claimant with the particulars of claim. This is not restricted to personal injuries claims. In *Thermos Ltd v Aladdin Sales and Marketing Ltd* The Independent, 13 December 1999, the judge held that expert evidence was unnecessary in many claims concerning the alleged infringement of registered designs for consumer articles.

The power under r 32.1 could be used to exclude evidence obtained by unlawful means, but covert video evidence obtained in breach of art 8 of the European Convention on Human Rights and by trespassing inside the claimant's home was admitted in *Jones v University of Warwick* [2003] 1 WLR 954.

19.3.5 Plans, photographs and models

Where a party intends to use photographs, plans, models and similar items as evidence at trial, then generally notice should be given to the other parties by the date for disclosing witness statements (CPR, r 33.6(4)).

19.3.6 Video evidence

Provided it is relevant, video evidence is generally admissible. A party may wish to use video evidence to illustrate a manufacturing process, or the scene of an accident (although photographs will usually be sufficient, and are far simpler to handle in court).

Rather more striking are surveillance videos used from time to time in personal injuries claims to test whether the claimant is as badly injured as is claimed. As video recordings fall into the wide definition of 'documents' for the purposes of CPR, Part 31, the usual rules on disclosure and inspection apply (see **Chapter 20**). Furthermore, there is an obligation to inform the court at the first opportunity that such evidence will be relied upon, as arrangements need to be made to ensure video equipment is available at trial, and extra time will be required at the trial for showing the evidence (*Rall v Hume* [2001] 3 All ER 248).

Use of videos at trial takes two forms. They can be used as part of a party's affirmative case. In this event the video tapes may need to be played in their entirety. Alternatively, a party may wish to use a video tape in cross-examination of the opposing party by playing certain parts of the video for comment by the witness being cross-examined in order to undermine the witness. Such use will usually be legitimate, even if an application for such use is made quite close to the trial date. However, a direction is likely to be made limiting the footage to be shown (in *Rall v Hume* a direction was made limited to 20 minutes).

19.4 Interim applications in multi-track cases

In multi-track cases the appropriate time to consider most forms of interim relief, if possible, is the first case management conference. PD 29, para 3.8, says that applications in multi-track cases must be made as early as possible so as to minimise the need to change the directions timetable, and that an application to vary a directions timetable laid down by the court (perhaps on its own initiative) must ordinarily be made within 14 days of service of the directions (para 6.2). If at all possible any applications contemplated by the parties should be issued in time to be heard at any case management conference fixed for the case.

19.5 Case summary

There will be occasions when the court will be assisted by a written case summary. This should be a short document not exceeding 500 words which is designed to assist the court in understanding and dealing with the issues raised in the case. It should give a brief chronology of the claim, state the factual issues that are agreed and those in dispute, and the nature of the evidence needed to decide them. Responsibility for preparing the document rests with the claimant, and if possible it should be agreed by the other parties.

19.6 Fixing the date for trial

The court will fix the trial date or the period in which the trial is to take place as soon as practicable: CPR, r 29.2(2). This may be possible when it gives allocation directions, but in complex cases this may have to be delayed, perhaps for a considerable period of time. Where fixing the trial date is postponed, it may be revisited either at a later case management conference, or on the application of the parties, or after further scrutiny by the court.

19.7 Pre-trial checklists

Directions will tell the parties when they must file their pre-trial checklists. These may be dispensed with. Pre-trial checklists will be sent out to the parties by the court for completion and return by the date specified in the directions given when the court fixed the date or period for trial: CPR, r 29.6. The specified date should be not less than eight weeks before the trial date or 'window': PD 29, para 8.1(3). The forms should be served by the court at least 14 days before they must be returned. Each party is under an obligation to return a completed pre-trial checklist before the specified date, and the claimant is required to pay a non-refundable fee of £100 and a hearing fee of £1,000. These fees are payable even if pre-trial checklists are dispensed with. The hearing fee is refundable in whole or part if the court is notified at least seven days before trial that the case has settled. There is a possible sanction of automatic striking out for non-payment after a reminder from the court: CPR, r 3.7. Further, both parties must file statements of costs (see **Figure 7.2**).

19.7.1   Purpose of pre-trial checklists

Pre-trial checklists are used to check that earlier orders and directions have been complied with, and to provide up-to-date information to assist the court with deciding when to hold the trial and how long it will take, and in making trial timetable directions. Once all the pre-trial checklists have been received, or the time limit has expired, the file will be placed before the procedural judge, who will make directions for trial, or direct that there should be a hearing under CPR, r 29.6(3) or pre-trial review.

19.7.2   Exchange of pre-trial checklists

The Civil Procedure Rules 1998 do not require the parties to exchange copies of their pre-trial checklists but doing so may avoid the parties giving conflicting or incomplete information to the court: PD 29, para 8.1(5). Getting this right may avoid the court feeling there is a need for a hearing under r 29.6(3) or pre-trial review.

19.7.3   Failure to file pre-trial checklists

If no one returns a pre-trial checklist by the specified date the court will usually make an order that the parties must do so within seven days of service of the order, failing which the claim and any counterclaim will be struck out: r 29.6(3). Where only some of the parties file pre-trial checklists, the court may fix a hearing under CPR, r 29.6(4). It may also fix a hearing under r 29.6(4) if any of the pre-trial checklists do not provide the necessary information, or if the court considers that such a hearing is necessary to decide what further directions should be given to complete the preparations for trial.

19.7.4   Hearings under rule 29.6(4)

Hearings under CPR, r 29.6(4), concentrate on making the decisions relevant to fixing the date of the trial. They are fixed for dates as early as possible, and the parties are given at least three clear days' notice of the date. Even if such a hearing is fixed because some of the parties did not file their pre-trial checklists, the court will normally fix or confirm the trial date and make orders about the steps to prepare the case for trial: PD 29, para 8.3(2). The court is likely to make further directions similar to those set out in **19.8.3** below.

The court is primarily concerned with whether the parties are, or soon will be, ready for trial, and with identifying the most convenient trial date or window given the constraints on court time and the availability of witnesses. It is not enough for a legal representative to attend with a list of dates to avoid: the court may question the reasons why experts and witnesses are said to be unable to attend, and if reasons are not given or are found to be inadequate, the court may proceed to fix the trial for the earliest free date: *Matthews v Tarmac Bricks and Tiles Ltd* [1999] CPLR 463, CA.

19.7.5   Listing in the Royal Courts of Justice

In non-specialist cases in the QBD and ChD proceeding in the Royal Courts of Justice in London, a direction will be given as early as possible (often the first case management conference) with a view to fixing the trial or trial window. It will often direct that the trial is not to begin before a specified date, or that it will be held within a specified period. The claimant must then, within the next seven days, take out an appointment with the Listing Officer and give notice of the appointment to the other parties. At the listing hearing the claimant must bring any case summary, the Particulars of Claim and any orders relevant to listing, and all parties must have details of the dates of availability of their witnesses, experts and counsel. The Listing Officer will try to provide the earliest firm trial date or trial window consistent with the case management directions.

19.8   Pre-trial review

If a pre-trial review is listed it is likely to take place about 8 to 10 weeks before trial. The purpose of a pre-trial review is to settle a statement of the issues to be tried, and to set a programme and budget for the trial. The pre-trial review gives the court a further opportunity to check the parties have complied with earlier orders and directions, and may help in promoting settlement. They are not held in all cases, but only in those that merit the additional hearing. The intention is that they should be conducted by the eventual trial judge.

19.8.1   Notice of pre-trial review

The fact there should be a pre-trial review may be set out in earlier directions made by the court of its own initiative or on a case management conference. The court may make the decision to hold a pre-trial review, or may actually fix the pre-trial review at a later stage, in which event it will give the parties at least seven clear days' notice of the hearing: CPR, r 29.7.

19.8.2   Attendance

The same rules about a fully informed representative being present apply to pre-trial reviews as apply to case management conferences. However, because the court may well use the hearing to decide a trial timetable it will often be advisable for trial counsel to attend.

19.8.3   Pre-trial review directions

The court will not readily go behind earlier directions, and will apply the same principles as are applied generally when the parties fail to comply with case management directions: PD 29, para 9.3.

Perhaps the most important task on a pre-trial review is to determine the timetable for the trial itself. This can lay down time limits for examination and cross-examination of witnesses, and for speeches. Doing this is intended to force advocates to focus their preparation, and to produce better managed trials. Other matters to be dealt with are:

(a) Evidence, particularly expert evidence. At this stage there should have been full disclosure and perhaps also discussions between the experts. It may be possible to make more rigorous directions about which experts really do need to be called at the trial, and which experts (or which parts of the expert evidence) can be taken from the experts' reports.

(b) A time estimate for the trial.

(c) Preparation of trial bundles.

(d) Fixing a trial date or week.

(e) Fixing the place of trial. This will normally be the court where the case is being managed, but it may be transferred depending on the convenience of the parties and the availability of court resources: PD 29, para 10.1.

19.8.4 Agreed pre-trial review directions

The parties are required to seek to agree the directions to be made on the pre-trial review, and may file an agreed order. The court may then make an order in the terms agreed, or make some other order, or reject the proposals and continue with the pre-trial review.

19.9 Variation of case management timetable

The parties may vary the timetable by consent provided doing so does not make it necessary to vary the dates for the return of allocation questionnaires, any case management conference, pre-trial review, return of pre-trial checklists or of the trial. Otherwise, any variation is only with the court's permission: CPR, r 29.5. As in fast track cases (see **18.9**), the courts are very reluctant to vacate trial dates if the only reason is that one of the parties has failed to keep to the directions timetable.

19.10 Trial

This will be considered further in **Chapter 33**.

Disclosure of documents

20.1 Introduction

20.1.1 What is disclosure?

Disclosure is the process whereby a party to a claim is obliged to disclose to the other party the existence of all documents which are or have been in his or her control which are material to the issues in the proceedings. Initially, disclosure is given by an exchange of lists of documents, and this should take place after allocation to the fast or multi-track. The other party is then entitled to inspect and take copies of the documents disclosed, except any document which is privileged.

20.1.2 Importance of disclosure

It may appear that the preparation of lists of documents is a routine and tedious step in a claim. However, many cases are lost or won by documents which are disclosed during this process, and effective use of the entitlement to disclosure can be one of the most powerful weapons in the litigant's armoury. Failure to make full or sufficient disclosure may lead to penalties in terms of adjournments and costs, and a court may draw adverse inferences as to the credit of a party failing to provide proper disclosure.

The importance of disclosure and the duties of practitioners and their clients with regard to disclosure cannot be over-emphasised. Counsel should remind both solicitors and their lay clients of their duties to ensure disclosure is properly undertaken. Indeed, it is advisable for a solicitor to begin the process of disclosure as early as possible. It is the duty of a solicitor to ensure that material documents are preserved. Further, the obligation upon parties to litigation is a continuing one. Thus, documents coming into existence or which came to the party's notice after the service of a list of documents must also be disclosed: CPR, r 31.11.

20.2 Disclosure by lists

The parties to fast track and multi-track proceedings are obliged to disclose to each other all the documents in their control that relate to the proceedings. This obligation covers not only documents that support the party making the list, but extends to documents that adversely affect that party, and which they would prefer to keep secret. Many litigants find it hard to believe that they are obliged to let their opponents see documents of this nature. However, lawyers are under professional duties to advise their clients on the scope of their obligations regarding the disclosure of documents, and cannot continue acting for clients who refuse to comply. As we saw in **Chapter 17**, the same does not apply in small claims track cases, where the obligation is simply to disclose the documents each party intends to rely upon.

Disclosure will usually (but not always; see *Smithkline Beecham plc v Generics (UK) Ltd* [2004] 1 WLR 1479) be made by serving lists of documents (see the example in **Figure 20.1**). As the name suggests, this is a document simply listing the documents that a party has relating to the case. A list must identify the documents in a convenient order and as concisely as possible. It must indicate which documents are said to be privileged (see **20.5** below), and which documents are no longer available and what has happened to them. Further, the list must contain a disclosure statement (see **20.4.5** below) unless this has been dispensed with (by the court or by agreement in writing between the parties).

However, the court may make directions requiring disclosure but dispensing with lists, or for disclosure to take place in stages, and the parties may agree to disclosure taking place in a similar informal, or staged, manner. For example, CPR, r 31.10(8), provides:

The parties may agree in writing—

> *(a) to disclose documents without making a list; and*
> *(b) to disclose documents without the disclosing party making a disclosure statement.*

20.3 Stage when disclosure takes place

Generally, directions made at the allocation stage or at a case management conference will include provision for disclosure and inspection of documents. The direction will state whether lists should be provided, and whether a disclosure statement is required (see below). It will also give a calendar date for the last day for compliance. Allocation takes place within a few weeks of the filing of defences, and disclosure is normally ordered for a few weeks thereafter. The result is that disclosure is often required about two months after the defence is filed.

As was seen in **Chapter 2**, a great proportion of the documents that might be disclosed during proceedings will be disclosed in compliance with the pre-action protocols. If full disclosure has taken place in this way, the court should be informed with the allocation questionnaires so the directions made on allocation reflect the correct position.

20.4 Documents required to be disclosed

The meaning of 'documents' is not restricted to paper writings, but extends to anything upon which evidence or information is recorded: CPR, r 31.4. Thus, recordings (whether audio, digital or video and including surveillance tapes) are disclosable.

Electronic documents, including e-mails, messages on mobile telephones, word processed documents and databases, are included in the definition. It also covers documents that are stored on servers and backup systems and electronic documents that have been 'deleted', and additional information stored and associated with electronic documents known as metadata (PD 31, para. 2A.1).

20.4.1 Documents in a party's control

Disclosure must be made of documents which are, or have been, in a party's control. 'Control' is defined as covering documents which are or have been in a party's physical possession, and also where a party had a right to possession or to inspect or take copies: CPR, r 31.8.

For example, a bailee or agent has physical possession of documents entrusted to him or her on behalf of the owner. An employer or principal has a right to possession of documents in the hands of an employee in the course of the employee's employment or an agent in the course of the agency. It is a question of fact whether the documents of a subsidiary are within the power of its parent company.

Documents to be disclosed are not limited to those which are within the jurisdiction (ie England and Wales). If a material document outside the jurisdiction is in a party's power, it must be disclosed (however, this rule does not apply to *Norwich Pharmacal* orders (**21.2**): *Mackinnon v Donaldson Lufkin and Jenrette Securities Corp* [1986] Ch 482).

20.4.2 Standard disclosure

An order to give disclosure is an order to give standard disclosure unless the court directs otherwise: CPR, r 31.5. The court may dispense with or limit standard disclosure. Further, the parties may agree in writing to dispense with or to limit standard disclosure. The nature of the documents that must be disclosed under standard disclosure is described by CPR, r 31.6, which provides:

Standard disclosure requires a party to disclose only—

(a) the documents on which he relies; and

(b) the documents which—

 (i) adversely affect his own case;

 (ii) adversely affect another party's case; or

 (iii) support another party's case; and

(c) the documents which he is required to disclose by a relevant practice direction.

Determining whether a document falls into sub-paras (a) or (b) is judged against the statements of case (*Paddick v Associated Newspapers Ltd* (2003) LTL 12/12/2003). In addition to disclosing documents relied upon, it can be seen that adverse documents must also be disclosed. There is a further obligation to disclose the documents which may be specified by a relevant Practice Direction. At the moment this does not take us much further, because there is no relevant Practice Direction.

Under the old, pre-1999, system discovery had to be given of documents falling into four categories, as explained by Brett LJ in *Compagnie Financiere et Commerciale du Pacifique v Peruvian Guano Co* (1882) 11 QBD 55. These were:

(a) documents that would be evidence upon any issue in the case;

(b) documents that would advance the case of the party seeking discovery;

(c) documents that would damage the case of the party giving discovery; and

(d) documents which could fairly lead to a train of inquiry which might have either of the consequences in (b) or (c).

Standard disclosure in accordance with CPR, r 31.6, is narrower than the old test in that it does not include train of inquiry documents.

20.4.3   Examples of disclosable documents

(a) In a claim concerning the satisfactory quality or fitness for purpose of a set of garage doors supplied by Closs Ltd, which Closs Ltd attempted to repair following their supply, the following documents, among others, would be required to be disclosed:

    (i)   All notes and plans relating to the construction of the doors.

    (ii)   All notes and reports relating to the repair of the doors.

    (iii) All communications, including notes and plans, between Closs Ltd and its subcontractors or any independent surveyor.

(b) In a claim for misrepresentation by Zipp Ltd, following its purchase of a business together with goodwill from Shady Ltd on the basis that the annual turnover was misrepresented, the following documents, amongst others, would be required to be disclosed:

    (i)   The past accounts of Shady Ltd for the business.

    (ii)   Accountant's or other reports prepared for Shady Ltd before the sale, projecting future growth.

(c) In a personal injuries claim the claimant may be required to disclose all his past hospital records and general practitioner's notes. This is so almost regardless of the nature of the dispute. The records will either confirm the claimant's injuries and their consequences, or will question those injuries or their extent, and will therefore support either the claimant's or defendant's case (*OCS Group Ltd v Wells* [2008] PIQR P18). Such documents are in the claimant's control by virtue of the Data Protection Act 1998 (see **21.3.9**) or by a simple consent to their release. However, there may be a question whether the requirement to give disclosure of this nature infringes art 8(1) of the European Convention on Human Rights.

(d) Where there was a dispute as to whether a contractual document was sent by e-mail, disclosure was ordered of the relevant hard disks, backups and server (*Marlton v Tektronix UK Holdings Ltd* (2003) LTL 10/2/2003).

20.4.4   Duty to search

When giving standard disclosure, a party is required to make a reasonable search for documents falling within the meaning of standard disclosure. The CPR, r 31.7(2), provides:

> *(2) The factors relevant in deciding the reasonableness of a search include the following—*
>   *(a)   the number of documents involved;*
>   *(b)   the nature and complexity of the proceedings;*
>   *(c)   the ease and expense of retrieval of any particular document; and*
>   *(d)   the significance of any document which is likely to be located during the search.*

The rule does not demand that no stone be left unturned (*Abela v Hammonds Suddards* (2008) LTL 9/12/2008). A wider search is likely to be necessary for primary evidence (going to the issues in the case) than for secondary evidence (which is merely an aid to assessing the primary evidence) (*Nichia Corporation v Argos Ltd* [2007] Bus LR 1753). Initially it is for the solicitor responsible for the disclosure process for each party to decide what constitutes a reasonable search (PD 31, para 2). Transparency where a limited search has been conducted is dealt with by r 31.7(3):

> *(3) Where a party has not searched for a category or class of document on the grounds that to do so would be unreasonable, he must state this in his disclosure statement and identify the category or class of document.*

A court asked to adjudicate on whether the search was sufficiently thorough has to decide whether the search was in fact reasonable (*Nichia Corporation v Argos*).

20.4.5 Disclosure statement

A list of documents must contain a 'disclosure statement' setting out the extent of the search that has been made and certifying the party understands the duty to disclose and that to the best of the disclosing party's knowledge the duty has been carried out. It must be signed by the client, not the solicitor. Where there are several defendants, each must sign (*Arrow Trading and Investments Est Ltd v Edwardian Group Ltd* [2005] 1 BCLC 696). Where a party has not searched for a category or class of document on the grounds that to do so would be unreasonable, this must be stated in the disclosure statement and the categories or classes of document not searched for must be identified. An example of a disclosure statement can be seen in **Figure 20.1**. Making a false disclosure statement, without an honest belief in its truth, may be punished as a contempt of court: CPR, r 31.23.

20.4.6 Duty of the solicitor to ensure full disclosure is made

It is the duty of a solicitor to ensure that the client does provide full disclosure as required by the rules. The duty is an active one. The client must be advised as to the requirements of disclosure and the solicitor must ensure (so far as possible) that the originals of all disclosable documents are preserved and made available for disclosure to the other side.

20.5 Privilege

Some classes of documents, although they must be disclosed (ie included in the list of documents), are nevertheless privileged from production and inspection (for further reading see *Evidence* manual). There are four main categories of privileged documents:

- documents protected by legal professional privilege;
- documents tending to criminate or expose to forfeiture the party who would disclose them;
- documents protected on the grounds of public policy; and
- without prejudice communications.

The burden of proof in a disputed claim for privilege rests on the person asserting the privilege (*Akzo Nobel Chemicals Ltd v Commission of the European Communities (cases T-125 and T-253/03)* [2008] Bus LR 348).

20.5.1 Legal professional privilege

Legal professional privilege protects the right of a person to obtain skilled advice about the law without the fear that what is discussed might be used against them at a later stage. It is a fundamental human right long established at common law, buttressed by art 8 of the European Convention on Human Rights, and forms part of Community law (*R (Morgan Grenfell and Co Ltd) v Special Commissioner of Income Tax* [2003] 1 AC 563).

This category may be divided into two classes, namely:

- Those that are privileged whether or not litigation was contemplated or pending.
- Those that are privileged only if litigation was contemplated or pending when they were made or when they came into existence.

20.5.1.1   **Privilege although no litigation pending**

Communications between a party and his or her solicitors are privileged from production, provided that they are confidential and written to or by the solicitor in a professional capacity and for the purpose of getting legal advice or assistance for the client, but not otherwise. Who the 'client' is may be obvious in the case of individuals, but in the case of corporations it will be restricted to those individuals who have been authorised by the corporation to retain the solicitors (*Three Rivers District Council v Governor and Company of the Bank of England (No. 5)* [2003] QB 1556). 'Legal advice' covers advising the client on the law and also advising the client on what should prudently be done in the relevant legal context (*Balabel v Air India* [1988] Ch 317). According to Lord Scott of Foscote in *Three Rivers District Council v Governor and Company of the Bank of England (No. 6)* [2005] 1 AC 610 in borderline cases determining whether communications are privileged depends on whether:

(a) the advice sought related to the rights, liabilities, obligations or remedies of the client under private or public law; and

(b) it was reasonable to expect the privilege to apply in the circumstances.

The same privilege also attaches to communications with a solicitor in the service of a party (eg a solicitor in a legal department of a company or government department), provided the communications relate to legal as opposed to administrative matters.

Instructions and briefs to counsel, and counsel's opinions, drafts and notes are also privileged. However, counsel's indorsement on a brief of the result of a hearing is not privileged.

20.5.1.2   **Privilege when litigation is contemplated or pending**

This category also falls to be considered in two parts.

Communications between a party's solicitor and a third party

Such communications, which come into existence after litigation is contemplated or commenced and are made with a view to such litigation, either for the purpose of obtaining or giving advice in regard to it, or of obtaining or collecting evidence which may be used in it, are privileged. The document in respect of which privilege is claimed must have come into existence at a time when litigation was contemplated or pending. Thus, it is not possible to attach privilege to enclosures to a letter to a solicitor simply because they were sent under cover of a letter which itself may be privileged.

Examples of documents which fall into this category and are privileged include:

• Witness statements obtained by a solicitor for the purpose of a contemplated or current action.

• Experts' reports, eg a surveyor's report, obtained by a solicitor for the purpose of a contemplated or current action.

Copies and translations of documents are privileged if the original was privileged, and are generally not protected from privilege if the originals were not privileged. By way of exception, a compilation of copies or translations of documents obtained from third parties may be protected by legal professional privilege if disclosing them may betray the trend of advice given by the solicitor to the client. This exception does not apply, however, where the original documents came from the client (*Sumitomo Corporation v Credit Lyonnais Rouse Ltd* [2002] 1 WLR 479).

Communications between the party personally and a third party

It is this category which presents most difficulties in practice. The general principle is that such documents are privileged if, and only if, the *dominant purpose* for which the document was prepared was for submission to a legal adviser in view of contemplated or pending litigation (see *Waugh v British Railways Board* [1980] AC 521). Thus, to ascertain whether a document in this category is protected by privilege, the issues which fall to be considered are whether:

(a) at the time when the document came into existence litigation was contemplated or pending; and

(b) the dominant purpose for which the document was prepared was for its submission to a legal adviser in view of the litigation.

As to (a), the Court of Appeal (*Re Highgrade Traders Ltd* [1984] BCLC 151; *Guinness Peat Properties Ltd v Fitzroy Robinson Partnership* [1987] 1 WLR 1027) has held that, if litigation is *reasonably in prospect*, documents brought into existence for the purpose of enabling solicitors to advise whether a claim should be made or resisted are protected by privilege, whether or not a decision to instruct solicitors has been made at that time, provided, of course, that such purpose is the dominant purpose of their creation.

As to (b), problems often arise where the document was prepared for a number of purposes. For example, in the case of an accident, the preparation of an accident report may be for the purpose of the avoidance of similar accidents in the future, as much as to determine blame in the individual case.

The dominant purpose of a document is not necessarily determined by reference to the intentions of its actual author. For example;

(a) Where a report has been prepared by an employee at the request of his employer, the dominant purpose will be ascertained by looking at the intention of the *employer* or the person requesting the report.

(b) Similarly, where a report has been prepared by an independent expert at the request of a potential party to a claim, the dominant purpose will again be determined by looking at the intention of the party, and not the expert.

(c) Also, where a document has been prepared at the request of insurers, the test will be the intention of the insurers at the time that the document was made.

In any event, the test is: What was the dominant purpose at the time when the document came into existence? The fact that the document may *subsequently* have been used by solicitors in the conduct of the litigation is irrelevant if the *original* purpose was different. The question of the dominant purpose is a matter of fact to be decided by the court in each particular case.

20.5.1.3 Extension to others providing legal services

The Courts and Legal Services Act 1990, s 63, extends legal professional privilege to communications with persons other than barristers and solicitors who are authorised to provide advocacy, litigation, conveyancing and probate services.

20.5.1.4 Loss of legal professional privilege by reason of fraud

A party is not entitled to assert legal professional privilege as a ground for refusing to disclose communications which have been made in furtherance of a fraudulent or illegal design. A party seeking disclosure of such communications should establish a strong prima facie case of fraud where fraud is one of the issues in the case. Where fraud is not an issue in the case, a prima facie case of fraud may be sufficient (*Kuwait Airways Corp v Iraqi Airways Co (No. 6)* [2005] 1 WLR 2734).

The privilege was lost on this ground in a case where a search order was obtained using information which had been gathered in breach of the Data Protection Act 1984 (*Dubai Aluminium Co Ltd v Al Alawi* [1999] 1 WLR 1964).

20.5.2   Documents tending to criminate or expose to a penalty

A party is entitled to claim privilege in respect of documents which may tend to criminate him or her (ie present a risk of criminal prosecution or exposure to a penalty). It has been held that subsequent committal proceedings for contempt of court are penal for this purpose (*Memory Corporation plc v Sidhu (No. 2)* [2000] 1 WLR 1443), but disqualification proceedings under the Company Directors Disqualification Act 1986 are regulatory rather than penal (*Re Westminster Property Management Ltd* The Times, 19 January 2000). The rule applies only to criminal liability or penal proceedings in the UK, and not to penal proceedings abroad. However, liability to a penalty under EC legislation forming part of the law in the UK by virtue of the European Communities Act 1972 is a penalty under the law of the UK. The privilege protects 'compelled' evidence only, not 'free standing' evidence, such as photographs found on a computer under a search order (*C plc v P* [2008] Ch 1).

By SCA 1981, s 72, privilege in respect of compliance with orders for disclosure or the answering of questions on the grounds of self-incrimination relating to infringements of intellectual property rights has been withdrawn. The section applies to proceedings in respect of the infringement of rights pertaining to intellectual property (eg patent and copyright) and passing-off. This provision has particular relevance to the operation and effect of search orders (see **16.5.3.5**). Similar provision removing the protection of the privilege against self-incrimination is provided for theft and fraud offences by the Theft Act 1968, s 31, and the Fraud Act 2006, s 13.

20.5.3   Protection on the grounds of public policy

Strictly this is not a head of privilege at all, and is often referred to as 'public interest immunity'. The rule is that if disclosure of a document would be injurious to the public interest it must be withheld. Thus, for example, diplomatic despatches, Cabinet minutes and documents dealing with matters of national defence are normally immune from disclosure. Unlike claims to privilege properly so-called, if disclosure would be injurious to the public interest there is no question of waiver of the protection, and if immunity is not raised by a party, it must be insisted on by the judge.

20.5.3.1   The test

The test is whether the production of a document would be injurious to the public interest or, in other words, whether the withholding of a document is necessary for the proper functioning of the public service. The fact that a document is a 'State Document' or marked 'confidential', or that disclosure might invoke public discussion or criticism of a government department is not sufficient. The court should balance the public interest in concealment against the public interest that the administration of justice should not be frustrated.

20.5.3.2 The principles

The principles defining this ground of privilege and the conditions of its exercise are found in the House of Lords decisions *Burmah Oil Co Ltd v Governor of the Bank of England* [1980] AC 1090 and *Conway v Rimmer* [1968] AC 910.

20.5.3.3 Procedure

Under CPR, r 31.19(1), a person (who need not be a party) may apply, without notice, for an order permitting him to withhold disclosure of a document on the ground that disclosure would damage the public interest. Often the person most likely to apply will be the Secretary of State for the government department asserting public interest immunity in the document. By r 31.19(2), unless the court otherwise orders, any order made under this rule must not be served on any other person, and must not be open to inspection by any other person. Claims for protection may alternatively be made in the list of documents served by a party (r 31.19(4)), or may be insisted upon by the court of its own initiative.

It is questionable whether these procedures, particularly the procedure under CPR, r 31.19(1), comply with art 6(1) of the European Convention on Human Rights. In *Rowe and Davis v United Kingdom* (2000) 30 EHRR 1, the European Court of Human Rights considered the procedural aspects of withholding evidence in criminal trials on the grounds of public interest. It was decided that withholding evidence on the grounds of public interest had to comply with the requirements of adversarial proceedings; equality of arms; and must incorporate safeguards to protect the interests of the accused. It was found that to comply with art 6(1) the accused had to be given information about the withheld information appropriate to the category of the evidence involved, and that it was for the trial judge (rather than a court on appeal) to decide whether the evidence should be withheld. The procedures under r 31.19 allow orders to be made without giving any information to the parties (or to just one side if one of the parties is the government department seeking to withhold disclosure), and for decisions to be made by judges other than the trial judge, which would seem to fall short of the safeguards contemplated by the Convention. In criminal trials there are the additional minimum rights given by art 6(3), which do not apply to civil cases, but this difference is unlikely to have a substantial effect on the implications of the decision in civil cases.

20.5.4 Waiver of privilege

With the exception of public interest immunity, the privilege in all cases is that of the client and not the legal adviser. Privilege is not waived by mere reference to the document in a statement of case or in written evidence. Waiver as to one or some of several documents does not amount to waiver of the others unless they relate to the same 'transaction' as the disclosed documents (*Fulham Leisure Holdings Ltd v Nicholson Graham & Jones* [2006] 2 All ER 599). If part of a document is put in evidence or read in court, privilege will be waived for the whole document, unless the remaining part deals with an entirely different subject matter.

Further, if a party relies upon a document, in respect of which he could have claimed privilege in an interim application, he or she will be taken to have waived privilege in respect of that document altogether (*Somatra Ltd v Sinclair Roche and Temperley* [2000] 1 WLR 2453).

Where a party mistakenly includes privileged documents in the first part of his or her list, the mistake may be rectified prior to inspection by notifying the other party and stating the grounds of the objection to producing them. Where a party inadvertently allows a privileged document to be inspected (see **20.6** below), the party who has inspected the document may use it or its contents only with the permission of the court (CPR, r 31.20).

A former client who sues its solicitors impliedly waives its privilege in all documents relevant to the claim to the extent necessary to enable the court to adjudicate the dispute fully and fairly (*Lillicrap v Nalder and Son* [1993] 1 WLR 94, CA). Thus if the defendant's solicitor alleges that even if there was negligence there was no causation, because the claimant never listened to the solicitor's advice, the implied waiver of privilege will extend to other transactions undertaken by the solicitor for the claimant and not just the transaction forming the basis of the claim. However, there are limits on the implied waiver of privilege in solicitors' negligence claims. In *Paragon Finance plc v Freshfields* [1999] 1 WLR 1183, CA, Freshfields had acted for the finance company in relation to a number of mortgage transactions. The finance company made a number of claims against insurance policies entered into in relation to the mortgages, which the insurer disputed. The finance company then retained a second firm of solicitors to pursue outstanding insurance claims, and later sued Freshfields for professional negligence. A question arose as to whether the finance company had, by suing Freshfields, impliedly waived its privilege in respect of the work done by the second firm in pursuing the insurance claims. It was held that by suing Freshfields the finance company had only put its relationship with that firm into the public domain, and had not done so in respect of the work done by the second firm, and so had not waived its privilege in respect of the work done by the second firm. See also *Farm Assist Ltd v Secretary of State for Environment Food and Rural Affairs* [2008] EWHC 3079 (TCC).

20.5.5   Without prejudice communications

The purpose of 'without prejudice' privilege is to enable the parties to negotiate, without risk of their proposals being used against them if negotiations fail.

Documents which form part of without prejudice negotiations between the parties, whether litigation was current or not, are privileged from production. Depending on the circumstances this may also be the case even if the words 'without prejudice' or the equivalent were not used. The privilege thus applies to joint settlement meetings, except to the extent they are stated to be without prejudice save as to costs (*Jackson v Ministry of Defence* [2006] EWCA Civ 46). However, conversely, the words 'without prejudice' are not necessarily conclusive and do not automatically render the document privileged. Without prejudice privilege applies to communications which are a genuine attempt to negotiate a settlement of a claim. It will not apply to a letter which merely asserts a party's alleged rights (*Buckinghamshire County Council v Moran* [1990] Ch 623), nor to letters seeking time to pay an admitted liability (*Bradford and Bingley plc v Rashid* [2006] 1 WLR 2066, HL). Nor will it apply to a very clear case of abuse of a without prejudice occasion (*Savings and Investment Bank Ltd v Fincken* [2004] 1 WLR 667).

If privilege is claimed, but challenged, the court has to examine the documents and decide whether they are truly without prejudice in nature. However, as a rule of good practice, if possible, a judge (or Master) other than the trial judge should decide such a dispute. If a challenge to privilege is raised before trial this should not present difficulty. However, if a challenge to privilege is raised during a trial in the County Court, it is possible for the trial judge to adjourn that particular question to the District Judge.

Without prejudice material will be admissible upon the issue as to whether or not the negotiations resulted in an agreed settlement. Without prejudice material in applications to dismiss for want of prosecution may also be used to explain apparent delays or to provide material about the 'innocent' party's conduct (*Family Housing Association (Manchester) Ltd v Michael Hyde and Partners* [1993] 1 WLR 354, CA).

The House of Lords have confirmed that a document, once privileged by reason it was without prejudice will always be privileged. Thus an admission made in without prejudice communications by one party will not be admissible in other proceedings against that party (*Rush and Tompkins Ltd v Greater London Council* [1989] AC 1280; *Ofulue v Bossert* [2009] 2WLR 749). The public policy rationale of the privilege has been said to be directed solely to protecting admissions, and if documents are to be used for a different purpose, such as to show the amount of compensation paid for an earlier injury, they are admissible (*Murrell v Healy* [2001] 4 All ER 345, a distinction which may be unsound as it is too subtle: *Ofulue v Bossert*).

Subsequent proceedings based on without prejudice statements made in earlier proceedings will be struck out as an abuse of process, unless the claimant in the subsequent proceedings can show that the statements relied upon were made improperly, or some other public interest reason in favour of their subsequent use (*Unilever plc v Procter and Gamble Co* [2001] 1 All ER 783).

20.5.6 Confidential material

Documents which are regarded as confidential (and also perhaps damaging to a party's case) are often, but incorrectly, thought to be privileged. Unless a document falls within one of the above categories of privilege it is not protected by privilege, whether the document is confidential in nature or damaging to the party giving disclosure, and must therefore be disclosed. Thus, a litigant is not entitled to claim privilege in respect of a document merely by reason that it was supplied in confidence by a third party.

However, protection (not strictly by way of privilege) will be given by the court in certain cases of confidentiality. Where a party claims secrecy in relevant material (eg a defendant in a patent infringement action who claims that a process is secret), the governing principle is that the court should order a controlled measure of disclosure. In each case the court must decide what measure of disclosure is appropriate, to whom it should be made, and upon what terms.

20.5.7 Secondary evidence

A party able to rely on privilege is entitled to refuse to produce a privileged document. Privilege does not operate (apart from public interest immunity) so as to prohibit the other side from proving the facts stated in the privileged material by other means.

20.5.8 Listing privileged documents

Documents in respect of which privilege is claimed must also be contained in the list. The description to be given in the list of the document is not for the purpose of enabling the other party to learn the contents of the document but to test the claim for privilege. Accordingly, a very concise description is sufficient.

However, the party claiming privilege in respect of any document must include in the list a sufficient statement of the grounds of the privilege claimed. For example:

(a) 'Correspondence between the defendant and his solicitors for the purpose of obtaining legal advice.'

(b) 'Documents which came into existence and were made by AB Ltd [being a sub-sidiary of the defendant], its officers or employees, after this litigation was in contemplation and in view of such litigation for the purpose of obtaining for and furnishing to the solicitors of the defendant evidence and other information for the use of those solicitors to enable them to advise the defendant in the conduct of the defence of this claim.'

20.6 Inspection

20.6.1 Entitlement to inspect documents

A party who has served a list of documents must allow the other parties, including co-de-fendants, to inspect the documents referred to in the list (other than any to which there is an objection to production, ie those in respect of which privilege is claimed). A party wishing to inspect must send a written notice to that effect to the other side, and the other side must give their permission within the next seven days: CPR, r 31.15(a), (b).

Normally, documents must be disclosed for inspection in their entirety, but there is scope for blanking out irrelevant passages (*GE Capital Corporate Finance Group Ltd v Bankers Trust Co* [1995] 1 WLR 172, CA).

The court has the power to give directions as to whether the inspection of documents should be by electronic means (eg by CD-ROM) or hard copy (see *Grupo Torras SA v Al Sabah* The Times, 13 October 1997).

20.6.2 Entitlement to copies of documents

By CPR, r 31.15(c), a party who is entitled to inspection may serve notice on the other party requiring the supply of copies of the documents upon undertaking to pay reason-able copying charges.

20.7 Orders for disclosure

20.7.1 Party failing comply with disclosure direction

Where a party fails to give disclosure as required by a disclosure direction, an application can be made for an order compelling this to be done. Before issuing the application the innocent party should write to the defaulting party warning that an application will be issued if the default is not remedied. The court is likely to consider making an 'unless' order with the effect that some sanction, such as striking out the claim or Defence, will take effect if disclosure is not given within a limited period of time.

20.7.2 Specific disclosure

20.7.2.1 Applying for specific disclosure

An application for specific disclosure may be used to challenge the sufficiency of a list of documents. It also has a wider use, and such an application may be made at any stage of a claim, for example:

(a) In interim injunctions (particularly in freezing injunctions and search orders), an order for specific disclosure is a powerful weapon indeed, as at the time of seeking a freezing order, the claimant may apply for an order that the defendant disclose the whereabouts of any assets and give disclosure of material documents (see *A v C* [1980] 2 All ER 347; *Bankers Trust Co v Shapira* [1980] 1 WLR 1274).

(b) Specific disclosure may be ordered against a claimant before service of the defence where it would assist the defendant to plead a full defence rather than an initial bare denial (*Dayman v Canyon Holdings Ltd* (2006) LTL 11/1/2006).

The CPR, r 31.12, provides:

(1) The court may make an order for specific disclosure or specific inspection.

(2) An order for specific disclosure is an order that a party must do one or more of the following things—

    (a) disclose documents or classes of documents specified in the order;

    (b) carry out a search to the extent stated in the order;

    (c) disclose any documents located as a result of that search.

(3) An order for specific inspection is an order that a party permit inspection of a document referred to in rule 31.3(2).

If it is established that the other side have not given standard disclosure the order will usually be made (PD 31, para 5.4). This procedure may also be used if a party wants disclosure of 'train of inquiry' documents (see *Peruvian Guano*), but on such an application the court will be particularly astute to apply the overriding objective (PD 31, para 5.4).

20.7.2.2 Making the application

An application for specific disclosure must specify the order asked for and be supported by evidence stating that, in the belief of the deponent, the other party has or has had certain specific documents relating to a matter in question. The evidence must show:

- that such documents are or were in the control of the other party; and

- that the specified documents are disclosable under standard disclosure, or should otherwise be disclosed in accordance with the overriding objective.

20.7.2.3 At trial

During the course of a trial, in particular as a result of cross-examination, the existence of previously undisclosed material documents is often revealed. In such a case an application for specific disclosure of the documents may be made to the judge.

20.8 Inspection of documents referred to

By CPR, r 31.14(1), a party may at any time serve on another, whose statements of case, witness statements or affidavits mention any document, a notice requiring the other party to produce that document for inspection. A document is 'mentioned' if there is a direct allusion to it. Thus, a witness statement saying 'he wrote to me' is a direct allusion to the covering letter (*Expandable Ltd v Rubin* [2008] 1 WLR 1099). The other party must permit inspection within seven days. If objection is taken to the production of any document, the notice must specify the document and state the grounds of the objection.

The power to order inspection must be exercised with reasonable restraint in relation to documents referred to in experts' reports (PD 31, para 7). It will not generally be exercised provided the material parts of the documents are set out in the report (*Lucas v Barking, Havering and Redbridge Hospitals NHS Trust* [2004] 1 WLR 220).

20.9 Order for inspection

If a party has difficulty in obtaining inspection of documents referred to in the other side's list of documents or any statement of case or written evidence an application can be made to the court for an order for specific inspection: CPR, r 31.12. The application must be supported by evidence.

20.10 Misuse of material obtained on disclosure

The fact that a party may be required to give disclosure and inspection of highly confidential and potentially damaging material is somewhat mitigated by the limited use which the other party may make of documents disclosed in the course of proceedings.

A party given disclosure may use the documents disclosed only for purposes connected with the proper conduct of that action: CPR, r 31.22(1). Any misuse of the documents may be restrained by injunction or punished as a contempt of court or by striking out subsequent proceedings based on documents disclosed in the course of earlier proceedings (see *Riddick v Thames Board Mills Ltd* [1977] QB 881). Permission to use the materials disclosed may be sought (see **16.5.2**).

The protection against subsequent use of disclosed documents is not, however, absolute. The CPR, r 31.22, provides:

(1) *A party to whom a document has been disclosed may use the document only for the purpose of the proceedings in which it is disclosed except where—*
  (a) *the document has been read to or by the court, or referred to, at a hearing which has been held in public;*
  (b) *the court gives permission; or*
  (c) *the party who disclosed the document and the person to whom the document belongs agree.*
(2) *The court may make an order restricting or prohibiting the use of a document which has been disclosed, even where the document has been read to or by the court, or referred to, at a hearing which has been held in public.*
(3) *An application for such an order may be made—*
  (a) *by a party; or*
  (b) *by any person to whom the document belongs.*

The prohibition on collateral use of documents is restricted to disclosure, and does not apply to documents used as exhibits to witness statements and affidavits or which are ordered to be disclosed after being referred to in witness statements and affidavits (*Cassidy v Hawcroft* [2000] CPLR 624).

The lifting on the ban against use outside the scope of the present proceedings after documents have been used in open court stems from a compromise reached arising from the proceedings in *Home Office v Harman* [1983] 1 AC 280, HL. It will be noticed from r 31.22(2) that after use at trial, the court may reimpose the restrictions on subsequent use, and by r 31.22(3)(a) such an application may be made 'by a party'. That expression was interpreted in *Singh v Christie* The Times, 11 November 1993, as meaning a party to the original proceedings in which the documents were disclosed, and not the parties to any subsequent proceedings in which the documents may be used. There is no obvious reason why this interpretation should not be applied to the rule as it appears in the Civil Procedure Rules 1998.

Once documents have been used in open court, an order restricting or prohibiting subsequent use will be made only if there are very good reasons for departing from the usual rule of publicity (*Lilly Icos Ltd v Pfizer Ltd* [2002] 1 WLR 2253). Merely asserting a document is confidential is insufficient. Specific reasons as to why a party would be damaged by subsequent use are required.

List of documents: standard disclosure

Notes

- The rules relating to standard disclosure are contained in Part 31 of the Civil Procedure Rules.
- Documents to be included under standard disclosure are contained in Rule 31.6
- A document has or will have been in your control if you have or have had possession, or a right of possession, of it **or** a right to inspect or take copies of it.

In the	
HIGH COURT OF JUSTICE QUEEN'S BENCH DIVISION	
Claim No.	HQ 09 487565
Claimant (including ref)	JERSEY LIPTON LIMITED
Defendant (including ref)	POOLE TECHTONICS LIMITED
Date	

Disclosure Statement

I, the above named

☐ Claimant   ☐ Defendant

☑ Party (if party making disclosure is a company, firm or other organisation identify here who the person making the disclosure statement is and why he is the appropriate person to make it)

> James Lipton, Managing Director of the Claimant Jersey Lipton Limited. I negotiated the relevant contract with the Defendant on behalf of the Claimant.

state that I have carried out a reasonable and proportionate search to locate all the documents which I am

required to disclose under the order made by the court on (date of order) | 13.11.2009

☑ I did not search for documents:-

☐ pre-dating

☑ located elsewhere than

> the Claimant company's offices and that of its solicitor

☑ in categories other than

> the contractual documents and correspondence relating to this contract

☐ for electronic documents

☑ I carried out a search for electronic documents contained on or created by the following:
(list what was searched and extent of search)

> the Claimant company's computer system

Figure 20.1   Specimen list of documents

☑ I did not search for the following:-

    ☑ documents created before

            | [start date] |

      documents contained on or created by the ☑ Claimant   ☐ Defendant

☐ PCs	☐ portable data storage media
☐ databases	☐ servers
☐ back-up tapes	☑ off-site storage
☑ mobile phones	☐ laptops
☑ notebooks	☑ handheld devices
☑ PDA devices	

      documents contained on or created by the ☑ Claimant   ☐ Defendant

☐ mail files	☐ document files
☑ calendar files	☑ web-based applications
☐ spreadsheet files	☑ graphic and presentation files

      documents other than by reference to the following keyword(s)/concepts
      (delete if your search was not confined to specific keywords or concepts)

I certify that I understand the duty of disclosure and to the best of my knowledge I have carried out that duty. I further certify that the list of documents set out in or attached to this form, is a complete list of all documents which are or have been in my control and which I am obliged under the order to disclose.

I understand that I must inform the court and the other parties immediately if any further document required to be disclosed by Rule 31.6 comes into my control at any time before the conclusion of the case.

☐ I have not permitted inspection of documents within the category or class of documents (as set out below) required to be disclosed under Rule 31(6)(b)or (c) on the grounds that to do so would be disproportionate to the issues in the case.

Signed | | **Date** | [date of list of documents] |

      (Claimant)(Defendant)('s litigation friend)

List and number here, in a convenient order, the documents (or bundles of documents if of the same nature, e.g. invoices) in your control, which you do not object to being inspected. Give a short description of each document or bundle so that it can be identified, and say if it is kept elsewhere i.e. with a bank or solicitor	**I have control of the documents numbered and listed here. I do not object to you inspecting them/producing copies.**

1. Letters from the Defendant to the Claimant	Various dates
2. Copy letters from the Claimant to the Defendant	Various dates
3. Bundles of specifications for the Claimant's Plastic mouldings machines	Undated
4. Bundles of advertising material	Undated
5. Purchase order, ref 8603578	Dated
6. Copy delivery note, ref XA07811	Dated
7. Copy invoice, ref ST 9922	Dated
8. Copy letters from Claimant's solicitors to Defendant	Various dates
9. Letters from Defendant's solicitors to Claimant's solicitors	Various dates
10. Statements of case, questionnaires and orders common to both parties	Various dates

---

List and number here, as above, the documents in your control which you object to being inspected. (Rule 31.19)

I have control of the documents numbered and listed here, but I object to you inspecting them:

1. Communications between the Claimant and its solicitor in its professional capacity for the dominant purpose of obtaining or given legal advice.
2. Instructions to, opinions of, and statements of case settled by Counsel in this claim.
3. Communications between the Claimant's officers, employees and agents when litigation was pending for the dominant purpose of obtaining information or evidence for use in this claim.

Say what your objections are

I object to you inspecting these documents because:

They are protected from inspection by legal professional privilege.

List and number here, the documents you once had in your control, but which you no longer have. For each document listed, say when it was last in your control and where it is now.

I have had the documents numbered and listed below, but they are no longer in my control.

The originals of the copy documents numbered 2, 6, 7 and 8 in the first section of this list, which were delivered or sent to the Defendant or the Defendant's solicitors on their respective dates.

Special disclosure orders

21.1 Introduction

The main features of the procedures described in this chapter, together with search orders (see **Chapter 16**), are shown in **Figure 21.1**. This chapter deals with a number of special rules that supplement the general rules governing disclosure. Search orders, which are a special form of disclosure, have already been dealt with in **Chapter 16**. Disclosure of documents has been considered in **Chapter 20**, and requests for further information are discussed in **Chapter 22**.

21.2 *Norwich Pharmacal* orders

21.2.1 The principle

A *Norwich Pharmacal* order is a procedure whereby it is possible to find out the identity of an alleged wrongdoer.

The classic statement of the principle is by Lord Reid in *Norwich Pharmacal Co v Customs and Excise Commissioners* [1974] AC 133, 175, HL:

[The authorities] seem to me to point to a very reasonable principle that if through no fault of his own a person gets mixed up in the tortious acts of others so as to facilitate their wrongdoing he may incur no personal liability but he comes under a duty to assist the person who has been wronged by giving him full information and disclosing the identity of the wrongdoers. I do not think that it matters whether he became so mixed up by voluntary action on his part or because it was his duty to do what he did. It may be that if this causes him expense the person seeking the information ought to reimburse him. But justice requires that he should cooperate in righting the wrong if he unwittingly facilitated its perpetration.

The facts were that Norwich owned the patent to a chemical used for immunising poultry. Statistics published by the Commissioners revealed that the number of importations of the chemical was higher than those brought in by Norwich. Norwich were unable to take direct steps to protect their patent, so they brought proceedings against the Commissioners to compel them to disclose the identities of the other importers. It was held that although Norwich had no substantive cause of action against the Commissioners, the Commissioners had facilitated the wrongdoing of the importers and were ordered to disclose their identities.

The key factor, therefore, is that the person against whom the order is sought has facilitated the wrongdoing.

In *P v T Ltd* [1997] 4 All ER 200, the court extended the principle by holding that an order could be obtained for disclosure to assist a prospective claimant to obtain the information and documents necessary to bring a possible action in tort even though it could not be ascertained (without the information sought by the order) whether the person to be identified had actually committed a tort against the prospective claimant. *Ashworth Hospital Authority v MGN Ltd* [2002] 1 WLR 2033 makes it clear that the jurisdiction is not restricted to tort claims.

The principle was further extended by *Murphy v Murphy* [1999] 1 WLR 282, where an order was made against a settlor to disclose to a potential beneficiary the names and addresses of the trustees under a settlement, to enable the potential beneficiary to communicate with the trustees with a view to being considered for the distribution of trust property held on discretionary trusts. Obviously, the trustees were not accused of any wrongdoing.

21.2.2 Disclosure of additional information

Norwich Pharmacal orders are principally used as a procedure to identify an alleged wrongdoer. In *Mercantile Group (Europe) AG v Aiyela* [1994] QB 366, CA, however, the order related to more extensive information. In that case judgment was entered against the defendant, and a *Mareva* (freezing) injunction was subsequently granted in aid of execution. There was prima facie evidence that the defendant's wife was mixed up in the defendant's attempts to frustrate the judgment, and she was ordered, under the *Norwich Pharmacal* principle, to disclose financial information about herself and the defendant. In non-freezing injunction applications there is a great reluctance to go further than requiring the respondent to disclose the identity of the wrongdoer and to provide documents. An application for the respondent to provide written evidence about the underlying cause of action was refused as too broad and oppressive in *BNP Paribas v TH Global Ltd* [2009] EWHC 37 (Ch).

21.2.3 Mere witness rule

Someone who observes the facts giving rise to a cause of action between two other people can be called as a witness at trial. A witness can be compelled to attend to give oral evidence or to produce documents by serving a witness summons (**33.12.6**). But, until trial, the witness can refuse to answer questions and to disclose documents. Subject to the procedure discussed at **21.4** below, a witness must not be joined as a party for the sole purpose of obtaining disclosure.

In *Norwich Pharmacal* situations one of the most difficult questions is as to whether the respondent is a mere witness or is someone who has got mixed up with and facilitated another's wrongdoing. A case falling on the wrong side of the line was *Ricci v Chow* [1987] 1 WLR 1658, CA. The claimant alleged that the journal published by the Seychellois National Movement defamed him. The defendant was the Secretary General of the Movement, but had nothing to do with the printing and publication of the article, and had in no way facilitated its preparation. The fact that he was aware of the identities of the alleged tortfeasors did not justify making a *Norwich Pharmacal* order against him.

21.2.4 Defendant a tortfeasor

In *X Ltd v Morgan-Grampian (Publishers) Ltd* [1991] 1 AC 1, HL, it was held that where the claimant had a cause of action against the defendant (against whom the claimant sought disclosure of the identity of an unknown tortfeasor) connected with the cause of action against the unknown tortfeasor, the defendant was amenable to the full scope of the court's wide power to order disclosure on notice, irrespective of the *Norwich Pharmacal* jurisdiction. In most such cases this will include disclosure of the identity of the unknown tortfeasor.

Once the identity of the unknown tortfeasor is known they can be made a party to the claim against the existing defendant (who is also a tortfeasor) or separate proceedings can be commenced against them.

21.2.5 Of general application

British Steel Corporation v Granada Television Ltd [1981] AC 1096, HL is authority for the proposition that *Norwich Pharmacal* orders are not restricted to any particular categories of cases.

The Contempt of Court Act 1981, s 10, does, however, provide a statutory privilege against the disclosure of journalist's sources in certain defined circumstances (see *X Ltd v Morgan-Grampian (Publishers) Ltd; Goodwin v United Kingdom* (1996) 22 EHRR 123, and *Camelot Group plc v Centaur Communications Ltd* [1999] QB 124, CA).

21.2.6 Real interest in suing

A *Norwich Pharmacal* order will not be made for the mere gratification of curiosity. The claimant must have a real and unsatisfied claim against the unknown wrongdoer which cannot be brought unless the facilitator reveals the wrongdoer's identity (*British Steel Corporation v Granada Television Ltd*). This is best fulfilled if the wrongdoer's name is sought for the purpose of bringing proceedings against him or her. In *British Steel* Lord Wilberforce said he would have been prepared, if necessary, to hold that, given a cause of action, '. . . an intention to seek redress, by court action or otherwise, would be enough'. Other methods of redress could include dismissal or deprivation of pension. This fairly wide approach has been confirmed in *X Ltd v Morgan-Grampian (Publishers) Ltd* [1991] 1 AC 1, HL and *Ashworth Hospital Authority v MGN Ltd* [2002] 1 WLR 2033.

21.2.7 Remedy is discretionary

The remedy (being equitable) is discretionary. Therefore, even if the basic conditions are made out, there may be public interest reasons for refusing relief. The applicant will generally be expected to have exhausted other avenues for discovering the information (*Mitsui and Co Ltd v Nexen Petroleum Ltd* [2005] 3 All ER 511), and the court will weigh factors such as the seriousness of the conduct of the alleged wrongdoer (*Interbrew SA v Financial Times Ltd* The Times, 4 January 2002, at first instance).

21.2.8 Procedure

The claimant issues a claim form against the facilitator, claiming disclosure of the identity of the wrongdoer. An interim application seeking disclosure of the wrongdoer's identity is then made, supported by written evidence. Once the identity of the wrongdoer is disclosed, the proceedings started against the facilitator have achieved their aim and fresh proceedings should be commenced against the wrongdoer, or the facilitator should be released from the proceedings if there are wrongdoers as other parties

(*Australia and New Zealand Banking Group Ltd v National Westminster Bank plc* The Times, 14 February 2002).

In *Loose v Williamson* [1978] 1 WLR 639, Goulding J held the order may be granted without notice if this is justifiable on the facts. The claimant sighted three fishing boats poaching on his shell fishery. He noted the identification numbers of two of the boats. He sought *Norwich Pharmacal* orders without giving notice against the owners of those two boats for disclosure of the identities of those on board their boats and for the identity of the third boat. The order was made because the claimant would suffer irreparable harm if the fishing continued, whereas the defendants would suffer no harm by disclosing.

21.2.9   Costs

A claimant will normally be required to pay the legal costs and any other expenses incurred by a blameless defendant in complying with a *Norwich Pharmacal* order. It may be possible to recover such costs and expenses from the wrongdoer if liability is eventually established, provided it was foreseeable that the claimant would need to make a *Norwich Pharmacal* application before bringing the substantive proceedings (*Totalise plc v Motley Fool Ltd (No. 2)* The Times, 10 January 2002).

21.3   Pre-action disclosure

21.3.1   Jurisdiction

Under SCA 1981, s 33(2), and CCA 1984, s 52(2), the court has power to make an order for pre-action disclosure against the likely defendant. Such an order can only be made if four conditions are fulfilled:

- the applicant appears likely to be a party to subsequent proceedings;
- the defendant appears likely to be a party; and
- the defendant appears likely to have or to have had relevant documents in his or her possession, custody or power; and
- advance disclosure is desirable to dispose of the anticipated proceedings fairly, or to prevent the need to commence proceedings, or to save costs.

21.3.2   Likely to be a party

Despite earlier authorities, in *Black v Sumitomo Corporation* [2002] 1 WLR 1569, it was held there is no requirement that it be likely that proceedings would be issued, but merely that the persons involved were likely to be parties if subsequent proceedings were issued. In this context, 'likely' means 'may well' rather than 'more probably than not'. This means that generally the court should not embark at this stage on investigating justiciability or the elements of the cause of action (*Total E & P Soudan SA v Edmunds* [2007] EWCA Civ 50). If the claim is weak, that is more appropriately considered as part of the discretion whether to make the order (*Snowstar Shipping Co Ltd v Graig Shipping plc* (2003) LTL 3/7/2003).

21.3.3   Documents covered

The CPR, r 31.16(3)(c), provides that an order for pre-action disclosure can only be made if the documents the applicant wants to be disclosed would be included in the respondent's obligation to give standard disclosure if proceedings were started. In the case of a class of documents, the applicant must show that the whole class would be covered by standard disclosure (*Hutchison 3G UK Ltd v O2 (UK) Ltd* [2008] EWHC 55 (Comm)). Further, by r 31.16(3)(d) the applicant needs to establish that pre-action disclosure is desirable in order to:

- dispose fairly of the anticipated proceedings; or
- assist the dispute to be resolved without proceedings; or
- save costs.

It follows that the court has to be clear what the issues are likely to be in the anticipated proceedings, and must make sure that the documents being asked for are likely to adversely affect the case of one side or the other. If the applicant already has sufficient material to plead a claim, it is unlikely to be 'desirable' to order pre-action disclosure (*First Gulf Bank v Wachovia Bank National Association* (2005) LTL 15/12/2005).

21.3.4   Discretion

Once the conditions are satisfied, the court has to undertake a balancing exercise to determine whether pre-action disclosure is 'desirable' in one of the three ways set out in r 31.16(3)(d) (*Bermuda International Securities Ltd v KPMG* [2001] CPLR 252). The court will also consider factors such as the strength of the substantive claim, the degree to which the documents sought are likely to support the proposed claim (or whether they are merely 'train of inquiry' documents), and the cost of complying (*Black v Sumitomo Corporation* [2002] 1 WLR 1569).

In *Shaw v Vauxhall Motors Ltd* [1974] 1 WLR 1035, CA, Buckley LJ said that s 33(2) should not '. . . be used to encourage fishing expeditions to enable a prospective plaintiff to discover whether he has in fact got a case at all'. Ormrod LJ said that if a claimant is going to ask the court to exercise its discretion to grant him an order under s 33(2), it is only fair that he should commit himself by letter or other written evidence '. . . to at least either a description of the accident and how it happened, or a statement that he does not know how it happened'.

21.3.5   Procedure

Applications for pre-action disclosure are made by issuing an ordinary application notice supported by written evidence in the anticipated substantive proceedings (but before the substantive proceedings are themselves issued).

Notice of the hearing must be given to the likely defendant.

21.3.6   The order

If the basic conditions are fulfilled, the court may, not must, order the defendant to disclose the relevant documents and to produce them to the applicant, or to the applicant's legal, medical or professional advisers. Thus, in appropriate cases, the applicant may be precluded from seeing the documents. The order is limited to such documents as the defendant ought to disclose by way of standard disclosure.

The CPR, r 31.16(4) and (5), provide:

> (4) An order under this rule must—
>> (a) specify the documents or the classes of documents which the respondent must disclose; and
>> (b) require him, when making disclosure, to specify any of those documents—
>>> (i)   which are no longer in his control; or
>>> (ii)   in respect of which he claims a right or duty to withhold inspection.
> (5) Such an order may—
>> (a) require the respondent to indicate what has happened to any documents which are no longer in his control; and
>> (b) specify the time and place for disclosure and inspection.

21.3.7 Costs

Under CPR, r 48.1, whenever the court makes an order for pre-action disclosure (or for disclosure against non-parties, see **21.4**), it will order the applicant to pay the respondent's costs, unless it was unreasonable for the respondent to have opposed the application. As the starting point is that the applicant must pay the respondent's costs, it will not usually be unreasonable to resist the application (*SES Contracting Ltd v UK Coal plc* (2007) 33 EG 90 (CS)). It may be unreasonable where the respondent had an obligation to provide the documents in compliance with a pre-action protocol. Even where the respondent is regarded as acting unreasonably, costs against the respondent should be limited to the costs of the application, with the applicant still paying the costs of the exercise of disclosing the documents (*Bermuda International Securities Ltd v KPMG* [2001] CPLR 252).

21.3.8 Directions to commence substantive proceedings

The CPR, r 25.2(3), provides that where the court grants an interim remedy before a claim has been commenced, it may give directions requiring a claim to be commenced. A special rule, however, applies to applications for pre-action disclosure, with r 25.2(4) creating a distinction between s 33 and s 52 orders and other types of pre-action orders. Rule 25.2(4) provides that the court need not direct that a claim be commenced where a pre-action disclosure order is made. The reason for the distinction is that pre-action disclosure orders may result in the claimant deciding not to bring substantive proceedings at all, as recognised in *Dunning v United Hospitals Board of Governors* [1973] 1 WLR 586, and it would not make sense to require the claimant to bring a substantive claim in such circumstances.

21.3.9 Data protection

Under the Data Protection Act 1998, s 7, on making a request in writing and paying a fee (if applicable; see the Data Protection (Subject Access) (Fees and Miscellaneous Provisions) Regulations 2000, SI 2000/191), an individual is entitled to have communicated to him in an intelligible form any personal data relating to that individual and any information about the source of that data. For this purpose 'data' means information which is processed automatically (generally by computer), and also information recorded as part of a filing system, or which forms part of an accessible record (which, by the Data Protection Act 1998, s 68, means health, education and accessible public records). Personal data is defined as meaning data relating to a living individual who can be identified from that data (or other information in the possession of the data controller), and includes expressions of opinion about the individual. There are various exemptions and further detailed provisions, such as a restriction on revealing information that would identify other individuals without their consent (s 7(4)). A number of statutory instruments provide even more detail in respect of certain types of data. Health records are dealt with by the Data Protection (Subject Access Modification) (Health) Order 2000, SI 2000/413, art 5 of which provides that personal data consisting of information as to the physical or mental health of a person is exempt from the disclosure requirement in s 7 of the Act to the extent that disclosure would be likely to cause serious harm to the physical or mental health of any person. Similar provision is made for education records (Data Protection (Subject Access Modification) (Education) Order 2000, SI 2000/414) and social work records (Data Protection (Subject Access Modification) (Social Work) Order 2000, SI 2000/415).

The data controller is required to comply with a request promptly, and can be ordered to comply by the High Court or a County Court (Data Protection Act 1998, ss 7(9) and 15(1)). There are different versions of s 7(9) substituted where the data comprises health, education or social work records (SI 2000/413, 414 and 415), the variations allowing a person who may suffer serious harm through compliance with a request for disclosure to apply to the court for an order preventing compliance with the request. For the purpose of determining whether the applicant is entitled to the information under the Data Protection Act 1998, s 7, the court may require the information to be made available for inspection by the court (but not the applicant, who will not be allowed to inspect the information until after a determination in his favour (s 15(2)).

In *Durant v Financial Services Authority* [2004] FSR 28, the claimant sought an order under the Act for the disclosure of a manual file dealing with a complaint he had made to the Financial Services Authority about a bank. The order was refused for a number of reasons:

(a) The file did not contain 'personal data', because its focus was the complaint about the bank, not biographical information about the applicant.

(b) A manual filing system will only be covered if it is of sufficient sophistication to provide the same or similar ready accessibility as a computerised filing system.

(c) The court has an untrammelled discretion whether to grant an order, but the main factor is that access under the Act is mainly for the purpose of correcting inaccuracy, whereas in this case the main purpose was gathering information to make further claims against the bank.

An inquiry agent who may be in breach of the Data Protection Act 1998 may be ordered to disclose the identity of the customer on whose behalf the inquiry agent was acting, and of any sub-agent who gathered the information (*Hughes v Carrutu International plc* [2006] EWHC 1791(QB)).

21.4   Production of documents against non-parties

21.4.1   Jurisdiction

Under SCA 1981, s 34(2), and CCA 1984, s 53, the court has power to order a non-party to produce documents before trial. In the absence of this power witnesses could only be required to produce documents in response to a witness summons, which would mean the documents could only be required (in the absence of consent) to be produced at trial.

The SCA 1981, s 34(2), is similar to s 33(2), but here the application has to be made after the proceedings are issued, whereas the purpose of s 33(2) is to decide whether to issue substantive proceedings. Under s 34(2) the application is made against a witness, whereas under s 33(2) the application is against a potential defendant.

21.4.2   Conditions

The conditions that must be satisfied are set out in CPR, r 31.17(3):

The court may make an order under this rule only where—

> *(a) the documents of which disclosure is sought are likely to support the case of the applicant or adversely affect the case of one of the other parties to the proceedings; and*
>
> *(b) disclosure is necessary in order to dispose fairly of the claim or to save costs.*

Disclosure against non-parties will therefore only be granted (limb (a) above) where the documents sought are likely to be relevant (as opposed to disclosable under standard disclosure) (see *American Home Products Corp v Novartis Pharmaceuticals UK Ltd* (2001) LTL 13/2/2001). The court should primarily consider relevance in the context of the statements of case, and should not embark on determining disputes of substance as to whether the documents are relevant (*Clark v Ardington Electrical Services* (2001) LTL 4/4/2001). 'Likely' in r 31.17, as in r 31.16 (see **21.3.2**), means 'might well' as opposed to 'more probable than not' (see *Three Rivers District Council v Governor and Company of the Bank of England (No 4)* [2003] 1 WLR 210).

Where the first limb is satisfied, it is also necessary to consider limb (b), and the court may refuse the order in its discretion, or impose some limit on disclosure, such as by ordering disclosure of documents only between stated dates. Further, the court will not make an order if it is not satisfied that the documents sought in fact exist, so in *Re Howglen Ltd* [2001] 1 All ER 376 an application was made in general terms for documents against a non-party bank for bank records and interview notes. An order was made limited to the notes of three interviews identified in the evidence in support.

It will sometimes be possible to make an application under the Data Protection Act 1998, or the Bankers' Books Evidence Act 1879, as an alternative to making an application for non-party disclosure under SCA 1981, s 34, or CCA 1984, s 53.

21.4.3   Procedure

An application for disclosure against a non-party can be made at any time after substantive proceedings have been issued. It is made by application notice, and must be supported by written evidence: CPR, r 31.17(2).

21.4.4 The order

The CPR, r 31.17(4) and (5), provide:

> (4) An order under this rule must—
> (a) specify the documents or the classes of documents which the respondent must disclose; and
> (b) require the respondent, when making disclosure, to specify any of those documents—
>   (i) which are no longer in his control; or
>   (ii) in respect of which he claims a right or duty to withhold inspection.
> (5) Such an order may—
> (a) require the respondent to indicate what has happened to any documents which are no longer in his control; and
> (b) specify the time and place for disclosure and inspection.

21.5 Inspection of property

There are wide powers to order inspection, examination, testing, experimenting on and photographing property which is relevant to proceedings. In contrast to search orders, these powers include in some circumstances jurisdiction to order the respondent to allow the applicant, and the applicant's advisers and experts, entry onto the respondent's premises. The rules provide for three separate situations, which are considered below.

21.5.1 Before issue of proceedings

21.5.1.1 Jurisdiction

The SCA 1981, s 33(1), provides:

> On the application of any person in accordance with rules of court, the High Court shall, in such circumstances as may be specified in the rules, have power to make an order providing for any one or more of the following matters, that is to say—
>
> (a) the inspection, photographing, preservation, custody and detention of property which appears to the court to be property which may become the subject-matter of subsequent proceedings in the High Court, or as to which any question may arise in any such proceedings; and
> (b) the taking of samples of any such property as is mentioned in paragraph (a), and the carrying out of any experiment on or with any such property.

21.5.1.2 Conditions

The only condition that must be fulfilled is that the property may become the subject-matter of subsequent proceedings.

21.5.1.3 Procedure

Pre-action inspection orders are applied for by issuing an ordinary application notice in the anticipated proceedings supported by written evidence, but before those proceedings are issued. The CPR, r 25.5, provides:

> (2) The evidence in support of such an application must show, if practicable by reference to any statement of case prepared in relation to the proceedings or anticipated proceedings, that the property—
> (a) is or may become the subject matter of such proceedings; or
> (b) is relevant to the issues that will arise in relation to such proceedings.

(3) A copy of the application notice and a copy of the evidence must be served on—(a) the person against whom the order is sought . . .

Like pre-action disclosure applications (see **21.3.6**), the court will not usually give a direction for commencing the substantive proceedings as the decision to commence will usually turn on the nature of the evidence gathered from the inspection (see CPR, r 25.2(4)).

21.5.2 After issue of proceedings, property in the possession of a party

21.5.2.1 The general rules

In many cases one party will have possession of property which the opponent's expert will need to inspect before an expert opinion can be reached. This problem arises where, for example, a surveyor needs to inspect land in relation to an alleged obstruction of ancient lights, or where an engineer needs to examine and test a machine after a factory accident, or where it is claimed goods are not of satisfactory quality. Thus, among the general interim remedies available to the court set out in CPR, r 25.1, are powers to make:

(1) . . .

(c) an order—

(i)   for the detention, custody or preservation of relevant property;

(ii)   for the inspection of relevant property;

(iii) for the taking of a sample of relevant property;

(iv)   for the carrying out of an experiment on or with relevant property; . . .

(d) an order authorising a person to enter my land or building in the possession of a party to the proceedings for the purposes of carrying out an order under sub-paragraph (c); . . .

(2) In paragraph (1)(c) . . . 'relevant property' means property (including land) which is the subject of a claim or as to which any question may arise on a claim.

Orders for inspection are commonly sought at the allocation stage. They can be asked for in a covering letter sent with the completed allocation questionnaire (the letter should be disclosed to the other parties at the same time), or in draft consent directions filed with the allocation questionnaire. Otherwise, such orders may be made on the case management conference or on an application issued for the purpose at any time after proceedings have been issued, or, in respect of a defendant, after giving notice of intention to defend. No written evidence is necessary.

21.5.2.2 Restriction on applications

The main restriction on such applications is that the rule is limited to physical things. In *Ash v Buxted Poultry Ltd* The Times, 29 November 1989, Brooke J held he had inherent jurisdiction to order the defendants to allow the claimant to make a video film of the defendant's manufacturing process.

21.5.3 After issue of proceedings, property in the possession of a non-party

21.5.3.1 Jurisdiction

The SCA 1981, s 34(3), provides:

On the application, in accordance with rules of court, of a party to any proceedings, the High Court shall, in such circumstances as may be specified in the rules, have power to make an order providing for any one or more of the following matters, that is to say—

(a) *the inspection, photographing, preservation, custody and detention of property which is not the property of, or in the possession of, any party to the proceedings but which is the subject-matter of the proceedings or as to which any question arises in the proceedings;*

(b) *the taking of samples of any such property as is mentioned in paragraph (a) and the carrying out of any experiment on or with any such property.*

The county courts have an identical power under CCA 1984, s 53(3).

21.5.3.2   Procedure

An order for inspection of property against a non-party is sought by issuing an application notice supported by evidence during the course of the substantive proceedings. The CPR, r 25.5, provides:

(3) *The evidence in support of such an application must show, if practicable by reference to any statement of case prepared in relation to the proceedings . . . , that the property—*

    (a) *is . . . the subject matter of such proceedings; or*

    (b) *is relevant to the issues that will arise in relation to such proceedings.*

(4) *A copy of the application notice and a copy of the evidence in support must be served on—*

    (a) *the person against whom the order is sought; and*

    (b) *in relation to an application under section 34(3) of the Supreme Court Act 1981 or section 53(3) of the County Courts Act 1984, every party to the proceedings other than the applicant.*

21.6   Interim delivery-up of goods

21.6.1   Jurisdiction

The Torts (Interference with Goods) Act 1977, s 4(2), provides:

On the application of any person in accordance with rules of court, the High Court shall, in such circumstances as may be specified in the rules, have power to make an order providing for the delivery up of any goods which are or may become the subject matter of subsequent proceedings [for wrongful interference] in the Court, or as to which any question may arise in the proceedings.

21.6.2   Principles

A number of guidelines have been suggested by the Court of Appeal in *CBS UK Ltd v Lambert* [1983] Ch 37:

- There should be clear evidence that the defendant is likely to dispose of the goods in order to deprive the claimant.
- There must be some evidence that the defendant acquired the goods wrongfully.
- The order should not be made if it will act oppressively against the defendant.

Often, the court needs to balance the claimant's immediate need for the goods against the defendant's grounds for retaining them.

21.6.3   The order

The order may provide for delivery to the claimant or a person appointed by the court. As an alternative to an order for delivery up, the court may make an order for preservation and detention of the goods.

Type of order	Type of case	Against	Stage	Type of application
Search order, entry and removal	Real possibility of defendant destroying vital material	Defendant	On issue of claim	Without notice
Norwich Pharmacal, identity of tortfeasor	Unknown defendant	Facilitator	Pre-action	Claim form and application on notice
SCA 1981, s 33(1), inspection of property	General application	Person with possession of property which may become the subject matter of subsequent action	Pre-action	Application notice before issue
SCA 1981, s 33(2), pre-action disclosure	General application	Likely Defendant	Pre-action	Application notice before issue
SCA 1981, s 34(2), disclosure of documents	General application	Non-party	After issue	Application notice
SCA 1981, s 34(3), inspection of property	General application	Non-party	After issue	Application notice
Detention, Custody, Preservation, Inspection, Samples, Observation, Experiments	General application	Party with possession of property	After issue	Allocation directions (generally)

Figure 21.1   Special disclosure and inspection orders

In *CBS United Kingdom Ltd v Lambert* the Court of Appeal said the order:

- should clearly specify the chattel to be delivered up;
- should not authorise the claimant to enter the defendant's land without the defendant's permission;
- should make adequate provision for the safe custody of the goods; and
- should give the defendant liberty to apply.

21.6.4 Procedure

Applications under the Torts (Interference with Goods) Act 1977 are among the general interim remedies available under CPR, r 25.1. Being an interim application, CPR, Parts 23 and 25, apply, so an application notice must be issued, usually on notice, supported by written evidence. In urgent cases the application can be made without notice and even before issue of originating process.

Requests for further information

22.1 Introduction

We have already seen how parties can obtain disclosure of documents, and thus, among other things, be in a better position to assess the strengths and weaknesses of the other side's case. Additionally, the judicious (and legitimate!) use of the request for further information can ensure that your opponent's statement of case has been set out in such a way as to make the issues between the parties absolutely clear. Nevertheless, there may be many times when it would be helpful if you could obtain further information from the other side without being limited to the other side's statement of case. In most cases, one simply has to wait for the exchange of witnesses' statements or wait until the trial—after all, it is then that the evidence is given and examined. However, there are circumstances in which it may be appropriate to ask for further information about matters raised in the witness statements or from documents inspected in the process of disclosure. The process of seeking further information extends to seeking information as the case develops, and there will be many cases where requests for further information are made early on to clarify the statements of case, and also at a later stage to clarify the evidence.

22.2 Procedure

The procedure for requesting further information can be used to expose deficiencies in the other side's statement of case. Such requests should be made shortly after the relevant statement of case is served. The procedure can also be used to seek clarification of any matter in dispute, or to seek information about any such matter, even though the point in question is not contained in or referred to in a statement of case (CPR, r 18.1). The procedure can therefore be used to try to find out about facts that might be expected to be contained in the witness statements (in which case the application would normally be expected to be made after the exchange of witness statements). The procedure can be used by the court of its own initiative for a variety of purposes, including finding out information for case management purposes. It is doubtful whether Part 18 can be used to seek information about the defendant's insurance cover, even if this will save unnecessary costs in seeking to maximise the damages claim where the defendant may not be able to pay without insurance (*West London Pipeline and Storage Ltd v Total UK Ltd* [2008] 1 CLC 935, not following *Harcourt v FEF Griffin* [2007] PIQR Q177).

A party seeking clarification or information (the first party) should first serve on the party from whom it is sought (the second party) a written request for that clarification or information stating a date by which the response to the request should be served. The date must allow the second party a reasonable time to respond. The request should be made by e-mail if this is reasonably practicable (PD 18, para 1.7). It should be concise and strictly confined to matters which are reasonably necessary and proportionate to enable the first party to prepare its own case or to understand the case that has to be met. A request may be made by letter (as an attachment) if the text of the request is brief and the reply is likely to be brief, otherwise the request should be made in a formal request for further information.

A request which is not in the form of a letter may, if convenient, be prepared in such a way that the response may be given on the same document. To do this the numbered paragraphs of the request should appear on the left-hand half of each sheet so that the paragraphs of the response may then appear on the right.

Unless the request is in the format described in the previous paragraph and the second party uses the document supplied for the purpose, a response must:

(a) be headed with the name of the court and the title and number of the claim;

(b) in its heading identify itself as a response to that request;

(c) repeat the text of each separate paragraph of the request and set out under each paragraph the response to it; and

(d) refer to and have attached to it a copy of any document not already in the possession of the first party which forms part of the response.

The second party must serve the response on the first party, and must file at court and serve on every other party a copy of the request and of the response. The response should be verified by a statement of truth.

If the second party objects to answering a request, or if the second party considers the time given by the first party to be too short, the second party should inform the first party of the objection promptly and within the time stated for the answers by the first party. Objections could include the disproportionate nature of the request, or that it infringes privilege, or otherwise infringes the overriding objective.

If a request for further information is not responded to, the first party is entitled to apply to the court for an order requiring the second party to reply in a stated period of time. There is no need to inform the second party of the application for such an order if the second party failed to make any response as set out in the previous paragraph within the time stated by the first party, and provided at least 14 days have passed since the request was served (PD 18, para 5.5(1)).

22.3 Principles

PD 18, para 1.2, provides:

A request should be concise and strictly confined to matters which are reasonably necessary and proportionate to enable the first party to prepare his own case or to understand the case he has to meet.

Until 1999 it was not unusual for parties to serve interrogatories and requests for further and better particulars (the predecessors of the present request for information) which were incredibly long and detailed. It was not unusual to ask 30 or 50 questions, many with several sub-questions. There was always the suspicion that such requests were mainly designed to rack up costs, or to make it difficult for the other party to answer, so that applications for 'unless' orders (orders with sanctions) could be made. Applying the overriding objective, and as PD 18, para 1.2, makes clear, such an approach is no longer tolerated, and any requests made for information should be reasonably necessary and proportionate.

22.3.1 Relevance to the issues

Requests will not be allowed unless they are relevant to the matters in issue. This might allow requests which may open a train of inquiry tending to establish the existence or non-existence of material facts (*Marriott v Chamberlain* (1886) 17 QBD 154), but the court will be astute in such a case to apply the overriding objective to ensure the inquiry is kept under control. Requests asked for the purposes of future actions will be refused.

22.3.2 'Fishing' requests

'Fishing' requests are disallowed.

If the question is asked by a party '. . . in order that he may find out something of which he knows nothing now, which might enable him to make a case of which he has no knowledge at present' it is fishing and will be disallowed (per Lord Esher MR in *Hennessey v Wright (No. 2)* (1888) 24 QBD 445, at 448, CA).

22.3.3 Questions as to the credibility of witnesses

Questions going to credibility of witnesses, as opposed to liability or damages, are not allowed (*Thorpe v Greater Manchester Chief Constable* [1989] 1 WLR 665, CA).

22.3.4 Scandalous requests

Scandalous requests are disallowed. These include insulting or degrading questions, as well as those which are irrelevant or impertinent to the issues.

22.3.5 Oppressive requests

Oppressive requests are also disallowed.

A question is oppressive if it places an undue burden on the party required to answer. As Collins MR said in *White v Credit Reform Association* [1905] 1 KB 653, at 659:

> A question becomes oppressive when it exceeds the legitimate requirements of the particular occasion. Such questions have some relevance to the issues, and the approach of the court is to ask whether the benefit in obtaining an answer countervails the inconvenience imposed on the opponent.

Thus, in *Parnell v Walter* (1890) 24 QBD 441, the Court of Appeal regarded a question asking for the precise circulation of a newspaper to be oppressive, and limited the required answer to giving the best information available in round figures. Similarly, a question in *Kirkup v British Railway Engineering Ltd* [1983] 1 WLR 1165, directed to noise levels in the whole of the defendant's operations, was limited by Croom-Johnson J on appeal to the works where the claimant was employed.

Kirkup is also authority for the proposition that a question is oppressive if not precisely formulated.

22.3.6 Necessary for disposing fairly of the claim

For example, a request in a debt claim which was designed to compel the defendant to acknowledge a debt under what is now the Limitation Act 1980, s 29, and thereby defeat an accrued limitation defence, may be disallowed as unnecessary for disposing fairly of the claim (*Lovell v Lovell* [1970] 1 WLR 1451, CA).

22.3.7   Overriding objective

The second party can object in his reply to a request on the ground that compliance will involve disproportionate expense (PD 18, para 4.2(2)). This may be because answering will require expensive enquiries. It may also arise where using the request procedure needlessly increases costs, for example where the information will be provided in any event during disclosure or the exchange of witness statements (*Hall v Selvaco Ltd* The Times, 27 March 1996, CA). There may, however, be good reasons for making a request even where the matter might be included in a witness statement (*Griebart v Morris* [1920] 1 KB 659, where the claimant had no knowledge of the accident due to the injuries suffered).

22.3.8   Requests instead of striking out

A request for further information may be the proportionate method for dealing with a statement of case which does not provide full information, rather than the more drastic approach of applying to strike out (*Deutsche Morgan Grenfell Group plc v Inland Revenue Commissioners* [2007] 1 AC 558, HL).

22.4   Requests for further information in search orders and freezing orders

Clauses requiring defendants to provide further information are included as standard in the model freezing and search orders in PD 25. Clause 9 of the standard freezing injunction order requires the defendant to provide information confirmed on affidavit giving details of all his assets. Clause 18 of the standard search order requires the defendant to provide information confirmed on affidavit of the whereabouts of all listed items, the names and addresses of the persons who supplied them or to whom they have been supplied, and dates and quantities of each transaction.

22.5   Collateral use

The CPR, r 18.2, says that the court may direct that information provided whether voluntarily or after an order must not be used for any purpose other than for the proceedings in which it is given. Consideration should be given to asking for such a direction whenever sensitive information is to be given in answer to a request for information.

IN THE CENTRAL LONDON COUNTY COURT   Claim No. 09 CL 43762

BETWEEN

Mrs ELEANOR JANE WELDON   Claimant

and

(1) Mr JAMES ARTHUR WILLIAMS

(2) D. STOKES (HAULAGE LIMITED)   Defendants

REQUEST FOR FURTHER INFORMATION UNDER PART 18

Made on behalf of Eleanor Jane Weldon (the first party) to D. Stokes (Haulage) Limited (the second party) dated 19th October 2009. These requests are to be answered no later than by 16th November 2009.

1. Is the first defendant employed or has the first defendant been employed by the second defendant? If yes, say in what capacity, what his principal duties are and have been, and the date his employment with you commenced and, if it be the case, the date his employment with you ended.

2. Was a van registration number LN02 YSJ ('the van') owned by the second defendant, and was the van operated by the second defendant, on 27th November 2008?

3. Was the van operating in London N10 on 27th November 2008?

4. Did the first defendant drive the van in Newlands Road, London N10 on 27th November 2008?

5. Did the van collide with a stationary car in Newlands Road, London N10 on 27th November 2008?

TAKE NOTICE that Donald Stokes, a director of the second defendant D. Stokes (Haulage) Limited, is required to answer these requests.

Dated the 19th October 2009, by Messrs Buchanan & Co of 23 The Hard, London N10, - solicitors for the claimant.

Figure 22.1   Request for further information

Limitation

23.1 Introduction

This chapter deals with the substantive rules on the limitation periods applicable to various classes of proceedings, which are discussed in **23.2** to **23.6**. A reasonable limitation period will not infringe art 6(1) of the European Convention on Human Rights, nor will it infringe EU law (*Aprile SRL v Amministrazione Delle Finanze Dello Stato (No. 2)* [2000] 1 WLR 126, ECJ). Likewise, the extinction of title rule after 12 years' adverse possession was held by the ECJ in *JA Pye (Oxford) Ltd v United Kingdom (Application No. 44302/02)* (2007) 23 BHRC 405 not to infringe art 1 of the First Protocol to the ECHR.

23.2 Limitation: general

Limitation is a procedural defence and if relied upon details must be given in the defence: PD 16, para 13.1. The expiry of a limitation period will not be taken by the court of its own motion. The basic policy is that defendants should not be perpetually at risk of proceedings being brought, and should not have to defend stale claims. Fixed periods have been laid down for bringing various categories of cases (see **Figure 23.1**), although there has been a tendency in more recent legislation towards granting some flexibility (see **23.5**).

Effluxion of time usually has the effect of extinguishing the claimant's remedy. In cases of adverse possession of land and conversion, expiry of the limitation period has the additional effect of extinguishing the claimant's title (see eg **23.3.3.3**).

The following table (fig 23.1) sets out the limitation periods for a selection of different categories of cases. It is not comprehensive.

	Class of action	Limitation period
1.	Tort, other than 2-3 below	6 years (Limitation Act 1980 (LA 1980), s 2)
2.	Personal injuries claims in negligence, nuisance or breach of duty (including contract or statute)	3 years (LA 1980, s 11)
3.	Fatal Accidents Act 1976 claims on behalf of the deceased's dependants	3 years from the date of death or the dependant's date of knowledge
4.	Contract (other than personal injuries claims)	6 years (LA 1980, s 5)

Class of action	Limitation period
5. Recovery of land	12 years (LA 1980, s 15(1))
6. Actions by beneficiaries to recover trust property or in respect of breach of trust	6 years (LA 1980, s 21(3))
7. Contribution under Civil Liability (Contribution) Act 1978	2 years (LA 1980, s 10(1))

Figure 23.1   Limitation periods

23.3   Accrual of cause of action

The date on which time begins to run for limitation purposes depends on the nature of the cause of action. Before considering some of the rules relating to specific causes of action, we will deal with some general points.

23.3.1   General rules

In *Reeves v Butcher* [1891] 2 QB 509, 511, Lindley LJ said '. . . it has always been held that the statute runs from the earliest time at which an action could be brought.' This is the time when facts exist establishing all the essential elements of the cause of action (*Coburn v Colledge* [1897] 1 QB 702, 706 per Lord Esher MR). A distinction is drawn between the substantive elements, which must be present, and mere procedural bars which do not stop time running. Sometimes this can be a difficult distinction to draw (see *Sevcon Ltd v Lucas CAV Ltd* [1986] 2 All ER 104, HL). Further, there must be a party capable of suing and a party liable to be sued (*Thomson v Lord Clanmorris* [1900] 1 Ch 718, 729 per Vaughan Williams LJ (obiter)). This will not be so where, for example, goods are converted after the owner has died intestate. Time in such a case runs from after letters of administration are taken out. On the other hand, time continues during a period in which the defendant is an undischarged bankrupt (*Anglo Manx Group Ltd v Aitken* [2002] BPIR 215).

23.3.2   Contract

Time runs from breach of the contract.

23.3.3   Tort

23.3.3.1   Trespass and libel
These are actionable per se, without proof of damage, so time runs from the wrongful act.

23.3.3.2   Slander, nuisance, negligence and other torts not involving personal injuries or death
These require proof of damage, so time runs from the damage. Formerly, the fact that the damage may not have been discovered until some time later did not prevent time running. See now the rules relating to latent damage (**23.3.4**).

23.3.3.3 Conversion

Time runs from the converting event. Note the following special rules:

(a) Where a chattel is converted more than once, the original six-year period is not renewed by the subsequent conversions: LA 1980, s 3(1).

(b) At the end of the original six-year period, the true owner's title is extinguished: LA 1980, s 3(2).

(c) Subject to (d), there is no time limit at all in bringing a claim in respect of a stolen chattel: LA 1980, s 4(1), (2).

(d) Where a chattel is converted, then stolen at a later date, proceedings in respect of the theft are barred once the original owner's title is extinguished under s 3(2) in respect of the original conversion: LA 1980, s 4(1).

23.3.3.4 Personal injuries: date of knowledge

Time runs from accrual (usually the date of the accident, when the injury was sustained) or, if later, the injured person's date of knowledge: LA 1980, s 11(4). Under LA 1980, s 14(1), a claimant's 'date of knowledge' is the first date the claimant knew three (sometimes four) things.

For time to begin to run the claimant must know:

(a) That the injury was significant ie the claimant would reasonably have considered it sufficiently serious to justify instituting proceedings for damages against a defendant who did not dispute liability and was able to satisfy a judgment: LA 1980, s 14(2). This element is often relevant in asbestosis claims. The question is whether, given what the claimant knew or should have known about his injuries, a reasonable person with that knowledge would have considered the injuries sufficiently serious to justify commencing proceedings (*A v Hoare* [2008] 1 AC 844). Collateral considerations, such as whether it would be impolitic to sue one's employer, are irrelevant (*McCafferty v Metropolitan Police District Receiver* [1977] 1 WLR 1073, CA).

(b) That the injury was attributable to the alleged default. This element is often relevant in clinical negligence claims. Time runs under this element when the claimant (or the claimant's doctor) concluded there was a real possibility that the defendant's activities caused the claimant's injury, such that a reasonable person would then investigate the link further (*Kew v Bettamix Ltd* [2007] PIQR P210).

The final words of s 14(1) expressly state that 'knowledge that any acts or omissions did or did not, as a matter of law, involve negligence, nuisance or breach of duty' is irrelevant. Although it is the essence of the allegedly negligent act or omission which must be known by the claimant, there must be a degree of specificity in that knowledge (*Nash v Eli Lilly and Co* [1993] 1 WLR 782, CA).

(c) The identity of the defendant. Time may not run against an injured employee where the exact identity of an allegedly negligent employer is not clear from the employee's contract of employment (*Cressey v E Timm and Son Ltd* [2005] 1 WLR 3926, CA).

AND

(d) If it is alleged that the act or omission was of a person other than the defendant (eg in vicarious liability situations), the identity of that person and the facts supporting an action against the defendant.

'Knowledge' for this purpose turns on the nature of the information available to the claimant, and how a reasonable person in the claimant's position, suffering from any medical condition suffered by the claimant, would have acted (*Adams v Bracknell Forest Borough Council* [2005] 1 AC 76). Reasonable people can be expected to seek professional advice on the cause of any significant injuries they might have suffered. Knowledge detailed enough to enable the claimant's advisers to draft Particulars of Claim is not required before time begins to run, and is contrary to the final words of s 14(1) (see *Broadley v Guy Clapham and Co* [1994] 4 All ER 439, CA).

In *Spargo v North Essex District Health Authority* [1997] PIQR P235, Brooke LJ laid down the following principles:

(a) The knowledge required to satisfy s 14(1)(b) is a broad knowledge of the essence of the causally relevant act or omission to which the injury is attributable.

(b) A claimant who knows enough to make it reasonable to begin to investigate whether or not there is a case against the defendant has the requisite knowledge. This will be the case if the claimant so firmly believes that his or her condition is capable of being attributed to an act or omission which he or she can identify (in broad terms) that he or she goes to a solicitor to seek advice about making a claim for compensation.

(c) A claimant who thinks he or she knows of acts or omissions which should be investigated, but in fact is barking up the wrong tree; or whose knowledge is too vague or general; or who is not sure whether his or her condition could be attributable to the act or omission alleged to constitute negligence, and would need to check with an expert, will not have the requisite knowledge.

Further, s 14(3) provides that a person's knowledge includes knowledge which he or she might reasonably have been expected to acquire from observable facts and the taking of appropriate expert advice. Where a serious injury has been suffered as a result of allegedly negligent medical treatment, Stuart-Smith LJ indicated in *Forbes v Wandsworth Health Authority* [1997] QB 402, CA, that a period of 12 to 18 months may be reasonable for taking stock before seeking expert advice.

23.3.3.5   Fatal accidents

There are potentially two limitation periods in fatal accident claims. The claim vested in the injured person's estate under the Law Reform (Miscellaneous Provisions) Act 1934 accrues on the date of the accident. The claim for the benefit of the deceased's dependants under the Fatal Accidents Act 1976 accrues on death (*Reader v Molesworths Bright Clegg* [2007] 1 WLR 1082). Time may be delayed in the Fatal Accidents Act 1976 claim until the date of the relevant dependant's knowledge (LA 1980, s 12), again as defined in LA 1980, s 14 (see **23.3.3.4**).

23.3.4   Latent damage

LA 1980, ss 14A, 14B, were inserted by the Latent Damage Act 1986. They apply to negligence actions, other than personal injuries cases. They are restricted to negligence claims in tort, and do not include actions for breach of contractual duty founded on allegations of negligent or careless conduct (*Iron Trade Mutual Insurance Co Ltd v J K Buckenham Ltd* [1990] 1 All ER 808). Latent damage is often a problem in relation to defective buildings, but ss 14A, 14B apply to all types of non-personal injuries negligence cases, such as claims against solicitors for negligent drafting or advice.

LA 1980, s 14A, provides for two alternative periods, namely six years from accrual and, if later, three years from the 'starting date' (see **23.3.4.1** and **23.3.4.2**). Both are subject to a 'longstop' of 15 years (see **23.3.4.3**).

23.3.4.1   Six years from accrual

As stated in **23.3**, an action in tort accrues when all the essential elements exist. In an action against a solicitor for negligent advice, the claimant suffers actual damage and has a complete cause of action when the advice is acted on, such as by executing a document (*Forster v Outred and Co* [1982] 1 WLR 86, CA). Contrast *Pirelli General Cable Works Ltd v Oscar Faber and Partners* [1983] 2 AC 1, HL where consulting engineers designed an addition to the claimant's factory, including a chimney. The chimney was built in 1969. Unsuitable materials were used, and cracking developed in 1970. With reasonable diligence, the claimants could have discovered the cracks in 1972, but in fact only discovered them in 1977. It was held that the action accrued when the damage came into existence in 1970. Acting on the defendants' design, discoverability and actual discovery of the damage were all rejected as dates for the accrual of the action. Whether this is still the law must be open to question. *Pirelli* was interpreted as falling within the *Hedley Byrne and Co Ltd v Heller and Partners Ltd* [1964] AC 485, HL principle in *Murphy v Brentwood District Council* [1991] 1 AC 398 at 466, where Lord Keith said that if the claimants had discovered the defect before any damage had occurred their cause of action would have accrued at that stage.

23.3.4.2   Starting date

The alternative period of three years runs from the earliest date the claimant knew:

(a) that the relevant damage was sufficiently serious to justify commencing proceedings;

(b) that the damage was attributable to the alleged negligence;

(c) the defendant's identity; and

(d) if it is alleged that the act or omission was of a person other than the defendant, the identity of that person and the facts supporting an action against the defendant.

These concepts mirror those for determining the claimant's date of knowledge in personal injuries cases (see **23.3.3.4**). 'Knowledge' in s 14A means knowing with sufficient confidence to justify embarking on the preliminaries to issuing proceedings. Under condition (b), it is enough for the claimant to have broad knowledge of the facts on which the complaint is based, combined with knowing as a real possibility that the alleged acts or omissions caused the damage under condition (a) (*Haward v Fawcetts* [2006] 1 WLR 682, HL).

23.3.4.3   Longstop

LA 1980, s 14B, provides a 15-year overriding time limit for negligence actions not involving personal injuries, after which such actions shall not be brought even if the cause of action has not yet accrued or the 'starting date' has not yet arrived. This 15-year period runs from the date of the act or omission which is alleged to constitute the negligence resulting in the claimant's damage.

23.3.5   Recovery of land

A number of very detailed rules are set out over four pages in LA 1980, Sch 1.

23.3.6   Contribution

Time runs from the date when the amount of the liability in respect of which contribution is sought was fixed (excluding any variation on appeal). Thus, if the amount was determined by a court, time runs from the date judgment was given (LA 1980, s 10(3)). In the case of split trials, time runs from the judgment on liability (*Aer Lingus v Gildacroft Ltd* [2006] 1 WLR 1173, CA). If settled by compromise, time runs from the date the amount was agreed (LA 1980, s 10(4)).

23.4   Calculating the limitation period

23.4.1   General rules

Time runs from the day following the day on which the cause of action arose, as parts of a day are disregarded (*Marren v Dawson, Bentley and Co Ltd* [1961] 2 QB 135). Time stops running when proceedings are 'brought'. If the court office is closed on what would otherwise be the last day of the limitation period, proceedings will be in time if brought on the next day on which the court office is open (*Kaur v S. Russell and Sons Ltd* [1973] QB 337, CA). A claim is brought for the purposes of the Limitation Act on the date the papers needed to issue the claim are delivered to the court, rather than the date of issue (PD 7, para 5.1; *St Helens Metropolitan Borough Council v Barnes* [2007] 1 WLR 879). The court will normally date-stamp the covering letter to record the date of receipt, which provides evidence of when the claim is brought: para 5.2.

23.4.2   Sets-offs and counterclaims

By virtue of LA 1980, s 35(1)(b), sets-offs and counterclaims are deemed to have been commenced on the same date as the original claim. This is often called the statutory relation back. As this provision may save claims which might otherwise be time barred, generally no such claim can be made after the expiry of the limitation period unless it is 'an original set-off or counterclaim'. To qualify as such, the set-off or counterclaim must be brought by a party who has not previously made any claim in the proceedings: s 35(3).

23.4.3   Additional claims under Part 20

Additional claims, other than counterclaims, are deemed to have been commenced on the date the additional claim form under Part 20 was issued: LA 1980, s 35(1)(a). It is questionable whether the cases on delivering the claim form to the court (see **23.4.1**) apply, because s 35(1)(a) uses the word 'commenced' rather than 'brought'.

23.4.4   Disability

Time does not run against a person under disability on the date the cause of action accrued: LA 1980, s 28. There are two categories:

(a) children (persons under the age of 18); and

(b) persons who lack capacity within the meaning of the Mental Capacity Act 2005 (LA 1980, s 38(2)). These are persons who lack capacity in relation to a matter through being unable to make a decision for themselves in relation to the matter because of an impairment of, or a disturbance in the functioning of, the mind or brain (see Mental Capacity Act 2005, s 2(1)).

Where the claimant suffers injury resulting in immediate unsoundness of mind, limitation does not run for the period of the disability. If, before attaining majority, a claimant becomes of unsound mind, the limitation period will only commence when the later disability ends. But, where a person of full age becomes of unsound mind after the accrual of a cause of action, time continues to run during the period of disability.

23.4.5 Acknowledgment

Limitation is renewed where the defendant acknowledges a claim in signed writing, or makes any payment towards the liability, provided the claim is not already barred (LA 1980, ss 29(5), (7) and 30). An acknowledgment in a privileged document cannot be used for this purpose, and an acknowledgment in a pleading takes effect on the date of the pleading (*Ofulue v Bossert* [2009] 2 WLR 749).

23.4.6 Fraud

By LA 1980, s 32(1)(a), the limitation period in an action based upon the fraud of the defendant does not run until the claimant either has, or could with reasonable diligence have, discovered the fraud. A suspicion of the defendant's dishonesty does not start time running (*Barnstaple Boat Co Ltd v Jones* [2008] 1 All ER 1124). The claim must be actually founded on fraud, as in deceit. The fact the defendant has incidentally been fraudulent or dishonest (as in many conversion cases) is not enough (*Beaman v ARTS Ltd* [1949] 1 KB 550, 558, CA).

23.4.7 Concealment

Where any fact relevant to the claimant's right of action has been deliberately concealed by the defendant, time does not begin to run until the claimant either discovers, or could with reasonable diligence have discovered, the concealment: LA 1980, s 32(1)(b). In *Kitchen v Royal Air Force Association* [1958] 1 WLR 563, CA, solicitors negligently failed to advise the claimant that she had a possible claim against an electricity company. The section came into operation when, later, the solicitor failed to inform her that the company had offered to pay £100 in compromise, so as not to reveal their earlier negligence. Moreover, s 32(1)(b) also operates where the defendant conceals facts relevant to the claimant's claim after time has started to run (*Sheldon v RHM Outhwaite (Underwriting Agencies) Ltd* [1996] AC 102, HL).

By s 32(2), the deliberate commission of a breach of duty in circumstances in which it is unlikely to be discovered for some time amounts to a deliberate concealment. In *Cave v Robinson Jarvis and Rolf* [2003] 1 AC 384, the House of Lords overruled previous Court of Appeal authorities including *Brocklesbury v Armitage and Guest* [2002] 1 WLR 598 (which had given an unduly wide interpretation for s 32(2)), and held that s 32 deprives a defendant of a limitation defence:

(a) where the defendant has taken active steps to conceal his breach of duty after he has become aware of it; and

(b) where the defendant is guilty of deliberate wrongdoing and conceals or fails to disclose it in circumstances where the wrongdoing is unlikely to be discovered for some time.

However, the mere fact the defendant intended to do the act complained of does not mean that s 32 applies to prevent time running. If the defendant is unaware of his alleged error or that he may have failed to take proper care, there is nothing for the defendant to disclose, and time is not prevented from running by s 32. Consequently, time will run where a surgeon negligently leaves a swab inside a patient; and where an anaesthetist negligently administers the wrong drug; and where a solicitor gives a client negligent advice. Time will not run if the surgeon deliberately left the swab inside the patient, or if the lawyer after giving negligent advice fails to disclose other facts which he is under a duty to disclose to the client which would have alerted the client to the negligent nature of the advice.

23.4.8 Mistake

Where the claimant's action is for relief from the consequences of a mistake, again time does not run until the mistake either is, or could with reasonable diligence have been, discovered: LA 1980, s 32(1)(c). In *Peco Arts Inc v Hazlitt Gallery Ltd* [1983] 1 WLR 1315, the claimant, on the recommendation of a specialist in nineteenth century drawings, bought a drawing from the defendants. It was an express term that it was an original drawing signed by the artist. Six years after purchase it was revalued by an art expert, and no doubts were cast on its authenticity. Five years later it was found to be a reproduction. The claimant claimed for recovery of the purchase price as money paid under a mutual mistake of fact. It was held that 'reasonable diligence' in the context of the claimant's action meant doing that which an ordinary prudent buyer of a valuable work of art would do, and that on the facts the claimant had exercised reasonable diligence.

23.4.9 Breach of trust

LA 1980, s 21(1), provides that no limitation period applies to actions brought by beneficiaries either:

(a) in respect of any fraud by a trustee; or

(b) to recover from a trustee property converted to the trustee's use.

Time was held to run in favour of the trustee in *Thorne v Head* [1894] 1 Ch 599, who had negligently left trust funds with a solicitor who then embezzled it. The trustee was not a party to or privy to the fraud.

23.5 Discretionary extension of limitation periods

23.5.1 General

Some of the prescribed periods may be extended in the discretion of the court. Thus, the three month period for making an application for judicial review may be extended applying the overriding objective. In defamation cases, if the claimant discovers the relevant facts after the expiry of the one-year basic period, an action can be brought within one year of the facts becoming known, but only with the permission of the court: LA 1980, s 32A.

23.5.2 Personal injuries cases

23.5.2.1 Principles

Perhaps more important is the equitable discretion of the court to disapply the primary limitation period in personal injuries cases. LA 1980, s 33, provides:

> (1) *If it appears to the court that it would be equitable to allow an action to proceed having regard to the degree to which—*
>
> > (a) *the provisions of section 11 or 12 of this Act prejudice the plaintiff or any person whom he represents; and*
> >
> > (b) *any decision of the court under this subsection would prejudice the defendant or any person whom he represents; the court may direct that those provisions shall not apply to the action, or shall not apply to any specified cause of action to which the action relates.*
>
> > . . .
>
> (3) *In acting under this section the court shall have regard to all the circumstances of the case and in particular to—*
>
> > (a) *the length of, and the reasons for, the delay on the part of the plaintiff;*
> >
> > (b) *the extent to which, having regard to the delay, the evidence adduced or likely to be adduced by the plaintiff or the defendant is or is likely to be less cogent than if the action had been brought within the time allowed by section 11 or (as the case may be) by section 12;*
> >
> > (c) *the conduct of the defendant after the cause of action arose, including the extent (if any) to which he responded to requests reasonably made by the plaintiff for information or inspection for the purpose of ascertaining facts which were or might be relevant to the plaintiff's cause of action against the defendant;*
> >
> > (d) *the duration of any disability of the plaintiff arising after the date of the accrual of the cause of action;*
> >
> > (e) *the extent to which the plaintiff acted promptly and reasonably once he knew whether or not the act or omission of the defendant, to which the injury was attributable, might be capable at that time of giving rise to an action for damages;*
> >
> > (f) *the steps, if any, taken by the plaintiff to obtain medical, legal or other expert advice and the nature of any such advice he may have received.*

The leading authority on s 33 is *Thompson v Brown* [1981] 1 WLR 747, where the House of Lords held that the discretionary power to disapply the primary limitation period is unfettered, the court being required to take into account all the circumstances of the case. A tortfeasor only deserves to have his obligation to pay damages removed if the passage of time has significantly compromised his ability to defend the claim (*Cain v Francis* [2009] LS Law Medical 82).

If the delay was caused by the claimant's solicitors' negligence, that is a highly relevant factor, because the strength of an alternative claim will directly affect the degree to which the claimant is prejudiced by the time limit in s 11. However, as Lord Diplock mentions at p 750, instructing new and strange solicitors may cause some prejudice to the claimant.

The factors set out in LA 1980, s 33(3)(a) and (b), are addressing the period between the expiry of the primary limitation period, as extended, if appropriate, by the claimant's date of knowledge under s 14 (*Long v Tolchard* [2001] PIQR P2, CA). If an extended period has been granted by reference to s 14, the court is likely to give only limited weight under s 33 to the reasons for any delay beyond that extended period (*KR v Bryn Alyn Community (Holdings) Ltd* [2003] QB 1441). Wrong advice from the claimant's lawyers is relevant for the purposes of s 33(3)(a) and (f), and the claimant is not to be criticised for this type of error by his or her lawyers (*Das v Ganju* [1999] PIQR P260, CA). One of the things s 33(3)(b) requires the court to consider is the extent to which it is possible to have a fair trial of all the issues. If the claimant has a strong, or even a cast iron, case against the original tortfeasor, that is an important factor to place into the balance that has to be struck, but, like all the other factors, is not determinative of the application, which may still be decided against the claimant (*Long v Tolchard*).

Section 33 was further considered by the House of Lords in *Donovan v Gwentoys Ltd* [1990] 1 WLR 472. The claimant was injured at work in 1979 when aged 16. She had received advice from her union representative about sickness pay, but he did not mention claiming damages. The claimant attained her majority on 25 April 1981. She eventually consulted a solicitor on 6 April 1984. Limitation expired on 25 April 1984. The defendants were notified of the claim in September 1984, and proceedings were issued on 10 October 1984. The accident papers in 1979 referred to a wrist injury, but the details of the claimant's injury sent to the defendants in January 1986 revealed the substantial claim was for a knee injury. The defendants set up the Limitation Act in defence, and the claimant applied for a direction under s 33(1).

Lord Griffith adopted the following passage from the dissenting judgment of Stuart-Smith LJ in the Court of Appeal:

The time of the notification of the claim is not one of the particular matters to which the court is required to have regard under section 33(3), although it may come in under paragraph (e). But to my mind it is an extremely important consideration . . .

Lord Griffith held that the balance of prejudice in the case came down heavily in favour of the defendants. It would not be equitable to require the defendants to meet such a stale claim which they would have the utmost difficulty in defending, whereas the claimant would suffer only the slightest prejudice in being required to sue her solicitors.

In early notification cases where there is no defence on liability, financial prejudice to the defendant should not be taken into account (*Cain v Francis* [2009] LS Law Medical 82).

23.5.2.2   Procedure

An application under s 33 to disapply the limitation period is considered to be a final rather than interim matter (see *Hughes v Jones* The Times, 18 July 1996, CA). It should therefore be dealt with by a judge having trial jurisdiction over the claim (which means that District Judges can only deal with these applications in County Court fast track cases). It is incumbent on the claimant to disclose all relevant circumstances at the hearing of the application, and if this is breached, the decision may be set aside (*Long v Tolchard* [2001] PIQR P2, CA).

Whether to exercise the jurisdiction under s 33 can come before the court in the following instances:

- by way of a cross-application by the claimant if the defendant applies for summary judgment or to strikeout;
- on an application by application notice supported by evidence by the claimant;
- by way of a trial of limitation as a preliminary issue; or
- may be left to be dealt with at trial.

23.5.3   Issuing a second claim

At one time it was held that the Limitation Act 1980, s 33, could only be used to disapply limitation if the claimant had not previously brought proceedings in respect of the accident in question (*Walkley v Precision Forgings Ltd* [1979] 1 WLR 606). This meant that s 33 could not be used if proceedings had been brought within limitation, but did not proceed to trial for any reason, and a second claim was then issued outside the limitation period. This restriction was removed by *Horton v Sadler* [2007] 1 AC 307.

23.5.4 Categorisation of injury claims

Personal injury claims are all governed by the three-year limitation period in LA 1980, s 11, which may be extended by the date of knowledge provisions in s 14 and the discretionary extension of time under s 33. This is so whether the claim is founded on tort, breach of statutory duty or breach of contract (s 11). The only exception relates to defective product claims (for which see s 11A). At one time it was thought there was a distinction between cases involving intentional trespass to the person (which were thought to be subject to the six-year limitation period in s 2) and unintentional trespass and negligence claims (see *Stubbings v Webb* [1993] 2 AC 498). This distinction is now recognised as being false (see *A v Hoare* [2008] 1 AC 844).

A negligent failure by an education authority to improve the consequences of the claimant's dyslexia by appropriate teaching, or a negligent failure to treat a physical injury, are both claims for personal injuries (*Adams v Bracknell Forest Borough Council* [2005] 1 AC 76). A claim in professional negligence against a solicitor arising out of the firm's handling of a divorce ancillary relief claim, which included a claim for anxiety and stress arising out of the firm's alleged mishandling of her claim, became, for that reason, a claim in respect of personal injuries and subject to the three-year limitation period rather than the usual six-year period in claims in tort and breach of contract (*Oates v Harte Reade and Co* [1999] PIQR P120).

23.6 Equitable remedies

By LA 1980, s 36(1), the usual time limits do not apply to claims for specific performance, injunctions or other equitable relief, except insofar as they may be applied by analogy (see *Cia de Seguros Imperio v Heath (REBX) Ltd* [2001] 1 WLR 112). The defences of laches and acquiescence are preserved by LA 1980, s 36(2). In considering these defences, the courts assess the hardship caused to the defendant by the delay, any effect upon third parties, and the balance of justice in granting or refusing the relief claimed. In keeping with equitable principles, the court has a wide discretion, and no firm maximum period has been laid down. See generally *Weld v Petre* [1929] 1 Ch 33 and *Jones v Stones* [1999] 1 WLR 1739.

Amendment

24.1 Introduction

This chapter considers:

- The procedural rules relating to the amendment of statements of case and misjoinder of parties.
- The rather complex rules that apply when a party seeks to amend after the expiry of a relevant limitation period.

24.2 Amendment: general

In many cases, a party to a claim may wish to amend a statement of case after it has been served. Sometimes, a claimant who wishes to add a claim for a new cause of action, or to join a new defendant, will have to amend the claim form, as well as the particulars of claim, or the defendant may wish to amend the defence. Further, it has to be admitted, even lawyers are not perfect, and an occasional slip may have to be amended. Amendments may be allowed either by consent or by a court order. The usual position is that the party making an amendment must pay the costs of and occasioned by the amendment.

In **24.3** to **24.5** we will first consider the general rules, which can be divided into amendment with and without the permission of the court. We will then, in **24.6**, consider the problems relating to amendment of parties.

24.3 Amendment without permission

By CPR, r 17.1(1), a party is allowed to amend a statement of case at any time before it has been served on any other party. Once it has been served a statement of case can only be amended with the consent of the other parties or the permission of the court. As we have seen previously, the term 'statements of case' is defined as the claim form, particulars of claim, the defence, reply, additional claims under Part 20 and any further information given in relation to them: CPR, r 2.3(1).

The right to amend without permission is therefore largely restricted to amendments to the claim form and particulars of claim in the period between issue and service, which could be as long as four months. Other statements of case could fall to be amended without permission in the period between filing and service, but in most cases this will be a very short period of time.

A party served with a statement of case amended without permission can object to the amendment by issuing an application notice seeking an order disallowing the amendment pursuant to CPR, r 17.2. Such an application should be made within 14 days of service of the amended statement of case: r 17.2(2).

24.4 Amendment by consent

Any amendment (other than one altering the parties to the claim) is allowed with the written consent of all other parties: CPR, rr 17.1(2)(a), 19.4(1). An unreasonable refusal of consent may result in the loss of the usual order that the party asking to amend must pay the costs of and occasioned by the amendment (*La Chemise Lacoste SA v Skechers USA Ltd* (2006) LTL 24/5/2006).

24.5 Amendment with permission

24.5.1 Principles

The CPR, r 17.1(2), provides:

If his statement of case has been served, a party may amend it only—

(a) *with the written consent of all other parties; or*
(b) *with the permission of the court.*

A court asked to grant permission to amend will base its decision on the overriding objective. Generally, disposing of a case justly should mean that amendments should be allowed to enable the real matters in controversy between the parties to be determined. The usual costs rule is that the party granted permission to amend must pay the other parties their 'costs of and arising from' the amendment (PD 17 and PD 19). It has been held that: 'However negligent or careless may have been the first omission, and however late the proposed amendment, the amendment should be allowed if it can be made without injustice to the other side. There is no injustice if the other side can be compensated by costs,' (per Brett MR in *Clarapede v Commercial Union Association* (1883) 32 WR 262). There is a public interest in allowing a party to deploy its real case, provided it is relevant and has a real prospect of success (*Cook v News Group Newspapers Ltd* (2002) LTL 21/6/2002).

However, this is not always the case. Lord Griffiths in *Ketteman v Hansel Properties Ltd* [1987] AC 189, HL, has said,

. . . it is not the practice invariably to allow a defence which is wholly different from that pleaded to be raised by amendment at the end of the trial even on terms that an adjournment is granted and that the defendant pays all the costs thrown away . . . Whether an amendment should be granted is a matter for the discretion of the trial judge and he should be guided in the exercise of the discretion by his assessment of where justice lies. Many and diverse factors will bear upon the exercise of this discretion.

Turning to the facts, during the final stages of the trial it became apparent that the defendants were likely to lose on the merits. During closing speeches they were granted permission to amend their defence to plead a limitation defence. They could have raised the defence at an earlier stage, and the House of Lords agreed with the Court of Appeal that such an amendment should not have been allowed. If the application had been made earlier, preferably before the trial, it is unlikely the defendant would have encountered difficulties in amending.

The principles in these cases were approved in the post-CPR case of *Charlesworth v Relay Roads Ltd* [2000] 1 WLR 230, where Neuberger J described them as representing a fundamental assessment of the functions of the court and having a universal and timeless validity.

The interrelation between the *Clarapede* and *Ketteman* principles was considered by the Court of Appeal in *Easton v Ford Motor Co Ltd* [1993] 1 WLR 1511. *Clarapede* governs all applications made in the early stages of litigation through to the period immediately before trial. In the latest stages of litigation, and particularly the closing stages of the trial, *Ketteman* will apply. There is a grey area between the two. So, for example, an amendment sought at trial to plead a set of facts that only emerges with the evidence at the trial will generally be permitted, because allowing a party to plead a case consistent with the real facts is consistent with the overriding objective (*Binks v Securicor Omega Express Ltd* [2003] 1 WLR 2557). On the other hand, lateness combined with a weak case justified refusal of permission to amend in *Savings and Investment Bank Ltd v Fincken* [2004] 1 WLR 667.

In any case, the court may refuse an amendment if it will serve no useful purpose (*Re Jokai Tea Holdings Ltd* [1992] 1 WLR 1196, CA), or if the proposed amendments have no real prospects of success (*Oil and Mineral Development Corporation Ltd v Sajjad* (2001) LTL 6/12/2001; *Clarke v Slay* [2002] EWCA Civ 113).

24.5.2 Withdrawal of pre-commencement admission

After proceedings are issued, an admission made before proceedings were commenced may be withdrawn, but requires either the consent of all parties or the court's permission (CPR, r 14.1A(3)(b)). In deciding whether to give permission, the court is required by PD 14, para 7.2, to have regard to all the circumstances of the case, including:

(a) the grounds upon which the applicant seeks to withdraw the admission, including whether or not new evidence has come to light which was not available at the time the admission was made;

(b) the conduct of the parties, including any conduct which led the applicant into making the admission;

(c) any prejudice that may be caused to any person if the admission is withdrawn;

(d) the prejudice that may be caused to any person if the application is refused;

(e) the stage in the proceedings at which the application to withdraw is made, and in particular in relation to the trial date or window;

(f) the prospects of success (if the admission is withdrawn) of the claim or part of the claim in relation to which the admission was made; and

(g) the interests of the administration of justice.

24.5.3 Procedure

A party seeking permission to amend must issue an application notice. Generally no evidence is required in support, but the proposed amended statement of case must be filed with the application: PD 17, para 1.2(2).

The traditional way of amending is to retype the statement of case showing the original wording in ordinary black type, but with the amendments made in, or underlined in, red. Any words deleted are shown crossed through in red ink. Re-amendments are shown in green ink. Subsequent amendments are shown first in violet and then yellow inks: PD 17, para 2.4. However, there are two other options:

(a) by using monochrome typeface, but with a numeric code indicating the amendments (PD 17, para 2.2(2)); or

(b) by simply retyping the document incorporating the changes and omitting deleted text (PD 17, para 2.2). However, the court may, if it thinks it desirable, direct that the amendments be shown in one or other of the ways described above.

If there is a substantial change the document should be re-verified by a statement of truth (PD 17, para 1.4).

The amended statement of case should be endorsed 'Amended [Particulars of Claim] by Order of District Judge [Chelmsford] dated [19th November 2008]'.

24.6 Addition and substitution of parties

24.6.1 Main rules

If an amendment involves the removal, addition or substitution of a party the court will consider CPR, Part 19, which provides a code for dealing with such situations (as well as providing a code for intervention by non-parties (see **8.7**)). Permission for such amendments must be sought if the alteration is to be made after service of the claim form: r 19.4(1).

The main test when considering a change involving the addition or substitution of a party is whether the amendment is 'desirable': see CPR, r 19.2(2)-(4). Nobody, however, may be added as a claimant unless they consent in writing: CPR, r 19.4(4).

The CPR, r 19.2, provides so far as is material:

(2) *The court may order a person to be added as a new party if—*
    (a) *it is desirable to add the new party so that the court can resolve all matters in dispute in the proceedings; or*
    (b) *there is an issue involving the new party and an existing party which is connected to the matters in dispute in the proceedings, and it is desirable to add the new party so that the court can resolve that issue.*
(3) *The court may order any person to cease to be a party if it is not desirable for that person to be party to the proceedings.*
(4) *The court may order a new party to be substituted for an existing one if—*
    (a) *the existing party's interest or liability has passed to the new party; and*
    (b) *it is desirable to substitute the new party so that the court can resolve the matters in dispute in the proceedings.*

Court fees are payable when new parties are brought in.

24.6.2 Procedure for making changes in the parties

Any change involving the addition or substitution of a party will involve amending the statements of case, and can only be made by order of the court: see CPR, r 19.2(2)-(4). The application may be made by an existing party or by a person who wishes to become a party: CPR, r 19.4(2). There is an express provision requiring evidence in support of an application under r 19.2(4) for the substitution of a new party where an existing party's interest has passed (eg on death), and that type of application can be made without notice: r 19.4(3). Any other type of application for addition or substitution does not strictly have to be supported by written evidence, though the circumstances may make this desirable. Further, any other type of addition or substitution application is usually made on notice to all other parties.

If a proposed change in the parties is agreed by the court, the order must be served on all the parties and also on anyone affected by the order: CPR, r 19.4(5). An order granting permission to make such an amendment may include consequential directions (r 19.4(6) and PD 19, para 3.2) dealing with:

- filing and serving of the amended claim form and particulars of claim on any new defendant, usually within 14 days;
- serving other relevant documents on the new party;
- providing the new defendant with a response pack for the purpose of admitting, defending or counterclaiming;
- serving the order on all parties and any other person affected by it; and
- the management of the proceedings.

24.6.3   Effect of addition or substitution of a new party

A person added as a defendant by amendment becomes a party for the first time when the amended proceedings are served (*Ketteman v Hansel Properties Ltd* [1987] AC 189, HL).

24.7   Amendment after the limitation period

24.7.1   General rule

The Limitation Act 1980, s 35(3), provides:

Except as provided by section 33 of this Act or by rules of court, neither the High Court nor any county court shall allow a new claim . . . , other than an original set-off or counterclaim, to be made in the course of any action after the expiry of any time limit under this Act which would affect a new action to enforce that claim.

A 'new claim' is defined in s 35(2) as:

any claim by way of set-off or counterclaim, and any claim involving either—

(a) the addition or substitution of a new cause of action; or
(b) the addition or substitution of a new party

Relevant rules of court, made under s 35(4), are CPR, rr 17.4 and 19.5.

24.7.2   Amendment after the limitation period to add/substitute a new cause of action

The Limitation Act 1980 (LA 1980), s 35, provides that a new cause of action may be added to existing proceedings after the expiry of the limitation period only if:

(a) it is an original set-off or counterclaim made by a party who has not previously made any claim in the action (s 35(3)); or

(b) the court disapplies the personal injuries limitation period under LA 1980, s 33 (s 33 is explained at **23.5.2** above) (s 35(3)); or

(c) it arises out of the same, or substantially the same, facts as are already in issue (s 35(5)(a)).

An original set-off or counterclaim ((a) above) arises when the party making the counterclaim has not previously counterclaimed and is on the opposite side of the record to the defendant to the counterclaim (*Law Society v Wemyss* [2008] EWHC 2515 (Ch)). To avoid unfair evasion of the rules on limitation, amendments under this provision may be refused in the court's discretion if the counterclaim is being used as an offensive weapon, or if it is radically different to the existing claim.

Whether amendments involve the same or substantially the same facts as those already in issue is determined by comparing the bare minimum of essential facts abstracted from the original pleading with the bare minimum of facts required in the amended pleading (*P and O Nedlloyd BV v Arab Metals Co* [2007] 1 WLR 2483). The writ served in *Brickfield Properties Ltd v Newton* [1971] 1 WLR 863 claimed damages against the defendant architect for negligent supervision of certain works. After the limitation period had expired, a statement of claim was served claiming damages both for negligent design and negligent supervision. The defendant applied to strike out the allegation of negligent design. The Court of Appeal held that the statement of claim could not stand without amending the writ. It was further held that the design and supervision claims arose out of 'substantially the same facts' ((c) above), and in its discretion the court allowed the amendment of the writ. However, Spanish fishermen were refused permission to amend their claim to add further claims for compensation for breach of Community law (in being prevented from fishing by unlawful UK legislation) in respect of additional vessels. This was because the facts they needed to prove were largely specific to each boat, and so the additional claims did not arise out of substantially the same facts as were already in issue (*R v Secretary of State for Transport, ex p Factortame Ltd (No.7)* [2001] 1 WLR 942).

In *Goode v Martin* [2002] 1 WLR 1828, the claimant sought permission to amend her claim after the expiry of limitation to plead that, on the alternative version of the facts pleaded in the defence, the defendant would still be liable to her. The judge held that there was no power to allow the amendment, because r 17.4(2) allows such amendments if the new claim arises out of the same or substantially the same facts 'as a claim in respect of which [the claimant] has already claimed', and the facts relied upon were pleaded by the defendant. The Court of Appeal held that the Human Rights Act 1998, s 3, allowed it to read the words 'are already in issue on' into this rule, with the effect that the court had power to allow the amendment as it was based on facts put in issue by the defence.

24.7.3   Amendment after the limitation period to add/substitute a new party

There are four situations where such an amendment will be allowed. The first is in relation to personal injury cases (s 35(3)), the remaining three are where it is necessary to add/substitute a new party (s 35(5)(b)).

24.7.3.1   Limitation Act 1980, s 33

This is where a new party is added or substituted when the court disapplies the personal injury limitation period under s 33 (see s 35(3) and CPR, r 19.5(4)). The addition of the new party will also be allowed if the decision under s 33 is left until trial (r 19.5(4)(b)).

24.7.3.2   Claim cannot properly be carried on without new party

The CPR, r 19.5(3), provides that the addition or substitution of a new party after the expiry of a limitation period may be necessary if:

> *(b)   the claim cannot properly be carried on by or against the original party unless the new party is added or substituted as claimant or defendant. . .*

The rule gives no further guidance on when claims cannot 'properly' be carried on without the amendment. It is possible that the rule gives a general discretion to the court to consider whether evading the provisions of the Limitation Act by amendment would be 'proper'. However, this is unlikely to be what the rule envisages. The former provisions (RSC Ord 15, r 6(6)), giving effect to this part of the LA 1980, s 35, laid down five categories of cases where errors in naming parties gave rise to a legal bar to obtaining a remedy, and it was only in these five categories where it was considered 'necessary' (the same word used in the present rules in r 19.5(2)(b) in this context) to add a party once limitation had expired. It is most likely that it will only be 'proper' to add or substitute a party under r 19.5(3)(b) where a legal impediment such as those set out in the old Ord 15, r 6(6), exists, a view which is strongly supported by *Merrett v Babb* [2001] QB 1174. The old categories were where:

(a)   property was vested in the new party at law or in equity and the claimant's claim was in respect of an equitable interest in that property which was liable to be defeated unless the new party was joined; or

(b)   the relevant cause of action was vested in the new party and the claimant jointly but not severally; or

(c)   the new party was the Attorney-General and the proceedings should have been brought by relator proceedings (see **8.2.13**) in his name; or

(d)   the new party was a company in which the claimant was a shareholder and on whose behalf the claimant was suing to enforce a right vested in the company; or

(e)   the new party was sued jointly with the defendant and was not also liable severally with him and failure to join the new party might have rendered the claim unenforceable.

It will be appreciated that these categories were rather narrow. Joint, but not several, entitlement or liability (grounds (b) and (e) above) may arise where a contract is, by its terms, made jointly with numerous persons. An example is *Roche v Sherrington* [1982] 1 WLR 599 where it was alleged that loans were made to the defendant from moneys in a joint account in the names of three persons. In such a case, under CPR, r 19.3, all three must be made parties to the claim, as defendants if they do not consent to acting as claimants unless the court gives permission to the contrary.

24.7.3.3   Alteration of capacity

The third situation is provided by CPR, r 17.4(4):

> *The court may allow an amendment to alter the capacity in which a party claims if the new capacity is one which that party had when the proceedings started or has since acquired.*

'Capacity' in this rule is used in the sense of legal competence or status to bring or defend a claim. The rule could not be used where a claimant wrongly issued proceedings in her own right (because the cause of action had vested in her trustee in bankruptcy), and thereafter took an assignment from the trustee, and asked for permission to amend to plead the assignment. This was because both before and after the proposed amendment the claimant was purporting to sue in her personal capacity, so there was no 'alteration of capacity' (*Haq v Singh* [2001] 1 WLR 1594). Nor will a change of capacity after limitation be allowed if the amendment requires the addition of a party unless the rules on addition of parties after limitation are also satisfied (*Roberts v Gill* [2009] 1 WLR 531).

24.7.3.4   Correcting a mistake

The fourth situation is provided by CPR, rr 17.4(3) and 19.5(3)(a), which allow the correction of the name of an existing party after the expiry of the limitation period even if the effect is to substitute a new party. Rule 17.4(3) provides:

The court may allow an amendment to correct a mistake as to the name of a party, but only where the mistake was genuine and not one which would cause reasonable doubt as to the identity of the party in question.

Whether a mistake would cause reasonable doubt as to the identity of the party has to be determined objectively based on what is said in the claim form and the context of the claim (*Abb Asea Brown Boveri Ltd v Hiscox Dedicated Corporate Member Ltd* [2007] EWHC 1150 (Comm)).

The alternative route to correct a mistake after the expiry of limitation is r 19.5(3)(a), which provides that such an amendment may be made where:

(a) *the new party is to be substituted for a party who was named in the claim form in mistake for the new party* . . .

Adelson v Associated Newspapers Ltd [2008] 1 WLR 585 decided that on an application under r 19.5(3)(a):

(a) the mistake must have been made by the person responsible for issuing the claim form;

(b) the new party would have been named in the claim form if the mistake had not been made;

(c) the mistake must be as to name rather than identity;

(d) permission to amend should be refused if it will cause injustice; and

(e) all that can be done is to substitute the new party. Rule 19.5(3)(a) does not allow the addition of an extra party (*Broadhurst v Broadhurst* [2007] EWHC 1828 (Ch)).

24.7.3.5   Applications made just before the expiry of limitation

Provided an application to add a new cause of action or new party by amendment is made, and effected by service of an amended claim form (see **24.6.2**) before the expiry of the limitation period, the rules considered in this section (**24.7.3**) do not apply. However, if an application to add a cause of action or a party is made before the expiry of limitation, but service of the amended claim form is not effected until after the expiry of the limitation period, the amendment will be bad unless it falls within one of the exceptions discussed in **24.7.3.1** to **24.7.3.4** (*Bank of America National Trust and Savings Association v Chrismas* [1994] 1 All ER 401). Consequently, if an order to add a new cause of action or a new party is made close to the expiry of limitation where none of the exceptions will apply, the order should impose a condition that service on the additional defendants must be effected before the expiry of the limitation period.

Similarly, where an application for permission to amend to add a party or a cause of action is issued before the expiry of the limitation period, but the application is heard after limitation has expired, the Court can only grant permission to amend if the amendment is permitted by one of the exceptions in **24.7.3.1** to **24.7.3.4** (*Welsh Development Agency v Redpath Dorman Long Ltd* [1994] 1 WLR 1409, CA).

24.8   Amendments after the limitation period affecting accrued rights

24.8.1   General rule

Amendments (usually by the defendant) which would prejudice the rights of the opposite party (usually the claimant) existing at the date of the proposed amendment are not generally allowed. Thus in *Cluley v RL Dix Heating* (2003) LTL 31/10/2003 the claimant sued the defendants for breach of contract. After expiry of the limitation period the defendants sought permission to amend their Defence. The original Defence admitted the contract and denied breach. The proposed amendment denied there was any contract with the claimant, and alleged the claimant should have sued other parties. The amendment was disallowed, because, limitation having expired against the other parties, the claimant could not be put in the same position as if the proposed Defence had been served at the proper time.

24.8.2   Exceptions

(a) If fresh evidence comes to light after the expiry of the limitation period, and the defendants are not at fault in seeking to amend at that stage, they may be allowed to amend notwithstanding any prejudice caused to the claimant by the expiry of the limitation period (*Weait v Jayanbee Joinery Ltd* [1963] 1 QB 239, CA).

(b) If an amendment to the Defence introduces facts which the claimant must have known all along, it may be allowed notwithstanding the expiry of the limitation period, provided the defendant seeking to amend was not previously aware of those facts (*Turner v Ford Motor Co Ltd* [1965] 2 All ER 583, CA).

Renewal of proceedings

25.1 Introduction

There are two rules, neither of which is very onerous in a usual case, which are designed to prevent unduly stale claims being litigated. They are:

(a) the prescribed periods of limitation for commencing proceedings, after which, with certain exceptions, the proposed defendant will have a Limitation Act defence; and

(b) the periods prescribed by the Civil Procedure Rules 1998 over which an originating process is valid after issue for the purpose of service.

These two rules are cumulative. For example, the limitation period for claims for breach of contract is six years, and the period of validity of a claim form is usually four months. If the claimant uses these periods to the full, the defendant need not be served until six years and four months after the breach.

If the claimant has reasons for not effecting service of the claim form during its period of validity, an extension may be granted either by consent or on making a without notice application to the court. Consent for an extension is only effective if given by the written agreement of the parties (see CPR, r 2.11, and *Thomas v Home Office* [2007] 1 WLR 230).

25.2 Period of validity

25.2.1 How long does a claim form remain valid?

This is best explained by reference to CPR, r 7.5, which provides:

(1) *Where the claim form is served within the jurisdiction, the claimant must complete the step required by [**Figure 3.3** in **Chapter 3**] in relation to the particular method of service chosen, before 12.00 midnight on the calendar day four months after the date of issue of the claim form.*

(2) *Where the claim form is to be served out of the jurisdiction, the claim form must be served in accordance with Section IV of Part 6 within six months of the date of issue.*

Time starts running on the day after the date of issue. Thus, if a claim form to be served within the jurisdiction is issued on 11 September 2009, the four month period of validity would start running on 12 September, with the result that the last moment on which the step chosen for serving the claim (such as posting by first class post) could be taken would be 12.00 midnight on 11 January 2010 (see *Smith v Probyn* The Times, 29 March 2000). Time continues to run even if a stay is imposed (*Aldridge v Edwards* [2000] CPLR 349).

25.2.2   Application to extend the period of validity

If the claimant does not take the step required for service of the claim form within the relevant six or four month period an application may be made to the court to have its validity extended. This application should ordinarily be made before the validity of the claim expires, although there is power under CPR, r 7.6, to make an order extending the validity of the claim form even after it has expired. Rule 7.6 provides:

(1) *The claimant may apply for an order extending the period for compliance with rule 7.5.*

(2) *The general rule is that an application to extend the time for compliance with rule 7.5 must be made—*

   (a) *within the period specified by rule 7.5; or*

   (b) *where an order has been made under this rule, within the period for service specified by that order.*

(3) *If the claimant applies for an order to extend the time for compliance after the end of the period specified by rule 7.5 or by an order made under this rule, the court may make such an order only if—*

   (a) *the court has failed to serve the claim form; or*

   (b) *the claimant has taken all reasonable steps to comply with rule 7.5 but has been unable to do so; and*

   (c) *in either case, the claimant has acted promptly in making the application.*

25.2.3   Service of an invalid claim form

Such service is not a nullity, but it is an irregularity. The defendant should acknowledge service in the normal way. Simply acknowledging service does not waive the irregularity.

The defendant should then apply for an order setting aside service of the claim form under CPR, Part 11. The application must be supported by evidence verifying the facts on which the application is based. However, if there is delay in acknowledging service, or in seeking to set such service aside, or if the defendant fails to state an intention to defend, such (and similar) conduct may be held to be a waiver of the irregularity in service.

A claimant in this situation may cross-apply for a retrospective order for an extension to the period of validity of the claim form. Any such cross-application will be dealt with in accordance with the restrictions laid down in r 7.6 (see **25.2.2** and **25.3**). A claimant who cannot meet the requirements of r 7.6 (or who is facing a challenge to an order for an extension, see **25.5**), cannot, subject to three exceptions, find alternative relief under any of the general provisions in Parts 3 and 6. This is because the Court of Appeal in three decisions (*Kaur v CTP Coil Ltd* (2000) LTL 10/7/2000, *Vinos v Marks & Spencer plc* [2001] 3 All ER 784, and *Godwin v Swindon Borough Council* [2002] 1 WLR 997) has decided in effect that r 7.6 is a self-contained code dealing with applications to extend time for service. Consequently, it is not possible in these cases to ask the court to exercise the general power to extend time (r 3.1(2)(a)), to grant relief from sanctions (r 3.9), or to remedy an error of procedure (r 3.10). The exceptions are:

(a) to apply retrospectively for an order for alternative service under r 6.15(2) (see **3.8.6**);

(b) that in exceptional cases it may be possible to obtain an order dispensing with service under r 6.16 (see **3.8.7**); and

(c) an order under r 3.10 can be made to remedy an error in an application notice which was issued while the claim form was current, which sought permission to extend time for service of the particulars of claim (forgetting to ask for permission to extend the claim form as well) (*Steele v Mooney* [2005] 1 WLR 2819) or where there has been a technical defect in service (see *Phillips v Symes (No. 3)* [2008] 1 WLR 180).

25.3 Principles to be applied

The form of CPR, r 7.6, shows that a different approach will be taken depending on whether or not the application to extend the period of validity of the claim form is made while the claim form is still valid.

25.3.1 Applications made during the period of validity

No criteria are laid down in CPR, r 7.6(2), itself indicating how the discretion to extend during the period of validity of the claim form should be exercised. Accordingly, the application will be decided by applying the overriding objective. Dealing with a case justly will include dealing with it if at all possible, but the court will also be mindful of the need to deal with cases expeditiously and the importance of not side-stepping the effect of the Limitation Act.

Typically, extensions are sought where there are problems in tracing the defendant for the purpose of service. Granting permission is discretionary, and may be refused if the claimant encounters problems after leaving service to the last minute. In *Mason v First Leisure Corporation plc* (2003) LTL 26/8/2003, it was held to be inappropriate to extend time where the extra time was sought in a personal injuries claim to prepare the particulars of claim, schedule of loss and damage, and medical evidence.

In *Hashtroodi v Hancock* [2004] 1 WLR 3206, the court refused to grant an extension where the reason for failing to serve within the period of validity was the incompetence of the claimant's legal advisers. The court felt it appropriate to give only general guidance on the principles to be applied under r 7.6(2), namely:

(a) the discretion to extend the period of validity of a claim form should be exercised in accordance with the overriding objective; and

(b) the reason for the failure to serve within the specified period is a highly material factor. If there is a very good reason for the failure to serve, an extension will usually be granted. The weaker the reason, the more likely the court will be to refuse an extension. If there is no more than a weak reason, the court is very unlikely to grant an extension (*Collier v Williams* [2006] 1 WLR 1945).

25.3.2 Applications made after the expiry of the period of validity

For applications after the claim form has expired, fairly exacting criteria have been laid down by CPR, r 7.6(3) (see **25.2.2**). It will be seen that there should have been efforts to serve, and that there must be no unexplained delay in making the application (albeit the application is made after the expiry of the period of validity). If the claimant has been making efforts to serve, it is not all that likely that the claimant will simultaneously forget about the period of validity.

The rule is most likely to assist claimants who believe the court is effecting service, and later discover this is not the case. A failure by the court to serve because it completely overlooks the claim form comes within r 7.6(3)(a) just as much as where the court tries unsuccessfully to effect service (*Cranfield v Bridgegrove Ltd* [2003] 1 WLR 2441). In this situation the court will usually grant an extension.

25.3.3 If time is required, but there are no grounds for an extension

In this situation the claimant must serve the claim form, ie serve 'protective proceedings'. If there are continuing negotiations, or if the claimant has not completed the necessary inquiries, the best course is then to obtain an extension of time for the service of the particulars of claim, either by agreement with the defendant or by order of the court.

25.3.4 Period of any extension

In *Baly v Barrett* The Times, 19 May 1989, HL, it seemed there was a local practice of granting initial extensions for periods of 12 months. Lord Brandon said that that practice was wrong—it is always for the claimant to show that the period of extension sought is justified.

25.4 Procedure on renewal

An application to extend the period of validity is made by issuing an application notice, which is dealt with without giving notice: CPR, r 7.6(4)(b). The application must be supported by evidence which must include:

- all the circumstances relied on;
- the date of issue of the claim;
- the expiry date of any previous extension; and
- a full explanation as to why the claim has not been served.

Once the order has been made, the application notice and evidence in support must be served with the order on the party against whom the order was sought, unless the court otherwise orders: CPR, r 23.9. The order will contain a notice informing the defendant of the right to apply to set aside the order granting the extension, and any application to set aside must be made within seven days of service of the order: r 23.10.

25.5 How to challenge an order extending the validity of a claim

The first the defendant will know about the order will be when the claim form is served.

The claim should be acknowledged in the usual way, stating an intention to defend. An application should then be made on notice supported by written evidence for an order to set aside the order extending the validity of the claim form (and see **25.2.2**).

If the court forms the view that the extension should not have been granted, one of the most important factors in deciding whether to set aside service is whether the defendant is prejudiced by the order granting the extension (*Mason v First Leisure Corporation plc* (2003) LTL 26/8/2003). This usually involves a careful consideration of the correspondence between the parties in the period of validity of the claim form, including considering whether the defendant gave any encouragement to the claimant to incur expense in progressing the claim.

26

Security for costs

26.1 Introduction

There are circumstances where a defendant who has been sued feels that, given the strength of the defence, there is a good chance of defeating the claim, but is worried that, in the event of winning, the claimant would be unable to meet any order for costs made at trial. It can also happen that an impecunious claimant can begin a 'nuisance action', which has little prospect of success, but which is guaranteed to cause inconvenience and annoyance to the defendant, whatever the eventual result.

In order to protect a defendant in this situation, there is provision to make an application that the claimant provide security for costs. If this application is granted, the claimant will be required to pay a specific amount of money into court within a specified time period.

Normally the proceedings will be temporarily halted until the claimant complies with the order. The money will be held to provide a fund out of which the defendant's costs can be paid, in the event of the defendant being successful.

26.2 Conditions for granting security for costs

Security for costs can only be ordered if one of the conditions set out in CPR, r 25.13(2), is satisfied. The conditions are:

(a) the claimant is—

    (i)   resident out of the jurisdiction; but

    (ii) not resident in a Brussels Contracting State, a Lugano Contracting State or a Jurisdiction Regulation State, as defined in the CJJA 1982, s 1(3);

(b) [revoked]

(c) the claimant is a company or other body (whether incorporated inside or outside Great Britain) and there is reason to believe that it will be unable to pay the defendant's costs if ordered to do so;

(d) the claimant has changed his or her address since the claim was commenced with a view to evading the consequences of the litigation;

(e) the claimant failed to give his or her address in the claim form, or gave an incorrect address in that form;

(f) the claimant is acting as a nominal claimant, other than as a representative claimant under Part 19, and there is reason to believe that he or she will be unable to pay the defendant's costs if ordered to do so;

(g) the claimant has taken steps in relation to his or her assets that would make it difficult to enforce an order for costs against him or her.

Residence outside the jurisdiction for the purposes of ground (a) above is a question of fact. In *Re Little Olympian Each Ways Ltd* [1995] 1 WLR 560, Lindsay J was only prepared to hold that a Jersey registered limited company was 'resident out of the jurisdiction' after a detailed analysis of its activities, and on the basis that its central control and management was exercised in Jersey and hence outside the jurisdiction.

Subparagraph (ii) of ground (a) is based on the decision of the Court of Appeal in *Fitzgerald v Williams* [1996] QB 657. Under the old rules there was no equivalent to subparagraph (ii), so security for costs could, potentially, have been ordered merely because the claimant was outside the jurisdiction. In *Fitzgerald v Williams* it was held that this potentially offended against what is now the EC Treaty, art 12, as being covertly discriminatory against EC residents on the grounds of nationality. As EC nationals protected by art 12 will more or less coincide with the persons against whom judgments can be enforced under the Jurisdiction Regulation, this should no longer be an issue. Subparagraph (ii) also aims to rectify the problem identified in *De Bry v Fitzgerald* [1990] 1 WLR 522, which is that, as it is relatively cheap and easy to enforce English judgments under the Brussels and Lugano Conventions and Jurisdiction Regulation in the courts of other contracting States, there is little reason for granting security for costs against claimants residing in such countries purely on the basis that the claimant is resident outside the jurisdiction. The result is that security for costs under ground (a) is broadly limited to claimants residing outside the European Union.

Ground (c) applies to limited companies registered under the Companies Acts, and also unlimited companies, companies with a single member (*Jirehouse Capital v Beller* [2009] 1 WLR 751) and other corporations. It is the only ground specifically tied to impecuniosity.

Security for costs was ordered against the claimant in *Aoun v Bahri* [2002] 3 All ER 182 on ground (g) because the claimant had sold his home in Australia, and objectively that made it more difficult to enforce a costs order against him. Under ground (g) there is no need to show that the steps taken were 'with a view to' making enforcement more difficult.

26.3 Parties to an application for security for costs

Normally, applications for security for costs are made by defendants against claimants. They can also be made by claimants against defendants in respect of the costs of any counterclaim (but if the counterclaim is a set-off it is most unlikely that security will be ordered: *Ashworth v Berkeley-Walbrook Ltd* The Independent, 9 October 1989, CA). Further they may be made by a third party against the defendant making an additional claim under Part 20, or against an appellant to an appeal (or a respondent who cross-appeals): see CPR, r 25.15.

By r 25.14, an order for security for costs may also be made against someone other than a claimant if the court is satisfied that the person against whom the order is sought either:

(a) assigned the claim to the claimant with a view to avoiding the possibility of a costs order being made against him or her; or

(b) has contributed or agreed to contribute to the claimant's costs in return for a share of any money or property which the claimant may recover in the proceedings.

26.4 Discretion to grant security for costs

Once it has been established that the case comes within one of the conditions set out in **26.2** or **26.3** above, the court has a general discretion whether to grant an order for security. In exercising this discretion the court will have regard to all the circumstances of the case, and consider whether it would be just to make the order: see CPR, rr 25.13(1)(a) and 25.14(1)(a).

An order for security for costs does not infringe art 6(1) of the European Convention on Human Rights, although the right of access to the courts has to be taken into account (*Nasser v United Bank of Kuwait* [2002] 1 WLR 1868). In exercising its discretion there are conflicting authorities on whether the court should consider the substantial body of pre-CPR case law on the subject. In *Nasser v United Bank of Kuwait,* the court said the decision has to be made applying the overriding objective, and by affording a proportionate protection against the difficulty identified by the ground relied upon as justifying security for costs in the case in question. Thus, where security is sought against a claimant outside the Brussels and Lugano Convention and Jurisdiction Regulation States, the order should reflect the obstacles in the way, or the costs, of enforcing an English judgment for costs against the particular claimant or in the particular country concerned. In the context of applications against impecunious limited liability companies, it is suggested that one of the key factors will be that it is generally unjust for a defendant to have to defend with no realistic prospect of recovering its costs even if successful, but that security should not be in an amount that would stifle an apparently genuine claim. On the other hand, in *Vedatech Corp v Seagate Software Information* [2001] EWCA Civ 1924, an appeal was allowed because the judge had failed to take into account the fact that a Part 36 offer had been made, with the court expressly referring to pre-CPR cases such as *Sir Lindsay Parkinson and Co Ltd v Triplan Ltd* [1973] QB 609 (which had held that the fact a defendant had paid money into court was a relevant factor in exercising the discretion to order security for costs).

It is suggested that the following factors should be taken into account:

(a) The risk of not being able to enforce a costs order, and/or the difficulty or expense of being able to enforce a costs order, if the defendant is awarded costs.

(b) The merits of the claim, where this can be investigated without holding a mini-trial (*Porzelack v Porzelack (UK) Ltd* [1987] 1 WLR 420; *Swain v Hillman* [2001] 1 All ER 91). This has an impact on the risk of needing to enforce a costs order against the claimant.

(c) Whether the defendant may be able to recover costs from someone other than the claimant.

(d) The impact on the claimant of having to give security. In some cases a substantial order for security will effectively deprive the claimant of the ability to take the claim to trial. Where the claimant is sheltering in a tax haven the court is unlikely to be very sympathetic, but where the claimant's inability to pay has been caused by the defendant's conduct complained of in the claim, a substantial order may unjustly stifle the claim (*Interoil Trading SA v Watford Petroleum Ltd* (2003) LTL 16/7/2003).

(e) Delay in making the application. Generally the application should be made shortly after proceedings are commenced, and delay may be reflected either in refusing the application or reducing the amount of security ordered. Apparent delay may be explained if the circumstances were not known by the defendant (*Underwriting Members of Lloyd's Syndicate 980 v Sinco SA* [2009] EWCA Civ 130).

26.5 Procedure

26.5.1 Application

The defendant issues an application notice which is heard on notice by a Master or District Judge. The application must be supported by written evidence establishing the condition on which the application is based and providing evidence dealing with the relevant discretionary factors.

26.5.2 Effect of the order

Where the application is successful, the Master will state the amount to be paid and the time within which the claimant must comply with the order. Usually proceedings will be stayed, pending payment of the money. In the Commercial Court the practice is to give the claimant a reasonable time to provide the security, and the defendant liberty to apply for an order dismissing the claim in the event of default (Commercial Court Guide, appendix 16, para 6).

26.5.3 Amount of the payment

While the amount of security ordered is entirely at the court's discretion (*Procon (Great Britain) Ltd v Provincial Building Co Ltd* [1984] 1 WLR 557), the amount should be neither illusory nor oppressive *(Hart Investments Ltd v Larchpark Ltd* [2008] 1 BCLC 589). It is helpful to give the court an estimate of costs of the proceedings (*T. Sloyan and Sons (Builders) Ltd v Brothers of Christian Instruction* [1974] 3 All ER 715), probably in the form of a statement of costs (see **Figure 7.2**).

The order for security can cover both future costs and those already incurred.

The amount of security may be increased by a further application to the court.

26.5.4 The effect of non-compliance

The court may dismiss the claim, and will do so where it considers that:

- the claimant is not pursuing the claim sufficiently diligently;
- there is no real likelihood of the money being paid; and
- the time limit for complying with the order has been ignored (*Speed Up Holdings Ltd v Gough and Co (Handly) Ltd* [1986] FSR 330).

26.5.5 Discharge or variation of the order

It is open to a claimant to apply to discharge or vary an order for security for costs, if the claimant can show the court that there has been a significant change in the circumstances since the making of the order (*Gordano Building Contractors Ltd v Burgess* [1988] 1 WLR 890, CA).

26.5.6 After the trial

If the defendant is successful, as has been said, the money held as security can be used to pay all, or part of his or her costs. Any surplus (unlikely!) must be returned.

If the claimant is successful, the money given as security will be returned, even where there has been a stay of execution pending appeal.

Part 36 offers

27.1 Introduction

It is in the public interest, and generally in the interests of the parties too, that if possible civil disputes should be settled rather than proceeding through to trial. The court system would become clogged up if too many cases went to trial, and there are substantial costs savings for the parties if they can settle their disputes in the early stages. To point the parties in the right direction, the overriding objective encourages the parties to cooperate and the court may suggest ADR procedures where these are appropriate. In addition, Part 36 provides a formal system for making offers to settle which will have costs and other consequences if they are not accepted.

Part 36 deals with a number of situations where formal offers might be made: by claimants or defendants; before or after proceedings are issued; and where the relief claimed is or is not money.

A party who receives a realistic formal offer is best advised to settle the claim by accepting the offer. If a formal offer is refused, the litigation will continue, but Part 36 operates by awarding costs from the expiry of the offer period to the party making the offer if the offeree ultimately fails to do better than the terms of the offer.

The current version of Part 36 came into operation on 6 April 2007. The previous version used a combination of payments into court for money claims, and what used to be called 'Calderbank offers' for non-money claims. Payments into court were abolished as from 6 April 2007, and the current system is based around making 'offers to settle' in all types of claims.

27.2 Offers to settle

An offer to settle within the meaning of CPR, Part 36 (a 'Part 36 offer'), may be made at any time, including before the commencement of proceedings (r 36.3(2)(a)) or in appeal proceedings (r 36.3(2)(b)). Parties are not obliged to use the Part 36 format when making an offer to settle, but if they do not, the consequences in rr 36.10, 36.11 and 36.14 do not apply (r 36.1(2)).

27.2.1 Formalities

A Part 36 offer must:

(a) be made in writing (CPR, r 36.2(2)(a)). Although a Part 36 offer may be made in a letter, it is better to use form N242A (see PD 36, para 1.1);

(b) state on its face that it is intended to have the consequences of Part 36 (r 36.2(2)(b));

(c) if made at least 21 days before trial, specify a period of not less than 21 days within which the defendant will be liable for the claimant's costs in accordance with r 36.10 if the offer is accepted (rr 36.2(2)(c) and 36.2(3)). This 21-day period is called the 'relevant period' in Part 36. In cases where an offer is made less than 21 days before the start of the trial, the relevant period is the period up to the end of the trial or such other period as the court may determine (r 36.3(1)(c)(ii)). The relevant period can be extended by consent or if the court extends time under r 3.1(2)(a) (*Martin v Randall* [2007] EWCA Civ 1155);

(d) state whether it relates to the whole of the claim or part of it or to an issue that arises in the claim, and if so, which part or issue (r 36.2(2)(d)). An offer may relate solely to liability (r 36.2(5)); and

(e) state whether it takes into account any counterclaim (r 36.2(2)(e)).

27.2.2 Terms of the offer

A Part 36 offer needs to state the terms of the proposed compromise, which should be sufficiently precise and certain for an effective contract to be formed if the offer is accepted. It is important to be clear on whether the offer is in full and final settlement of all matters in dispute between the parties, or defined matters between the parties, and whether the offer takes into account matters such as any cross-claim or previous interim payment. The terms of the offer must include the costs consequences of acceptance (see **27.2.1**, para (c)).

27.2.3 Additional formalities for money claims

Part 36 offers made by defendants in claims for money must offer to pay a single sum of money (CPR, r 36.4(1)). An offer to pay all or part of a sum of money at a date later than 14 days following the date of any acceptance is not treated as a Part 36 offer unless the offeree accepts the offer (r 36.4(2)). The single sum offered is treated as inclusive of all interest to the end of the relevant period (r 36.3(3)).

27.2.4 Deduction of benefits in personal injuries claims

When making a Part 36 offer in a claim for damages for personal injuries, the defendant should state (CPR, r 36.15(3)) either:

(a) that the offer is made without regard to any liability for recoverable amounts under the Social Security (Recovery of Benefits) Act 1997; or

(b) that the offer is intended to include any deductible amounts under the 1997 Act. In such a case, the defendant's offer should state the amount of gross compensation; the name and amount of any deductible benefit or lump sum; and the net amount after deduction of recoverable amounts (r 36.15(6)).

27.2.5 Personal injuries claims for future pecuniary loss

Claims for future pecuniary loss in personal injuries claims are governed by the Damages Act 1996, s. 2(1). A number of additional formalities have to be included in a Part 36 offer in such a case (see CPR, r 36.5). The formalities include specifying whether the offer is for compensation in the form of:

(a) a lump sum to cover the whole claim; or

(b) a mix of a lump sum and periodical payments in respect of the claim for future pecuniary losses; or

(c) periodical payments for the claim for future pecuniary losses.

27.2.6   Offers in provisional damages claims

A Part 36 offer made in a claim which includes a claim for provisional damages must specify whether the offer includes an award of provisional damages (CPR, r 36.6(2)). The offer must by r 36.6(3) also state:

(a) that the sum offered is in satisfaction of the claim for damages on the assumption that the claimant will not develop the disease or suffer the deterioration specified in the offer; and

(b) that the offer is subject to the condition that the claimant must make any claim for further damages within a specified period.

27.2.7   Defence of tender before claim

A defendant who wishes to rely on a defence of tender before claim must make a payment into court of the amount said to have been tendered (CPR, r 37.2). This is a narrow exception to the abolition of payments into court. The payment in should be paid at the time of filing the defence (*Greening v Williams* (1999) *The Times*, 10 December 1999). Money paid into court in support of a defence of tender before claim may not be paid out without the court's permission, except where it is accepted without needing permission and the defendant agrees that the sum in court can be used to satisfy the offer (r 37.3). The rule (see **27.10**) that Part 36 offers must not be communicated to the trial judge does not apply to tenders before claim (r 36.13(3)(a)).

27.2.8   Clarification

If the terms of a Part 36 offer are unclear, the offeree may ask the offeror to clarify the offer (CPR, r 36.8(1)). The request should be made within seven days of service of the offer, and the offeror should respond within seven days of receiving the request (r 36.8(2)). If the offeror fails to provide the requested clarification, the offeree is entitled to apply for an order that it be provided. Such an order will also specify the date when the Part 36 offer is to be treated as having been made (r 36.8(3)).

27.3   Making a Part 36 offer

A Part 36 offer is made when it is served on the offeree (CPR, r 36.7(1)). One of the prescribed methods of service in r 6.20 should be used (see **3.8.5** and **3.11**). Where the offeree is legally represented, the offer must be served on the legal representative (PD 36, para 1.2).

27.4   Acceptance of a Part 36 offer

27.4.1   Notice of acceptance

A Part 36 offer is accepted by serving written notice of acceptance (there is no prescribed form, so a letter will suffice) on the offeror (CPR, r 36.9(1)). It is also necessary to file the notice of acceptance with the court (PD 36, para 3.1). In most cases the offeror should serve the notice of acceptance during the relevant period. When this happens the defendant must pay the claimant's standard basis costs up to the date of notice of acceptance (see r 36.10(1), (3)). The claimant is entitled to 100 per cent of his assessed costs, and the court has no jurisdiction to order payment of only a proportion of those costs (*Lahey v Pirelli Tyres Ltd* [2007] 1 WLR 998).

27.4.2   Late acceptance

Notice of acceptance may be served after the relevant period. This is effective only if the offer has not been withdrawn before service of the notice of acceptance (CPR, r 36.9(2)) or, if *Wakefield v Ford* [2009] EWHC 122(QB) is correct, if the offer is not construed as being open only for a limited time. Where the offeree effectively accepts an offer to settle after the relevant period, the parties may agree the liability for costs, but if they do not, the court will make an order for costs (r 36.10(4)(b)). Although the court may order otherwise, the order for costs will usually provide that:

(a) the claimant is entitled to costs up to the expiry of the relevant period; and

(b) the offeree will be liable for the offeror's costs for the period from the expiry of the relevant period to the date of acceptance.

Even where the late acceptance is of a claimant's offer to settle (rather than a defendant's offer), costs ordered under r 36.10(4) should be on the standard basis, although enhanced interest on costs after expiry of the relevant period may be appropriate (*Fitzpatrick Contractors Ltd v Tyco Fire and Integrated Solutions (UK) Ltd* [2009] EWHC 274 (TCC)).

A notice of acceptance served after the trial has started will only be effective if the court's permission is given (r 36.9(3)(d)). A notice of acceptance served after the end of the trial but before judgment is handed down is only effective if the parties agree (r 36.9(5)).

27.4.3   Acceptance relating to part of the claim

An acceptance of a Part 36 offer relating to only part of the claim results in a settlement of the claim and the claimant's entitlement to costs only if the claimant abandons the balance of the claim (CPR, r 36.10(2)). If the balance is not abandoned, that part proceeds to trial, and the court has a discretion on the costs of the compromised part of the claim.

27.4.4   Permission to accept

The court's permission is required for an acceptance of a Part 36 offer where:

(a) the Part 36 offer is made by some, but not all, of a number of defendants and CPR, r 36.12(4), applies (r 36.9(3)(a));

(b) the claim is for damages for personal injuries, the offer is intended to include any deductible amounts, and further deductible benefits or a deductible lump sum have been paid to the claimant since the date of the offer (r 36.9(3)(b)). In this situation the application must state the net amount offered in the Part 36 offer, the deductible amounts accrued at the date of the offer, and those that have subsequently accrued. The application must be accompanied by a copy of the current certificate of recoverable amounts (PD 36, para 3.3);

(c) an apportionment is required under r 41.3A (Fatal Accidents Act claims) (r 36.9(3)(c));

(d) the trial has started (r 36.9(3)(d)); or

(e) any of the parties is a child or protected party (r 21.10).

27.4.5 Stay on acceptance

If a Part 36 offer is accepted, the claim will be stayed (CPR, r 36.11(1)). The stay will be on the terms of the offer where the Part 36 offer relates to the whole claim (r 36.11(2)). A stay under r 36.11(1) does not affect the power of the court to enforce the terms of the Part 36 offer, nor to deal with any question of costs or interest on costs relating to the proceedings (r 36.11(5)).

27.4.6 Time for payment

Unless the parties agree otherwise in writing, where a Part 36 offer to pay money is accepted, payment must be made within 14 days of the acceptance (CPR, r 36.11(6)(a)).

27.5 Rejection of a Part 36 offer

There is no need for the offeree to give an express rejection of a Part 36 offer. Making a counter-offer, surprisingly, does not operate as a rejection of a Part 36 offer (CPR, r 36.9(2)). Doing nothing or counter-offering allows the offeree to serve a late notice of acceptance (**27.4.2**) if the offer has not been withdrawn (or if the offer is not construed as time limited). Whether it is possible to accept after rejecting is unclear from r 36.9(2).

27.6 Withdrawing a Part 36 offer

27.6.1 Before the expiry of the relevant period

Before the expiry of the relevant period, a Part 36 offer may be withdrawn or its terms changed in a way less advantageous to the offeree only with the court's permission (CPR, r 36.3(5)). Permission is sought by making an application in accordance with Part 23 (PD 36, para 2.2(1)).

27.6.2 After the expiry of the relevant period

After expiry of the relevant period and provided the offeree has not previously served notice of acceptance, the offeror may withdraw the offer or change its terms to be less advantageous to the offeree without the permission of the court (CPR, r 36.3(6)). This is done by serving written notice on the offeree (r 36.3(7)). A change in the terms of a Part 36 offer (whether it is an improved offer or one which is less advantageous to the offeree) takes effect when written notice of the change is served on the offeree (rr 36.2(2)(a), 36.7(2)).

27.6.3 Effect of a withdrawn Part 36 offer

A withdrawn Part 36 offer ceases to have the effect on costs and interest of a subsisting Part 36 offer (CPR, r 36.14(6)(a)). However, r 44.3 requires the court to consider an offer to settle which does not have the costs consequences set out in Part 36 in deciding what order to make about costs. This gives the court a wide discretion, to be exercised applying the overriding objective. In a suitable case the court can even treat a withdrawn Part 36 offer as having the same costs consequences as if it had not been withdrawn (*Trustees of Stokes Pension Fund v Western Power Distribution (South West) plc* [2005] 1 WLR 3595).

27.7 Failing to obtain judgment more advantageous than a Part 36 offer

There are costs and interest consequences (see CPR, r 36.14(1)) where a Part 36 offer is not accepted and either:

(a) the claimant fails to obtain a judgment more advantageous than the Part 36 offer if made by the defendant; or

(b) judgment is entered against the defendant which is at least as advantageous to the claimant as the proposals set out in the Part 36 offer if made by the claimant.

The consequences in r 36.14 do not apply where the Part 36 offer has been withdrawn, or changed to terms less advantageous to the offeree than the judgment, or if the Part 36 offer was made less than 21 days before the trial (unless the court abridges time).

The most straightforward situation is where the offeror says its offer is the same or higher (defendant's offer) or lower (claimant's offer) than the judgment. Where the offer includes interest, the court must recalculate the interest included in the judgment to find the sum in interest that would have been awarded on the relevant date (*Blackham v Entrepose UK* [2004] EWCA Civ 1109). Where there are deductible benefits etc the question is whether the claimant has failed to recover, after deduction of recoverable amounts, a sum greater than the net sum stated in the Part 36 offer in compliance with r 36.15(6)(c).

Remarkably, an offer to settle may also be 'more advantageous' than a judgment when it is less (defendant's offer) or more (claimant's offer) than the judgment (adjusted for interest and state benefits), but by an insignificant amount. In *Carver v BAA plc* [2009] 1 WLR 113, CA, judgment was entered for just under £5,000 in a claim said to be worth about £20,000. The judgment was (after adjustment for interest) £51 more than the defendant's offer to settle. Nevertheless, the judgment was held not to be more advantageous than the offer, because no reasonable claimant would have embarked on litigation which cost the claimant £80,000, together with the stress and anxiety involved in taking the case to trial, for a gain of only £51.

27.7.1 Offers made by defendants

Where the judgment is not more advantageous than a Part 36 offer made by a defendant, unless the court considers it unjust to do so, the court will order:

(a) the defendant to pay the claimant's costs up to the expiry of the relevant period applying the usual principle that costs follow the event (CPR, r 44.3(2)(a));

(b) the claimant to pay the defendant's costs from the expiry of the relevant period (r 36.14(2)(a));and

(c) the claimant to pay interest on the defendant's costs (r 36.14(2)(b)).

27.7.2 Offers made by claimants

Where the judgment is at least as advantageous as a Part 36 offer made by a claimant, unless the court considers it unjust to do so, the court will order:

(a) interest on the judgment (excluding interest) awarded at a rate not exceeding 10% above base rate for some or all of the period since the expiry of the relevant period. Where interest is also awarded under the County Courts Act 1984, s 69, or the Supreme Court Act 1981, s 35A, the total rate of interest may not exceed 10% above base rate (CPR, r 36.14(5));

(b) the defendant to pay the claimant's costs after the expiry of the relevant period on the indemnity basis; and

(c) interest on those indemnity basis costs at a rate not exceeding 10% above base rate.

27.7.3 Unjust to make usual costs and interest orders

In considering whether it would be unjust to make an order under CPR, r 36.14(2) or (3), on costs or interest, the court will, by r 36.14(4), take into account all the circumstances of the case, including:

(a) the terms of the Part 36 offer;

(b) the stage in the proceedings when the Part 36 offer was made, and in particular the period between the offer and the start of the trial;

(c) the information available to the parties at the time when the Part 36 offer was made; and

(d) the conduct of the parties with regard to giving or refusing to give information for the purposes of enabling the offer to be made or evaluated.

27.8 Effect of non-compliance with Part 36

Minor defects in Part 36 offers are likely to be corrected under CPR, r 3.10, which gives the court a discretion to correct errors in procedure. An offeree who keeps quiet about a defect in a Part 36 offer is unlikely to be allowed to rely on the defect because of their failure to cooperate (*Hertsmere Primary Care Trust v Administrators of Balasubramanium's Estate* [2005] 3 All ER 274).

In *Trustees of Stokes Pension Fund v Western Power Distribution (South West) plc* [2005] 1 WLR 3595, the defendant made an offer which did not comply with Part 36. The defendant then withdrew the offer. At trial the claimant was awarded slightly less than the offer. Despite the non-compliance with Part 36, the court took the offer into account on costs because:

(a) it was expressed in clear terms, stating whether it took into account any counter-claim and interest;

(b) it was expressed to be open for acceptance for 21 days;

(c) it was a genuine offer, and not a sham; and

(d) the defendant was clearly good for the money.

The fact the offer was withdrawn was held on the facts to be irrelevant, because the claim had been exaggerated (it was over 30 times more than the amount recovered), and the claimant was never going to accept an offer in the same range as the amount in the event found at trial.

27.9   Advising on Part 36 offers

It will be seen from **27.7** that making a reasonable Part 36 offer is an effective way for a defendant to put costs pressure on a claimant. To gain maximum effect the offer:

(a) should be made as early as possible, because the costs benefit only covers the period from the 22nd day after serving the notice of payment into court. Advice on this subject should therefore usually be included in opinions and conferences with clients, even in the early stages of the progress of a dispute; and

(b) should be pitched at a figure which the claimant cannot dismiss as derisory, but not so high that the defendant is paying more than the claim is worth.

Counsel advising a claimant who has received a Part 36 offer has to be careful to explain the costs risks of rejecting the offer, but must also be wary of advising the client to accept less than the claim is worth. If advice has to be given on the day of the trial, counsel should concentrate on giving clear practical advice that can be readily understood by the client, rather than giving the client a catalogue of every factor that might bear on whether the offer should be accepted (*Moy v Pettman Smith* [2005] 1 WLR 581).

27.10   Non-disclosure

The fact there has been a Part 36 offer (except in the case of a defence of tender or where parties agree to disclose in writing) must not be disclosed to the trial judge until all questions of liability and quantum of damages have been decided: CPR, r 36.13. This is to prevent the judge being influenced by the offer. It also means a defendant cannot argue that claims for continuing damages or continuing interest should be restricted to the period before a Part 36 offer (*Johnson v Gore Wood & Co (No. 2)* The Times, 17 February

2004). The embargo on disclosure does not apply to interim applications (*Experience Hendrix v Times Newspapers Ltd* [2008] EWHC 458 (Ch)).

If the claimant's case does not appear to be going well at trial, it may become advisable to accept the offer. This will require the judge's permission (r 36.9(3)(d)), which will not normally be given without the agreement of the defendant.

If the Part 36 offer is disclosed by such an application or by inadvertence, the trial judge has a discretion to continue to hear the case or refer it to another judge. The judge may allow the case to proceed if satisfied that no injustice will be done (*Garratt v Saxby* [2004] 1 WLR 2152).

27.11 Part 36 offers in appeals

A Part 36 offer which is made before trial has effect in relation to the costs of the proceedings up to the final disposal of the proceedings at first instance (CPR, r 36.3(4)). Costs protection for appeal proceedings may be obtained by making a separate Part 36 offer in the appeal proceedings (rr 36.3(2)(b), 36.3(4)).

Halting proceedings

28.1 Introduction

This chapter deals with a number of matters which can arise when a claim does not proceed smoothly from issue of process to trial. These are:

(a) Striking out (**28.2**), whereby a litigant or the court can attack the validity of a party's statement of case, or complain that the proceedings are an abuse of the court's process. This may result in part or the whole of a statement of case being struck out, and possibly with judgment being entered.

(b) Sanctions for breach of court orders and directions (**28.3**).

(c) Stays (**28.4**), are temporary halts in proceedings ordered by the court. They are only ordered for good reason, such as where it is likely the claim will not proceed to trial, so that further steps will be a waste of costs. In practice, such halts often end up being permanent.

(d) Discontinuing (**28.5**), amounts to a total abandonment of a claim or counterclaim, and entitles the other side to recover its costs incurred up to that time.

If the court strikes out a statement of case or dismisses an application or an appeal as being totally without merit, the court must record that fact on its order (CPR, rr 3.3, 3.4, 23.12, 52.10). Doing so may be the precursor to making a civil restraint order restraining a party from making further applications or issuing certain claims (r 3.11 and PD 3C), or to making a vexatious litigant order under SCA 1981, s 42.

28.2 Striking out

28.2.1 Introduction

If particulars of claim are struck out, the claim will be stayed or dismissed. If a defence is struck out, judgment is entered for the claimant. If the claimant claims damages, then judgment is for damages to be assessed.

28.2.2 Grounds for striking out

The grounds for striking out are contained in CPR, r 3.4(2), which is set out at **5.9**. Rule 3.4(1) says that the reference to a statement of case in this rule includes reference to part of a statement of case. It is therefore possible for the court to strike out just part of a statement of case where the document is not entirely bad.

The rules in CPR, r 3.4, do not apply to interim applications, which may only be struck out in the court's inherent jurisdiction (*Port v Auger* [1994] 1 WLR 862).

28.2.3 General principle

Striking out has traditionally been said to be appropriate only in plain and obvious cases, per Lord Templeman in *Williams and Humbert Ltd v W and H Trade Marks (Jersey) Ltd* [1986] AC 368, HL. Cases requiring prolonged and serious argument are therefore unsuitable for striking out. This approach was approved in *Three Rivers District Council v Bank of England (No. 3)* [2003] 2 AC 1.

28.2.4 Procedure

The court may exercise its power to strike out on application by a party or on its own initiative, and may do so at any time: PD 3, para 4.1. However, applications by parties should be made as soon as possible, and generally before track allocation: PD 3, para 5.1. Many applications to strike out can be made simply by issuing an application notice, there being no need for evidence in support. However, if any facts need to be proved in order to show why a statement of case should be struck out, then written evidence will be needed, and should be filed and served in the usual way: PD 3, para 5.2. The jurisdiction to strike out is closely related to that governing summary judgment, and in many cases it may be appropriate to seek both in the alternative: PD 3, para 1.7.

28.2.5 No reasonable cause of action or defence

A number of examples of situations where the power to strike out on the ground of failing to disclose a reasonable cause of action or defence are given by PD 3. A claim may be struck out if it sets out no facts indicating what the claim is about (such as a claim simply saying it is for 'Money owed £5,000'), or if it is incoherent and makes no sense, or if the facts it states, even if true, do not disclose a legally recognisable claim against the defendant. A defence may be struck out if it consists of a bare denial or otherwise fails to set out a coherent statement of facts, or if the facts it sets out, even if true, do not amount in law to a defence to the claim.

Paragraphs 2 and 3 of PD 3 deal with situations where court officials see, when asked to issue claims or on receipt of defences, that the contents of the relevant document fail to meet these standards. The official may decide to consult the judge, who may on his or her own initiative make an order staying the proceedings or striking out the claim or defence. The judge may or may not give the party a hearing before making such an order, or may make an order under CPR, Part 18, requiring additional information about the defective statement of case with a sanction in default. An order can also be made that the document is to be retained by the court and not served until any stay imposed is lifted.

In *Taylor v Inntrepreneur Estates (CPC) Ltd* (2001) LTL 7/2/2001, the claimant brought a claim seeking a declaration that a lease agreement had come into force, damages for breach of the lease, and damages for misrepresentation resulting from having entered into the alleged lease. On the documents it was clear that throughout the parties had negotiated on a 'subject to contract' basis. It was held that as no written agreement had been signed, no lease had been entered into. It followed that there was no reasonable cause of action, and the claim was struck out.

If a striking out order is made the judge may enter such judgment as the other party may appear entitled to: PD 3, para 4.2.

If the statement of case could be saved by amendment, then the proper order is for permission to amend rather than striking out (*Republic of Peru v Peruvian Guano Co* (1887) 36 Ch D 489 at 496 (per Chitty J); *Brophy v Dunphys Chartered Surveyors* The Times, 11 March 1998, CA).

The fact that the limitation period applicable to a cause of action has expired does not mean that there is no cause of action, but rather that there is a defence to that claim. If the particulars of claim discloses that the cause of action arose outside the limitation period the defendant may apply for the particulars of claim to be struck out on the ground they are an abuse of the process of the court, or alternatively seek a preliminary trial of that issue (see **33.3**).

28.2.6   Abuse of process

PD 3, para 1.5, says a statement of case may be an abuse of process where it is vexatious, scurrilous or ill-founded. An example is where a person seeks to re-litigate a question which has already been adjudicated by a court of competent jurisdiction even though the matter is not strictly speaking *res judicata (Hunter v Chief Constable of West Midlands Police* [1982] AC 529, HL). The underlying public interest is that there should be finality in litigation, and that a party should not be vexed twice in the same matter. An application to strike out for abuse of process must be made before filing a defence on the merits. If a defence is filed, the defendant will be taken to have acquiesced, and any later application will be dismissed (*Johnson v Gore Wood and Co* [2002] 2 AC 1).

In considering whether the second claim is an abuse it is necessary to decide not merely that the second claim could have been brought in the earlier claim, but whether it should have been brought in the first claim. The court has to make a broad, merits-based judgment taking account of all the public and private interests involved, and all the facts. This is a decision which has only one answer: it is not a matter of discretion (*Aldi Stores Ltd v WSP Group plc* [2008] BLR 1). The crucial question is whether, in all the circumstances, the claimant is misusing or abusing the process of the court (*Johnson v Gore Wood and Co* [2002] 2 AC 1). Mr Johnson was a shareholder in a company which had sued the defendant solicitors. That first claim was settled, with the compromise agreement containing a clause seeking to limit the defendant's liability to Mr Johnson personally. Mr Johnson then sued the solicitors in his personal capacity, and the defendant applied to strike out his personal claim as an abuse. Certain heads of claim were struck out, as they merely reflected losses suffered by his company, but others were arguably recoverable in his own right, and it was held that even though his personal claim could have been joined with the first claim by the company, it was not on the facts an abuse to have brought the personal claim by separate proceedings.

Destruction of evidence before proceedings are commenced in an attempt to pervert the course of justice may result in a claim or defence being struck out. Destruction of evidence after proceedings are issued may be visited by striking out if a fair trial is no longer achievable (*Douglas v Hello! Ltd* (2003) 153 NLJ 175).

28.2.7   Obstructing the just disposal of the claim

Poorly drafted statements of case may be struck out as likely to obstruct the just disposal of the proceedings. This may be appropriate where the pleading is unclear and not readily cured by amendment, or where it seeks to reverse the burden of proof (*Prince Radu of Hohenzollern v Houston* [2009] EWHC 398 (QB)). An overly pedantic approach may be contrary to the overriding objective (*Deutsche Morgan Grenfell Group plc v Commissioners of Inland Revenue* [2007] 1 AC 558).

28.3 Sanctions

The power to impose sanctions for non-compliance with its orders and directions is the means by which the courts can ensure that their case management decisions are complied with, and that they retain control over the conduct of litigation. The most draconian sanction that may be imposed is striking out. The CPR, r 3.4(2)(c) (see **28.2.2** above), provides that the court may strike out all or part of a statement of case if it appears that there has been a failure to comply with a rule, practice direction or court order. Striking out the whole of a party's statement of case ought to be reserved for the most serious, or repeated, breaches or defaults. In less serious cases of default or breach the court may be prepared to impose a sanction which, to use a phrase used in some of the recent cases under the old rules, 'fits the crime'. Rule 3.4 itself states that the power to strike out may be exercised over the whole or just a part of a statement of case. For example, a party may be in default of an order to provide further information on a single issue in a case where several issues are raised. A suitable sanction in such circumstances may be striking out the part of the statement of case dealing with that issue.

As alternatives to striking out, the court may impose costs sanctions including ordering a party to pay certain costs forthwith. It may also debar a party in default from adducing evidence in a particular form or from particular witnesses. Alternatively, the court may impose sanctions that limit or deprive a party, if successful, of interest on any money claim, or which increase the amount of interest payable by the party in default.

Further, there are various provisions in the Civil Procedure Rules 1998 and practice directions that automatically impose various sanctions in default of due compliance. For example, r 35.13 provides that a party who fails to disclose an expert's report may not use the report at the trial or call the expert to give evidence orally unless the court gives permission. A more severe sanction is imposed by r 3.7, which provides for the striking out of claims for non-payment of allocation, listing, and hearing fees where the claimant fails to pay the fee after the time set by a notice of non-payment. An example from the Practice Directions is PD 32, para 25.1, which provides that, if an affidavit, witness statement or exhibit does not comply with the requirements of CPR, Part 32, or PD 32, the court may refuse to admit it as evidence and may refuse to allow the costs arising from its preparation. This last example differs from the previous two in that it provides for sanctions which the court may choose to impose, whereas the other two provide for sanctions which apply unless the court grants relief.

28.3.1 Non-compliance with directions

It is to be anticipated that from time to time one or other of the parties to proceedings will be unable to keep to the directions timetable that will have been imposed by the court. This will not generally be a problem provided the parties cooperate and can still keep to the directions relating to the 'key' dates relating to filing allocation questionnaires, case management conferences, pre-trial reviews, filing pre-trial checklists, and trial: CPR, rr 26.3(6A), 28.4 and 29.5. If the non-compliance is through events outside the control of the defaulting party or is otherwise not deliberate, normally it would be expected that the parties would cooperate in compliance with r 1.4(2)(a) and resolve the difficulty by agreeing a new timetable that preserved the 'key' dates. Provided there is no express provision barring variation by the parties, the time specified by any provision of the Civil Procedure Rules 1998 or by the court for doing any act may be varied by the written agreement of the parties: r 2.11. If non-compliance cannot be resolved without, say, impinging on one of the 'key' dates, or if the other side insist on compliance, the matter is likely to come before the court.

An 'innocent' party faced with an opponent who has not complied with the court's directions is not permitted to either:

- sit back and wait for the other side's default to get worse by the additional passage of time; or
- make an immediate application for an order.

Instead, the correct procedure is that laid down in PD 28, para 5 (for fast track cases), and PD 29, para 7 (which is in identical terms and applies in multi-track cases). The references that follow are to the fast track practice direction (PD 28). The innocent party must first write to the defaulting party referring to the default and warn the defaulting party of the intention to apply for an order if the default is not rectified within a short reasonable period: para 5.2. This will usually be seven or 14 days. If there is continued default, the innocent party may apply for an order to enforce compliance or for a sanction to be imposed or both: para 5.1. Any application for such an order must be made without delay: para 5.2. If the innocent party does delay in making the application, the court may take the delay into account when it decides whether to make an order imposing a sanction or whether to grant relief from a sanction imposed by the rules or any practice direction.

28.3.2   Court's approach on breach of orders or directions

The general approach that will be adopted where there has been a breach of case management directions is set out in PD 28, para 5.4 (fast track), and PD 29, para 7.4 (multi-track), respectively. Paragraphs 5.4 and 7.4 provide as follows:

(1) *The court will not allow a failure to comply with directions to lead to the postponement of the trial unless the circumstances of the case are exceptional.*

(2) *If it is practicable to do so the court will exercise its powers in a manner that enables the case to come on for trial on the date or within the period previously set.*

(3) *In particular the court will assess what steps each party should take to prepare the case for trial, direct that those steps are taken in the shortest possible time and impose a sanction for non-compliance. Such a sanction may, for example, deprive a party of the right to raise or contest an issue or to rely on evidence to which the direction relates.*

(4) *Where it appears that one or more issues are or can be made ready for trial at the time fixed while others cannot, the court may direct that the trial will proceed on the issues that are or will then be ready, and order that no costs will be allowed for any later trial of the remaining issues or that those costs will be paid by the party in default.*

(5) *Where the court has no option but to postpone the trial it will do so for the shortest possible time and will give directions for the taking of the necessary steps in the meantime as rapidly as possible.*

(6) *Litigants and lawyers must be in no doubt that the court will regard the postponement of a trial as an order of last resort. The court may exercise its power to require a party as well as his legal representative to attend court at a hearing where such an order is to be sought.*

28.3.3   Final orders and unless orders

Minor breaches are usually dealt with by allowing the defaulting party a limited period of time to comply, together with an adverse costs order in respect of any interim application needed to bring the matter before the court (*Colliers International Property Consultants v Colliers Jordan Lee Jafaar Bhd* [2008] 2 Lloyd's Rep 368). If the matter is more serious the court will make it plain it requires compliance by stating a revised deadline is 'final', or will enforce compliance by making an 'unless' order with a stated sanction in default. Breach of a final order usually results in a sanction being imposed on a further application to the court (*Sports Network Ltd v Calzaghe* [2008] EWHC 2566 (QB)). Breach of an unless order results in the immediate imposition of the stated sanction (see **28.3.6**). Unless orders should only be made if the court is satisfied that in all the circumstances such a sanction is appropriate (*Marcan Shipping (London) Ltd v Kefalas* [2007] 1 WLR 1864). An important question is whether the court will go further, and strike out a party's statement of case as an immediate sanction for procedural default.

28.3.4   Immediate imposition of sanction

The Court of Appeal in *Biguzzi v Rank Leisure plc* [1999] 1 WLR 1926 affirmed a decision to strike out for wholesale disregard for the court's rules. Nevertheless, the Master of the Rolls commented that striking out would not always be the correct approach. Instead, the court should impose a proportionate sanction aimed at ensuring the punishment fits the crime. These include making orders for indemnity costs, for paying money into court, and awarding interest at higher or lower rates. By a proper exercise of case management powers it should be possible for the courts to ensure parties do not disregard timetables, whilst producing a just result.

However, *Biguzzi v Rank Leisure plc* must not be understood as promoting an unduly lenient approach to the imposition of sanctions. Each case has to be considered on its own facts, with the court seeking to do justice between the parties in the light of the overriding objective. There will, accordingly, be a number of cases where there has been serious default where immediate striking out is appropriate. In *UCB Corporate Services Ltd v Halifax (SW) Ltd* [1999] CPLR 691, the claimant had repeatedly failed to comply with court directions and provisions in the rules, and there was an unexplained delay of two years, at which point the defendant made an application to strike out. The claimant was regarded as being guilty of a total disregard of court orders, amounting to an abuse of process. Accordingly, the judge was held to have been entitled to strike out the claim rather than imposing a lesser penalty.

Both parties have obligations regarding compliance with court directions and the provisions of the CPR, and are required to cooperate with each other (see r 1.4(2)(a)). Where both sides are in breach of directions, it is difficult to justify imposing a sanction purely on the claimant, provided it is reasonably possible to have a fair trial notwithstanding the breach (*Western Trust and Savings Ltd v Acland and Lensam* (2000) LTL 19/6/2000).

In *Taylor v Anderson* [2003] RTR 305, it was held that striking out on the ground of delay is only appropriate where there is a considerable risk that it will be impossible to have a fair trial. In cases where a fair trial is still possible, the court should consider imposing some lesser sanction.

Axa Insurance Co Ltd v Swire Fraser Ltd [2000] CPLR 142 was a case where the Court of Appeal held the judge had been wrong to strike out the claim despite a protracted failure to provide further information. It was said that proof of prejudice is not a requirement for an order for striking out under r 3.4(2)(c). That said, prejudice to the innocent party is clearly an important factor, and where it is present, such as in *Purdy v Cambran* [1999] CPLR 843, where the defendant's expert died in the period of delay, it may offset an argument that striking out would be a disproportionate sanction. Where there is no prejudice, the court may well decide that the default can be characterised as relatively minor, and accordingly impose some lesser sanction. A striking out order was set aside in *Grundy v Naqvi* (2001) LTL 1/2/2001 on the ground that this was a disproportionate response to a failure to comply with an order to disclose witness statements. The defaulting party had some reason for not having complied (in that she wanted to amend her statement of case, which would have impacted the content of the witness statements), albeit she was also guilty of delay in seeking permission to amend. An order was made requiring the defaulting party to pay £50,000 into court. A sanction limited to indemnity costs was imposed despite protracted delay in *Royal Bank Invoice Finance Ltd v Bird* (2001) LTL 19/2/2001, as striking out the claim or discharging a freezing injunction (the other options) were regarded as too draconian and unjust.

28.3.5 Avoiding sanctions being imposed

The court has a general power to extend and abridge time: CPR, r 3.1(2)(a). A party who will be unable to comply with an order or direction in time (or who is already in breach) and who has not been able to agree an extension with the other side (perhaps because the Civil Procedure Rules 1998 do not allow such an agreement, such as an extension to the period for service of a Defence beyond 28 days; see r 15.5), may make an application under this rule asking the court to extend time for compliance.

The discretion given to the court under the rule is unfettered other than by the general requirement to abide by the overriding objective. There is a fundamental difference between applying for an extension of time before a time limit has expired, and seeking relief from a sanction after the event (*Robert v Momentum Services Ltd* [2003] 1 WLR 1577). In simple time applications the principal consideration is whether there is any prejudice caused to the other side through the delay in taking the step in question. The court is not required to consider the checklist of factors set out in r 3.9, discussed at **28.3.8**.

On other occasions, a default may arise through the defective performance of the requirements of a rule, practice direction or court order. For example, it may be that the wrong form was used, or that it was sent to the wrong address (but still came to the attention of the other side), or that the document used was not completed correctly. These are errors of procedure. By r 3.10, such errors do not invalidate the step purportedly taken, unless the court so orders. The court may make an order invalidating a step if it was so badly defective that the other side were mislead, or where the defects are so great that it would not be right to regard the purported performance as performance at all. Further, by r 3.10(2), the court may make an order to remedy any error of procedure. A defaulting party should consider seeking such an order where there is an objection made regarding defective performance.

28.3.6 Form of unless orders

Like all other orders, orders with sanctions must specify the time within which the step under consideration must be taken by reference to a calendar date and a specific time: CPR, r 2.9. The sanction part of the order may take the form of an 'unless' provision. This is to the effect that if the terms of the order are breached, the other party may file a request for judgment to be entered and costs: r 3.5. Such an order may read:

Unless by 4.00 pm on Friday 20th November 2009 the defendant do file and serve a list of documents giving standard disclosure, the Defence shall be struck out and judgment entered for the claimant for damages to be decided by the court.

28.3.7 Non-compliance with order imposing a sanction

If a party fails to comply with a rule, practice direction or court order imposing any sanction, the sanction will take effect unless the defaulting party applies for and obtains relief from the sanction: CPR, r 3.8. Therefore unless orders in the form that a claim 'shall' or 'will' be struck out or dismissed mean that on expiry of the time limit the claim is struck out or dismissed automatically, and no further order from the court is necessary (PD 3, para 1.9). Rule 3.8 goes on to provide that extensions cannot be agreed between the parties. The innocent party may still need to request the entry of judgment (common law remedies) or to apply for judgment (equitable relief) (r 3.5). On such an application the court's function is limited to deciding what order should properly be made to give effect to the sanction which has already taken effect (*Marcan Shipping (London) Ltd v Kefalas* [2007] 1 WLR 1864). A defaulting party can apply to have such a judgment set aside (r 3.6(1)), which is considered applying the principles governing relief from sanctions (r 3.6(4)).

28.3.8 Relief from sanctions

As mentioned in the previous section, a party in breach of a rule, practice direction or order imposing a sanction for non-compliance may apply for relief from the sanction. This is done by issuing an application notice, which must be supported by evidence. On such an application the CPR, r 3.9, provides that the court will consider all the circumstances, and then sets out a list of the following nine factors which will be considered:

- the interests of the administration of justice;
- whether the application for relief has been made promptly;
- whether the failure to comply was intentional;
- whether there is a good explanation for the failure;
- the extent to which the party in default has complied with other rules, practice directions, court orders, and any relevant pre-action protocol;
- whether the failure to comply was caused by the party or his legal representative;
- whether the trial date or the likely trial date can still be met if relief is granted;
- the effect which any failure to comply had on each party; and
- the effect which the granting of relief would have on each party.

In most cases where a party is seeking relief from sanctions, the judge must consider each of the factors in r 3.9 systematically, give each its appropriate weight, and strike a balance applying the overriding objective. Failing to do so is likely to mean that the decision is wrong in principle (*Woodhouse v Consignia plc* [2002] 1 WLR 2558). According to *Hansom v E Rex Makin* (2003) LTL 18/12/2003, the question of whether it is possible to have a fair trial is an important factor in applications for relief from sanctions, but not to the same extent as in applications for striking out as a sanction, where this factor is paramount (see **28.3.4**). In *Woodward v Finch* [1999] CPLR 699, the Court of Appeal refused to interfere with the judge's decision to grant relief, despite a history of non-compliance and the fact that the excuse put forward for not complying with an unless order was not a good one. The main reasons were that relief had been applied for promptly; the default was more muddle-headedness than anything else; the trial date could still be met; there was not much effect on either party through the default; and refusing relief would have a devastating effect on the claimant.

28.3.9   Non-compliance with applicable pre-action protocols

If, in the opinion of the court, there is non-compliance with a pre-action protocol various sanctions may be imposed (see **2.7** for details). In order to ensure the parties are not taken by surprise over alleged breaches which may be investigated years later at trial on the question of costs, the parties are required to plead in the claim form or particulars of claim (and respond in the defence) as to whether or not the relevant pre-action protocol was complied with (PD Pre-action conduct, para 9.7).

28.3.10   Second claims

If a claim is dismissed within the limitation period for breach of an unless order, a second claim based on the same cause of action would normally be struck out as an abuse of process (*Janov v Morris* [1981] 1 WLR 1389, CA).

28.4   Stays

28.4.1   Introduction

The SCA 1981, s 49(3), recognises and preserves the High Court's inherent power to stay proceedings pending before the court either of its own motion, or on the application of any person, whether or not a party to the proceedings. The County Court has the same power by virtue of County Courts Act 1984, s 38.

While a stay is in operation no steps may be taken in the claim other than an application to remove the stay. However, time continues to run for the purposes of the period of validity of the claim form (*Aldridge v Edwards* [2000] CPLR 349). A stay is not equivalent to discontinuance or the granting of judgment, and so the proceedings remain in existence. The stay may therefore be removed by the court if proper grounds are shown (*Cooper v Williams* [1963] 2 QB 567).

28.4.2   Procedure

Stays are applied for by issuing an application notice. Evidence in support is generally desirable.

28.4.3   Grounds

Examples of grounds upon which a party may apply for a stay of proceedings are:

(a) Where the claimant in a personal injuries action refuses to undergo a medical examination (*Edmeades v Thames Board Mills Ltd* [1969] 2 QB 67, CA), which is fully considered at **29.3.2** and **29.3.3**.

(b) Where the dispute is governed by an arbitration agreement and the defendant wishes the dispute to go to arbitration in accordance with the agreement (Arbitration Act 1996, s 9).

(c) Where the defendant wishes to argue *forum non conveniens* after permission has been granted without notice for service of originating process outside the jurisdiction.

(d) Where there are related criminal proceedings which should be disposed of before the civil claim proceeds (PD 23, para 11A).

28.4.4 Further examples

The following examples are further situations where a stay may be imposed:

(a) The usual order on a successful application for security for costs provides for the proceedings to be stayed until the amount specified in the order is paid into court.

(b) Proceedings are stayed where a party accepts a Part 36 offer.

(c) Where a first claim is struck out for default with costs, a second claim based on the same facts may be stayed pending payment of the costs of the first claim (*Sinclair v British Telecommunications plc* [2001] 1 WLR 38).

28.4.5 Stay by consent

A claim may be stayed as part of a consent judgment on the joint application of the parties. This applies to 'the stay of proceedings, either unconditionally or upon conditions as to the payment of money' and to 'the stay of proceedings upon terms which are scheduled to the order' but which are not otherwise part of it (a 'Tomlin order'). Tomlin orders are considered further at **37.3.2**.

28.5 Discontinuance

28.5.1 Introduction

Discontinuance means that the claimant gives up entirely all or part of a claim brought against the defendant in an action.

This is to be contrasted with abandonment, which means that the claimant gives up only some particular remedy against the defendant, but wishes to proceed on the rest.

28.5.2 Permission to discontinue

In general, a claimant may discontinue without needing to obtain the court's permission: CPR, r 38.2(1). In the following cases, however, permission is required:

(a) where an interim injunction has been granted (r 38.2(2)(a));

(b) where an undertaking to the court has been given (r 38.2(2)(a));

(c) where the claimant has received an interim payment (r 38.2(2)(b)); or

(d) where there is more than one claimant (r 38.2(2)(c)).

Permission may always be given by the court, but in situation (c) above there is the alternative of obtaining consent from the defendant, and in situation (d) above there is the alternative of obtaining consent from the other claimants.

28.5.3   Procedure

Discontinuance is effected by the claimant filing a notice of discontinuance in Form N279 with the court and serving copies on all other parties.

28.5.4   Effect

Discontinuing has the effect of bringing the entire claim, or the part of the claim identified in the notice of discontinuance, to an end. It also renders the claimant liable to pay the defendant's costs of the claim, or the part of the claim, that has been discontinued, unless the court orders otherwise: CPR, r 38.6. If a claim is discontinued after a defence has been filed, the claimant is not allowed to commence a second claim arising out of the same or substantially the same facts without the court's permission: r 38.7.

28.5.5   Setting aside a notice of discontinuance

A defendant may, within 28 days of service of a notice of discontinuance, apply to have the notice set aside: CPR, r 38.4. There have been cases in the past where claimants have served notice of discontinuance for tactical purposes, aiming to deprive the defendant of some right or legitimate expectation. Setting aside accordingly may be appropriate where some underhand motive or effect can be identified.

Expert evidence

29.1 Introduction

29.1.1 General rule

At common law there is a general rule that witnesses must state facts not opinions. To allow witnesses to express their opinions is regarded as an intrusion on the role of the tribunal of fact.

There are effectively two exceptions to this general rule: certain types of evidence given by non-expert witnesses, and the evidence given by expert witnesses.

29.1.2 Non-expert witnesses

A non-expert witness is allowed to express an opinion or impression where the facts perceived are too complicated or too evanescent in their nature to be recollected or separately and distinctly narrated. The Civil Evidence Act 1972 (CEA 1972), s 3(2), puts this into statutory form:

It is hereby declared that where a person is called as a witness in any civil proceedings, a statement of opinion by him on any relevant matter on which he is not qualified to give expert evidence, if made as a way of conveying relevant facts personally perceived by him, is admissible as evidence of what he perceived.

Some examples, which are not intended to be exhaustive, of matters on which a non-expert witness may state an opinion as a compendious way of stating facts are:

- Estimations of speed and distance.
- The identity of persons or articles.
- The state of the weather.
- The condition of articles.
- The age of persons or articles.

29.1.3 Expert witnesses

An expert differs from witnesses of fact in a number of respects in addition to that relating to opinion evidence. An expert witness may rely on published and unpublished material in reaching conclusions, draw on his or her own experience and that of colleagues, and may refer to research papers, learned articles, and letters during the course of giving testimony, such documents being themselves admitted in evidence and supporting any inferences which can fairly be drawn from them.

29.2   Admissibility of expert evidence

29.2.1   When will expert evidence be admissible?

In order for expert evidence to be admissible the following conditions must be satisfied:

(a) the matter must call for expertise;

(b) the evidence must be helpful to the court in arriving at its conclusions (*Midland Bank Trust Ltd v Hett Stubbs and Kemp* [1979] 1 Ch 379, which might be just another way of saying the same thing as in point (a));

(c) there must be a body of expertise in the area in question (*Barings plc v Coopers and Lybrand* The Times, 7 March 2001);

(d) the particular witness must be suitably qualified as an expert in the particular field of knowledge; and

(e) permission to rely on the expect evidence must be obtained from the court.

29.2.2   The matter must call for expertise

29.2.2.1   Art or science

Regarding the first condition, the inquiry has to be into a matter of art or science which is likely to be outside the experience and knowledge of the tribunal of fact. Expert help is therefore unnecessary on matters relating to normal human nature and behaviour. See the *Evidence* manual.

This distinction can be illustrated by *Liddell v Middleton* [1996] PIQR P36, CA. This was an action in negligence arising out of a road traffic accident. Stuart-Smith LJ commented that in cases of this type expert evidence from accident reconstruction experts is both necessary and desirable to assist the judge where there are no witnesses capable of describing what happened, where deductions have to be made from circumstantial evidence from the scene, or where deductions are to be drawn as to the drivers' speeds and positions immediately before the collision from the positions of the vehicles after the accident, marks on the road, or damage to the vehicles. In these instances the expert provides the court with the necessary scientific assistance which the court does not possess as an ordinary layman. On the other hand, where the only material available to the expert are the accounts of the eyewitnesses, the expert will be usurping the function of the judge in expressing an opinion about speeds of the vehicles or whether any of the drivers could have done anything to avoid the accident: in these circumstances drawing the necessary inferences and finding the necessary facts are within the ordinary knowledge of the layman, and therefore an expert's opinion on these matters is irrelevant and inadmissible.

29.2.2.2   Handwriting evidence

It is provided by the Criminal Procedure Act 1865, s 8, that:

Comparison of a disputed Writing with any Writing proved to the satisfaction of the Judge to be genuine shall be permitted to be made by Witnesses; and such Writings, and the Evidence of Witnesses respecting the same, may be submitted to the Court and Jury as evidence of the Genuineness or otherwise of the Writing in dispute.

Despite its title, this statute applies to civil cases as much as it applies to criminal proceedings. It seems to be clear that, despite the use of the word 'Witnesses' rather than the phrase 'expert witnesses', a comparison of handwriting can only be done with the assistance of a handwriting expert (*R v Tilley* [1961] 1 WLR 1309, CCA and *R v O'Sullivan* [1969] 1 WLR 497, CA). A different point arose in *Lockheed-Arabia Corp v Owen* [1993] QB 806 where the disputed writing was the signature on a cheque. By the time of the trial the original had been stolen in a burglary of the claimant's solicitors' offices, but a photocopy of the cheque was available. It was held that the photocopy was a 'disputed writing' within the meaning of the section, and a comparison with a control sample of writing could be undertaken by a handwriting expert at trial. The fact the original was not available only went to weight.

29.2.3   The witness must be suitably qualified as an expert in that field

As to the fourth condition, the question is whether the witness has sufficient skill and knowledge in relation to the field in question. See the ***Evidence*** manual.

There is no absolute requirement that the witness be professionally qualified, there being several areas where expertise is obtained through experience rather than study. However, generally, the proposed expert must be fully professionally qualified in the relevant area, and should often be to the forefront of those practising in that area. For example, in an ordinary personal injuries claim it is usual to obtain the expert opinion of a consultant orthopaedic surgeon rather than a general practitioner.

As to how senior an expert to instruct, the parties will need to bear in mind the costs rules in CPR, Part 44 and r 35.4(4), and that experts' fees that are unreasonably high will be reduced down to reasonable figures.

Furthermore, an acknowledged expert is only permitted to give an opinion within his or her own science, so, for example, an orthopaedic surgeon will not be allowed to talk about the injuries to a claimant's teeth.

29.2.4   Opinions on ultimate issues

It used to be that a witness was, at common law, prohibited from giving an opinion on an ultimate issue. For example, in a running down claim an accident reconstruction expert used not to be able to say that the defendant had driven negligently, that being one of the very issues for the court to decide. This condition has been abolished in civil cases by the CEA 1972, s 3(1) and (3). Nevertheless, rather than attempting to make findings of fact, experts should express their opinions based on clearly identified assumed facts (*JP Morgan Chase Bank v Springwell Navigation Corp* [2007] 1 All ER (Comm) 549).

29.2.5   Conflicts with expert evidence

It is a common occurrence that the parties will adduce conflicting expert evidence. When this happens the duty of the judge is to make findings of fact and resolve the conflict (*Sewell v Electrolux Ltd* The Times, 7 November 1997). Where there is a conflict between an expert and lay witnesses, generally the judge should refuse to accept the lay evidence in preference to uncontradicted expert evidence (*Re B (A Minor)* [2000] 1 WLR 790). However, the judge is not obliged to accept expert evidence if there are sufficient grounds for rejecting it, such as where it does not speak to a relevant issue (see *R v Lanfear* [1968] 2 QB 77), or where the judge does not believe the expert or is otherwise unconvinced by it (*Dover District Council v Sherred* The Times, 11 February 1997). Also, there are cases where lay evidence may be preferred to expert evidence, such as where attesting witnesses are preferred to a handwriting expert over a contested will (*Fuller v Strum* [2002] 1 WLR 1097). Ultimately, cases are decided by the judge, not the experts, and it is possible for the judge to reject even the evidence of a jointly instructed expert (*Armstrong v First York Ltd* [2005] 1 WLR 2751).

29.3 Obtaining facilities for inspection by experts

29.3.1 Non-medical cases

Orders under CPR, r 25.1(1)(c), (d), for inspection of land and chattels, and for taking samples, conducting tests, etc are normally sought at the allocation stage (see **7.6** and **21.5.2**). Normally it is obvious from the nature of the dispute that such orders are in the interests of justice, and they are usually made with very little discussion.

29.3.2 Medical cases

There is no such general power to order a litigant claiming in respect of personal injuries to submit to a medical examination on behalf of the defendant. The reason for this seems to be that any type of medical examination is an infringement of the fundamental human right to personal liberty, and it would be objectionable to make a direct order for such with power to commit if the claimant refused.

However, the court can achieve much the same result by the indirect method of ordering a stay of the proceedings if the claimant refuses a medical examination on behalf of the defendant (see *Edmeades v Thames Board Mills Ltd* [1969] 2 QB 67, CA).

29.3.3 When will a stay of proceedings be ordered?

The principle laid down by Lord Denning MR in the above case, was that a stay would be ordered if it was just and reasonable to do so. Put another way, the court would order a stay if the conduct of the claimant in refusing a reasonable request was such as to prevent the just determination of the cause. Thus the test is twofold:

- Is it reasonable to order an examination? and, if so,
- Is the claimant's conduct in refusing an examination such as to prevent the just determination of the cause?

(See the judgment of Scarman LJ in *Starr v National Coal Board* [1977] 1 WLR 63, CA.)

However, whether or not a stay is granted is entirely within the discretion of the court, and it will only grant a stay if the applicant satisfies it that a stay is required in the interests of justice. The facts of each individual case, and the parties' reasons for asking for, or resisting, the proposed medical examination, are all matters which must be taken into consideration; and each party is under a duty to provide the court with the necessary material to enable the proper exercise of its discretion.

29.3.4 Where the examination poses a risk to health

Further problems arise if the proposed medical examination involves risk to health, or may be of an unpleasant nature. In assessing whether or not a refusal is reasonable, the court will 'weigh' the proposed examination on a scale, ranging from examinations involving no serious technical assault but only an invasion of privacy, to examinations involving a risk of injury or to health.

The degree of reasonableness in the claimant's objections to the proposed examination would bear a close correlation to its position on the scale. The test is then to balance the weight of reasonableness of the defendant's request against the weight of reasonableness of the claimant's objections, in order to ensure a just determination of the case (see *Prescott v Bulldog Tools Ltd* [1981] 3 All ER 869).

29.3.5 Conditions imposed by the claimant

29.3.5.1 Permissible conditions

As we have seen, whether a stay will be ordered may depend on whether the claimant is being reasonable. Sometimes a claimant is only prepared to submit to a medical examination upon certain conditions. Any or all of the following conditions have been held to be generally permissible:

(a) That the defendant pay the claimant's loss of earnings in attending the examination.

(b) That the defendant pay the claimant any out-of-pocket expenses in attending the examination, such as fares and subsistence.

(c) That the doctor will not discuss the cause of action with the claimant, except in so far as this is relevant for medical purposes.

(d) That the claimant have a friend, relative or a legal executive or partner from his or her solicitors present. (But see *Whitehead v Avon County Council* The Times, 3 May 1995, CA, where the Court of Appeal upheld a decision that the claimant's action be stayed unless she submitted herself to a psychiatric examination without a friend or relation being present throughout the examination.)

It is usually unreasonable for a claimant to refuse examination by a named doctor but it may be reasonable for the claimant to refuse an examination by a named doctor, for example, where:

(a) A female claimant has an injury which she would prefer to have examined by a female doctor (or, perhaps, a male claimant has an injury which he would prefer to have examined by a male doctor).

(b) There are substantial grounds for doubting the competence, honesty or professional honour of the doctor.

(c) There are substantial grounds for doubting whether the doctor will be able to produce a report which is full, complete and not misleading.

From *Starr's* case, it is clear that the courts will only readily entertain objections which are personal to the claimant. Objections as to the bona fides or competence of the defendant's doctor have to be regarded with considerable caution and care, due to the gravity of the allegations.

29.3.5.2 Where the claimant wishes to have a nominated doctor present

Matters become a little more difficult if the claimant wishes to impose a condition that a doctor nominated by him or herself be present at the examination. The reasonableness test will be applied, and in most cases it will be held that the presence of a lay person should be sufficient reassurance for the claimant. It will have to be a very strong case to overcome the disadvantages of increased costs and delay involved in having two doctors present. (See *Hall v Avon Area Health Authority (Teaching)* [1980] 1 WLR 481, CA.)

The situation is, of course, different, if the parties agree that there should be a joint medical examination of the claimant. In this case both doctors play an active part in the examination, and it is often a useful procedure prior to agreeing medical evidence, or to focus the medical issues.

29.3.5.3 Automatic disclosure of the medical report generally unjustifiable

It can rarely be a justifiable condition to insist on automatic disclosure of the resulting medical report, as this amounts to an advance requirement to waive legal professional privilege (see *Megarity v D J Ryan and Sons Ltd* [1980] 1 WLR 1237, CA). An exception was recognised in *Hookham v Wiggins Teape Fine Papers Ltd* [1995] PIQR P392, CA, if past delay in the proceedings or the proximity of the trial justifies such a condition in the particular circumstances.

29.3.6 Not restricted to personal injuries cases

The power to order a stay where a claimant refuses a reasonable request for a medical examination is not restricted to personal injuries cases. In *Jackson v Mirror Group Newspapers Ltd* The Times, 29 March 1994, CA, a libel action was stayed until the claimant submitted to a medical examination by the defendant's medical expert. The action involved an alleged defamatory statement that the claimant's face had been disfigured by cosmetic surgery. Restricting the defendant's expert to comment on the basis of photographic evidence when the claimant's expert had the opportunity of a full examination would have put the defendant at an unfair disadvantage.

29.4 Medical examination of defendant

Cosgrove v Baker (CA, 14 December 1979) was interpreted by *Lacey v Harrison* The Times, 22 April 1992, as deciding that in exceptional circumstances the court could order a defendant's defence to be struck out unless he or she submitted to a medical examination on behalf of the claimant where the defendant's liability depended on his or her medical condition. The most important consideration is whether the defendant, in refusing a reasonable request, is preventing the just determination of the case.

29.5 Legal professional privilege

29.5.1 General rule regarding experts' reports

Experts' reports, whether medical or non-medical, and whether obtained by the claimant or the defendant, if made for the purpose of pending or contemplated litigation, are privileged. Therefore, the exchange of experts' reports cannot, subject to the exception mentioned at **29.3.5.3**, properly be made the subject of an interim order (*Worrall v Reich* [1955] 1 QB 296, CA).

29.5.2 The CEA 1972, s 2

The CEA 1972, s 2, although it does not alter this rule directly, provides under s 2(3) that rules of court may be made

> . . . *enabling the court in any civil proceedings to direct, with respect to medical matters or matters of any other class . . . that the parties . . . shall . . . disclose to the other or others in the form of one or more expert reports the expert evidence . . . which he proposes to adduce as part of his case at the trial . . .*

Further, by s 2(5), rules of court may also make provision prohibiting a party who fails to comply with a direction to disclose expert evidence ' . . . from adducing, except with the leave of the court, any oral expert evidence whatsoever . . .'. Disclosure amounts to a waiver of privilege in the disclosed report, but not to earlier drafts of the report (*Jackson v Marley Davenport Ltd* [2004] 1 WLR 2926).

Relevant rules are contained in CPR, Part 35, and are considered at **29.6** to **29.9**.

29.6 Directions regarding expert evidence

Generally, expert evidence is not allowed in small claims track cases, so the discussion that follows is principally aimed at fast track and multi-track cases.

Directions dealing with expert evidence will usually be made when the case is allocated to the fast track or multi-track, or on the case management conference. Experts should be served with a copy of any order containing directions which may affect them (PD 35, para 6A).

When considering expert directions, the starting point is that no party may call an expert or put in evidence an expert's report without the court's permission. In the absence of a direction, therefore, expert evidence is inadmissible. In deciding whether to grant permission, and if so to what extent, the court will seek to restrict expert evidence to that which is reasonably required to resolve the proceedings. The primary rules are:

> 35.1 *Expert evidence shall be restricted to that which is reasonably required to resolve the proceedings.*
>
> 35.4—(1) *No party may call an expert or put in evidence an expert's report without the court's permission.*
>
> 35.13 *A party who fails to disclose an expert's report may not use the report at the trial or call the expert to give evidence orally unless the court gives permission.*

Traditionally, if expert evidence was permitted, both parties would instruct competing experts. This is still possible, and the most likely approach in multi-track cases. Recently, there has been a move towards the joint instruction of a mutually acceptable expert, who it is intended will produce a report which is objective and not biased towards either side. This is in fact the favoured approach in fast track cases.

29.6.1 Joint instruction of experts

Where two or more parties wish to submit expert evidence on a particular issue, CPR, r 35.7(1), provides that the court may direct that the evidence on that issue is to be given by one expert only. If the court makes such a direction, unless the parties agree on the expert to be instructed, the court may select an expert from a list submitted by the parties, or direct how the expert should be selected. Once selected, each instructing party may give instructions to the expert, sending a copy to the other instructing parties.

The fast track practice direction (PD 28) provides that where the court is to give directions of its own initiative and it is not aware of any steps taken by the parties other than service of statements of case, its general approach will be to give directions for a single joint expert unless there is good reason not to do so. If the parties agree directions in a fast track case, primarily they will be expected to have agreed to the joint instruction of experts, but they may agree to instruct their own experts, with subsequent mutual exchange of reports. Of course, the court may disagree with separate instruction, and may force the parties into jointly instructing experts.

The multi-track practice direction (PD 29), on the other hand, says that where the court is proposing on its own initiative to make an order that evidence on a particular issue is to be given by a single expert, the court must, unless the parties consented to the order, list a case management conference. This reflects the fact that separate instruction of experts is far more acceptable in multi-track cases.

There will be some reluctance to insisting on the joint instruction of a medical expert if one of the parties in a multi-track case objects to this course being taken (*Knight v Sage Group plc* (1999) LTL 28/4/99).

In many cases receipt of the jointly instructed expert's report will be all that is needed by way of obtaining expert evidence on the issue. It may be appropriate to ask written questions (see **29.6.3**), but the single expert should not be seen in conference by one side without the other side's written consent (*Peet v Mid-Kent Healthcare Trust* [2002] 1 WLR 210). In most cases the report prepared by the joint expert should be the evidence in the case on the issues it covers, and the report should not be amplified or tested in cross-examination at trial. Although this is the normal situation, there is a discretion to allow amplification or cross-examination, but such questioning should be restricted as far as possible (*Peet v Mid-Kent Healthcare Trust* [2002] 1 WLR 210).

In a small number of cases one of the parties may have more than fanciful grounds for seeking to challenge all or part of the joint expert's report. In such cases the court has a discretion to allow one or both parties to instruct their own experts (*Daniels v Walker* [2000] 1 WLR 1382). Factors bearing on the exercise of the discretion include the reasons for seeking another report, the nature of the case and the amount at stake, the effect of allowing another expert to report and its impact on delay and the trial (*Cosgrove v Pattison* [2001] CPLR 177). *Daniels v Walker* is also important because Lord Woolf MR pointed out that the overriding objective of dealing with claims justly means that it will generally be unnecessary to resort to Human Rights Act 1998 points (even under art 6(1)) on case management decisions, and counsel have to take a responsible attitude about raising such points.

29.6.2 Letters of instruction

Detailed guidance on the information to be provided to experts when they are instructed is given by the Experts Protocol in PD 35, para 8.1. The main obligation is to explain the purpose of the report, describe what needs to be investigated, and to explain the issues in the case. All the necessary background information should also be provided. An example of a letter of instruction is shown in **Figure 2.4**.

29.6.3 Written questions to experts

The CPR, r 35.6, provides:

> (1) *A party may put to—*
>   (a) *an expert instructed by another party; or*
>   (b) *a single joint expert appointed under rule 35.7, written questions about his report.*
> (2) *Written questions under paragraph (1)—*
>   (a) *may be put once only;*

(b) *must be put within 28 days of service of the expert's report; and*

(c) *must be for the purpose only of clarification of the report, unless in any case—*

  (i)   *the court give permission; or*

  (ii) *the other party agrees.*

Questions must be purely for clarification if they are put to the expert without permission, but it is possible to ask about matters not in the expert's report (as long as they are within the expert's expertise) with the consent of the other side or the court's permission (*Mutch v Allen* [2001] CPLR 200, CA). Despite the apparently adversarial format of r 35.6(1) above, it does not prevent a party putting written questions to his own expert (*Stallwood v David* [2007] 1 All ER 206). Directions given allowing expert evidence to be introduced will usually provide a date by when questions should be put to the expert. The expert's answers to such questions are treated as part of the expert's report (r 35.6(3)). Rule 35.6(4) provides:

(4) *Where—*

  (a) *a party has put a written question to an expert instructed by another party in accordance with this rule; and*

  (b) *the expert does not answer that question, the court may make one or both of the following orders in relation to the party who instructed the expert—*

    (i)   *that the party may not rely on the evidence of that expert; or*

    (ii) *that the party may not recover the fees and expenses of that expert from any other party.*

29.6.4 Without prejudice discussion

The court may, at any stage, direct a discussion between experts for the purpose of requiring the experts to identify the issues in the proceedings and, where possible, reach agreement on the issues. Such a direction will normally also provide that following the discussion the experts must prepare a statement for the court showing:

- those issues on which they agree; and
- those issues on which they disagree with a summary of their reasons for disagreeing.

In *Aird v Prime Meridian Ltd* The Times, 14 February 2007, CA, directions were given for mediation, with a joint statement to be prepared by the parties' experts. A draft joint statement was headed 'without prejudice', but the final version had these words removed. The mediation failed to settle the case. It was held that the joint statement did not acquire without prejudice status by being used in the mediation, so was admissible in the proceedings.

29.6.5 Mutual exchange

Where directions allow the parties to each instruct their own expert, the usual practice is for mutual disclosure (ie exchange of reports) within a specified period.

However, in exceptional circumstances, and to save costs, sequential disclosure may be ordered with disclosure by one party only and the other party permitted to defer disclosure of any reports, eg where a defendant has not had a medical examination and it is likely that the claimant's report will be agreed. Another example was *Kirkup v British Railway Engineering Ltd* [1983] 1 WLR 1165. In this case the statement of claim was in very general terms, and the defendant had decided on policy grounds (in order to reduce costs) not to ask for particulars, as it had been flooded with 8,661 similar claims by its employees. One principal issue in each case was the noise level in the various workshops where the employees had been working, often stretching over the whole working life of the employee. To obviate the need on the part of the defendants of writing a thesis on noise generally in engineering workshops, a sequential disclosure order was made.

29.7 Form of experts' reports

By virtue of CPR, r 35.10, and PD 35, para 2.2, an expert's report must:

(a) give details of the expert's qualifications;

(b) give details of any literature or other materials the expert has relied on in making the report;

(c) contain a statement setting out the substance of all facts and instructions given to the expert that are material to the report. By CPR, r 35.10(4), and PD 35, para 4, the instructions referred to will not be protected by privilege, but cross-examination of the experts on the contents of the instructions will not be allowed without consent of the party who gave the instructions or unless the court permits it;

(d) make clear which facts stated in the report are within the expert's own knowledge;

(e) say who carried out any test or experiment which the expert has used for the report, give the qualifications of the person who carried out the test or experiment, and say whether or not the test or experiment has been carried out under the expert's supervision;

(f) where there is a range of opinion on the matters dealt with in the report, summarise the range of opinion, and give reasons for the expert's opinion;

(g) contain a summary of the conclusions reached;

(h) state any qualifications to the report; and

(i) contain a statement that the expert understands his or her duty to the court and has complied with that duty.

In addition:

(j) an expert witness should never assume the role of an advocate (PD 35, para 1.3);

(k) an expert should consider all material facts, including those which might detract from the opinion (PD 35, para 1.4);

(l) an expert witness should make it clear when a question falls outside his or her expertise, or when an opinion is provisional because the facts are not fully available (PD 35, para 1.5).

An expert's report must be verified by a statement of truth in the form:

I confirm that in so far as the facts stated in my report are within my own knowledge I have made clear which they are and I believe them to be true, and that the opinions I have expressed represent my true and complete professional opinion.

If an expert changes his or her mind on a material matter after the exchange of reports, that change of view should be communicated to the other parties (and, if reports have been lodged at court, to the court: PD 35, para 1.6).

29.8   Choice of expert

The Civil Procedure Rules 1998 place a lot of emphasis on the importance of experts remaining independent of the parties, and state that the expert's primary duty is to the court rather than the party paying his fees. The CPR, r 35.3, provides:

(1) *It is the duty of an expert to help the court on the matters within his expertise.*

(2) *This duty overrides any obligation to the person from whom he has received instructions or by whom he is paid.*

An expert who has caused significant expense to be incurred through flagrant, reckless disregard of his duties to the court may be ordered to pay those costs (*Phillips v Symes (No. 2)* [2005] 1 WLR 2043). In *Stevens v Gullis* [2000] 1 All ER 527, CA, an expert instructed by one of the parties demonstrated by his conduct that he had no conception of the requirements imposed on experts by the Civil Procedure Rules. This included failing to state in his report that he understood his duty to the court and failing to set out his instructions, and also in failing to cooperate with the other experts in signing an agreed memorandum following a without prejudice meeting of experts. It was held that in the circumstances he should be debarred from giving evidence in the case. On the other hand, provided the expert understands his primary duty is to the court, there is no objection to an employee of one of the parties being instructed as an expert witness (*Field v Leeds City Council* [2000] 1 EGLR 54; *R (Factortame Ltd) v Secretary of State for Transport, Local Government and the Regions (No. 8)* [2003] QB 381).

29.9   Putting experts' reports in evidence

The CPR, r 35.11, provides that where a party has disclosed an expert's report, any party may use that expert's report as evidence at the trial. This rule gives the parties an absolute right to rely on the expert reports disclosed by other parties, unrestricted by any discretion in rr 35.1 and 35.7 (*Shepherd Neame Ltd v EDF Energy Networks (SPN) plc* [2008] Bus LR Digest D43).

Witness statements

30.1 Introduction

The rules providing for the exchange of the parties' witnesses' statements are an important element in producing an open system for trial preparation. Witness statements are used as a means of putting evidence before the court in interim applications (see **10.2.4**) and as a means of disclosing to the opposite side the evidence that will be given by the witnesses intended to be called at trial. Although these purposes are quite different, witness statements follow the same format whatever their purpose. The provenance of the rules has been confirmed by the Courts and Legal Services Act 1990, s 5.

30.2 Directions for the exchange of witness statements

The main rules relating to the use of witness statements are to be found in CPR, rr 32.4 and 32.10:

32.4—(1) A witness statement is a written statement signed by a person which contains the evidence which that person would be allowed to give orally.

(2) The court will order a party to serve on the other parties any witness statement of the oral evidence which the party serving the statement intends to rely on in relation to any issues of fact to be decided at the trial.

32.10 If a witness statement or witness summary for use at trial is not served in respect of an intended witness within the time specified by the court, then the witness may not be called to give oral evidence unless the court gives permission.

When directions are made on allocating a case to the fast track or multi-track, or at a case management conference, the court will make provision for the date by when witness statements must be exchanged. Witness statements are not usually exchanged in small claims track cases, so, like **Chapter 29**, the following discussion is largely limited to fast track and multi-track cases.

Normally mutual exchange is required, and it usually takes place a few weeks after disclosure and inspection of documents. Part of the reason why witness statements are exchanged after disclosure of documents is that the witnesses may need to comment on some of the documentation in their statements. If a witness statement is not served within the time specified in the directions, the witness may only be called with permission.

The statements that need to be exchanged are those of the witnesses a party intends to call at trial. There is no obligation to disclose statements from 'witnesses' who will not be called at trial.

30.3   Format of exchanged statements

The statement should represent the witness's evidence in chief. It will contain a formal heading with the title of the proceedings. In the top right-hand corner it should state the party on whose behalf it is made; the initials and surname of the witness; whether it is the first, second etc statement of the witness; the references of the exhibits included; and the date it is made. See **Figure 10.1**. The opening paragraph should give details of the witness's occupation or description, and if relevant state the position he holds and the name of his employer, and should also state if he or she is a party in the proceedings, or employed by a party.

The text of the statement must, if practicable, be in the witness's own words. It should be expressed in the first person. It is usually convenient to follow the chronological sequence of events. Each paragraph should, so far as possible, be confined to a distinct portion of the subject. The statement should indicate sections of its content that are made only from knowledge and belief as opposed to matters within the witness' own knowledge, and should state the sources of any matters of information and belief. All numbers, including dates, should be expressed in figures. Documents referred to in the statement should be formally exhibited (*Tweed v Parades Commission for Northern Ireland* [2007] 1 AC 650). The statement must include a signed statement that the witness believes the facts it contains are true. False statements may be punished as contempt of court (see **5.8**). The form of statement of truth is: 'I believe that the facts stated in this witness statement are true.'

Witness statements must be produced on durable A4 paper with a 35 mm margin and typed on one side of the paper only. Wherever possible they should be securely bound in a manner that will not hamper filing. If they are not securely bound each page should bear the claim number and initials of the witness.

30.4   Witness summaries

A party who is unable to obtain signed statements before the time prescribed for exchange may apply for permission to serve witness summaries instead of witness statements. Witness summaries are simply summaries of the evidence that would have been included in a witness statement. They could be unsigned draft statements, or even just an indication of the issues it is hoped the witness could deal with. Such orders can only be granted if the party is unable to obtain the relevant witness statement. Unless the court orders otherwise, a witness summary must be served within the period in which a witness statement would have had to be served.

30.5   Failure to comply with a direction

The general principles and factors relevant to late service under the Civil Procedure Rules are discussed at **28.3.2** and **28.3.6** above.

In *Mealey Horgan plc v Horgan* The Times, 6 July 1999, the defaulting party served its witness statements about two weeks later than required by directions as extended, and six weeks before trial. Buckley J said that making an order depriving the defaulting party of its evidence would be out of proportion to the default. Such a response would be appropriate only if there had been deliberate flouting of court orders, or inexcusable delay which would otherwise result in the adjournment of the trial. In *Cowland v District Judges of the West London County Court* (1999) LTL 20/7/99, the Court of Appeal held that the claimants should have been given permission to call a witness on the day of the trial despite not having served a witness statement. The witness could give evidence on the key issue, was available to both parties (and there is no property in a witness), and there was no material prejudice that could not be guarded against by an order for costs.

On the other hand, permission to serve the statement of one witness late was refused in *Coore v Chief Constable of Leicestershire* (1999) LTL 10/5/99, CA. Although the court made comments to the effect that the case was based on the exercise of the discretion to allow late service, the main reason given is to the effect that the witness did not address the essential issue in the case.

30.6 Privilege and use of opponents' statements

If a statement is made by a person and the party who took the statement decides not to call the maker of the statement at trial or to use the statement at trial then the statement will be privileged if made for the purpose of pending or contemplated litigation. If, however, a person is to be called at trial, their witness statement will have to be disclosed to the other side on the exchange of witness statements. The exchange of such a witness statement created some debate as to whether, after disclosure, the statement remained protected by legal professional privilege so that the party receiving it could not use it without some further act of waiver of privilege. This would be particularly important if the party who disclosed the statement later decided for some reason not to call the maker of the statement at trial. However, there can be no doubt that once a witness statement has been exchanged the privilege is waived (*Re Rex Williams Leisure plc* [1994] Ch 350, CA).

The CPR, r 32.5(5), provides that where the party who has disclosed a witness statement does not use it at trial, '. . . any other party may put the witness statement in as hearsay'. The discretion provided by the word 'may' in this rule is intended to be given to the party receiving the witness statement, but was interpreted by the Court of Appeal in *McPhilemy v Times Newspapers Ltd (No. 2)* [2000] 1 WLR 1732 as being vested in the court. In *McPhilemy v Times Newspapers Ltd (No. 2)* the party who disclosed a witness statement decided against calling the witness. The opposite side then attempted to put the statement into evidence for the purpose of proving that its contents were untrue. The Court of Appeal held that the trial judge had been right to prevent this because of the general rule of evidence that a party is not allowed to adduce evidence that his own witnesses are not to be believed on their oaths (with the exception of hostile witnesses).

30.7 Use of witnesses' statements at trial

30.7.1 Examination-in-chief

Exchanged witness statements stand as the witnesses' evidence in chief unless the court otherwise orders. A witness may, however, and provided the court considers there is good reason not to confine the witness to the contents of the disclosed statement, amplify his or her witness statement and give evidence in relation to new matters that have arisen since the statement was served: CPR, r 32.5(3), (4). The CPR, r 32.5, provides:

(1)   If—
   (a)   a party has served a witness statement; and
   (b)   he wishes to rely at trial on the evidence of the witness who made the statement, he must call the witness to give oral evidence unless the court orders otherwise or he puts the statement in as hearsay evidence.
(2)   Where a witness is called to give oral evidence under paragraph (1), his witness statement shall stand as his evidence in chief unless the court orders otherwise.
(3)   A witness giving oral evidence at trial may with the permission of the court—
   (a)   amplify his witness statement; and
   (b)   give evidence in relation to new matters which have arisen since the witness statement was served on the other parties.
(4)   The court will give permission under paragraph (3) only if it considers that there is good reason not to confine the evidence of the witness to the contents of his witness statement.

Unless such additional evidence is to be called, the examination-in-chief of the witnesses can be very short. They will be called, take the oath, and asked for their names and addresses (and often their occupations). They will then be asked to turn to the pages in the trial bundles (for which see **33.7**) where their statements can be found, and asked whether the document they have been shown is their statement, signed by them, and that its contents are true to the best of their knowledge and belief. They are then asked to wait in the witness box for cross-examination.

30.7.2   Cross-examination

The CPR, r 32.11, provides:

Where a witness is called to give evidence at trial, he may be cross-examined on his witness statement whether or not the statement or any part of it was referred to during the witness's evidence in chief.

30.7.3   Copies for the public

Where a direction is made that an exchanged statement shall stand as a witness's evidence in chief, members of the public present in court may not be able to follow the case and the principle that justice should be administered in open court would be undermined. CPR, r 32.13, therefore enables members of the public to request to inspect such statements, and, if this happens, the court must make them available on payment of a prescribed fee. This right does not, in all probability, extend to documents exhibited to the statements (*GIO Personal Investment Services Ltd v Liverpool and London Steamship Protection and Indemnity Association Ltd* [1999] 1 WLR 984, CA). It is also subject to the court refusing to make the statements available for some sufficient reason, such as disclosure being contrary to the interests of justice or national security, or because of the nature of any expert medical evidence in a statement.

30.8 Implied undertaking

After a statement has been exchanged, CPR, r 32.12, provides that it may be used only for the purpose of the present proceedings unless and to the extent that:

- the witness gives consent in writing; or
- the court grants permission; or
- it has been put in evidence at a hearing in public.

Hearsay in civil cases

31.1 Common law rule against hearsay

The hearsay rule is one of the oldest of the exclusionary rules in the law of evidence, having developed at the same time as the modern form of trial by jury.

At common law, a witness who was testifying could not repeat either:

(a) what he had himself said outside the witness box on an earlier occasion (the rule against narrative); or

(b) assertions of other persons, whether oral, written or by conduct (the strict hearsay rule).

An assertion is hearsay when it is tendered to establish the truth of that asserted. It is not hearsay when tendered to establish the fact that an assertion was made or the manner in which it was made.

It is also necessary to distinguish between hearsay and real evidence. Real evidence consists of physical objects which are produced for inspection by the court. Thus, a watch may be produced to prove it is defective, or a dog to prove it is vicious. An automatic recording, eg a tape recording, video recording or computer printout can be an item of real evidence and, if so, will be admissible provided there is prima facie evidence that it is authentic and sufficiently intelligible. The question is whether any specific recording is real evidence or hearsay. This turns on whether the recording or printout contains information produced with human intervention: if not, it is real evidence.

31.2 Civil Evidence Act 1995

31.2.1 Admissibility of hearsay in civil cases

The Civil Evidence Act 1995 (CEA 1995) abolished the common law rule against hearsay for civil cases, and the admissibility of hearsay is now governed by statute. This appears from s 1(1), which provides:

In civil proceedings evidence shall not be excluded on the ground that it is hearsay.

Hearsay includes multiple hearsay (s 1(2)(b)). However, hearsay will not be admissible if the maker of the statement would not have been competent as a witness (s 5), such as through being too young or of unsound mind.

31.2.2 Notice procedure

Section 2 of the CEA 1995 provides, in effect, that rules of court may:

- specify classes of proceedings in which a party intending to rely on hearsay evidence must give advance notice to the other parties;
- make provision for the other parties to request particulars of the hearsay evidence intended to be adduced; and
- prescribe the manner and time for complying with the above.

The rules are contained in CPR, rr 33.2 and 33.3, which provide:

> 33.2—(1) *Where a party intends to rely on hearsay evidence at trial and either—*
>> (a) *that evidence is to be given by a witness giving oral evidence; or*
>> (b) *that evidence is contained in a witness statement of a person not being called to give oral evidence;*
>>> *that party complies with section 2(1)(a) of the Civil Evidence Act 1995 by serving a witness statement on the other parties in accordance with the court's order.*
>
>> (2) *Where paragraph (1)(b) applies, the party intending to rely on the hearsay evidence must, when he serves the witness statement—*
>>> (a) *inform the other parties that the witness is not being called to give oral evidence; and*
>>> (b) *give the reason why the witness will not be called.*
>
>> (3) *In all other cases where a party intends to rely on hearsay evidence at trial, the party complies with section 2(1)(a) of the Civil Evidence Act 1995 by serving a notice on the other parties which—*
>>> (a) *identifies the hearsay evidence;*
>>> (b) *states that the party serving the notice proposes to rely on the hearsay evidence at trial; and*
>>> (c) *gives the reason why the witness will not be called.*
>
>> (4) *The party proposing to rely on the hearsay evidence must—*
>>> (a) *serve the notice no later than the latest date for serving witness statements; and*
>>> (b) *if the hearsay evidence is to be in a document, supply a copy to any party who requests him to do so.*
>
> 33.3 *Section 2(1) of the Civil Evidence Act 1995 (duty to give notice of intention to rely on hearsay evidence) does not apply—*
>> (a) *to evidence at hearings other than trials;*
>> (aa) *to an affidavit or witness statement which is to be used at trial but which does not contain hearsay evidence;*
>> (b) *to a statement which a party to a probate action wishes to put in evidence and which is alleged to have been made by the person whose estate is the subject of the proceedings; or*
>> (c) *where the requirement is excluded by a practice direction.*

Hearsay evidence is frequently given by witnesses who repeat what they were told on a previous occasion, and, as the witness statements are supposed to set out the evidence the witnesses are intended to say in chief, hearsay evidence will usually be set out in the exchanged witness statements. The CPR, r 33.2(1), says that if the hearsay evidence is set out in a witness statement served in accordance with the usual directions on exchange of witness statements, there is no need for a hearsay notice. There is also no need for a hearsay notice where a witness statement which includes hearsay evidence is used on an interim hearing (r 33.3(a)).

A single hearsay notice may deal with the hearsay evidence of more than one witness.

The duty to give notice may be waived by the parties (s 2(3)). A failure to comply with the duty to give notice does not affect the admissibility of the hearsay evidence, but may adversely affect the weight of the evidence and may be penalised in costs (see s 2(4)).

31.2.3   Adducing hearsay evidence at trial

By s 6(3), the CEA 1995 does not affect the continued operation of the Criminal Procedure Act 1865, ss 3, 4 and 5, which relate to impeaching hostile witnesses by cross-examination, and the use of inconsistent statements.

If a party adduces hearsay evidence without calling the maker of the statement, the CEA 1995, s 3, provides that the other parties may be allowed by the Rules of Court to call the maker, whose hearsay statement will be treated as the witness's evidence in chief, and who will be cross-examined by the party calling the witness.

The relevant provision in the rules is CPR, r 33.4, which provides:

(1) *Where a party—*
   (a) *proposes to rely on hearsay evidence; and*
   (b) *does not propose to call the person who made the original statement to give oral evidence, the court may, on the application of any other party, permit that party to call the maker of the statement to be cross-examined on the contents of the statement.*
(2) *An application for permission to cross-examine under this rule must be made not more than 14 days after the day on which a notice of intention to rely on the hearsay evidence was served on the applicant.*

The application will need to be made by issuing an application notice. Consideration should be given to supporting the application with evidence in writing, although there is no strict requirement for this.

If the maker of a hearsay statement is called as a witness at trial, the general rule is that the oral testimony of the witness is all that can be adduced (see CEA 1995, s 6(2)). However, this general prohibition does not prevent the introduction of:

(a) the exchanged witness statement of the witness (see **Chapter 30**); or

(b) a previous consistent statement made by the witness adduced to rebut an allegation of fabrication; or

(c) a previous hearsay statement with the permission of the court. Permission is likely to be granted, for example, where, through the passage of time since the events under consideration, or through the onset of some disease, the witness finds it difficult or impossible to remember the relevant events, or otherwise gives confused or incoherent evidence, but did make a statement about the events soon after they occurred (but outside the time allowed for the use of memory-refreshing documents). See, for example, *Morris v Stratford-on-Avon Rural District Council* [1973] 1 WLR 1059, a case under the CEA 1968.

31.2.4   Assessing the weight of hearsay evidence

The weight to be attached to hearsay evidence is dealt with by the CEA 1995, s 4. This provides that in assessing weight, all the relevant circumstances must be considered.

These include the ease of calling the maker of the statement, how contemporaneous the statement was with the events it describes, whether it involves multiple hearsay, any editing, and any motive the maker or recorder may have had to conceal or misrepresent matters: CEA 1995, s 4(2).

By s 5(2) evidence is admissible to attack or support the credibility of the maker of the hearsay statements introduced at trial, unless under the rules of evidence a denial by the witness would have been final. This means that evidence on collateral matters cannot be introduced to attack a hearsay statement, subject to the usual exceptions, namely that the witness has been convicted of a crime, the fact that the witness is biased in favour of the party calling him or her, and the fact that he or she has made a statement inconsistent with the present hearsay statement.

If a party wishes to attack the credibility of the maker of a hearsay statement, CPR, r 33.5, provides:

> (1) Where a party—
>   (a) proposes to rely on hearsay evidence; but
>   (b) does not propose to call the person who made the original statement to give oral evidence; and
>   (c) another party wishes to call evidence to attack the credibility of the person who made the statement,
>   the party who so wishes must give notice of his intention to the party who proposes to give the hearsay statement in evidence.
> (2) A party must give notice under paragraph (1) not more than 14 days after the day on which a hearsay notice relating to the hearsay evidence was served on him.

The court will also take into account any failure to comply with the notice requirements.

31.2.5 Preservation of certain common law exceptions to the hearsay rule

The CEA 1995, s 7, preserves the continued operation of the following five common law exceptions to the hearsay rule:

- Published works dealing with matters of a public nature.
- Public documents.
- Records of certain courts, Crown grants, pardons and commissions.
- Evidence of a person's reputation for good or bad character.
- Evidence of reputation or family tradition for the purposes of proving pedigree, the existence of a marriage, public or general rights, and for identifying persons or things.

Under the CEA 1968, the common law exception to the hearsay rule relating to the proof of informal admissions was preserved by s 9 of the 1968 Act. Under the 1995 Act, informal admissions are treated in the same way as other forms of general hearsay, and are admissible under s 1(1) and subject to the notice requirements in s 2.

31.2.6 Business and public records

Under the CEA 1995, s 9(1), business (which includes any activity regularly carried on over a period of time, whether for profit or not) and public authority (which includes any public or statutory undertaking or government department) records (which are defined in s 9(4) as records in whatever form) may be received in evidence without further proof. A document will, by s 9(2), be regarded as such a record if a certificate signed by an officer of the business or authority is produced to the court. A document purporting to be such a certificate is deemed by s 9(2) (a) to have been duly given by an appropriate officer and signed by him or her. These provisions are designed to facilitate the easy proof of records without the need to call anyone as a witness at the trial. However, if the document contains hearsay a hearsay notice should still be served.

By s 9(3), the fact of an absence of an entry in the records of a business or public authority may be proved by an affidavit sworn by an officer of the relevant body. This is useful, as it is notoriously difficult to prove a negative.

Admissions, notices to admit, and trial documents

32.1 Introduction

It makes good sense to delimit the areas of conflict, as to do so saves both time and expense. The subject matter of this chapter deals with aspects of the law relating to admissions by the parties to litigation. We will deal first with admissions of fact, and then admissions in respect of documents. The final part of the chapter will deal with documents to be used at trial.

32.2 Admissions of fact

32.2.1 What are admissions?

Admissions are statements, whether express or implied, whether oral or written, which are wholly or partly adverse to a party's case. Admissions may be either formal or informal.

32.2.2 Formal admissions

Formal admissions may be made by the statements of case or otherwise in writing, including admissions made in compliance with a notice to admit (see **32.3**) or on a case management conference or other directions hearing (see **19.3.3**).

32.2.3 Informal admissions

Informal admissions are simply items of evidence and may be disproved or explained away at trial by evidence to the contrary. Although they are hearsay, in that they are assertions made other than by a person while giving oral evidence at trial and are adduced as evidence of the facts asserted, they are admissible in evidence by virtue of Civil Evidence Act 1995, s 1.

Where the informal admission is made by a party personally, the only conditions of admissibility are:

- that the statement must be at least partly adverse;
- that the statement was made in the same legal capacity as that in which the party is now suing or being sued; and
- that the statement is received in its entirety.

Employees and agents may make admissions which are admissible against a party if they have express or implied authority to talk about the subject in question. It is to be noted that generally employees and agents have a wider authority to act than to speak about what they have done.

32.2.4   Withdrawing admissions

Withdrawing pre-action admissions was considered at **2.2.3**. Where an admission has been pleaded, the court may allow it to be withdrawn by amendment (CPR, r 14.1(5)). This was considered at **24.5.2**. Unless permission is granted, a party who has made an admission is not allowed to adduce evidence at trial to contradict it.

32.3   Notice to admit facts

A party may seek further to limit and define the issues at trial after the directions stage by serving a notice to admit. A specimen notice appears at **Figure 32.1**. The CPR, r 32.18, provides:

> (1) *A party may serve notice on another party requiring him to admit the facts, or the part of the case of the serving party, specified in the notice.*
> (2) *A notice to admit facts must be served no later than 21 days before the trial.*
> (3) *Where the other party makes any admission in response to the notice, the admission may be used against him only—*
>   (a) *in the proceedings in which the notice to admit is served; and*
>   (b) *by the party who served the notice.*
> (4) *The court may allow a party to amend or withdraw any admission made by him on such terms as it thinks just.*

Under the old rules, if the other side failed to make the requested admissions within 14 days after service of the notice and if those facts were later proved at trial, the costs of proving those facts and the costs occasioned by and thrown away as a result of that failure would be borne by him or her unless the court ordered otherwise: see RSC Ord 62, r 6(7). Under the Civil Procedure Rules 1998 there is no express rule dealing with the consequences of not making a positive response to a notice to admit facts. However, the costs rules in Part 44, and in particular r 44.3(6), are wide enough to achieve the same result.

Notices to admit are a judicially favoured procedure. In *Baden v Société Générale pour Favoriser le Développement du Commerce et de l'Industrie en France SA* [1985] BCLC 258, CA, Sir John Donaldson MR said that notices to admit and the costs penalties are of the greatest importance in the administration of justice and ought to be more frequently used. The reason is that judicial time is saved and the costs of litigation reduced if the issues in dispute are sharply defined before trial.

However, the procedure should not be abused by issuing notice to admit facts which are at the centre of the dispute. In such circumstances, the court is unlikely to impose any costs penalty for failing to make the requested admissions.

32.4   Deemed admission of the authenticity of disclosed documents

A party served with a list of documents may find that they are deemed to have admitted the authenticity of documents disclosed by the other side. The relevant rule is CPR, r 32.19, which provides:

> (1) *A party shall be deemed to admit the authenticity of a document disclosed to him under Part 31 (disclosure and inspection of documents) unless he serves notice that he wishes the document to be proved at trial.*

(2) A notice to prove a document must be served—
(a) by the latest date for serving witness statements; or
(b) within 7 days of disclosure of the document, whichever is the later.

The reference to 'disclosure' in r 32.19(2)(b) is presumably intended to be a reference to 'inspection'. If a party believes that documents disclosed by the other side are fabricated or have been tampered with, they must serve a notice to prove. There is a prescribed form for the notice, Form N268.

The purpose of the rule is to prevent the necessity and cost of formal notices to admit documents disclosed in a list of documents. In practice this rule catches the vast majority of documents relevant to litigation.

32.5 Proof of documents

32.5.1 Best evidence rule

There was a very old common law rule that the contents of a document had to be proved by primary evidence. The rule was often said to be an aspect of the best evidence rule. The best primary evidence of a document was the original, although it was held in *Slatterie v Pooley* (1840) 6 M & W 664 that an informal admission was primary evidence of the contents of a document against the party making the admission.

32.5.2 Abolition of the best evidence rule

The best evidence rule was abolished for civil claims by the Civil Evidence Act 1995, s 8, which provides:

(1) Where a statement contained in a document is admissible as evidence in civil proceedings, it may be proved—
(a) by the production of that document, or
(b) whether or not that document is still in existence, by the production of a copy of that document or of the material part of it,
authenticated in such manner as the court may approve.
(2) It is immaterial for this purpose how many removes there are between a copy and the original.

When secondary evidence is given of a document, the contents of the document can be proved by copies of the original, whether these be manuscript copies, or photocopies or some other method, including copies of copies. The only condition is that the copy must be authenticated in such manner as the court may approve.

It was held that once secondary evidence has been adduced, the original cannot be adduced to contradict the secondary evidence (*Collins v Gashon* (1860) 2 F & F 47).

32.5.3 Agreed trial bundles

All the documents in agreed trial bundles (see **33.7**) are admissible as evidence of their contents unless the court orders otherwise or another party serves written notice objecting to the admissibility of specified documents (PD 32, para 27.1). The originals of the documents in the trial bundle should be available at the trial (PD 39, para 3.3).

Notice to admit facts

In the Central London County Court	
Claim No.	CL 938878
Claimant (include Ref.)	CLIVE SHERRILL
Defendant (include Ref.)	DORADOWN (MACHINE FITTINGS) LIMITED

I (We) give notice that you are requested to admit the following facts or part of case in this claim:

1. That the machine referred to in paragraph 2 of the Particulars of Claim was designed to be operated with steel guards in place.
2. That the steel guards designed for use with the machine were removed for maintenance four days before the Claimant's accident.
3. That the steel guards were not in place on the day of the Claimant's accident.
4. That the Claimant's accident was not caused or contributed to by the negligence of the Claimant.

I (We) confirm that any admission of fact(s) or part of case will only be used in this claim.

Signed _____   **Position or office held** _____
(Claimant)(Defendant)('s Solicitor)   (If signing on behalf of firm or company)

Date _____

- -

Admission of facts

I (We) admit the facts or part of case (set out above)(in the attached schedule) for the purposes of this claim only and on the basis that the admission will not be used on any other occasion or by any other person.

1. Admitted.
2. Admitted.
3. The Claimant is required to prove that the steel guards were not in place on the day of the Claimant's accident. Maintenance of the guards was completed two days before the Claimant's accident, and they would have been refitted at that time.
4. The Defendant maintains its allegations as to causation and contributory negligence as set out in the Defence.

Signed _____   **Position or office held** _____
(Claimant)(Defendant)('s Solicitor)   (If signing on behalf of firm or company)

Date _____

The court office at

is open between 10 am and 4 pm Monday to Friday. Address all communication to the Court Manager quoting the claim number

N266 - w3 Notice to admit facts (4.99)   *Printed on behalf of The Court Service*

Figure 32.1   Specimen notice to admit

Notice to prove documents at trial

In the	Central London County Court

Claim No.	CL 938878
Claimant (include Ref.)	CLIVE SHERRILL
Defendant (include Ref.)	DORADOWN (MACHINE FITTINGS) LIMITED

I (We) give notice that you are requested to prove the following documents disclosed under CPR Part 31 in this claim at the trial:

1. Letter from Messrs. Armstrong and Graham to the Defendant dated the 5th April 2007.
2. Letter from Messrs. Hope & Co to the Defendant dated the 11th May 2007.

Signed

(Claimant)(Defendant)('s Solicitor)

Position or office held
(If signing on behalf of firm or company)

Date

The court office at

is open between 10 am and 4 pm Monday to Friday. Address all communication to the Court Manager quoting the claim number

N268 - W3 Notice to prove documents at trial (4.99)   Printed on behalf of The Court Service

Figure 32.2   Notice to prove documents

33 Trial

33.1 Introduction

The vast majority of claims commenced in the civil courts of this country never reach trial. Proceedings may fail to reach the trial stage for many reasons. Judgment may be entered in default or on an application for summary judgment. The proceedings may be struck out as an abuse of process, or as a result of a sanction, or discontinued. Most frequently, however, the parties avoid trial by negotiating a settlement of their dispute. One of the factors constraining the parties to settle their differences is the great cost of trial. The cost of any individual trial depends on a number of matters, including its length, complexity, the seniority of counsel instructed, and the fees of any experts who are required to attend. However, it can be said that the costs of many trials far exceed the costs of all the interim proceedings involved in the case prior to trial.

If the dispute between the parties cannot be resolved by negotiation, either party may seek to have it determined by the court. Although individual litigants may have their own motives for bringing their cases to trial, such as to have their day in court or to vindicate themselves in public, the primary purpose of having a trial is to decide finally the dispute between the parties by a judgment of the court.

33.2 Pre-trial checklists and fixing the date of trial

These topics have already been considered in the context of the discussion of fast track cases (see **18.3**, **18.6** and **18.10**) and multi-track cases (see **19.2**, **19.6** and **19.7**). Essentially, directions made either on track allocation or at a case management conference or other directions hearing will fix a date for filing pre-trial checklists, and trial dates will be fixed as soon as possible. In fast track cases this means at the allocation stage. In multi-track cases, fixing the trial date as soon as possible may mean doing this at the allocation stage, but may mean doing so considerably later. If a trial date is given at an early stage it may be altered later perhaps after the court considers the pre-trial checklists. Trial dates may either be fixtures, which obviously means that the trial will commence on a specific date, or may be given by means of a trial 'window' of up to three weeks.

The rules give the courts a great deal of flexibility regarding how they will deal with trials. As discussed in **Chapters 18** and **19** the court can lay down trial timetables prescribing how the time available for the trial will be used, and allocating specified, limited times, for examination-in-chief, cross-examination and so on. Another power available to the court is to direct that one or more issues should be dealt with before the others as preliminary issues.

33.3 Preliminary issues

33.3.1 Introduction

As a general rule, it is in the interests of the parties and the administration of justice that all issues arising in a dispute are tried at the same time. However, there are a number of rare and exceptional cases where some question or issue can be more conveniently or economically dealt with before or separately from the main trial. There are three main types of order that can be made:

- the trial of a preliminary issue on a point of law;
- the separate trial of preliminary issues or questions of fact; and
- the separate trials of the issues of liability and damages.

33.3.2 Procedure

A party raising a preliminary issue must usually apply by application notice or at a case management conference or pre-trial review. The court may alternatively make such an order of its own initiative. Very occasionally, the trial judge may order a question or issue to be tried first before the main trial.

The order will formulate the question that is to be tried, and must do so precisely so as to avoid difficulties of interpretation. If the issue is one of law, the court will further order the issue to be tried:

- on the statements of case; or
- on a case stated; or
- on an agreed statement of facts.

33.3.3 When is taking a preliminary issue desirable?

In *Allen v Gulf Oil Refining Ltd* [1981] AC 101, HL, Lord Roskill said:

The preliminary point procedure can in certain classes of case be invoked to achieve the desirable aim both of economy and simplicity. But cases in which invocation is desirable are few.

His Lordship gave two examples of situations where the procedure may be appropriate:

(a) Where 'a single issue of law can be isolated from the other issues in a particular case, whether of fact or of law, and its decision may be finally determinative of the case as a whole.'

(b) Where the 'facts can be agreed and the sole issue is one of law.'

The House of Lords has protested against orders for the trial of preliminary points of law on assumed facts. In *Tilling v Whiteman* [1980] AC 1, Lord Scarman said they were '. . . too often treacherous short cuts. Their price can be delay, anxiety and expense.' The danger is that if the court, perhaps on appeal, decides against the point of law, the case has to go back to the court of first instance to be tried.

There appears to be a slightly increased willingness to order the trial of preliminary issues under the Civil Procedure Rules 1998. The way it is put in the Chancery Guide, for example, at para 3.11, is that costs can sometimes be saved by identifying decisive issues, or potentially decisive issues, and ordering that they be tried first. The decision of one issue, which in itself may not be decisive, may still be appropriate because it may enable the parties to settle the remainder of their dispute.

33.4 Jury trial

33.4.1 Cases where jury trial is appropriate

In the County Court (CCA 1984, s 66) and in the Queen's Bench Division of the High Court (SCA 1981, s 69) a party may apply for the claim to be tried by jury if there is in issue either:

(a) a claim in fraud; or

(b) a claim in respect of libel, slander, malicious prosecution or false imprisonment.

The prima facie right to trial by jury in such cases is subject to the court otherwise being of the opinion that the trial requires prolonged examination of documents or accounts, or any scientific or local investigation which cannot conveniently be made with a jury. Further, the right to a trial by jury must be applied for within 28 days of service of the defence (CPR, r 26.11), otherwise the right to trial by jury may be lost although the court retains a discretion to order trial by jury (see by analogy *Cropper v Chief Constable of the South Yorkshire Police* [1990] 2 All ER 1005, CA).

It is to be noted that even in the cases mentioned at (a) and (b) above there is no prima facie right to trial by jury in the Chancery Division.

Both the County Court and Queen's Bench Division have in addition a discretion to allow trial by jury in other cases. However, the usual rule is that all other cases are tried by judge alone (*Williams v Beesley* [1973] 1 WLR 1295, HL).

33.4.2 Majority verdicts

Juries in the County Court are eight strong. If they fail to agree on a verdict within a reasonable period of time a majority verdict of 7:1 may be accepted (see Juries Act 1974, s 17). In the High Court juries are 12 strong, and majority verdicts of 11:1 and 10:2 are permissible (and 10:1 and 9:1 after the discharge of jurors on the ground of evident necessity).

33.4.3 Releasing jurors in lengthy trials

Judges in jury trials should inquire of prospective jurors whether they will suffer inconvenience or hardship by having to serve for the estimated length of the trial, and excuse those who will be so affected (*Practice Direction (Juries: Length of Trial)* [1981] 1 WLR 1129).

33.5 Rights of audience

Rights of audience are governed by the Courts and Legal Services Act 1990 (CLSA 1990) as amended and the regulations made by the various legal professional bodies. Counsel have unrestricted rights of audience. Solicitors have to comply with the Law Society advocacy qualifications to conduct High Court trials.

In addition, parties can conduct their own cases as litigants in person, and express permission may be given to an individual by the court (CLSA 1990, s 27(2)(c)).

33.6 Pre-trial matters

In advance of trial the parties should use their best endeavours to agree on the issues or the main issues, and it is their duty so far as possible to reduce or eliminate the expert issues. A list of agreed issues should be delivered with the skeleton arguments (for which see **33.8**).

Also, in multi-track cases a pre-trial review may be held. This is usually conducted by the trial judge, is held usually about eight weeks before the start of the trial, and should be attended by the advocates who are to represent the parties at trial. Its functions include ensuring all parties will be ready for trial, to avoid the need for late adjournments or adjournments after the trial begins, to ensure the main issues are identified, and to provide directions for the efficient conduct of the hearing, including a trial timetable.

33.7 Trial bundles

Trial bundles should be filed by the claimant not more than seven and not less than three days before the start of the trial (CPR, r 39.5(2)). The responsibility for preparation of the trial bundles rests with the legal representative of the claimant. The court may give directions requiring the parties to use their best endeavours to agree on the contents of the trial bundles (PD 32, para 27.1). In no circumstances should rival bundles be lodged. All the documents contained in agreed trial bundles are admissible as evidence of their contents at the hearing, unless the court orders otherwise or a party gives written notice objecting to the admissibility of particular documents (para 27.2). PD 39, para 3, lays down detailed rules for trial bundles. Unless the court otherwise orders, the trial bundle should include:

(a) the claim form and all statements of case;

(b) a case summary and/or a chronology where appropriate;

(c) requests for further information and responses to the requests;

(d) all witness statements to be relied on as evidence;

(e) any witness summaries;

(f) any notices of intention to rely on hearsay evidence under r 33.2;

(g) any notices of intention to rely on evidence (such as a plan, photograph etc) under r 33.6 which is not:

    (i)   contained in a witness statement, affidavit or expert's report,

    (ii)   being given orally at trial,

    (iii) hearsay evidence under r 33.2;

(h) any medical reports and responses to them;

(i) any experts' reports and responses to them;

(j) any order giving directions as to the conduct of the trial; and

(k) any other necessary documents.

The trial bundle should normally be contained in ring binders or lever arch files. It should be paginated continuously throughout, and indexed with a description of each document and the page number. If any document is illegible a typed copy should be provided and given an 'A' number. The contents of the bundles should be agreed if possible. If there is any disagreement, a summary of the points in dispute should be included. Bundles exceeding 100 pages should have numbered dividers. Where a number of files are needed, each file should be numbered or distinguishable by different colours. If there is a lot of documentation a core bundle should also be prepared containing the most essential documents, and which should be cross-referenced to the supplementary documents in the other files. Identical bundles with the same colour coded files have to be supplied to all the parties plus the bundle for the court and a further one for the use of the witnesses at the trial.

33.8   Skeleton arguments, reading lists and authorities

Skeleton arguments are compulsory in the High Court (*Practice Direction (Civil Litigation: Case Management)* [1995] 1 WLR 262) and on appeals (PD 52, paras 5.9 and 7.6). They are used partly in order to enable the judges to do effective pre-reading, and are not used as a substitute for oral argument in court. Their purpose is to identify, not to argue points. They should therefore be as succinct as possible, concisely summarising that party's submissions in relation to each of the issues, and citing the main authorities relied upon (which may be attached). Authorities used should be from the official series of law reports in preference to reports in other series, and with the *Weekly Law Reports* and *English Reports* being used in preference to the *All England Law Reports* and *All England Law Reports Reprint* (*Bank of Scotland v Henry Butcher and Co* The Times, 20 February 2003). Law reports of applications attended by one party only; applications for permission to appeal; applications that only decide the application is arguable; and county cases (other than to illustrate damages in personal injuries claims or to illustrate current authority where no higher authorities are available), should not be cited unless they establish a new principle or extend the law (*Practice Direction (Citation of Authorities)* [2001] 1 WLR 1001). The same *Practice Direction* says that skeleton arguments will have to justify reliance on decisions that merely apply decided law to the facts, and also decisions from other jurisdictions. (Decisions of the European Court of Justice and organs of the European Convention on Human Rights are treated as domestic authorities for this purpose.) Further, for each authority cited, the skeleton must state the proposition of law the case demonstrates, and refer to the passages in support. Any bundle or list of authorities must contain a certificate by the advocate that these requirements have been complied with. Skeletons should be lodged at Court and served on the other parties three days before the hearing. (In appeals different time periods for service of skeleton arguments apply.)

Further guidance on drafting skeleton arguments can be found in the **Drafting** manual, **Chapter 23**, which also contains sample skeleton arguments for an interim application and a civil trial.

In all QBD and ChD claims where bundles must be lodged, the claimant or applicant must at the same time lodge:

- a reading list for the judge who will conduct the hearing;
- an estimated length of reading time; and
- an estimated length for the hearing.

This must be signed by all the advocates who will appear at the hearing. Each advocate's name, business address and telephone number must appear below his or her signature. In the event of disagreement about any of these matters, separate reading lists and estimates must be signed by the appropriate advocates. See *Practice Direction (R.C.J.: Reading Lists and Time Estimates)* [2000] 1 WLR 208.

Lists of any authorities which will be relied on at trial must be given to the court by 5 pm on the day before the hearing and to counsel for the other side in good time before the hearing. If an extract from Hansard is to be used in accordance with the principles in *Pepper v Hart* [1993] AC 593 as interpreted by *Wilson v First County Trust (No. 2)* [2004] 1 AC 816, copies should be served on the other parties and the court, together with a brief summary of the argument based on the extract, five working days before the hearing (*Practice Direction (Hansard: Citations)* [1995] 1 WLR 192). Lists of any authorities and copies of any reports of cases on the interpretation of the European Convention on Human Rights must be served and filed at least three days before the hearing (PD 39, para 8.1).

33.9 Hearing in public or in private

The general rule, buttressed by art 6(1) of the European Convention on Human Rights, is that all trials are heard in open court. The general rule does not, however, impose an obligation to make special arrangements for accommodating members of the public. By way of exception to the general rule, the CPR, r 39.2(3), provides that hearings may be conducted in private if:

- publicity would defeat the object of the hearing;
- it involves matters relating to national security;
- it involves confidential information (including information relating to personal financial matters) and publicity would damage that confidentiality;
- a private hearing is necessary to protect the interests of any child or patient;
- it is a hearing of an application made without notice and it would be unjust to any respondent for there to be a public hearing;
- it involves uncontentious matters arising in the administration of trusts or in the administration of a deceased's estate; or
- the court considers this to be necessary, in the interests of justice.

Further, the court may order that the identity of any party or witness must not be disclosed if it considers non-disclosure necessary in order to protect the interests of that party or witness (CPR, r 39.2(4)).

Even though a hearing may be in private, the judgment given will normally not be a secret document and thus will usually be considered a public document (*Forbes v Smith* [1998] 1 All ER 973).

33.10 Adjournment

The CPR, r 3.1(2)(b), gives the court a general power to adjourn.

Whether or not a litigant should be granted an adjournment is a matter within the judge's discretion, but the discretion must be exercised judicially and in accordance with the overriding objective. For example, in *Joyce v King* The Times, 13 July 1987, CA, the defendant was granted one adjournment, but was unable to obtain legal aid in time for the rearranged hearing. Without legal aid she was unable to get her expert, whose testimony was essential if she was to defend the case, to attend. Even though Mrs King was acting in person, the judge decided to refuse a second adjournment because Mrs King had been given several weeks' notice of the hearing and had applied to adjourn at a late stage. The Court of Appeal set aside the judgment for the claimant and remitted the case for a fresh hearing, because it was clear that it was not possible for Mrs King to obtain justice without the adjournment. See *Blackstone's Civil Practice*, para 59.10.

Other sufficient reasons for granting adjournments would include vital witnesses being unavoidably out of the country or too ill to attend trial.

Adjournments sought because of a failure to comply with directions will not be allowed unless the circumstances are exceptional (PD 28, para 5.4(1); PD 29, para 7.4(1)). The need for exceptional circumstances only applies to adjournments based on default in complying with directions, not to adjournments based on circumstances outside the control of the parties (*Collins v Gordon* (2008) LTL 21/1/2008). Late adjournments, even with the consent of the other parties, may be visited by costs sanctions and wasted costs orders.

33.11 Non-attendance

If both parties fail to attend the hearing the proceedings are likely to be struck out (CPR, r 39.3).

If one side fails to attend, the court may allow the trial to proceed in the absence of that party. If it is the claimant who fails to attend, the claim and any defence to any counter-claim will usually be struck out, and judgment will almost certainly be entered for the defendant. If the defendant is absent, the claimant will usually still need to prove the claim to the satisfaction of the court although the court may strike out the defence and any counterclaim under r 39.3(1)(c). Any judgment obtained in the absence of one party may be set aside (r 39.3(3) and *Shocked v Goldschmidt* [1998] 1 All ER 372, CA).

The main factors that are considered on an application to reinstate following striking out for non-attendance are (r 39.3(5)):

(a) whether the application to reinstate has been made promptly;

(b) whether there is a good excuse for not attending. Claimants, in particular, are expected to keep in contact with their solicitors, and so have limited grounds for saying they were unaware of a hearing date (*Neufville v Papamichael* (1999) LTL 23/11/99); and

(c) whether the absent party has a reasonable prospect of success if the trial is reconvened.

There is no residual discretion to reinstate if one of the factors is missing (*Barclays Bank plc v Ellis* The Times, 24 October 2000). One of the factors is making the application to reinstate promptly. This means 'with alacrity' (*Regency Rolls Ltd v Carnall* (2000) LTL 16/10/2000).

Where a party fails to appear, or fails to give due notice to the court of any inability to appear, the court may summon that party to explain the failure, and may impose a fine not exceeding level 3 (CLSA 1990, s 12).

33.12 Witnesses

33.12.1 Oral testimony

The general rule is that evidence is to be given orally and in public: CPR, r 32.2.

33.12.2 Hearsay

Generally, the evidence of witnesses who cannot attend trial may be adduced at trial under the provisions of the Civil Evidence Act 1995. However, in these circumstances the evidence will not usually be under oath nor will it have been tested in cross-examination.

33.12.3 Evidence by deposition

Where the potential witness is too old, frail or ill to attend trial, or is likely to give birth at about the time of the trial, or will leave the country before the trial, it may be appropriate to apply for an order that the witness's evidence be taken on oath before trial under CPR, r 34.8-34.12. The examination, which includes cross-examination, is conducted before a judge, examiner of the court or such other person as the court may appoint. The examination can be conducted at any place, including, for instance, the witness's bedside. The evidence is reduced into writing in the form of a deposition which is signed by the witness. The examiner may make a special report as to the conduct of the witness during the examination, reporting matters such as whether the witness fainted or became violent.

A deposition is receivable in evidence at trial, but the party relying on it should serve notice of the intention to rely on it at least 21 days before the trial. The court retains a power to require the deponent to attend trial and give oral evidence: r 34.11(4).

33.12.4 Examination out of the jurisdiction

The High Court has power on its own behalf under CPR, r 34.13-34.24, and on behalf of a County Court under CCA 1984, s 56, to order:

(a) the examination of a witness outside the jurisdiction before the British consular authority as a special examiner; or

(b) the issue of a letter of request to the judicial authorities of the relevant country to take a witness's evidence. Evidence obtained under a letter of request may be given either orally or in answer to written questions. A letter of request may alternatively, according to *Panayiotou v Sony Music Entertainment (UK) Ltd* [1994] Ch 142, be confined to the production of specified documents in the possession of a person outside the jurisdiction.

33.12.5 Television link

The court may allow a witness to give evidence through a video link or by other means: CPR, r 32.3. PD 32, Annex 3, contains detailed guidance. In *Polanski v Conde Nast Publications Ltd* [2005] 1 WLR 637, a claimant who was a fugitive facing a risk of extradition to the United States if he entered this country was allowed to give evidence by video link.

33.12.6 Witness summons

If a witness is reluctant to attend trial, for example, if the witness has a job and is not prepared to take leave, attendance can be compelled by issuing and serving a witness summons (CPR, r 34.2-34.7) (see **Figure 33.1**). Issuing a witness summons is purely administrative, and a fee must be paid. Service must be effected personally and not less than seven days before the witness is required to attend court. Conduct money, namely a sum sufficient to cover the witness's expenses in travelling to and from court and compensation for loss of time, must be tendered on service of the witness summons if the witness is to be liable to committal proceedings for failing to attend court.

There are two types of witness summons:

(a) to attend court to give oral testimony; and

(b) to produce documents at court. A witness summons is to be used for obtaining documentary evidence, not for the purpose of obtaining disclosure which might lead to the obtaining of evidence after enquiries are made (*Macmillan Inc v Bishopsgate Investment Trust* [1993] 1 WLR 1372, CA). The documents to be produced must be sufficiently described, although classes of documents may be described compendiously (*Panayiotou v Sony Music Entertainment (UK) Ltd* [1994] Ch 142). The CPR, r 34.2(4)(b), allows the court to direct that a witness summons may require a witness to produce documents on such date as the court may decide, which may be substantially earlier than the main trial. This device enables a witness summons to operate in a manner similar to disclosure, but against a witness as opposed to a party.

Witness summonses are issued to ensure that witnesses who are able to give relevant evidence are available in court. A person who is served with a witness summons, but is unable to give relevant evidence, may apply to have the witness summons set aside.

33.13 The day of the hearing

33.13.1 The usual sequence of events

Provided the claimant has the burden of proof on at least one issue, the claimant will start. The sequence is as follows:

(a) Claimant's opening speech (opening speeches should be succinct).

(b) Claimant's evidence. Witnesses are called and:

    (i)   sworn (or affirm);

    (ii) examined-in-chief by the claimant (but it is likely that the witness statements shall stand as the evidence in chief of the witness);

    (iii) cross-examined by the defendant;

    (iv) re-examined by the claimant.

          Witnesses may be asked questions by the judge. They are sometimes ordered to leave the court at the start of the hearing so they do not hear the evidence given by other witnesses, unless they are experts or parties. However, it is quite common for witnesses to be present throughout the trial if the legal representatives for both sides do not object.

(c) If the defendant elects not to adduce evidence, the claimant then makes a closing speech, followed by the defendant's statement of his or her case. The next stage would then be (h) below. Otherwise:

(d) Defendant's opening speech (if any).

(e) Defendant's evidence.

(f) Defendant's closing speech.

(g) Claimant's closing speech.

(h) Judgment, which is often given immediately or is sometimes given after an adjournment for consideration.

(i) Consideration of costs. Normally, the party obtaining judgment has its own costs paid by the other side. Consideration is also given to the appropriate basis of assessment of costs, or the costs may be assessed summarily.

Where there are two or more defendants who are separately represented, they open their cases and adduce their evidence in the order their names appear on the record. Their closing speeches are then made in the same order.

If a point of law is raised or an authority is cited for the first time in a final closing speech, the other side is permitted to reply (confining the reply to the relevant point or authority).

The traditional sequence of events may be altered at the discretion of the trial judge, and may be subject to the rigours of a trial timetable.

33.13.2 Summary disposal of issues at the start of a trial

Under CPR, r 1.4(2)(c) (see **1.4.1**), a trial judge has a power to make an order excluding certain issues from the trial. This power is additional to those for striking out (**Chapter 28**) and summary judgment (**Chapter 12**), but should be used sparingly, and by applying the test of whether the issues in question have a real prospect of success. In most cases weak issues should be disposed of well before trial, and generally use of the procedure at trial is deprecated as potentially time wasting and expensive (see *Royal Brompton Hospital NHS Trust v Hammond* [2001] BLR 297, CA).

33.13.3 Second speeches

The judge may make a direction dispensing with opening speeches in non-jury trials. In such cases stages (a) and (d) in **33.13.1** would not apply. Nevertheless, it should be noted that a judge has a broad discretion as to the order of speeches at the trial. Even if the judge in question usually only allows counsel a single speech, an application may be made to allow second speeches if, for example, the case is one of complexity or importance.

33.13.4 Submission of no case to answer

A submission of no case to answer can be made by the defendant at the conclusion of the case for the claimant. Generally, defendants seeking to make a submission of no case to answer will be put to an election as to whether they will call any evidence. It is only in exceptional cases that they will not be put to this election (*Boyce v Wyatt Engineering* The Times, 14 June 2001). If they are put to their election, and decide to call no evidence, they can make a submission of no case to answer, which will be decided on the basis of whether the claimant's case has been established by the evidence on the balance of probabilities, and judgment will be entered for whichever party succeeds on the submission. In cases where the defendant is not put to an election, the submission is considered on the basis of whether the claimant's case has no real prospect of success (*Miller v Cawley* (2002) The Times, 6 September 2002). In such a case, if the submission is unsuccessful the defendant is allowed to call its evidence and the trial continues in the normal way.

33.13.5 Standard of proof

The civil standard of proof is proof on a balance of probabilities. The main exception is contempt of court, which must be proved beyond all reasonable doubt. If the party with the burden of proof fails to discharge that burden, the fact is treated as not having happened. If the burden of proof is discharged, the court treats the fact as having happened. There is no halfway house between the two (*Re B (Children) (Care Proceedings: Standard of Proof)* [2009] 1 AC 11). Inherent probabilities have to be taken into account as a factor 'to whatever extent is appropriate in the particular case' (Lord Nicholls of Birkenhead in *Re H (Minors) (Sexual Abuse: Standard of Proof)* [1996] AC 563 at 583), but do not alter the balance of probabilities test.

33.13.6 Noting judgment

If the judge gives a reasoned judgment, counsel must take a note of those reasons. This note should be as full as possible. If the court has facilities for mechanically recording judgments, counsel's notes will be used for advising on the merits of any appeal and drafting any necessary notice of appeal. If the judgment is not mechanically recorded, counsel's notes may also form the basis of the note of the judgment used in the Court of Appeal.

Whenever judgment has been given counsel will endorse their briefs with a short note of the orders made by the court before returning their papers to their instructing solicitors. Instructing solicitors may use this as the basis for drawing up the orders. Accuracy in noting the judgment is therefore of real importance. If the orders are at all complex, it is often prudent to consult counsel for the other side immediately after the hearing to ensure both parties are clear on what the court has ordered.

33.14 Conclusion

In addition to being the most expensive stage of most civil proceedings, the trial is usually the most important. Almost all aspects of civil litigation are focussed on the ultimate trial of the case. It is tempting to think that once judgment has been obtained (by trial or otherwise) the case is finished. However, in exceptional cases it may be appropriate to appeal all or part of the judge's decision. This is discussed in **Chapter 39**. Also, in many cases it will be necessary to enforce the judgment (see **Chapter 38**), and, unless there is agreement as to the amount of costs to be paid or a summary assessment of costs, the costs order will have to be assessed (see **Chapter 36**).

Witness Summons

In the	Central London County Court
Claim No.	CL 938878
Claimant (including ref)	CLIVE SHERRILL
Defendant (including ref)	DORADOWN (MACHINE FITTINGS) LIMITED
Issued on	

To

Mr. Jonathan Collins,
38 Belsize Road,
Enfield,
London N24

You are summoned to attend at *(court address)* 13-14 Park Crescent, London W1N 3PD

on   6th of January   at 10.30   (am)(pm)

(and each following day of the hearing until the court tells you that you are no longer required.)

[✓] to give evidence in respect of the above claim

[ ] to produce the following document(s) *(give details)*

The sum of £ 70   is paid or offered to you with this summons. This is to cover your travelling expenses to and from court and includes an amount by way of compensation for loss of time.

This summons was issued on the application of the claimant (defendant) or the claimant's (defendant's) solicitor whose name, address and reference number is:

Do not ignore this summons

If you were offered money for travel expenses and compensation for loss of time, at the time it was served on you, you must –

- attend court on the date and time shown and/or produce documents as required by the summons; and

- take an oath or affirm as required for the purposes of answering questions about your evidence or the documents you have been asked to produce.

If you do not comply with this summons you will be liable, in county court proceedings, to a fine. In the High Court, disobedience of a witness summons is a contempt of court and you may be fined or imprisoned for contempt. You may also be liable to pay any wasted costs that arise because of your non-compliance.

If you wish to set aside or vary this witness summons, you may make an application to the court that issued it.

The court office at   13-14 Park Crescent, London W1N 3PD

is open between 10 am and 4 pm Monday to Friday. When corresponding with the court, please address forms or letters to the Court Manager and quote the claim number

N20 Witness Summons (09.02)   *Printed on behalf of The Court Service*

Figure 33.1 Witness summons

References to the European Court

34.1 Introduction

If in the course of litigation before our national courts a question arises as to the interpretation of the Treaties establishing the European Community, or as to the interpretation or validity of any act of the institutions of the EC, that question can be referred to the European Court of Justice for a preliminary ruling if the English court considers that a decision on that particular question is necessary in order to enable it to give judgment. Article 234 of the EC Treaty provides:

(1) *The Court of Justice shall have jurisdiction to give preliminary rulings concerning:*
    (a) *the interpretation of this Treaty;*
    (b) *the validity and interpretation of acts of the institutions of the Community and of the ECB;*
    (c) *the interpretation of the statutes of bodies established by an act of the Council where those statutes so provide.*
(2) *Where such a question is raised before any court or tribunal of a Member State, that court or tribunal may, if it considers that a decision on the question is necessary to enable it to give judgment, request the Court of Justice to give a ruling thereon.*
(3) *Where any such question is raised in a case pending before a court or tribunal of a Member State, against whose decisions there is no judicial remedy under national law, that court or tribunal shall bring the matter before the Court of Justice.*

It also applies to interpretation of the Brussels Convention and the Jurisdiction Regulation (Civil Jurisdiction and Judgments Act 1982) and the Rome Convention (Contracts (Applicable Law) Act 1990).

(Similar provision is contained in art 150 of the Euratom Treaty.)

34.2 Mandatory references: Article 234(3)

The only court that is bound to refer a question to the European Court of Justice is a final court against whose decisions there is no judicial remedy under national law. This will usually be the Supreme Court, because it is the final court in the land from which no further appeal lies but there may be circumstances where the Court of Appeal or the High Court may be a final court (see *Chiron Corp v Murex Diagnostics Ltd* [1995] All ER (EC) 88).

However, a court against whose decision there is no judicial remedy is not obliged to refer a question to the European Court of Justice if either:

(a) the point has already been decided by the European Court (but a further reference can be made if the national court wishes the European Court to reconsider the point); or

(b) the correct application of Community law is obvious. The national court must, however, be convinced that the point is equally obvious to the courts of other Member States and the European Court (see *CILFIT (Srl) v Italian Ministry of Health* (Case 283/81) [1982] ECR 3415 and *Practice Direction (ECJ)* [1997] All ER (EC) 1).

Further, a final court is only obliged to refer a point if it is necessary to consider that point, ie if it is relevant (*CILFIT (Srl) v Italian Ministry of Health*).

34.3 Discretionary references: Article 234(2)

References under art 234(2) are not confined to final courts but are appropriate where a court or tribunal considers a decision on a point within art 234(1) is 'necessary to enable it to give judgment'. The courts generally have a wide discretion whether or not to refer a point to the European Court. However, while national courts are able to find that acts of Community institutions are valid, if a national court intends to question the validity of an act of a Community institution it must refer that question to the European Court (see *Foto-Frost v Hauptzollamt Lubeck-Ost* (Case 314/85) [1987] ECR 4199 and *Practice Direction (ECJ)* [1997] All ER (EC) 1).

In deciding whether a decision by the European Court on a point is 'necessary to enable it to give judgment' Lord Denning, in *HP Bulmer Ltd v J Bollinger SA* [1974] Ch 401, CA, took a narrow view of the word 'necessary' in that the point would be 'necessary' if it was conclusive of the case whichever way it was decided. This view has been subsequently disapproved. In *Polydor Ltd v Harlequin Record Shops Ltd* [1982] CMLR 413, for instance, it was said by Ormrod LJ that 'necessary' meant 'reasonably necessary' in ordinary English and not 'unavoidable'.

The discretion to refer a point is a wide discretion: see the **Remedies** manual for some of the factors which have been considered in some cases to be relevant in the exercise of that discretion.

34.4 Procedure

Only a judge may make an order of reference. The order of reference may be made by the court upon application by a party to the proceedings or on its own initiative. It can be made either at or before the trial or hearing (CPR, r 68.2). Usually the proceedings before the national court will be stayed until the question which has arisen is determined by the European Court. A domestic appeal can be brought against the decision to make a non-mandatory reference (*R (Horvath) v Secretary of State for the Environment, Food and Rural Affairs* [2007] NPC 83).

Questions referred for preliminary rulings must concern only the interpretation or validity of a provision of Community law, since the European Court does not have jurisdiction to interpret national law or to assess its validity. The questions referred to the European Court must be drafted with care and simplicity as they will be translated into a number of European languages as part of the referral process. A maximum of 10 pages is often sufficient to set out the context of a reference for a preliminary ruling (ECJ Information Note, PD 68 Annex, para 22). It should give a brief account of the subject matter of the dispute and the relevant findings of fact. It should set out any applicable national legislation, and give precise references for relevant national case-law. It should also identify relevant Community provisions, explain why the reference is being made, and summarise the arguments of the parties.

The senior master will send a copy of the order making the reference to the European Court (r 68.3(1)) at the Registry of the Court of Justice of the European Communities in Luxembourg. County Court references are sent to the senior master by the proper officer of the County Court for onward transmission to the European Court (r 68.3(2)) together with the court file (PD 68, para 2.2). The European Court Registry stays in contact with the national court until judgment is given, and sends various documents to the national court, including written observations, the report of the hearing, the opinion of the Advocate General, and the judgment of the European Court.

The European Court will exceed its jurisdiction if it disagrees with the findings of fact of the referring court (*Arsenal Football Club plc v Reed* [2003] 1 All ER 137). It is for the referring court to apply the relevant provision of Community law, as interpreted by the European Court, to the facts of the case (ECJ Information Note, PD 68 Annex, para 5).

34.5 Costs

The question of costs will normally be reserved to the ultimate hearing of the case before the national court, after the European Court had provided its ruling (see *Boots Co plc v Commissioners of Customs and Excise* [1988] 1 CMLR 433 and *R v Dairy Produce Quota Tribunal, ex p Hall and Sons (Dairy Farmers) Ltd* [1988] 1 CMLR 592).

Community Legal Service and financing litigation

35.1 Introduction

How a case will be paid for is always a major issue in any litigation. In this respect public funding is an important area to consider as is also who will ultimately pay the costs of litigation. The expensive nature of litigation often means that funding the costs of litigation is almost as important as the relief or remedy sought. There are a number of alternative ways of financing litigation, which will be considered in this chapter. However, the bulk of the chapter will be devoted to public funding.

35.2 Traditional retainer

The traditional method is for the client to pay the solicitor's costs of conducting a case at an agreed hourly rate. The Solicitors' Practice Rules require solicitors to provide their clients with client care letters which should include at least basic information about charging rates and when bills are likely to be sent and, if possible, an estimate of the future costs. The Solicitors' Code of Conduct (2007) also requires solicitors to consider which of the various options on funding is best suited to the client's circumstances. A breach of the costs provisions of the Solicitors' Code of Conduct does not render the retainer illegal, but can be taken into account in assessing the amount of costs payable (*Garbutt v Edwards* [2006] 1 WLR 2907).

Charge out rates are based on the salaries of the staff and fee earners working at the solicitor's office together with an element representing the firm's profits. The modern approach is to fix a single hourly rate for each fee earner (or grade of fee earner) in the firm taking these factors into account. A variation on this approach is to adopt widely accepted regional rates for different grades of fee earner. Grade A covers solicitors with over eight years' post qualification experience, including at least eight years in litigation. Grade B covers solicitors and legal executives with over four years' litigation experience. Grade C covers other solicitors and legal executives and other fee earners of equivalent experience. Grade D covers trainee solicitors, paralegals and other fee earners. An alternative method has been to quote a lower hourly rate, but to add a markup of a variable percentage (say 50% for ordinary litigation). Clients tend to find being quoted a simple hourly rate easier to understand. In addition, the client will be expected to pay for disbursements. These are sums paid by the firm during the course of litigation in respect of experts' and counsel's fees, the cost of making copies of photographs, and similar expenditure. It is normal for solicitors to ask for sums on account of costs when they are first retained, and periodically during the course of litigation.

35.3 Conditional fee agreements

As an alternative to a traditional retainer, the client and the solicitor's firm may agree to enter into a conditional fee agreement. Since 1998 it has been possible to enter into these agreements in all types of civil litigation other than family work. The basic idea of these agreements is that the client will not have to pay anything to the firm acting for him or her if the case is lost, but if it is successful the lawyer will be entitled to charge the client at the lawyer's usual rate plus a success fee. The success fee will be a percentage, up to 100%, of the costs otherwise chargeable to the client. A conditional fee agreement (CFA) does not have to provide for a success fee, but where it does, it reflects the estimated risks in the litigation.

Statutory authorisation for CFAs was conferred by the CLSA 1990, s 58. Before the introduction of this provision any form of fee agreement under which a lawyer was paid depending on the success of the claim was illegal and unenforceable. The illegality in the funding arrangement also meant that a successful party with an illegal funding arrangement could not recover costs from the losing party. Any concern that a CFA might be attacked by the opposite side as savouring of maintenance or champerty was removed by *Hodgson v Imperial Tobacco Ltd* [1998] 1 WLR 1056.

To be effective under the CLSA 1990, a CFA has to be in writing and have a success fee (if any) limited to 100%. A CFA will be enforceable even if there is a breach of these conditions, provided there is no materially adverse effect on the client or upon the proper administration of justice (*Hollins v Russell* [2003] 1 WLR 2487). In cases where counsel is instructed, there will be a CFA between the client and the solicitor, and a second CFA between the solicitor and counsel. Model forms of CFAs have been drafted in consultation between the Law Society and Bar Council.

Although entering into a CFA means that the client will not have to pay his or her own lawyer's costs if the case is lost, a major concern for most clients is whether they will then be liable to pay the other side's costs. The answer is that, in accordance with the rule that costs normally follow the event, they usually will. However, there are several insurance companies that provide policies designed precisely to cover this situation at reasonably modest cost. These policies are called After the Event (ATE) policies. A further question is whether the client or the solicitor should meet the disbursements payable (such as court and experts' fees). This will be dealt with in the CFA between the client and the solicitor. The result is that most clients entering into CFAs will have to pay a modest premium for insurance against the risk of paying the costs of the other side, and may (depending on their agreement with the solicitor) have to pay the disbursements.

At the end of the case, if it is successful, the client would hope to recover damages from the other side and also the base costs, and will also usually recover a substantial part of the success fee and any insurance premium (see **36.4.6**). The other side and the client may challenge the base costs and the level of the success fee by using the detailed assessment procedure described at **36.5.4** and **36.5.6**.

The lawyers acting under a CFA assess their uplift as the product of a number of factors, including the chances of losing and the disadvantage the lawyers face in delays in being paid (there are no payments on account in CFAs).

So that opponents know what they are up against, the lawyers acting under a CFA are required to disclose to the other side (as part of the pre-action protocol, and when they take the first step in litigation) that they are acting under a CFA (although there is no obligation to give details of the success fee).

35.4 Legal expenses insurance

Some clients have the benefit of legal expenses insurance, often as part of their motor or home insurance policies. This is often called Before the Event (BTE) insurance. In these cases the costs incurred on behalf of the client will be met by the legal expenses insurer. Often these insurers require the client's lawyers to provide advice on the merits of the claim from time to time so they can assess whether continuing the litigation can be justified under the terms of the insurance.

35.5 After the event insurance

A client needs to be told about the potential liability for the other side's costs if the case is unsuccessful. The usual rule is that the unsuccessful party in the proceedings is ordered to pay the successful party's costs: CPR, r 44.3(2). The other side's costs generally have to be paid out of the losing party's personal resources. It may be possible for the client to arrange After the Event insurance to cover the other side's costs. With the exception of insurance designed for use with CFAs, such insurance is usually quite expensive.

35.6 Legal aid

Under the Legal Aid Act 1988 (LAA 1988) a person could qualify for legal advice, assistance or representation, the cost of which was effectively payable out of public funds through the Legal Aid Board. Legal aid was replaced by the Community Legal Service from 1 April 2000.

35.7 Community Legal Service

Assistance under the Community Legal Service has been designed to ensure that public funds are used to support claims that most need assistance in this way. This is reflected in the categories of excluded cases, and the exacting criteria for granting public funding. These include cost-benefit considerations in deciding whether to grant help under the Community Legal Service.

35.7.1 Levels of service

There are the following 'levels of service' under the Community Legal Service. The idea is that the amount of public funding given to a case should be commensurate with its needs, so that limited funding will be given if that is all that is needed, but that full public funding will be given to the most deserving cases.

35.7.1.1 Legal help

This provides help on how the law applies to a particular case, and initial work done for a client, but not issuing or conducting court proceedings or providing advocacy services.

It is primarily supplied by franchise holders which are firms of solicitors, Citizens' Advice Bureaux, law centres, and independent advice agencies.

35.7.1.2   Help at court

This authorises legal representation for the purposes of a particular hearing, without the lawyer becoming the client's legal representative in the proceedings.

35.7.1.3   Legal representation

This covers individuals contemplating legal proceedings or who are parties to proceedings. It provides funding for 'litigation services', 'advocacy services', and all the legal assistance usually given before and during proceedings and in achieving or giving effect to any compromise. Legal representation is not a level of service in itself, but is sub-divided into:

(a) 'investigative help', which is aimed at cases which require substantial investigation before an assessment can be made whether legal proceedings are justified;

(b) 'full representation'. This provides funding for bringing or defending proceedings, which will be defined in the funding certificate, and which will also impose limitations on the scope of the work that can be done and the amount of costs that can be incurred; and

(c) 'controlled legal representation'. This covers work involving cases before a mental health review tribunal and asylum and immigration tribunals.

35.7.1.4   Family help

Family help is available for family disputes, and may include assistance in resolving a dispute through negotiation or otherwise. It does not cover representation at a final hearing or appeal. Family help (lower) is limited to steps up to the issue of proceedings. Family work (higher) can cover proceedings and representation at hearings other than contested final hearings.

35.7.1.5   Specific directions

Other services are not strictly levels of service covered by the main Community Legal Service scheme, but there is some public funding of other cases if a specific order or direction is made by the Lord Chancellor. This may happen in important test cases and possibly also for certain class actions.

35.7.2   Excluded categories

Public funding under the Community Legal Service is not available in damages claims for personal injuries or death (except that clinical disputes are within the scheme). Also excluded are:

- negligent damage to property;
- conveyancing;
- boundary disputes;
- wills;
- matters relating to trust law (except applications in relation to ownership or possession of the applicant's home);
- defamation and malicious falsehood;
- matters relating to partnership law;

- matters relating to the carrying on of a business; and
- attending asylum interviews.

35.7.3 Financial eligibility

Help under the Community Legal Service is only available to clients who are unable to afford to litigate. Rules laying down the financial criteria are to be found in the Community Legal Service (Financial) Regulations 2000, SI 2000/516 as amended. Effectively, State assistance is available only for the very poor.

35.7.4 Individual

It is a requirement for public funding that the assisted party must be an individual, so help under the Community Legal Service is not available to limited liability companies.

35.7.5 Criteria for funding

There are detailed rules in the Commission's Funding Code setting out the criteria for granting the different levels of help under the Community Legal Service. These are intended to reflect the requirements of the different levels of service, and also to ensure that public money is targeted at the cases that deserve or need it. For example, there are nine criteria for granting full representation:

(a) funding may be refused if there is alternative funding (other than by way of CFAs, but see (g) below) available;

(b) funding may be refused if there is a complaint system or ombudsman which should be tried first;

(c) funding may be refused if the application is premature;

(d) funding may be refused if another level of service is more appropriate;

(e) funding may be refused if it is unreasonable, for example, in the light of other proceedings;

(f) funding will be refused if the claim is likely to be allocated to the small claims track;

(g) funding will be refused in cases where funding under a CFA is suitable and if the client is likely to be able to enter into such an arrangement;

(h) funding will be refused if the prospects are unclear (for which investigative help may be appropriate); or the prospects are borderline (unless there are public interest reasons or overwhelming importance to the client reasons for funding); or if the prospects are poor;

(i) funding will or may be refused on cost-benefit grounds.

35.7.6 Cost-benefit criteria

Funding will be refused if the benefit to be gained does not justify the level of costs likely to be incurred.

In money claims, help under the Community Legal Service may, in general, only be granted if:

- the prospects are very good (80% plus, category A), and the value of the claim exceeds the likely level of the costs;

- the prospects are good (60-80%, category B), and the value of the claim is at least twice the likely level of costs;

- the prospects are moderate (50-60%, category C), and the value of the claim is at least four times the likely level of costs.

In non-money claims the test is whether the likely benefits justify the likely costs, such that a reasonable private paying client would be prepared to litigate.

Counsel advising on funding must use these categories, and generally follow the Bar Council Guidelines set out in Annexe E to the Code (see the *Professional Conduct* manual, and *Opinion Writing* manual, **Chapter 11**).

Funding may be allowed despite costs outstripping the benefits given the risks, if there is a wider public interest or if there is overwhelming importance to the client.

35.7.7   Statutory charge

Under the Access to Justice Act 1999 (AJA 1999), s 10(7), the sums expended by the Legal Services Commission in providing help under the Community Legal Service shall be a first charge on any property recovered or preserved for the assisted party or any other person in any proceedings or in any compromise or settlement of any dispute in connection with the funded services. The effect is that if the dispute includes (say) beneficial interests in a house, the house will become charged with (in effect) a second mortgage to secure the public money spent on behalf of a party. Taking a different example, if compensation is recovered for a publicly funded claimant, the compensation has to be paid to the Legal Services Commission in order to ensure that the first charge on the money recovered is discharged, and will only be released to the claimant once the publicly funded costs have been deducted from the money received from the defendant. 'The proceedings' covered by the statutory charge are not restricted to the actual proceedings in which the preservation or recovery takes place, but extend to all proceedings covered by the funding certificate (*Hanlon v Law Society* [1981] AC 124).

The effect of the statutory charge is to some extent mitigated by exemptions provided by the Community Legal Service (Financial) Regulations 2000, SI 2000/516, regs 44–52. Further, the Commission may postpone the enforcement of its charge if immediate repayment would be unreasonable and if the charge relates to property to be used as a home for the publicly funded client or his dependents (or, in family proceedings, to money to buy such a home). In such cases interest is payable on the amount covered by the statutory charge (reg 53).

35.7.8   Protection against costs

The AJA 1999, s 11(1) and (2), provide:

(1) *Except in prescribed circumstances, costs ordered against an individual in relation to any proceedings or part of proceedings funded for him shall not exceed the amount (if any) which is a reasonable one for him to pay having regard to all the circumstances including—*

    (a)   *the financial resources of all the parties to the proceedings, and*

    (b)   *their conduct in connection with the dispute to which the proceedings relate;*
           and for this purpose proceedings, or a part of proceedings, are funded for an individual if services relating to the proceedings or part are funded for him by the Commission as part of the Community Legal Service.

(2) *In assessing for the purposes of subsection (1) the financial resources of an individual for whom services are funded by the Commission as part of the Community Legal Service, his clothes and household furniture and the tools and implements of his trade shall not be taken into account, except so far as may be prescribed.*

'Costs protection' applies to LSC funded clients (see the Community Legal Service (Costs) Regulations 2000, SI 2000/441), other than LSC funded clients receiving assistance by way of:

(a) help at court;

(b) legal help, unless the litigant is subsequently granted legal representation or approved family help by the LSC in respect of the same dispute, in which case the work covered by legal help is also covered by costs protection; and

(c) family help.

Regulation 8 of SI 2000/441 provides that the non-funded party may serve and file a statement of resources, and if this is done at least seven days before the hearing where a s 11(1) costs order may fall to be determined, the LSC funded client must also make a statement of resources and produce it at the hearing. Unless they have competing interests in the proceedings, the LSC funded client's partner's resources are treated as the resources of the funded party (reg 7(3)). However, the first £100,000 of the value of the LSC funded client's home is ignored (reg 7(1)). Also ignored is the value of the LSC funded client's clothes and household furniture, unless the circumstances are exceptional (reg 7(2)). The court can take into account any damages recovered by a funded party who fails to beat a Part 36 payment, and any resulting costs liability under s 11(1) has priority over the Commission's first charge (*Cook v Swinfen* [1967] 1 WLR457).

The court is required to consider whether, but for costs protection, it would have made a costs order against the publicly funded party, and, if so, whether it would have specified the amount payable (reg 9(1)). If so (or if the court decides to make a reasonably modest order), and if the court considers it has enough information to do so, the court can immediately make an order under s 11(1) specifying the amount the publicly funded party shall pay (reg 9(2), (3)). Usually, the 'reasonable' sum that a publicly funded litigant should pay will be relatively modest, or nothing. Often the judge will be guided by the level of contribution indorsed on the certificate (*Mercantile Credit Co Ltd v Cross* [1965] 2 QB 205), but must not follow the certificate blindly, because the test at this stage is not the same as the rules governing the level of contribution (*Gooday v Gooday* [1969] P 1).

If the court does not make an immediate order under s 11(1), but decides it would have ordered costs against the publicly funded party but for the costs protection rule, the non-funded party has three months to request a hearing to determine the costs payable by the publicly funded party (reg 10(2)). Regulation 10 lays down a detailed procedure for the determination of the amount, if any, payable in such circumstances. Any later application can be entertained only up to six years from the order, and only on the grounds of significant change in the funded party's circumstances, or additional information coming to light about the funded party's resources, or other good reasons (reg 12, and PD Costs, para 23.16).

A final costs order (one made at trial) may be made providing for a publicly funded party to recover part of his or her costs from the other side, and for the publicly funded party to pay part of the costs of the other side (perhaps because different issues were decided in favour of and against the publicly funded party). In such a case the court can order the two costs orders to be set off against each other, and doing so does not infringe the costs protection rule in AJA 1999, s 11 (*Hill v Bailey* [2004] 1 All ER 1210).

In relation to interim costs orders against publicly funded litigants, the court may make an order that the costs (which may be assessed summarily; PD Costs, para 13.10) shall be set off against any future award in the claim of damages or costs against the non-funded party (*Lockley v National Blood Transfusion Service* [1992] 1 WLR 492).

35.7.9   Costs orders against the Legal Services Commission

In exceptional cases it is possible to obtain a costs order against the Legal Services Commission, where an assisted party loses a claim. Details of the requirements for making such an order are spelt out in the Community Legal Service (Cost Protection) Regulations 2000, SI 2000/824, reg 5, which lay down the following conditions (very similar conditions applied under the Legal Aid Act 1988, s 18):

(a) the proceedings must be finally decided in favour of the non-publicly funded litigant. Where an appeal may be brought, any order against the LSC will not take effect until the time limit for seeking permission to appeal has elapsed without permission being granted, or, if no permission is required, no appeal is brought within the time limit for bringing an appeal (PD Costs, para 21.20). Where an appeal is brought, any order against the LSC never takes effect, but a fresh application may be brought in the appeal court;

(b) the non-publicly funded litigant must make the application for a costs order against the LSC within three months of the making of a costs order under the Access to Justice Act 1999, s 11(1) (Community Legal Service (Costs) Regulations 2000, SI 2000/441, reg 10(3), although a later application can be made if there is a good reason for the delay (SI 2001/3812, reg 4)); and

(c) the court must be satisfied that it is just and equitable in the circumstances that provision for the costs should be made out of public funds.

Further, in respect of costs incurred in proceedings at first instance, the following additional conditions must be satisfied:

(d) the proceedings must have been instituted by the publicly funded litigant; and

(e) the non-publicly funded litigant is an individual and must show he or she will suffer financial hardship if the order is not made.

35.7.9.1   Financial hardship

In *Hanning v Maitland (No. 2)* [1970] 1 QB 580, decided when this element was 'severe financial hardship', Lord Denning MR suggested almost any litigant could prove 'severe financial hardship', except commercial concerns in a considerable way of business, insurance companies and 'wealthy folk' who would not feel the cost of litigation.

The financial resources of the spouse of the unassisted person would not normally be taken into account in deciding whether 'financial hardship' was likely (see *Adams v Riley* [1988] QB 372).

35.7.9.2   Procedure in applications against the Legal Services Commission

A non-publicly funded litigant may make an application for costs to be payable by the LSC at any time within three months of a s 11(1) costs order being made (Community Legal Service (Costs) Regulations 2000, reg 10(2)). The application (in form N244) must be accompanied by the receiving party's bill of costs (unless the full costs have already been determined), a statement of resources, and a notice to the effect that a costs order is being sought against the Commission (reg 10(3) and PD Costs, para 23.3). All these documents must be served on the publicly funded party and the Regional Director of the LSC (reg 10(4) and PD Costs, para 23.4). After being served with the application, the publicly funded litigant must file and serve a statement of resources within 21 days (for the purpose of determining his personal liability under the Access to Justice Act 1999, s 11(1)), and may serve written points of dispute concerning the bill of costs (PD Costs, para 23.5). If the publicly funded litigant does not provide a statement of resources, the court may make a s 11(1) determination without a hearing (PD Costs, para 23.6). Determination hearings are listed giving at least 14 days' notice (para 23.7), and may be heard by a costs judge or district judge (para 23.8). The Regional Director may appear at the hearing, or may instead rely on a written statement, which should be served and filed seven days before the hearing (para 23.10).

Costs

36.1 Introduction

Costs in small claims track cases was dealt with in **Chapter 17**. The special rules dealing with fast track trial costs were considered at **18.11**. It will be recalled that the overriding objective requires the courts to deal with cases in ways that will save expense and which are proportionate to the nature of the case (see **1.4.1** above and CPR, r 1.1(2)). The extent to which these aims have been achieved will become evident when the costs of the litigation come to be assessed at the end of the case. This chapter will consider the specific rules relating to costs in the Civil Procedure Rules 1998. It will then discuss interim costs orders, and then the system for quantifying costs in cases where there is a detailed assessment of costs.

36.2 General principles

The two main principles when it comes to deciding which party should pay the costs of an application or of the whole proceedings are:

(a) the costs payable by one party to another are in the discretion of the court (SCA 1981, s 51 and CPR, r 44.3(1)); and

(b) the general rule as stated in CPR, r 44.3(2), is that the unsuccessful party will be ordered to pay the costs of the successful party ('costs follow the event' in the pre-1999 terminology).

A successful party in normal circumstances is entitled to have an order for costs against the loser, with limited exceptions (*Actavis Ltd v Merck and Co Inc* (2007) LTL 7/8/2007). Exceptions include cases where a successful claimant recovers no more than nominal damages, or where the successful party acted improperly or unreasonably (CPR, r 44.3(4)), or where the issue on which a party succeeded is raised for the first time by amendment at a very late stage (*Beoco Ltd v Alfa Laval Co Ltd* [1995] QB 137).

In exercising its discretion on costs the court is required to have regard to all the circumstances, and in particular to the following matters (r 44.3(4) and (5)):

(a) the extent to which the parties followed any applicable pre-action protocol;

(b) the extent to which it was reasonable for the parties to raise, pursue or contest each of the allegations or issues;

(c) the manner in which the parties pursued or defended the action or particular allegations or issues;

(d) whether the successful party exaggerated the value of the claim;

(e) whether a party was only partly successful; and

(f) any admissible offer to settle.

The first of these factors is one of the methods by which pre-action protocols are enforced, albeit indirectly (the other being by a less tolerant attitude on applications by defaulting parties for more time and for relief from sanctions).

Factors (b) and (e) require the court to take into account the extent to which the overall winner was in fact successful on the various issues, heads of claim etc raised in the case. This is intended to support the aspects of the overriding objective relating to identifying the real issues in the case, and only pursuing those issues to trial: see CPR, r 1.4(2)(b), (c). Generally, a party who wins on primary liability is awarded its costs despite a finding of contributory negligence (*'Krysia' Maritime Inc v Intership Ltd* [2008] EWHC 1880). Where a claimant had litigated over two issues, abandoned one a few days before trial, and won at trial on the remaining issue, it was held that the trial judge was plainly wrong to award the claimant the entire costs of the claim, as that failed to reflect the fact that one of the main issues had been abandoned (*Winter v Winter* (2000) LTL 10/11/2000). Conversely, merely failing to recover as much in damages as had been claimed does not give grounds for reducing the successful party's costs (*Hall v Stone* (2007) The Times, 1 February 2008). Generally, when a party is partially successful, the trial judge should award one party a percentage of its costs rather than awarding costs on different issues to different parties, because a percentage order avoids a great deal of complication on assessment of costs (*English v Emery Reimbold and Strick Ltd* [2002] 1 WLR 2409).

Factor (c), which covers unreasonable conduct, could also be used against parties who fail to conduct litigation in accordance with the overriding ethos, such as those who are unreasonably uncooperative: see CPR, r 1.4(2)(a). In *Grupo Torras SA v Al-Sabah* (5 July 1999) a claim had been made against a number of defendants in conspiracy, dishonest assistance in breach of trust and related causes of action. The claims against the fourth, sixth and tenth defendants failed because the claimant failed to prove the essential element of dishonesty as against them. Mance LJ, who was the trial judge, held the fourth defendant would only recover 50% of his costs because, although he did not realise there was a fraud, he was involved in deliberately backdating relevant documentation. The sixth defendant only recovered one-third of his costs. He was the finance director of one of the companies, and had deliberately deceived the auditors and gave untrue evidence at trial. The tenth defendant was a professional man who had created false documentation, misled the auditors and gave untruthful evidence at trial. He too only recovered one-third of his costs.

Exaggeration of the value of a claim (factor (d)) will obviously be relevant where the claim is inflated for the purpose of bringing it in the High Court or to have the case allocated to a higher track than it deserves. It could also be used in cases where exaggeration of the claim makes it difficult for the defendant to assess its true value for the purposes of making an offer to settle.

36.3 Interim costs orders

If an order makes no reference to costs, none are payable in respect of the proceedings to which the order relates: CPR, r 44.13(1) and PD 23, para 13.2. Usually, however, the court will make some form of order saying who will pay the costs of any interim application.

Figure 36.1 sets out in tabular form the meanings of commonly used interim costs orders.

Term	Effect
Costs in any event or 'costs'	The party in whose favour the order is made is entitled to the costs of the interim application whatever other costs orders are made in the proceedings
Costs in the case/costs in the application	The party in whose favour the court makes an order for costs at the end of the proceedings is entitled to his costs of the interim application.
Costs reserved	The decision about costs is deferred to a later occasion, but if no later order is made the costs will be costs in the case.
Claimant's/defendant's costs in the case/application	If the party in whose favour the costs order is made is awarded costs at the end of the proceedings, that party is entitled to his or her costs of the interim application. If any other party is awarded costs at the end of the proceedings, each party bears its own costs for the interim application.
Costs thrown away	Where, for example, a judgment or order is set aside, the party in whose favour the costs order is made is entitled to the costs which have been incurred as a consequence. This includes the costs of: (a) preparing for and attending any hearing at which the judgment or order which has been set aside was made; (b) preparing for and attending any hearing to set aside the judgment or order in question; (c) preparing for and attending any hearing at which the court orders the proceedings or the part in question to be adjourned; (d) any steps taken to enforce a judgment or order which has subsequently been set aside.
Costs of and caused by/costs of and arising from	Where, for example, the court makes this order on an application to amend a statement of case, the party in whose favour the costs order is made is entitled to the costs of any preparing for and attending the application and the costs of consequential amendment to his or her own statement of case.
Costs here and below	The party in whose favour the costs order is made is entitled not only to his or her costs of the appeal, but also to his or her costs of the proceedings in any lower court.
No order as to costs/each party to pay his or her own costs	Each party is to bear his or her own costs of the interim application whatever costs order the court makes at the end of the proceedings except: <ul><li>trustees and personal representatives are entitled to their costs from the relevant fund</li><li>landlords and mortgagees may be able to recover their costs under the terms of the relevant agreement</li><li>orders made on applications without notice, where silence on costs means 'applicant's costs in the case' (r 44.13(1A)).</li></ul>

Figure 36.1   The meanings of common interim costs orders

The choice of order depends on the court's view of who won the interim application, and on the other factors set out in CPR, r 44.3. Case management hearings usually result in orders for costs in the case, as there is no 'winner'. An adversarial application won by the claimant will usually result in an order for 'claimant's costs'. Applications made without notice, and interim injunctions granted on the basis of the balance of convenience, usually result in 'costs reserved' (see *Desquenne et Giral UK Ltd v Richardson* [1999] CPLR 744, and *Picnic at Ascot Inc v Derigs* [2001] FSR 2).

36.3.1 Summary assessment of interim costs

The costs of interim hearings likely to last less than a day are likely to be dealt with by way of summary assessment there and then. The parties are required to file and serve statements of their costs not less than 24 hours before the hearing to assist with this process. Summary assessment should not be made of the costs of parties who are publicly funded or acting under a disability. Nor is summary assessment normally appropriate where an interim application lasts more than a day.

A failure to serve a statement of costs 24 hours in advance of the hearing should be met with a proportionate response (*MacDonald v Taree Holdings Ltd* [2001] CPLR 439). Options include:

(a) adjourning for a detailed assessment;

(b) adjourning to a later date for a summary assessment before the same judge, or for the summary assessment to be dealt with in writing; and

(c) adjourning for a short period to allow the unsuccessful party a chance to consider a late statement of costs, with the judge then considering the summary assessment, but with added leniency towards the paying party.

Where a court makes a summary assessment of interim costs, those costs will be stated in the order made by the court, and the costs will consequently be payable within 14 days of the date of the order (CPR, r 44.8). The court retains a discretion to decide when such costs are to be paid (r 44.3), but any application for an extension of time in which to pay such costs should be supported by evidence (*Pepin v Watts* The Independent, 6 November 2000, CA).

36.3.2 Detailed assessment of interim costs

Orders for costs will be treated as requiring detailed assessment unless the order specifies the sum to be paid or states that fixed costs are to be paid: PD Costs, para 12.2. Detailed assessments generally take place after the proceedings are concluded.

36.3.3 Representation by counsel

PD Costs, para 8.7, allows the court when making a costs order (including both interim costs orders and final costs orders made at trial) to state an opinion as to whether or not the hearing was fit for representation by one or more counsel. Paragraph 8.7(3) provides that the court should consider recording whether the hearing was fit for counsel in particular where the paying party asks for the court to express a view; where more than one counsel attended for a party; and where the judge thinks the hearing was not fit for counsel.

36.3.4 Notifying client

Where a costs order is made against a legally-represented client who is not present in court when the order is made, the solicitor representing the client is under a duty to inform the client of the costs liability within seven days of the order being made: CPR, r 44.2. The court may ask for proof that this has been done.

36.4 Final costs orders

36.4.1 Variations from winner recovering costs

Under the CPR, r 44.3(6), there are seven possible variations from the main rule that the unsuccessful party should pay the whole of the successful party's costs. These variations are:

(a) that a party must pay only a proportion of another party's costs;

(b) that a party must pay a specified amount in respect of the other side's costs;

(c) that a party must pay costs from or until a certain day only;

(d) that a party must pay costs incurred before proceedings have begun;

(e) that a party must pay costs relating only to certain steps taken in the proceedings;

(f) that a party must pay costs relating only to a certain distinct part of the proceedings, although an order of this type can only be made if an order in either of the forms set out at (a) or (c) would not be practicable (CPR, r 44.3(7)); and

(g) that a party must pay interest on costs from or until a certain date, including a date before judgment.

36.4.2 Order for costs in cases involving multiple parties

Where the claimant sues two defendants and is successful against one defendant but not the other, if costs were to follow the event, the unsuccessful defendant would have to pay the claimant's costs in respect of the claim against the unsuccessful defendant and the claimant would have to pay the costs incurred in respect of the claim against the successful defendant. However, if it was reasonable to join both defendants to the action, the court in its discretion may make a special order enabling the claimant to recover the costs paid to the successful defendant or for them to be paid by the unsuccessful defendant direct to the successful defendant (*Irvine v Commissioner of Police for the Metropolis* (2005) LTL 3/2/2005). There are two types of order: *Bullock* and *Sanderson*.

36.4.2.1 *Bullock* order

This is derived from *Bullock v London General Omnibus Co* [1907] 1 KB 264, CA. The claimant is ordered to pay the costs of the successful defendant and once paid the claimant is then allowed to recover these costs from the unsuccessful defendant in addition to the claimant's costs incurred in respect of the claim against the unsuccessful defendant. This is known as a *Bullock* order.

36.4.2.2 *Sanderson* order

This is derived from *Sanderson v Blyth Theatre Co* [1903] 2 KB 533, CA. The unsuccessful defendant is ordered to pay the successful defendant's costs direct to the successful defendant. Also, the unsuccessful defendant will have to pay the claimant's costs incurred in respect of the claim against the unsuccessful defendant. This order is appropriate where the claimant is publicly funded or insolvent as the order will ensure that the successful defendant is able to recover his or her costs. This order is known as a *Sanderson* order.

36.4.2.3 Choice of order

The choice of order is a matter for the discretion of the court, although the court will normally want to protect the successful defendant first against the risk of irrecoverable costs (see *Mayer v Harte* [1960] 1 WLR 770, CA). Nevertheless, likely hardship to a claimant and a desire to spread the burden of irrecoverable costs more equitably are justifiable considerations (see *Bank America Finance Ltd v Nock* [1988] AC 1002, HL).

36.4.3 Order for costs in cases involving additional claims under Part 20

The court has power to make such order as it thinks just. The following is a general guideline:

(a) Generally, if the claimant wins against the defendant, who then succeeds against the third party, the third party will be liable for the defendant's costs, including those that the defendant will have had to pay the claimant.

(b) However, if the defendant is considered to have defended the claimant's claim for his or her own benefit, the defendant may only be able to recover the costs of the third party action, against the third party.

(c) If the claimant loses against the defendant, and the defendant thus loses against the third party, it does not *necessarily* follow that the claimant will have to pay the costs of the third party. It may be that the defendant should not have joined the third party in any event.

(d) The claimant will have to pay the whole costs if it was inevitable that the defendant would have to join other parties, when meeting the claimant's claim.

(e) Where, for example, the claimant and the third party *both* lose to the defendant, generally each will be responsible only for the costs of the claim to which they were a party.

It should be noted that as costs between the *immediate* parties normally follow the event if, in case (a) above, the third party proves to be insolvent, the defendant will unfortunately still be responsible for paying the claimant's costs.

36.4.4 Joinder of causes of action

The joinder of causes of action is encouraged by the Civil Liability (Contribution) Act 1978, s 4, whereby a claimant who brings successive claims for damages in respect of the same damage is not entitled to costs in any proceedings other than the first claim, unless the court is satisfied that there were reasonable grounds for bringing separate claims.

36.4.5 Costs of counterclaims and set-offs

36.4.5.1 Where are separate orders appropriate?

Separate orders for costs are appropriate where the counterclaim is unrelated to the claim and the claimant succeeds on the claim and the defendant succeeds on the counterclaim, or where they both fail on their respective claims.

Thus, the order might be for judgment for the claimant on the claim with the costs of claim, and judgment for the defendant on the counterclaim with costs of counterclaim. According to *Medway Oil and Storage Co Ltd v Continental Contractors Ltd* [1929] AC 88, there would then be a division of costs between the claim and counterclaim, with the usual result that the costs relating to the claim would be far greater than the costs exclusively referable to the counterclaim.

36.4.5.2   Percentage orders

Where the claim and counterclaim are related, and the claimant and defendant are partially successful, the court should usually award a percentage costs order in favour of the party who has achieved overall success. See *English v Emery Reimbold and Strick Ltd* [2002] 1 WLR 2409 and *NF Burchell v Bullard* The Independent, 21 April 2005.

36.4.6   Conditional fee agreement costs orders

A party's 'costs' include any additional liability under a conditional fee funding agreement (CPR, r 43.2(1)(a)). The 'additional liability' under a CFA includes the percentage increase (or success fee), the insurance premium and/or the cost of membership, as the case may be (r 43.2(1)(o)). An order to pay a CFA litigant's costs will therefore include any additional liability under the agreement (PD Costs, para 9.1). A party and party costs order in favour of a CFA litigant does not, by virtue of r 44.3B, include:

(a) any proportion of the success fee that reflects the fact of postponement of payment to the CFA litigant's lawyers;

(b) any provision made by a membership organisation which exceeds the likely premium for insurance cover against the risk of paying the other side's costs;

(c) any additional liability incurred during any period in which the receiving party was in breach of the requirements (in r 44.15 and PD Costs, para 19) for providing information about the funding arrangement. The information is given using form N251. It must be filed and served when the claim is issued, or (if the CFA litigant is a defendant), when the first document is filed in response to the claim, or, if the funding agreement is entered into after proceedings have commenced, within seven days of entering into the agreement (para 19.2); or

(d) any percentage increase if there is a failure to comply with the requirements relating to disclosing the reasons for setting the percentage increase at the stated level. Relevant factors, such as the risk of losing and delay in payment, are set out in PD Costs, para 55.3.

The paying party can dispute the percentage increase, and any insurance premium. Generally, it will be reasonable to enter into After the Event insurance in conjunction with a CFA (*Callery v Gray* [2001] 1 WLR 2112 and *Callery v Gray (No. 2)* [2002] 1 WLR 2000), unless legal expenses insurance was available (*Sarwar v Alam* [2002] 1 WLR 125). Solicitors acting for prospective CFA clients need to consider whether there are alternative methods of funding available before the client enters into the CFA.

36.4.7   Against non-parties

Aiden Shipping Co Ltd v Interbulk Ltd [1986] AC 965, HL, is authority for the proposition that the SCA 1981, s 51, confers a very wide discretion on the court as to costs, which includes a power in appropriate cases to award costs against non-parties. Separate proceedings were taken by a ship owner against its charterers, and by the charterers against its sub-charterers. Although both disputes were almost identical, the proceedings were not consolidated. The House of Lords upheld the judge's costs order that the unsuccessful ship owner should pay the charterer's costs, such costs to include any costs the charterers had to pay the sub-charterers in the second set of proceedings.

Principles governing the exercise of the *Aiden Shipping* doctrine were laid down by the Court of Appeal in *Symphony Group plc v Hodgson* [1994] QB 179. Such orders are always exceptional. *Aiden Shipping* orders have been made in a number of cases, such as where a director has caused an insolvent company to bring or defend proceedings or where the non-party has been found to have maintained the action for the purposes of the law against maintenance and champerty (*McFarlane v EE Caledonia Ltd (No. 2)* [1995] 1 WLR 366). The most common basis for successful applications is where the non-party has funded the litigation (see also *Murphy v Young and Co's Brewery Ltd* [1997] 1 WLR 1591 and *Locabail (UK) Ltd v Bayfield Properties Ltd (No. 3)* The Times, 29 February 2000). In *Shah v Karanjia* [1993] 4 All ER 792, an application was refused principally because the non-party had not been separately represented at the trial, and the claim against him for costs had not been formulated against him until after the trial.

The CPR, r 48.2, lays down a statutory framework for the procedure to be followed on these applications. The person against whom the order will be sought must be added as a party (even though, apparently, there may be no substantive cause of action against that person), and that person must be given a reasonable opportunity to attend the hearing to give reasons why the court should not make the order. The determination of the application is a summary matter, with some relaxation of the normal rules of evidence.

36.4.8 Trustees

Where trustees are involved and the costs they have incurred have not been recovered from any other persons the court should order trustees to recover costs from the trust fund, whatever the result, provided the trustees have acted reasonably, in good faith, and for the benefit of the trust fund.

Similarly, the court will normally order the costs of claims by personal representatives on behalf of an estate to be recoverable from the estate. The same principle also applies to actions by mortgagees to protect mortgaged property.

However, where proceedings between trustees and beneficiaries are adversarial in nature, it is appropriate for the court to refuse to order the trustees' costs from the fund (*Holding and Management Ltd v Property Holding and Investment Trust plc* [1989] 1 WLR 1313, CA).

36.4.9 Costs of pre-commencement disclosure and disclosure against non-parties

These applications were considered at **21.3** and **21.4**. The general rule is that the applicant must pay the costs of the application: CPR, r 48.1, see **21.3.7**.

36.4.10 Costs after transfer

Subject to any order that may have been made by the original court, once a case is transferred the new court will deal with all questions as to costs, including the costs incurred before the transfer: CPR, r 44.13(3), (4).

36.4.11 Costs and track allocation

The special rules relating to costs in cases on the small claims track and fast track only apply once a claim is allocated to one of these tracks, but then apply also to the costs before allocation: CPR, r 44.9(1), (2). This means, for example, that where default judgment is entered on a small value claim before allocation the costs restrictions in Part 27 do not apply (although the fixed costs rules in Part 45 would be applied instead).

Where a claim exceeds the small claims limit, but is allocated to the small claims track under r 26.7(3), the small claims costs rules apply unless the parties agree to use the fast track costs rules (r 27.14(5), (6)). Where a small claim case is reallocated to another track, the fast track or multi-track costs rules apply only from the date of reallocation (r 27.15).

36.4.12 Costs on appeal

The recovery of costs by the successful party, which can include both the costs of the appeal and below, is normally subject to the discretion of the court.

Non-recovery of costs by a successful appellant may arise, in full or in part, where:

- the appeal is only partly successful; or
- the court's time has been wasted; or
- the appeal was successful only on a point not raised in the notice of appeal.

Non-recovery of costs by a successful respondent may arise, in full or in part, where:

- the appeal raised a novel question of general public importance;
- new points were raised which were never raised at the original hearing.

36.5 Quantification of costs

Once an order has been made as to costs the actual amount of costs a party will be able to recover from the other side will need to be quantified. This can be done in a number of ways.

36.5.1 Agreement between the parties

Agreement between the parties, as to the costs payable by one party to the other, avoids the time and expense involved in the assessment of costs.

It is not possible to agree costs in proceedings brought on behalf of a person under disability without the direction of the court.

36.5.2 Fixed costs

Some items of expenditure, particularly solicitors' charges in certain proceedings and on entering default judgments, are recoverable only as fixed costs.

36.5.3 Summary assessment

This involves the court determining the amount payable by way of costs immediately at the end of a hearing, usually on a relatively rough and ready basis. The starting point will be the statement of costs (see **Figure 7.2**). Courts sometimes develop conventional figures for specified costs for certain types of proceeding, such as the costs awarded for straightforward landlord and tenant possession proceedings. The courts tend to err on the side of caution when specifying the amount of costs to be paid, but it has been known for the amount specified to be relatively large. The court can call for whatever evidence is available at the time in deciding on the figure to be specified, such as looking at Counsel's Brief to see the brief fee, as well as hearing the advocates on the work involved in the matter. There are proposals for the introduction of 'benchmark costs' in the future. These are intended to impose moderate, standard amounts for costs for common interim applications.

36.5.4   Detailed assessment

A detailed assessment of costs involves leaving the quantification of costs to a costs officer, who will consider the amount to be allowed at an assessment hearing at some stage in the future after the parties have been given the opportunity of setting out the amount claimed and points of dispute in writing. Detailed assessments are carried out mainly by District Judges in the County Courts, and there is a special office, called the Supreme Court Costs Office, for the High Court. Generally the court has a discretion to decide whether to make a summary assessment or to order a detailed assessment if the costs cannot be agreed. However, where money is claimed by or ordered or agreed to be paid to or for the benefit of a child or patient the court in general must order a detailed assessment of the costs payable by the claimant to his or her solicitor: CPR, r 48.5.

36.5.5   Basis of quantification

There are two bases of assessment of costs: the standard basis and the indemnity basis. As its name suggests, the standard basis is the one usually applied in costs orders between the parties in litigation. The indemnity basis is used when a client is paying its own solicitor, and also when a trustee's costs are payable out of the trust fund. It can also be used between competing parties in litigation as a penalty for misconduct, or as a result of a successful claimant's Part 36 offer. Costs orders should identify the intended basis of quantification. On both bases the court will not allow costs which have been unreasonably incurred or which are unreasonable in amount.

On an assessment on the standard basis, which is the least generous basis, the CPR, r 44.4(2), provides that the court will:

(a) only allow costs which are proportionate to the matters in issue; and

(b) resolve any doubt which it may have as to whether costs were reasonably incurred or reasonable and proportionate in amount in favour of the paying party.

On an assessment on the indemnity basis there is no reference to proportionality, and any doubt on whether costs were reasonably incurred or were reasonable in amount is resolved in favour of the receiving party: CPR, r 44.4(3).

36.5.6   Procedure on detailed assessment of costs

Assessment proceedings must be commenced within three months of the judgment, order, award or other determination giving rise to the right to costs: CPR, r 47.7. This is done by serving on the paying party a notice of commencement in the relevant practice form together with a copy of the bill of costs: CPR, r 47.6(1). The paying party may dispute any item in the bill by serving the receiving party with points of dispute. These must be served within 21 days after service of the notice of commencement: CPR, r 47.9. If the paying party fails to serve points of dispute within the permitted time the receiving party may, on filing a request, obtain a default costs certificate: CPR, r 47.9(4) and 47.11. The receiving party has the right, but is not obliged, to serve a reply to any points of dispute. Any reply should be served on the party who served the points of dispute within 21 days after service: CPR, r 47.13. Hearings are relatively informal, with the points in dispute being taken in turn and both sides making submissions and the costs officer making rulings on each point in turn.

36.5.7 Predictable CFA costs

For certain road traffic claims and claims arising out of accidents etc at work, CPR, r 45.7 to 45.26, provide formulae for calculating the amount of costs to be added to the settlement figure and/or the percentage increase to be allowed for any CFA success fee. Different rates are allowed for different circumstances. For example, solicitors are allowed a 12.5% success fee if a road traffic claim concludes before trial, but 100% if such a claim concludes at trial (r 45.16).

36.6 Wasted costs order

36.6.1 Jurisdiction

Legal representatives may, by SCA 1981, s 51(6), be made personally liable for any wasted costs. Applications for wasted costs orders can be made against the legal representatives for the other side or against the legal representatives acting for the applicant (*Medcalf v Mardell* [2003] 1 AC 120). Applications can be made against legal or other representatives exercising rights of audience and rights to conduct litigation (s 51(13)). Applications against counsel are not restricted to their conduct in court, but extend to counsel's involvement in advising, drafting, and settling documents in relation to proceedings (*Medcalf v Mardell*). Costs are 'wasted' if they are incurred either:

- as a result of any improper, unreasonable or negligent act or omission by that legal representative; or
- before such an act or omission, but the court considers it unreasonable to expect the party to pay in the light of that act or omission.

The wasted costs may be simply disallowed on assessment, or an order may be made that the legal representative must pay the whole or some part of them.

36.6.2 Principles

The court must, according to *Re a Barrister (Wasted Costs Order) (No. 1 of 1991)* [1993] QB 293, apply a three-stage test:

- Has the lawyer acted improperly, unreasonably or negligently?
- If so, did such conduct cause the applicant to incur unnecessary costs?
- If so, was it in all the circumstances just to order the lawyer to compensate the applicant for the whole or part of the wasted costs?

Guidelines, particularly on the first stage, were laid down in *Ridehalgh v Horsefield* [1994] Ch 205, CA. 'Improper' conduct includes professional misconduct and also conduct considered improper by the consensus of professional opinion, even if it does not contravene the letter of the appropriate professional code of conduct. Pleading a case in fraud without a proper basis, in breach of the Bar Code of Conduct, may be 'improper' (*Medcalf v Mardell* [2003] 1 AC 120). The acid test for acting 'unreasonably' is whether the conduct admitted of a reasonable explanation. 'Negligent' must be understood in an untechnical way as denoting a failure to act with the competence to be reasonably expected of ordinary members of the profession. Pursuing a hopeless case will not be penalised under s 51(6) unless it amounts to an abuse of process. The reason is that barristers are subject to the 'cab rank' rule and are not allowed to pick and choose their cases, and many solicitors operate on a similar basis. A solicitor is not permitted to abdicate all responsibility by instructing counsel, but the more specialist the area the more reasonable it will be for a solicitor to rely on counsel's advice.

36.6.3 Procedure

By CPR, r 48.7, the court is required to give the legal representative a reasonable opportunity to attend a hearing to give reasons why the order should not be made. The court may also direct that notice be given to the legal representative's client. It was provided that for the purposes of such applications the court could direct that privileged documents were to be disclosed to the court and to the other party to the application for the order (see the 1999 version of CPR, r 48.7(3)). This particular provision was held to be ultra vires and also to infringe arts 6 and 8 of the European Convention on Human Rights by Toulson J in *General Mediterranean Holdings SA v Patel* [2000] 1 WLR 272, and has been deleted from the rules.

The procedure is intended to be summary, without detailed statements of case, formal disclosure of documents or requests for further information unless absolutely necessary. If the court makes an order it must specify the amount to be paid or disallowed. Wasted costs applications should normally be made at the end of the trial, and will generally be considered in two stages:

(a) at the first stage the applicant has to adduce evidence which, if unanswered, would be likely to lead to a wasted costs order, and that the wasted costs application appears to be justified having regard to the likely costs involved;

(b) at the second stage the court will give the legal representative an opportunity of putting forward his or her case.

What is 'summary' depends on the nature of the case. The fact that the costs proceedings may take some time to determine does not stop them being summary (*Robertson Research International Ltd v ABG Exploration BV* [1999] CPLR 756, Laddie J). However, if the application is speculative or bound to fail the court should summarily dismiss it (*Bristol and West plc v Bhadresa (No. 2)* [1999] CPLR 209). The court should limit the issues to be considered, and, if necessary, the length of cross-examination and submissions.

37

Judgments and orders

37.1 Introduction

This chapter is concerned with how judgments and orders pronounced in court and in chambers are converted into records which can be enforced. A judgment is a final decision in a claim while an order is an interim decision although it may end the claim, eg a final consent order.

There is a distinction between judgments (and orders), and the reasons given by the judge for the judgment (or order). A drawn-up judgment or order is simply a written record of the result. Compliance with the European Convention on Human Rights, art 6, requires reasons to be given for a judge's decision, which may be given orally or in writing. A written judgment (the reasons) is a different document from a drawn-up judgment. The level of detail required for reasons for a decision is the same under art 6 and under domestic law (*English v Emery Reimbold and Strick Ltd* [2002] 1 WLR 2409). There must be sufficient detail for an appeal court to understand the basis for the decision should there be an appeal. Reasons, even if short and even if for costs orders, must be clear, and cannot be left to inference (*Lavelle v Lavelle* The Times, 9 March 2004).

37.2 Drawing up orders and judgments

37.2.1 General rules relating to drawing up orders and judgments

The CPR, rr 40.2(2) and 40.3(1), provide that all judgments and orders have to be drawn up and sealed by the court, unless the court dispenses with the need to do so. Subject to the slip rule (**37.7**), once a judgment is drawn up the judge is *functus officio*, which operates as a bar to alterations to the judgment by the judge (*Earl of Malmesbury v Strutt and Parker* (2007) 42EG 294 (CS)).

In the county courts and in the Chancery Division, normally the court will take responsibility for drawing up, but:

- the parties usually have responsibility for drawing up orders in the Queen's Bench Division; or
- the court may order a party to draw up an order; or
- a party may, with the permission of the court, agree to draw up an order; or
- the court may direct a party to draw up the order subject to checking by the court before it is sealed; or

- the court may direct the parties to file an agreed statement of the terms of the order before the court itself draws up the order; or
- the order may be entered administratively by consent, in which event the parties will submit a drawn-up version of their agreement for entry.

A party who is required to draw up a judgment is allowed seven days to file the relevant document, together with sufficient copies for all relevant parties, failing which any other party may draw it up and file it for sealing: CPR, r 40.3(3) and 40.4(1).

Every judgment or order (apart from judgments on admissions, default judgments and consent judgments) must state the name and judicial title of the judge who made it: r 40.2(1). Where a party has asked for permission to appeal (see **39.5**), the order must state whether it is final, identify the appeal court, and state whether permission to appeal was granted (r 40.2(4)).

Once an order has been drawn up the court will serve sealed copies on the applicant and respondent, and also on any other person the court may order to be served: r 40.4(2). It will be the court that effects service unless one of the exceptions set out in r 6.3 applies. The court is given a specific power by r 40.5, to order service on a litigant as well as the litigant's solicitor.

Judgments and orders normally take effect from the day they are given or made, not from the time they are drawn up, sealed or served: r 40.7. However, the court is given the power to specify some later date from which the order shall take effect. A judgment for the payment of money (including costs) must be complied with within 14 days of the judgment, unless the court specifies some other date for compliance: r 40.11. This will include most orders that include a summary assessment of costs. The order may, instead of requiring immediate payment, impose an order for payment by instalments or defer the date for payment.

37.2.2 Special forms of judgment

37.2.2.1 Counterclaims

The court has power to give separate judgments when dealing with cases where there are claims and counterclaims. It also has power to order a set-off between the two claims, and simply enter judgment for the balance: CPR, r 40.13(2). Where it does so, it retains power to make separate costs orders in respect of the claims and counterclaims: r 40.13(3).

37.2.2.2 Interim payments

Detailed rules for the form of judgments given in cases where there have been interim payments are laid down in PD 25. In a preamble to the judgment in such a case there should be set out the total amount awarded and the amounts and dates of all interim payments. The total amount awarded should then be reduced by the total amount of the interim payments, with judgment being given for the balance. If the interim payments exceed the amount awarded at trial, by virtue of CPR, r 25.8(2), the judgment should set out any orders made for repayment, reimbursement, variation or discharge, and any award of interest on the overpaid interim payments.

37.2.2.3 Compensation recovery

In personal injuries cases where some or all of the damages are subject to recovery under the Social Security (Recovery of Benefits) Act 1997, the judgment should include a preamble setting out the amounts awarded under each head of damage, and the amount by which it has been reduced in accordance with the Act: PD 40B, para 5.1. The judgment should then provide for entry of judgment and payment of the balance.

37.2.2.4 Payment by instalments

A judgment for payment by instalments must state the total amount of the judgment, the amount of each instalment, the number of instalments and the date on which each is to be paid, and to whom the instalments should be paid: PD 40B, para 12.

37.2.2.5 Orders requiring an act to be done ('unless orders')

Orders requiring an act to be done, other than the payment of money, must specify the time within which the act must be done. The consequences of failing to comply with the order must also be set out: PD 40B, paras 8.1 and 8.2. There are two suitable forms of wording, and the first form should be used wherever possible. The second form should be used where the defaulting party does not attend: 'Unless the claimant serves his list of documents by 4.00 pm on Friday, 4 December 2009, his claim will be struck out and judgment entered for the defendant.' 'Unless the defendant serves his list of documents within 14 days of service of this order . . . .'

37.2.2.6 Penal notice

Injunction orders, whether prohibitory or mandatory, are intended to have penal consequences and can be punished as a contempt of court. These orders need to be endorsed with a penal notice in the following form (PD 40B, para 9.1):

If you the within-named [   ] do not comply with this order you may be held to be in contempt of court and imprisoned or fined, or [in the case of a company or corporation] your assets may be seized.

Undertakings given in lieu of injunctions are treated in the same way. A person giving an undertaking may also be required to sign a statement, which is indorsed on the court's copy of the order, to the effect that he or she understands the terms of the undertaking and the consequences of failure to comply with it: PD 40B, para 9.3.

37.3 Consent orders

37.3.1 Nature of consent orders

37.3.1.1 Using a consent order

A consent order can record the agreement of the parties in respect of certain interim matters and it may also be used to record the terms of a compromise when an action is settled.

37.3.1.2 Contractual nature of consent orders

As is inherent in the judgment of Buckley LJ in *Chanel Ltd v FW Woolworth and Co Ltd* [1981] 1 WLR 485, a consent order is based on a *contract* between the parties. The contractual nature of such orders was recognised as long ago as 1840, when in *Wentworth v Bullen* (1840) 9 B & C 840 it was pointed out that the contract is contained in what passes between the parties (usually an exchange of correspondence) and that the consent order is simply evidence of that contract. To be effective, strictly the necessary ingredients for a contract need to be present.

37.3.1.3 Consent order as an estoppel

A consent order can act as an estoppel, effective to prevent a party from alleging matters against the other which have been compromised by the agreement (see *Kinch v Walcott* [1929] AC 482). However, the wording of each order has to be looked at carefully to determine whether it will act as an estoppel. For example, if it is clear that, in arriving at a consent order, one party expressly reserved the right to proceed against the other on certain allegations, there will be no estoppel by reason of the order (see *Rice v Reed* [1900] 1 QB 54). Also, a previous consent order will not act as a bar to a later application if the later application is regarded as dealing with a different (albeit related) situation (*Kensington International Ltd v Republic of Congo* [2008] 1 WLR 1144).

37.3.1.4   Can a consent order be set aside or varied?

Before the consent order has been drawn up it is possible to apply back to the court to have it set aside or altered. However, good grounds are required for showing that the consent was procured through misrepresentation, mistake or any other ground for setting aside a contract (see *Dietz v Lennig Chemicals Ltd* [1969] 1 AC 170).

After the consent order is perfected the court has no power to vary it. In *De Lasala v De Lasala* [1980] AC 546, PC Lord Diplock said:

> Where a party seeks to challenge, on the ground that it was obtained by fraud or mistake, a judgment or order that finally disposes of the issues raised between the parties, the only ways of doing it that are open to him are by appeal from the judgment or order or by bringing fresh proceedings to set it aside.

However, there is a distinction between a real contract and a simple submission to an order. In *Siebe Gorman and Co Ltd v Pneupac Ltd* [1982] 1 All ER 377, at 380, Lord Denning MR said:

> It should be clearly understood by the profession that, when an order is expressed to be made 'by consent' it is ambiguous. One meaning is this: the words 'by consent' may evidence a real contract between the parties. In such a case the court will only interfere with such an order on the same grounds as it would with any other contract. The other meaning is this: the words 'by consent' may mean 'the parties hereto not objecting.' In such a case there is no real contract between the parties.

37.3.1.5   Enforcement

Generally, if either party fails to comply with a consent order, the innocent party can seek to enforce it in the same manner as any other court order.

37.3.2   Tomlin orders

37.3.2.1   Use and nature of a Tomlin order

Where complex terms of settlement are agreed, or terms are agreed which extend beyond the boundaries of the action, or where it is sought to avoid publicity of the terms agreed, the compromise can be embodied in a Tomlin order. The name is derived from a *Practice Note* [1927] WN 290, where Tomlin J said that in a case where terms of compromise have been arranged and it is proposed that the action be stayed on agreed terms to be scheduled to a consent order, the minutes should be drawn so as to read as follows:

> *And, the claimant and the defendant having agreed to the terms set out in the annexed schedule, it is ordered that all further proceedings in this action be stayed, except for the purpose of carrying such terms into effect. Liberty to apply as to carrying such terms into effect.*

37.3.2.2   Enforcement where the agreed terms are broken

If the agreed terms are broken, enforcement is a two-stage process.

First, the action must be restored under the liberty to apply, and an order obtained requiring the opponent to comply with the scheduled obligation that has been breached.

Secondly, if that order is not complied with it can then be enforced by committal or by levying execution as appropriate.

As is made clear in *EF Phillips and Sons Ltd v Clarke* [1970] Ch 322, at 325, provisions in the schedule can be enforced even if not part of the original action. As Goff J said:

> . . . provided [a Tomlin] order is in the normally appropriate form with a qualified stay and a liberty to apply, and provided the application is strictly to enforce the terms embodied in the order and the schedule and does not depart from the agreed terms, an order giving effect to the terms may be obtained under the liberty to apply in the original action, notwithstanding the compromise itself goes beyond the ambit of the original dispute and the provision sought to be enforced is something which could not have been enforced in the original action and which indeed, is an obligation which did not exist but arose for the first time under the compromise.

37.3.3   Entering consent orders

37.3.3.1   Administrative consent orders

In order to save time and costs, CPR, r 40.6, allows certain types of consent orders to be entered by a purely administrative process without the need for obtaining the approval of a judge. However, this process may not be used if any of the parties is a litigant in person: r 40.6(2)(b). The types of orders covered are:

- judgments or orders for the payment of money;
- judgments or orders for the delivery up of goods (other than specific delivery);
- orders to dismiss the whole or part of the proceedings;
- orders for stays on agreed terms which dispose of the proceedings, including Tomlin orders;
- orders setting aside default judgments;
- orders for the discharge from liability of any party; and
- orders for the payment, waiver or assessment of costs.

The consent order has to be drawn up in the agreed terms, has to bear the words 'By Consent', and be signed by the solicitors or counsel acting for each of the parties. In cases where terms are annexed in a schedule, provisions dealing with the payment of money out of court and for the payment and assessment of costs should be contained in the body of the order rather than in the schedule: PD 40B, para 3.5.

37.3.3.2   Consent orders approved by the court

If an order is agreed between the parties, but includes a provision going beyond the types of orders referred to in the previous section, or if one of the parties is a litigant in person, it will have to be approved by a judge (often a District Judge or Master). It will be drawn up as above. The name of the judge will not be known, so the draft will have to include a space for the judge's details to be inserted: PD 23, para 10.3. If all the parties write to the court expressing their consent, the court will treat that as sufficient signing of the consent order: PD 23, para 10.2. The court will not necessarily make the order in accordance with the agreement between the parties, as the court retains ultimate control, particularly over case management matters. However, it will always take the terms agreed between the parties into account in whatever order it decides to make: see, for example, PD 28, para 3.8.

In cases where the court's approval must be sought, either party may make the application for approval, and the application may be dealt with without a hearing: CPR, r 40.6(5), (6).

37.4 In the Court of Appeal

Orders are drawn up by the Court Associate, not by the parties.

37.5 In the Supreme Court

The practice in the new Supreme Court has yet to be published.

37.6 Interest on judgments

Under the Judgments Act 1838, s 17, and CCA 1984, s 74, simple interest, currently at 8% per annum, is payable on all High Court money judgments and County Court money judgments of £5,000 and more. In addition, a County Court judgment for any amount of money carries interest at 8% per annum if it is in respect of a debt which is a qualifying debt for the purposes of the Late Payment of Commercial Debts (Interest) Act 1998. A debt is a qualifying debt if it was created by virtue of an obligation under a contract to which the Act applies: s 3(1). Businesses, irrespective of size, and public sector bodies, can claim statutory interest at 8% above the 'reference rate', which is the Bank of England base rate for each six-month period starting on 30 June and 31 December. In addition, compensation is payable (£40 on debts up to £1,000; £70 on debts between £1,000 and £10,000 and £100 on debts of £10,000 and more).

Also of significance is *Thomas v Bunn* [1991] 1 AC 362, HL, where it was held that in cases where the claimant enters a judgment for damages to be decided by the court, 1838 Act interest on the main award runs from the date of the damages judgment, not the liability judgment. In personal injuries cases, interest on general damages before judgment is currently awarded at 2% per annum as opposed to 8% per annum under the Act. One effect of the decision is that it removes the interest rate disincentive on defendants admitting liability at an early stage, even though they still dispute quantum.

Under CPR, r 40.8, interest on costs runs from the date the judgment is given. As regards interest on costs after a claim is automatically struck out for non-payment of the fees payable at the allocation and pre-trial checklist stages, or after acceptance of an offer to settle, or after a claim is discontinued, by virtue of r 44.12, interest runs from the date of the event giving rise to the entitlement to costs (ie the date of striking out, acceptance, or the date of service of the notice of discontinuance).

37.7 Correction of errors in judgments or orders

Errors in judgments or orders as drawn up may sometimes be corrected. The CPR, r 40.12, provides:

(1) The court may at any time correct an accidental slip or omission in a judgment or order.

(2) A party may apply for a correction without notice.

The rule extends to accidental slips and errors made both by officers of the court and by the parties and their advisers. But the error must be an error in *expressing* the manifest intention of the court. If the intention of the court is in error, the remedy lies in an appeal.

If the contemplated type of error was made, but it was not 'accidental' as required by r 40.12, the court retains inherent jurisdiction to correct it. Thus, in *Hatton v Harris* [1892] AC 547 at 560, Lord Watson said:

> Where an error of that kind has been committed it is always within the competency of the court, if nothing has intervened which would render it inexpedient or inequitable to do so, to correct the record in order to bring it into harmony with the order which the Judge obviously meant to pronounce. The correction ought to be made on [application], and is not a matter either for appeal or rehearing.

37.8 Register of judgments

A register of money judgments is operated by Registry Trust Ltd under powers given by the Courts Act 2003, s 98. Courts provide periodic returns containing details of unsatisfied judgments to Registry Trust Ltd, and the register kept by the company is open to inspection on payment of prescribed fees. The information is regularly used by financial institutions for credit scoring purposes.

Enforcement

38.1 Introduction

A litigant who obtains a judgment or order does not thereby automatically obtain the remedy sought in the proceedings. Leaving aside the possibility of an appeal (a topic considered in **Chapter 39**), there is still the worry that the order will not be obeyed by the other side. Of course, most litigants will abide by the ruling of the court with reasonable promptness. But the court needs powers to enforce compliance by parties who fail to obey judgments and orders made against them, or else public confidence in the legal system would be lost.

The Tribunals, Courts and Enforcement Act 2007 will make a number of far-reaching revisions to the law relating to enforcement of money judgments. At the time of writing commencement dates have only been set for debt relief orders, but not for the other provisions dealing with enforcement. When they are brought into force there will be substantial changes to the rules of court. Many of these are preserved provisions of the RSC and CCR, which are currently found in the schedules to the CPR. This chapter will deal with the existing law. The new provisions will deal with:

(a) Information requests and orders (see **38.2**): Tribunals, Courts and Enforcement Act 2007, ss 95 to 105;

(b) Enforcement by taking control of goods (see **38.3**): Tribunals, Courts and Enforcement Act 2007, ss 62 to 70 and sch 12;

(c) Charging orders (see **38.5**): Tribunals, Courts and Enforcement Act 2007, ss 93 to 94;

(d) Attachment of earnings (see **38.7**): Tribunals, Courts and Enforcement Act 2007, ss 91 to 92 and sch 15;

(e) Administration orders (Tribunals, Courts and Enforcement Act 2007, s 106), and enforcement restriction orders (s 107); and

(f) Debt relief orders (Tribunals, Courts and Enforcement Act 2007, s 108 and sch 18 and 19) (which come into force on 6 April 2009), and debt management schemes (ss 109 to 123).

38.2 Obtaining information from judgment debtors

It may be that the judgment creditor (the person who has obtained a judgment for the payment of money) knows little or nothing about the judgment debtor's assets. Without further information he will be unable to make an intelligent choice between the methods of enforcement that are available. Informally further information can be obtained either personally or through an inquiry agent.

After judgment the court will provide formal assistance by the process of obtaining information from the judgment debtor. There is a prescribed form for the application, which will be dealt with by a court officer without a hearing (CPR, r 71.2). If the application complies with the requirements, an order will be made requiring the debtor to attend court, produce documents and answer questions. The 'debtor' for these purposes includes directors of a debtor company, even if a director is outside the jurisdiction (*Masri v Consolidated Contractors International (UK) Ltd (No. 4)* [2009] 2 WLR 699). The order to attend court has to be served personally not less than 14 days before the hearing (r 71.3). Once served, the debtor has seven days to ask the judgment creditor for a reasonable sum to cover the debtor's travelling expenses to court, which must be paid (r 71.4). The judgment creditor must swear an affidavit (a witness statement being insufficient) giving details of service of the order, any request for and payment of travelling expenses, and how much of the judgment remains unpaid. This affidavit must be filed two days before the hearing or produced at the hearing (r 71.5).

The nature of the examination was considered by the Court of Appeal in *Republic of Costa Rica v Stronsberg* (1880) 16 Ch D 8, where Jessell MR said that the judgment debtor 'must answer all questions fairly directed to ascertain from him what amount of debts is due, from whom due, and to give all necessary particulars to enable the plaintiffs to recover under a garnishee order.' And, according to James LJ 'The examination is not only intended to be an examination, but to be a cross-examination, and that of the severest kind.'

38.3 Execution against goods

Execution against a judgment debtor's goods is by way of a warrant of execution in the county court, and by way of the writ of *fieri facias* (abbreviated to *fi. fa.*) in the High Court. County Court judgments for £5,000 or more must be transferred to the High Court if to be enforced by this method. County Court judgments for less than £1,000 must be enforced in the County Court if enforced by this method. For judgments between £1,000 and £5,000 either court can enforce by this method. A judgment creditor seeking to enforce by either of these methods must complete the necessary forms, and pay the prescribed fee: see RSC Ord 46 and 47 and CCR Ord 26. Actual enforcement is the responsibility of the court bailiff (in the County Court) or the enforcement officer (in the High Court).

The bailiff, armed with the warrant of execution, or the enforcement officer, armed with the writ of *fi. fa.*, will call at the judgment debtor's premises and seek to gain entry. They are not entitled to break open outer doors, nor are they allowed to gain entry by putting a foot in the door and pushing their way in. Once lawfully inside the building, they can seize sufficient goods to satisfy the judgment debt. They can seize any type of goods, including money, bills of exchange, promissory notes and bonds, except protected goods. Clothing, bedding, furniture, household equipment and provisions necessary for satisfying the basic domestic needs of the debtor and his or her family, and such tools, books, vehicles and equipment as are necessary for the debtor's use in his or her employment, business or vocation, are protected goods. Goods belonging to other members of the debtor's family, goods on hire purchase, and goods belonging to a limited company which is not the debtor may not be seized.

Once goods have been seized, the bailiff or enforcement officer will either take them away, or may leave them in the premises having entered into a 'walking possession' agreement with some responsible person in the building. Under the terms of such an agreement the responsible person agrees not to remove or damage the goods, and authorises the bailiff or enforcement officer to re-enter the premises at any time to complete the enforcement process.

If the goods are taken away, the bailiff or enforcement officer will provide the debtor with an inventory, and will then arrange for them to be sold by an appointed broker or appraiser through a public auction. Purchasers acquire good title to the goods. Written accounts of the sale, and the application of the proceeds of sale, are then provided to the debtor, and the net proceeds of sale after various expenses are paid to the judgment creditor.

38.4 Third party debt orders

Where a judgment debtor is owed money from a third party, such as a bank or a trade debtor, the simplest and often most effective method of enforcement is by way of a third party debt order. For this purpose evidence that the judgment debtor had an account which in the past was in credit is sufficient, at least for the purposes of obtaining an interim order (*Alawiye v Mahmood* [2007] 1 WLR 79). Third party debt orders follow a two-stage process. The first stage is commenced by a without notice application verified by a statement of truth in the prescribed form and containing prescribed information (CPR, r 72.3). The application is considered, without a hearing by a judge (r 72.4(1)), who may make an interim third party debt order directing the third party not to make any payment which reduces the amount he owes the judgment debtor to less than the amount specified in the order. The judge will also fix a hearing to consider making the order final. The amount specified will be the total outstanding on the judgment or order being enforced, together with fixed costs (r 72.4(3)).

An interim order must be served on the third party who owes money to the judgment debtor not less than 21 days before the date fixed for the hearing to consider making the order final (r 72.5(1)(a)), and is binding on the third party when it is served on him (r 72.4(4)). If the third party is a bank or building society it must carry out a search to identify all accounts held by the judgment debtor, and must disclose to the court and the judgment creditor the account numbers, whether they are in credit, and if so, whether the balance is sufficient to cover the amount specified in the interim order or the amount in the account if insufficient (r 72.6(1) and (2)). A bank or building society is not required by r 72.6 to retain money in, or disclose information relating to, joint accounts (PD 72, para 3.2). A third party who is not a bank or building society has seven days after service to notify the court and the judgment creditor in writing if he claims not to owe any money to the judgment debtor or to owe less than the amount specified in the interim order (r 72.6(4)).

The interim order must also be served on the judgment debtor. This needs to be done not less than seven days after service on the third party, and not less than seven days before the date fixed for the hearing (r 72.5(1)(b)). Where service is effected by the judgment creditor a certificate of service must be filed not less than two days before the hearing, or must be produced at the hearing (r 72.5(2)). A judgment debtor who is an individual and who is suffering hardship in meeting ordinary living expenses as a result of the interim order may apply for a hardship payment order permitting one or more payments out of the account (r 72.7).

The second stage is when the court considers whether to make a final third party debt order on the date fixed when the interim order was made. A judgment debtor or third party objecting to the final order, or who knows or believes someone else has a claim to the money, must file and serve written evidence stating the grounds of any objection or details of the other claim not less than three days before the hearing (r 72.8). If the court is notified that another person has a claim to the money it will serve notice of the application and the hearing on that person (r 72.8(5)). At the hearing the court may make a final third party debt order, discharge the interim order, decide any issues or direct a trial of any issues (r 72.8(6)). A final third party debt order is enforceable as an order to pay money. By r 72.9(2) the third party is discharged as against the judgment debtor to the extent of the amount paid under the order.

38.5 Charging orders

A charging order, as its name suggests, is an order imposing a charge on specified property of a judgment debtor for the purpose of securing the amount of a judgment debt: see the Charging Orders Act 1979, s 1(1). The property that can be charged under a charging order includes (by s 2) a beneficial interest in land, a beneficial interest in government stock or in company shares, debentures or other securities. Charging orders have to be sought in the court where the judgment was obtained, except High Court judgments for less than £5,000 which have to be transferred to the County Court for this form of enforcement.

The first stage is to apply for an interim charging order by issuing an application notice in the prescribed form verified by a statement of truth (CPR, r 73.3(4)). This is considered, without a hearing, by a judge who will consider making an interim order and fixing a hearing to consider making a final charging order (r 73.4). It is usual to protect an interim order that relates to registered land by entering a unilateral or agreed notice under the Land Registration Act 2002, ss 32 and 34.

At least 21 days before the final hearing (which is the second stage) the judgment debtor, such other creditors as the court may direct, and certain other specified persons must be served with the interim charging order, application notice and any supporting documents (r 73.5(1)). Once it is served an interim charging order effectively prevents dealings with the assets charged pending the final hearing (r 73.6). If service is effected by the judgment creditor, a certificate of service must be filed at least two days before the final hearing, or produced at the hearing (r 73.5(2)). Any person objecting to the order being made final must file and serve written evidence setting out the grounds of the objection not less than seven days before the hearing (r 73.8). At the hearing the court may make a final charging order, discharge the interim order, decide any issues or direct a trial of any issues (r 73.8(2)).

By the Charging Orders Act 1979, s 1(5), when the court is deciding whether to make the order absolute, it is required to consider all the circumstances of the case, and in particular the personal circumstances of the debtor and whether any other creditor or creditors are likely to be unduly prejudiced by the making of the order. If the order is made absolute, it operates as a charge on the relevant property, converting the judgment creditor from an unsecured to a secured creditor. It does not provide the judgment creditor with an immediate right to any money, but it does provide a valuable safeguard in the event of the debtor becoming insolvent before paying, and it also provides the foundation for proceedings for enforcement by sale. While probably not strictly necessary if the interim order was registered, it is usual to register the final order if it relates to registered land.

38.6 Enforcement by sale

Proceedings to enforce a charge, whether obtained by a charging order or otherwise, have to be brought by separate proceedings commenced by Part 8 claim. Evidence is initially given by witness statement. If fully contested, the claim proceeds to trial, where an order may be made for the sale of the property charged.

38.7 Attachment of earnings

An attachment of earnings order is the most appropriate method of enforcement where the judgment debtor has no substantial assets other than salary. It is an order directed to the debtor's employer requiring the employer to make periodic deductions from the debtor's salary and to pay the sums deducted (less a £1 collection fee) to the collecting officer of the court. Attachment of earnings orders can only be made by the County Courts in respect of ordinary civil litigation, so a High Court judgment to be enforced in this manner will first have to be transferred to the County Court.

It is a pre-condition for the making of an attachment of earnings order that the judgment debtor has failed to make at least one payment due under the judgment. Thus, such orders can only be made where the judgment provides for payment by instalments that have fallen into arrears. The 'earnings' that may be attached are wages, salaries, fees, bonuses, commission and overtime payable under a contract of service, and also occupational pensions and statutory sick pay. It does not include State pensions or self-employed income; see the Attachment of Earnings Act 1971, s 24.

An application for an attachment of earnings order is a simple matter of completing the prescribed form and paying a court fee: CCR Ord 27. The court then sends a two-page questionnaire to the debtor asking detailed questions as to the debtor's financial circumstances, and which also contains a box where the debtor can make an offer to pay by instalments. On receipt of the form a court official can make an attachment of earnings order. Either party can object to the official's determination, in which event there is a hearing to consider the form of order that should be made. If the debtor does not cooperate, a 14-day committal order can be made. Often the court will make a suspended order, which will only be served on the employer if the debtor fails to pay the stated instalments.

An attachment of earnings order has two components:

(a) The debtor's protected earnings rate. This is related to the debtor's needs, and is the amount that must be earned each week or month before any money can be deducted under the order; and

(b) The normal deduction rate. This is the weekly or monthly instalment that the employer is required to deduct from the debtor's salary.

38.8   Judgment summons

This is a procedure under the Debtors Act 1869, s 5, for punishing a defaulting judgment debtor with a period in prison. It has ceased to be of general application and is now restricted to maintenance orders in family law and arrears of some taxes; see the Administration of Justice Act 1970, s 11.

38.9   Writs and warrants of delivery

Where the claimant obtains a judgment for *delivery of goods*, the means of enforcement is by writ of delivery (in the High Court: RSC Ord 45, r 4) or by warrant of delivery (in the County Court: CCR Ord 26, r 16). There are two types of writ (and warrant) of delivery, corresponding to the provisions of the Torts (Interference with Goods) Act 1977, s 3.

A writ (or warrant) to enforce the discretionary relief in s 3(2)(a) of the Act for delivery of the claimant's goods is known as a *writ (or warrant) of specific delivery*. It requires the enforcement officer (or bailiff) to seize the goods specified in the judgment. The judgment debtor does not have the alternative of paying the assessed value of the goods.

A writ (or warrant) to enforce the relief in s 3(2)(b) of the Act requiring delivery of the goods or damages in the alternative is known as a *writ (or warrant) of delivery*. It directs the enforcement officer (or bailiff) to seize the specified goods or to levy execution against the general goods of the judgment debtor to the assessed value of the specified goods, in the latter case with the result that the claimant's remedy is converted into one for damages.

38.10   Writ or warrant of possession

A judgment for the possession of land is *invariably* secured through High Court writs (RSC Ord 45, r 3) or County Court warrants (CCR Ord 26, r 17(1)) of possession. The claimant applies for the writ or warrant of possession simply by filing forms with the court and paying the court fee. Enforcement is dealt with by the enforcement officer (High Court) or bailiff (County Court).

It is usual to inform the police before enforcing possession, as entry *may be gained by force*. The claimant will usually need to be on hand in order to make the land secure after possession has been obtained.

In the County Court, CCA 1984, s 111(1), provides: 'For the purposes of executing a warrant to give possession of any premises, it shall not be necessary to remove any goods from those premises.' In the High Court, on the other hand, execution is not considered to be completed until all the goods and persons in the premises have been removed.

In *R v Wandsworth County Court* [1975] 1 WLR 1314, Lord Widgery CJ said 'it has always been the law that the bailiff, when lawfully enforcing a warrant for possession, turns out everybody he finds on the premises, even though they are not the parties.'

38.11   Receivers by way of equitable execution

Receivership orders are made where it is impossible to use any of the other legal methods of enforcement. By the order the receiver will be authorised to receive rents, profits and moneys receivable in respect of the judgment debtor's interest in specified property. If necessary, the receiver may bring proceedings in the judgment debtor's name to obtain moneys payable to the judgment debtor which do not amount to debts (which could be attached by a third party debt order), such as a claim to be indemnified.

In *Maclaine Watson and Co Ltd v International Tin Council* [1988] Ch 1 (at first instance), Millett J said that the test is 'that there should be no way of getting at the fund except by the appointment of a receiver'. It operates by removing a hindrance arising out of the nature of the property which prevents execution at law.

An application for the appointment of a receiver may be made without notice, but is made by issuing an application notice supported by written evidence (CPR, r 69.3). The evidence needs to address the circumstances making the appointment of a receiver desirable, and must also address the suitability of the person nominated to act as the receiver. If an order is made, it is usually served on the receiver and all the parties to the proceedings, and the court may direct that it be served on other interested persons (r 69.4). The receiver may be required to provide security to cover his liability for any acts and omissions as a receiver (r 69.5). Once appointed a receiver will be remunerated (often out of the income of the property managed by the receiver), and the receiver will be required to provide accounts for his dealings with the property (r 69.8). Once the receiver's duties are completed the receiver or any party may apply for the receiver to be discharged (r 69.10).

38.12   Committal for breach of an order or undertaking

38.12.1   What is committal for breach?

Defiance of court orders is only one, but the most common, form of contempt of court. Others include contempts in the face of the court and writing works calculated to interfere with the course of justice.

Committal for breach means that the person in breach is sent to prison for a period not exceeding two years: see Contempt of Court Act 1981, s 14(1). There are two purposes behind doing this. One is to punish for the past contempt, the other to secure compliance with the court order.

As an alternative to committing to prison, by RSC Ord 52, r 9, the court has the power to fine or take security. Further alternatives are to give a strong reprimand; to grant an injunction restraining a repetition of the contempt; and, in an appropriate case, to make a summary award of damages.

38.12.2   Procedure for the issue of a committal order

The application is by claim form or application notice (RSC Ord 52, r 4 and CCR Ord 29, r 1(4)):

(a) The applicant is required to identify the provisions of the order (injunction) that are alleged to have been broken, and the ways in which it is alleged that the injunction has been broken. The acts need not be set out as counts in an indictment.

(b) The applicant must file affidavit evidence in support.

(c) The respondent is served by personal service with the notice and affidavits not less than three clear days before the hearing.

(d) The hearing is before a judge. At the hearing the judge must be satisfied that the breach has been proved *beyond reasonable doubt.*

(e) If so satisfied, the judge can make an immediate or suspended committal order for a fixed period not exceeding two years.

38.13 Writ of sequestration

This too is a process for punishing contempt. It has become well known through its use in trade union cases. The writ is addressed to four sequestrators requiring them to enter the contemnor's lands and to seize the contemnor's personal property and to hold the same until the contempt is purged: see RSC Ord 46, r 5.

Appeals

39.1 Introduction

'Can I appeal?' is a familiar question to any member of the Bar. Frequently clients are anxious to know whether they can appeal in the event of an unsuccessful claim or defence long before their case is even heard. For others, it is the most pressing question after judgment is pronounced. It is therefore vital for you to retain at the very least a working knowledge of the appeals procedure, the grounds (if any) upon which an appeal may be brought, whether permission to appeal is required, and the time limit within which an appeal must be brought.

Some appeals can be brought as of right. Most other decisions can be appealed with permission. However, it is comparatively rare for decisions, particularly after trial, to be appealed. In recent times a total of about 1,600 appeals are completed each year in the Court of Appeal, of which just over 25% are successful. Each year there are about 50 civil appeals to the House of Lords, of which about a third achieve some success.

Counsel has a heavy responsibility when called upon to advise on the merits of an appeal. Lord Donaldson MR, in an annual review, put it in this way:

> The question which the adviser may ask himself is whether, looking at the matter objectively, there are sufficient grounds for believing not only that the case should have been decided differently, but that in all the circumstances it can be demonstrated to the satisfaction of the Court of Appeal that there are grounds for reversing the judge's findings. In considering this question the adviser must never forget the financial risk which an appellant undertakes of having not only to pay his own costs of the appeal, but those of his opponent and, for this purpose, the adviser has two clients if the litigant is [publicly funded]. Nor must he underrate the effect upon his client of the emotional and other consequences of a continued state of uncertainty pending an appeal. In a word, one of the most important duties of a professional legal adviser is to save his clients from themselves and always to remember that, whilst it may well be reasonable to institute or to defend particular proceedings at first instance, a wholly new and different situation arises once the claim has been fully investigated by the court and a decision given.

39.2 Civil appeals framework

The basic civil appeals structure is, by the Access to Justice Act 1999 (Destination of Appeals) Order 2000, SI 2000/1071 (the 'Destination of Appeals Order'), PD 52, para 2A.1, and the Constitutional Reform Act 2005, as follows:

(a) County Court District Judges may be appealed to the County Court Circuit Judge;

(b) High Court Masters and District Judges may be appealed to a High Court Judge;

(c) County Court Circuit Judges may be appealed to a High Court Judge;

(d) High Court Judges may be appealed to the Court of Appeal; and

(e) Court of Appeal decisions may be appealed to the Supreme Court (which replaced the House of Lords under the provisions of the Constitutional Reform Act 2005, ss 23-60 in September 2009).

These basic routes of appeal also apply in relation to Deputy Judges and their equivalents, such as Deputy District Judges (who are treated as if they were District Judges), and recorders who are treated as County Court Circuit Judges.

39.2.1   Exceptions: direct appeals to Court of Appeal

Appeals are made to the Court of Appeal rather than to a High Court judge (categories (b) and (c) above) if the hearing in the lower court was either:

(a) a final decision made in a multi-track claim or in specialist proceedings (Destination of Appeals Order, art 4); or

(b) itself an appeal from a County Court District Judge (in other words, the current appeal is a second appeal; see Destination of Appeals Order, art 5).

39.2.1.1   Final decisions in multi-track and specialist claims

If the exception in sub-para (a) of **39.2.1** applies, an appeal is taken to the Court of Appeal. This is so even if the final decision was by a District Judge or Master (*Tanfern Ltd v Cameron-MacDonald* [2000] 1 WLR 1311). The exception, however, does not apply to claims allocated to the multi-track under CPR, r 8.9(c).

A decision is 'final' if it would determine (subject to any possible appeal or detailed assessment of costs) the entire proceedings whichever way the court decided the issues before it (Destination of Appeals Order, art 1(2)(c)). Further, a decision is treated as final where it is made at the conclusion of part of a hearing or trial which has been split into parts, and would, if made at the conclusion of that hearing or trial, be a final decision because it determines the entirety of that part of the claim (art 1(3)).

This means that if a judge makes a final decision on any aspect of a claim, such as limitation, or on part of a claim which has been directed to be tried separately, this is a final decision within the meaning of the provision. On the other hand, orders striking out the proceedings or a statement of case, and orders giving summary judgment, are not final decisions, because they are not decisions that would finally determine the entire proceedings whichever way the court decided the issues before it (*Tanfern Ltd v Cameron-MacDonald* [2000] 1 WLR 1311). See PD 52, para 2A.2.

If a non-specialist claim has never been allocated to a track, an appeal will not be to the Court of Appeal even if the judge would have allocated the claim to the multi-track had track allocation been considered (*Clark (Inspector of Taxes) v Perks* [2001] 1 WLR 17). This can arise, for example, if the claim is dealt with as an assessment of damages.

39.2.1.2   Destination of second appeals

Appeals will come within sub-para (b) of **39.2.1** where they are second appeals. Thus, where an interim application is first dealt with by a Master or District Judge, a first appeal will be to the Circuit Judge (for County Court claims) or High Court Judge (for High Court claims). A second appeal based on the same application, which will be an appeal either from the Circuit Judge or High Court Judge, is, by virtue of the exception, always to the Court of Appeal.

39.2.2 Appeals in Part 8 claims

Although Part 8 claims are automatically allocated to the multi-track by CPR, r 8.9(c), the exception laid down in the Destination of Appeals Order, art 4, does not apply to this category of claim. Therefore appeals in these claims, even from final orders, follow the general routes of appeal. Where the normal appeal court is not the Court of Appeal, a court granting permission to appeal in such a case from a final order should consider whether to order the appeal to be transferred to the Court of Appeal under r 52.14.

39.2.3 Appeal centres in High Court appeals

County Court and District Registry appeals to a High Court Judge must be brought in the District Registry for an appeal centre on the Circuit in which the lower court is situated (PD 52, para 8.4). A list of appeal centres for each of the six Circuits can be seen in para 8.2.

39.2.4 Transfer of appeals to the Court of Appeal

If the normal route for a first appeal from a decision of a District Judge or Master would be to a Circuit Judge or to a High Court Judge, either the lower court or the appeal court may order the appeal to be transferred to the Court of Appeal. This may be done if it is considered that the appeal will raise an important point of principle or practice or there is some other compelling reason for the Court of Appeal to hear it (CPR, r 52.14(1)). This power cannot be used by the lower court if it refuses permission to appeal (**39.5**), because in such a case there is no appeal (*7E Communications Ltd v Vertex Antennentechnik GmbH* [2007] 1 WLR 2175). The Master of the Rolls has a similar power to divert appeals to the Court of Appeal (Access to Justice Act 1999, s 57(1)).

39.2.5 Appeals to the Supreme Court

There is an exceptional power for appeals to be taken directly from the High Court to the Supreme Court (Administration of Justice Act 1969, ss 12, 13 and 15, which continue in force after the commencement of the Constitutional Reform Act 2005). There are a number of conditions that must be complied with. These include the High Court Judge certifying that the appeal is a suitable one for the leapfrog procedure (as it raises a point of general public importance based on statutory interpretation or on which there is binding Court of Appeal authority), and the Supreme Court giving permission to use the procedure. It is anticipated that most appeals to the Supreme Court will continue by the conventional route, via the Court of Appeal.

39.3 Appeal notices

An appellant must file an appeal notice in form N161 in order to initiate an appeal. Filing may be done electronically (PD 52, para 15.1B). The appeal notice must set out the grounds on which it is alleged the judge below went wrong. If permission to appeal is required (see **39.5**), the appeal notice must include a request for such permission: CPR, r 52.4(1). If permission to appeal out of time is required (see **39.4** and **39.11**), an application for such permission must be made to the appeal court (r 52.6(1)), which is usually made in the appeal notice.

An appellant seeking, for the first time, to rely on any issue or to seek any remedy under the Human Rights Act 1998 must include information complying with PD 16, para 15.1, in the appeal notice (PD 52, para 5.1A). By CPR, r 52.11(5), a party may not rely at the hearing of the appeal on a matter not contained in his or her appeal notice unless the appeal court gives permission.

39.4 Time for bringing an appeal

An appeal is brought by filing the appeal notice. This must be done within 21 days after the date of the decision of the lower court, unless the lower court has directed some other period for bringing the appeal (which should not normally exceed 35 days): CPR, r 52.4(2), and PD 52, para 5.19. Once an appeal notice has been filed it must be served on each respondent as soon as practicable, and in any event within seven days after being filed: r 52.4(3).

39.5 Permission to appeal

39.5.1 General rule

With four minor exceptions, permission is required for appeals: CPR, r 52.3(1). The exceptions where decisions may be appealed without permission are those from:

- committal orders;
- a refusal to grant habeas corpus;
- secure accommodation orders under the Children Act 1989, s 25; and
- costs assessments by court officials (as opposed to costs judges).

If permission to appeal is required it should initially be sought orally from the court below at the end of the hearing. If permission is refused, an application for permission can be renewed to the appeal court (by including a request for permission in the appeal notice; see CPR, r 52.3(2)). In appeals to the Court of Appeal, permission to appeal is first considered on the papers by a single Lord Justice. If permission is refused, the appellant may request the question of permission to be reconsidered at a hearing: r 52.3(4). If the court considers a paper application for permission to appeal is totally without merit, it may make an order that the person seeking to appeal may not request a reconsideration at a hearing (r 52.3(4A)).

The basic test for granting permission is whether the appeal has a real prospect of success: r 52.3(6)(a). As discussed at **39.12.2** to **39.12.6**, there are restricted grounds for mounting a successful appeal. A fanciful prospect of success is not enough. Another factor is the general importance of the issue raised by the appeal. If the point is not of particular general importance, and if the costs of appealing do not justify the amount at stake, permission is unlikely to be granted. The court considering a request for permission is not required to analyse whether the grounds of the proposed appeal will succeed, but merely whether there is a real prospect of success (*Hunt v Peasegood* The Times, 20 October 2000). There is some reluctance in giving permission to appeal against case management decisions. In these cases the court will also consider whether the issue is of sufficient significance to justify the costs of an appeal; the procedural consequences of an appeal (such as losing a trial date); and whether it would be more convenient to determine the point after trial (PD 52, para 4.5).

39.5.2 Permission in second appeals

Permission is required from the Court of Appeal (and cannot be given by the court below) for all appeals to that court from a decision of a County Court or the High Court which was itself made on appeal (CPR, r 52.13(1)). The Access to Justice Act 1999, s 55, provides that the Court of Appeal will not give permission unless it considers that either:

(a) the appeal would raise an important point of principle or practice; or

(b) there is some other compelling reason for the Court of Appeal to hear it.

39.5.3 Reconsideration of whether to grant permission

There is no appeal from a decision of the appeal court, made at an oral hearing, to allow or refuse permission to appeal to that court (Access to Justice Act 1999, s 54(4)). However, where the appeal court, without a hearing, refuses permission to appeal, the person seeking permission may request the decision to be reconsidered at a hearing (CPR, r 52.3(4)). A request for reconsideration of whether to grant permission to appeal must be filed within seven days after service of the notice that permission has been refused (r 52.3(5)), and the request must be served on the respondent (PD 52, para 4.14). Notice of the hearing will be given to the respondent, but he is not required to attend unless the court requests him to do so (para 4.15).

39.5.4 Limiting the issues on granting permission

By CPR, r 52.3(7), an order giving permission to appeal may limit the issues to be heard and be made subject to conditions. If a court confines its permission to some issues only, it should expressly refuse permission on any remaining issues. Those other issues may then only be raised at the hearing of the appeal if limited permission was given on the papers, and then only with the appeal court's permission (PD 52, paras 4.18 to 4.21).

39.6 Documentation

39.6.1 Appellant's documents

When filing the appellant's notice, the appellant must also file a number of additional copies of the notice and his skeleton argument (to include copies for every respondent), a sealed copy of the order being appealed, and an appeal bundle. Appeal bundles have to contain the documentation listed in PD 52, para 5.6A, and must be put together in compliance with detailed rules stated in PD 52, para 15.4. For appeals to the Court of Appeal, if the appeal bundle exceeds 500 pages, it is necessary to file a core bundle containing no more than 150 pages being the documents which are central to the appeal (PD 52, para 15.3). The courts are extremely strict about appeal bundles, and insist that they only contain documents which are directly relevant to the issues under appeal (PD 52, para 5.6(2)).

39.6.2 Skeleton argument

Form N163 should be used (or used as a cover sheet) for the skeleton arguments. It should include a time estimate, and should be lodged with the appellant's notice (PD 52, paras 5.9 and 5.10). Lists of relevant persons, chronologies and glossaries of technical terms are often usefully included with skeleton arguments. See the detailed discussion at 33.8.

39.6.3 Bundle of authorities

For Court of Appeal hearings, advocates for the parties must agree and lodge a bundle of no more than 10 authorities to be relied upon at the hearing (PD 52, para 15.11). Relevant passages must be marked, and the file must contain a certificate signed by the advocates that they have complied with the requirements in para 5.10(3) to (5) about identifying propositions and not citing unnecessary authorities. The file must be lodged at least seven days before the hearing.

39.6.4 Record of the judgment of the lower court

If the judgment of the lower court was recorded, an approved transcript should accompany the appellant's notice (PD 52, para 5.12). Photocopies are not acceptable. If there is no official transcript, the next best is the lower court judge's written judgment duly signed by the judge. If the lower court's judgment was oral and not recorded, the advocates should confer and submit, if possible, an agreed note of the judgment to the judge for signature. If the note cannot be agreed, both versions should be submitted with a covering letter explaining the situation.

39.6.5 Final deadline

The Court of Appeal will often forgive late filing, but has a strict final deadline for lodging all the materials necessary for the appeal (PD 52, para 15.11B). This provides that if any documentation is not filed at least seven days before the hearing, the appeal may be listed before the presiding Lord Justice, when severe sanctions are likely to be imposed.

39.7 Service of appellant's notice on the respondent

By CPR, r 52.4(3), unless the appeal court orders otherwise, an appellant's notice must be served on each respondent as soon as practicable, and in any event not later than seven days after it is filed. A copy of the appellant's skeleton argument should be served at the same time (PD 52, para 5.21) unless this is impracticable, in which case it should be served within 14 days of filing the notice (para 5.9(2)).

39.8 Respondent's notice

Generally no response is required from the respondent until permission is granted. Respondents are served with certain documents before permission to appeal is granted, but the purpose of this is to ensure the respondent is informed of any landmarks in the appeal process. Respondents should only file submissions at the permission stage if those submissions are addressed to the point that the appeal will not meet the threshold test for permission, or if there was some material inaccuracy in the papers placed before the court, or if the court gives some specific decision (*Jolly v Jay* The Times, 3 April 2002). If the appeal court grants permission, the appeal court will send the parties copies of the order granting permission and any other directions given by the court (PD 52, para 6.3(2), (3)). The appeal bundle must be served by the appellant on the respondents within seven days of receiving the order granting permission (para 6.2).

A respondent may oppose an appeal in one of three ways:

(a) by simply arguing that the decision of the court below was correct for the same reasons as given by the judge below. Such a respondent need not serve a respondent's notice;

(b) by arguing that the decision of the court below was correct, but for reasons different from or additional to those given by the lower court. Such a respondent is not appealing as such, so there is no question of seeking permission to cross-appeal. However, a respondent's notice is required for the purpose of setting out the different or additional reasons (PD 52, para 7.2);

(c) by asking the appeal court to vary the order of the lower court. This amounts to cross-appealing, and permission to appeal must be sought on the same basis as for an appellant (PD 52, para 7.1). A respondent's notice is required for setting out the grounds on which it is to be argued that the order of the court below should be varied.

Generally, a respondent's notice must be filed within such period as may be directed by the lower court. Where the court makes no such direction, the notice must be filed within 14 days after the date laid down by CPR, r 52.5(5), relevant to the circumstances of the appeal. This date will be either:

(a) the date the respondent was served with the appellant's notice in cases where permission to appeal was given by the lower court or permission to appeal was not required; or

(b) the date the respondent was served with notification that the appeal court gave the appellant permission to appeal; or

(c) the date the respondent was served with notification that the application for permission to appeal and the appeal itself are to be heard together.

Unless the appeal court orders otherwise, a respondent's notice must be served on the appellant and any other respondent as soon as practicable, and in any event not later than seven days after it is filed (r 52.5(6)).

39.9 Respondent's skeleton argument

The respondent must provide a skeleton argument for the court in all cases where he or she proposes to address arguments to the court. It should conform to the principles applicable to the appellant's skeletons, but should also seek to answer the arguments in the appellant's skeleton. It may be included in the respondent's notice, or may be lodged and served no later than 14 days after filing the respondent's notice (PD 52, para 7.7).

39.10   Appeal questionnaires

For Court of Appeal cases, the Civil Appeals Office will send the appellant an appeal questionnaire. This must be returned within 14 days, and must include the appellant's advocate's time estimate for the hearing, confirmation that the transcript for the lower court's hearing has been requested, and confirmation that copies of the questionnaire and appeal bundle have been served on the respondents (PD 52, para 6.5).

A respondent who disagrees with the time estimate must inform the court within seven days of receipt of the questionnaire. Where the appeal court is the High Court, use of appeal questionnaires is optional (para 8.12).

39.11   Extending time for appealing

Any application to extend the time for appealing should be made to the appeal court (CPR, r 52.6), and permission to appeal out of time cannot be granted by agreement between the parties. The general principles discussed at **28.3.8** on obtaining relief from sanctions apply on such an application (*Sayers v Clarke Walker* [2002] 1 WLR 3095).

39.12   Nature of appeal hearings

39.12.1   Review of the decision below

By CPR, r 52.11(1), every appeal will be limited to a review of the decision of the lower court unless:

- a practice direction makes different provision for a particular category of appeal; or
- the court considers that in the circumstances of an individual appeal it would be in the interests of justice to hold a rehearing.

There are very few exceptions, and those that exist are of a technical nature (see, eg PD 52, para 9.1). An appeal from a decision in an interim application is technically a review rather than a rehearing even if in practice the appeal court will have to consider all the papers before the lower court (*McFaddens Solicitors v Chandrasekaran* [2007] EWCA Civ 220). This means that for almost all appeals, the appeal court will allow an appeal only where (r 52.11(3)) the decision of the lower court was:

- wrong; or
- unjust because of a serious procedural or other irregularity in the proceedings in the lower court.

The way it was put by Lord Fraser of Tullybelton in *G v G* [1985] 1 WLR 647, is that the appeal court '. . . should only interfere when it considers that the judge of first instance has not merely preferred an imperfect solution which is different from an alternative imperfect solution which the Court of Appeal might or would have adopted, but has exceeded the generous ambit within which a reasonable disagreement is possible.'

The House of Lords allowed an appeal in *Designers Guild Ltd v Russell Williams (Textiles) Ltd* [2000] 1 WLR 2416 on the ground that the Court of Appeal had approached the issue on the appeal more in the manner of a court of first instance making original findings of fact rather than an appellate court reviewing findings already made.

39.12.2   Discretion

Many, if not most, interim applications turn on the exercise of the court's discretion. In almost all cases the discretion is conferred on the judge or Master first dealing with the application. On an appeal the court is only entitled to substitute its own exercise of discretion in such limited circumstances as where the judge at first instance:

- failed to exercise any discretion at all;
- went wrong in principle;
- made a mistake of law;
- took into account irrelevant matters;
- misinterpreted the facts;
- exercised the discretion in a way in which no reasonable judge could have exercised it.

39.12.3   Decisions by juries

Juries usually give general verdicts, and usually it is impossible to attack them on appeal. One possible ground is that the verdict, whether on liability or damages, is one which no properly directed jury could reasonably have found upon the evidence. The Court of Appeal has power where the damages awarded are excessive or inadequate to substitute a proper sum for the sum awarded by the jury: CPR, r 52.10(3).

39.12.4   Credibility of witnesses

The trial judge sees the witnesses giving evidence, the appeal court does not. Having the advantage of having seen the demeanour and manner of the witnesses in court, the trial judge's findings on the credibility of witnesses will be upset on appeal only if the appeal court is convinced that the judge was plainly wrong (*Powell v Streatham Manor Nursing Home* [1935] AC 243, HL).

39.12.5   Inferences

There is a distinction between:

- facts deposed to by witnesses and found by the trial judge; and
- inferences of fact drawn from those facts.

The appeal court is not at the same disadvantage as in **39.12.4** in drawing inferences. If, on full consideration, the appeal court concludes that the judge's inferences were wrong, it will overrule the decision below.

39.12.6   Points not raised below

An appellant cannot, as a rule, raise on appeal points of law or fact not raised at the trial below (*Clouston and Co Ltd v Corry* [1906] AC 122, HL; *Mullarkey v Broad* [2009] EWCA Civ 2). However, a respondent may seek to support the findings of the trial judge on any ground, including any not raised below, provided such ground is included in the respondent's notice.

39.13 Stay of execution

Initiating an appeal does not have the automatic effect of staying execution on the judgment or order under appeal: CPR, r 52.7. Stays can nevertheless be sought, generally either from the court appealed from or the court appealed to.

In considering an application for a stay, the courts act on the principle that in general successful litigants must not be deprived of the fruits of the litigation. In *Linotype-Hell Finance Ltd v Baker* [1993] 1 WLR 321, Staughton LJ said a stay could be granted if an appellant would face financial ruin without it, provided the appeal had some prospect of success. Although the court has to balance the advantages to the parties and exercise its common sense in deciding whether to grant a stay of execution, the starting principle is that there has to be good reason for depriving the successful party of the fruits of its judgment at first instance (see *Winchester Cigarette Machinery Ltd v Payne (No. 2)* The Times, 15 December 1993, CA). The appellant needs to show some special circumstance taking the case out of the ordinary.

39.14 Court of Appeal procedure

If the parties are attempting a last-minute settlement of an appeal, they are under a duty to inform the judges of the appeal court, to avoid the judges undertaking unnecessary preparation (*Tasyurdu v Secretary of State for the Home Department* The Times, 16 April 2003).

Substantive appeals to the Court of Appeal are generally heard by three-judge courts (SCA 1981, s 54(2)), but in a number of situations the court is duly constituted if it consists of two judges. These include appeals from interim orders, from County Court orders, and from final orders made by Masters and High Court District Judges: see SCA 1981, s 54(4). Where a two-judge court is divided, either party may apply for a rehearing before a three-judge court. Fortunately, this is extremely rare. The Court of Appeal also has a power, to be exercised only in exceptional cases, to rehear an appeal where new facts come to light after first deciding the appeal (*Taylor v Lawrence* [2003] QB 528 and CPR, r 52.17).

Before the hearing the judges will have read the notice of appeal, any respondent's notice, the judgment under appeal and the skeleton arguments. At the beginning of the hearing the Presiding Lord Justice will state what other documents and authorities have also been read. Accordingly, it is not usually necessary for counsel to open the facts, but to proceed to the strongest ground of appeal. If, exceptionally, it would be helpful to the court for counsel to open the appeal, the Presiding Lord Justice notifies counsel before the hearing. Counsel should avoid reading passages of transcript *in extenso*, and should go immediately to the relevant passages in the judgments of cases which have been pre-read by the court. Lay clients should be forewarned of these arrangements, so as not to be left with the impression that their cases are not being given a fair hearing: *Practice Direction (Court of Appeal: Procedure)* [1995] 1 WLR 1191.

39.15 Fresh evidence

The *Ladd v Marshall* [1954] 1 WLR 1489 principles are that the Court of Appeal may receive fresh evidence (other than as to matters occurring since the date of hearing) only if it is satisfied that such evidence:

- could not have been obtained with reasonable diligence for use at the hearing;
- would probably have an important influence on the result of the case; and
- is apparently credible.

Since the introduction of the CPR, the *Ladd v Marshall* principles remain relevant as matters which must necessarily be considered, although not as strict rules (*Banks v Cox* (2000) LTL 17/7/2000, CA). Strong grounds have to be shown before fresh evidence will be admitted, and the *Ladd v Marshall* principles will be looked at with considerable care (*Hertfordshire Investments Ltd v Bubb* [2000] 1 WLR 2318). Fresh evidence going to the credit of one of the parties was admitted on the appeal in *Hamilton v Al Fayed (No. 1)* [2001] EMLR 394 applying the *Ladd v Marshall* principles, although it was recognised that fresh evidence as to credit would rarely have a sufficient impact on the result.

39.16 Orders for a new trial

One of the Court of Appeal's powers on appeal is to order a new trial: see SCA 1981, s 17, and CPR, r 52.10(2). This is more of a live issue if the case was tried with a jury. Grounds for making such an order include misdirecting the jury; leaving to the jury questions which are for the judge; and irregularities in relation to the jury (such as jurors conversing with strangers after retiring to consider the verdict). Other grounds, such as improper admission or rejection of evidence, could occur in trials by judge alone. Even if such grounds are established, a new trial will generally only be ordered if the Court of Appeal is of the opinion that some substantial wrong or miscarriage has been thereby occasioned. This means that a new trial will not be ordered unless there is a doubt whether the verdict below was correct on either liability or remedy (*Bray v Ford* [1896] AC 44, HL).

INDEX